The Divided Academy

Other Books by Everett Carll Ladd, Jr.

TRANSFORMATIONS OF THE PARTY SYSTEM: POLITICAL COALITIONS FROM THE NEW DEAL TO THE 1970S, *with C. D. Hadley, W. W. Norton, 1975.*

POLITICAL PARTIES AND POLITICAL ISSUES: PATTERNS IN DIFFERENTIATION SINCE THE NEW DEAL, *with C. D. Hadley, Sage Professional Papers in Political Science, 1973.*

ACADEMICS, POLITICS, AND THE 1972 ELECTION, *with Seymour M. Lipset, American Enterprise Institute for Public Policy Research, 1973.*

PROFESSORS, UNIONS, AND AMERICAN HIGHER EDUCATION, *with Seymour M. Lipset, Carnegie Commission on Higher Education, 1973.*

IDEOLOGY IN AMERICA: CHANGE AND RESPONSE IN A CITY, A SUBURB, AND A SMALL TOWN, *Cornell University Press, 1969, and W. W. Norton, Norton Library, Paperback edition with new preface, 1972.*

AMERICAN POLITICAL PARTIES: SOCIAL CHANGE AND POLITICAL RESPONSE, *W. W. Norton, 1970.*

NEGRO POLITICAL LEADERSHIP IN THE SOUTH, *Cornell University Press, 1966, and Atheneum, 1969.*

Other Books by Seymour Martin Lipset

EDUCATION AND POLITICS AT HARVARD, *with David Riesman, McGraw-Hill, 1975.*

FAILURE OF A DREAM? ESSAYS IN THE HISTORY OF AMERICAN SOCIALISM, *(editor), with John Laslett, Anchor Doubleday, 1974.*

ACADEMICS, POLITICS, AND THE 1972 ELECTION, *with Everett C. Ladd, American Enterprise Institute for Public Policy Research, 1973.*

PROFESSORS, UNIONS, AND AMERICAN HIGHER EDUCATION, *with Everett C. Ladd, Carnegie Commission on Higher Education, 1973.*

REBELLION IN THE UNIVERSITY, *Little, Brown, 1972.*

THE POLITICS OF UNREASON: RIGHT-WING EXTREMISM IN AMERICA, 1790–1970, *with Earl Raab, Harper & Row, 1970, Torch Books paperback, 1972.*

REVOLUTION AND COUNTERREVOLUTION: CHANGE AND PERSISTENCE IN SOCIAL STRUCTURE, *Basic Books, 1968, and Anchor Doubleday, revised 1970.*

STUDENTS IN REVOLT, *(editor), with Philip Altbach, Daedalus Library, Beacon Press, 1969.*

POLITICS AND THE SOCIAL SCIENCES, *(editor), Oxford University Press, 1969.*

AGRARIAN SOCIALISM: THE COOPERATIVE COMMONWEALTH FEDERATION IN SASKATCHEWAN, *University of California Press, 1950, revised 1968.*

SOCIOLOGY AND HISTORY: METHODS, *(editor), with Richard Hofstadter, Basic Books, 1968.*

STUDENT POLITICS, *(editor), Basic Books, 1967.*

PARTY SYSTEMS AND VOTER ALIGNMENTS, *(editor), with S. Rokkan, Free Press, 1967.*

THE FIRST NEW NATION: THE UNITED STATES IN HISTORICAL AND COMPARATIVE PERSPECTIVE, *Basic Books, 1963, and Anchor Doubleday, 1967.*

CLASS, STATUS, AND POWER: SOCIAL STRATIFICATION IN COMPARATIVE PERSPECTIVE, *(editor), with Reinhard Bendix, Free Press, 1966.*

ESTUDIANTES UNIVERSITARIOS Y POLITICA EN EL TERCER MUNDO, *Editorial Alfa, Montevideo, 1965.*

POLITICAL MAN: THE SOCIAL BASES OF POLITICS, *Doubleday, 1960, Anchor Doubleday, 1963.*

UNION DEMOCRACY, *with Martin Trow and James S. Coleman, Free Press, 1956, Anchor Doubleday, 1962, and Free Press paperback, 1975.*

SOCIAL MOBILITY IN INDUSTRIAL SOCIETY, *with Reinhard Bendix, University of California Press, 1959.*

The Divided Academy

PROFESSORS AND POLITICS

by **Everett Carll Ladd, Jr.**
and **Seymour Martin Lipset**

Sponsored by
The Carnegie Commission on Higher Education

MC GRAW-HILL BOOK COMPANY

New York   St. Louis   San Francisco
Düsseldorf   Johannesburg   Kuala Lumpur   London   Mexico
Montreal   New Delhi   Panama   Paris   São Paulo
Singapore   Sydney   Tokyo   Toronto

The Carnegie Commission on Higher Education,
2150 Shattuck Avenue, Berkeley, California 94704
has sponsored preparation of this volume as
part of a continuing effort to obtain and present
significant information for public discussion.
The views expressed are those of the authors.

THE DIVIDED ACADEMY
Professors and Politics

This book was set in Palatino by B. Handelman Associates,
Inc. It was printed and bound by The Maple Press Company.
The designer was Elliot Epstein. The editors were
Nancy Tressel and Janine Parson for McGraw-Hill Book Company
and Verne A. Stadtman and Karen Seriguchi for the
Carnegie Commission on Higher Education. Audre Hanneman
edited the index. Milton J. Heiberg supervised the production.

Library of Congress Cataloging in Publication Data
Ladd, Everett Carll.
The divided academy: professors and politics.

Sponsored by the Carnegie Commission on Higher
Education.
Includes bibliographical references.
1.   College teachers—United States—Political
activity.   2.   United States—Politics and government.
I.   Lipset, Seymour Martin, joint author.   II.   Carnegie
Commission on Higher Education.   III.   Title.
LA227.3.L33   378.1'2   74-17247
ISBN 0-07-010112-4

1 2 3 4 5 6 7 8 9 MAMM 7 9 8 7 6 5

*For Paul F. Lazarsfeld
who showed the way
in studying the
academic mind*

Contents

Foreword

Whenever there is political tension between society and the nation's campuses, concern is likely to be expressed about the influence of college and university professors. During the early 1950s, college and university campuses were frequent hunting grounds of the red hunters who were searching for imported ideologies within the faculties. And, in the 1960s, when the campuses were centers of opposition to the Vietnam War and of support for civil rights activities, there were those who partially wrote off students who became visibly involved in such efforts as "dupes of their radical professors." The obvious question raised by such episodes is, What really are the politics of academic men and women in the United States? And the question becomes increasingly important as we begin to realize how frequently university professors are involved in society's concerns—not only in teaching the young, but also in advising the leaders of government and industry, and in exercising leadership themselves in the discovery and analysis of new ideas.

In this book, Professors Everett Carll Ladd, Jr., and Seymour Martin Lipset provide some important answers to the question. In analyzing information obtained from the more than 60,000 professors who responded to the Carnegie Commission's Survey of Student and Faculty Opinion in 1969 and by making a supplementary survey of their own in 1972, they have been able to construct a detailed, up-to-date profile of the political orientation of the faculty members of American colleges and universities.

The authors find the dominant orientation of professors to be liberal, and they trace the causes of the orientation to the nature of intellectual activities that involve a questioning of the status quo and a critical attitude toward conventional wisdom. They substantiate this linkage between liberality and intellectuality by presenting evidence that ties liberality to the more intellectually oriented disciplines and to the higher achievers in scholarly endeavors. In reaching this conclusion, they also challenge the assertion that political liberality is predominant only among those faculty members who have the least stake in preserving the prevailing structure of academic life.

The findings of Professors Ladd and Lipset will be of great value to us as we consider the possible responses of academics to changes on the campus and in society in the future. We are, therefore, fortunate that their study was made and that it was undertaken by two such skillful and insightful scholars. They add greatly to our understanding of the American professoriate and of its many interactions with the campus and with society.

Clark Kerr

Chairman
Carnegie Commission
on Higher Education

May 1975

Preface

Studies of the politics of higher education have been written from various perspectives, so we should specify here at the outset the orientation and concerns which guided our work. Social change, which has so dominated the American experience historically, includes ascensions and declines of an array of interest collectivities. In postindustrial America, one prominent ascension involves intellectuals, together with a large segment of the population associated with the application of trained intelligence. Advanced technology and science makes extraordinary demands upon the intellectual community for skills necessary to its utilization, maintenance and, above all, its extension or further elaboration. With about 25 percent of the adult population now having been exposed to formal higher education, and with nearly one-third of all current high school graduates going on to earn at least a bachelor's degree, the potential audience for the communication of abstract ideas dwarfs that of all prior historical-societal experience. An elaborate structure for the communication of ideas—from the more than 2,500 colleges and universities on through the print and electronic media—contributes further to the central place of intellectuals and their apprentices.

Some additional statistics, general though they are, help to round out this picture of a major transformation and ascension of a social collectivity. In 1973, the number of teachers exceeded 2.7 million, with 600,000 in institutions of higher education. More than 8 million students were enrolled in degree-credit programs within the country's colleges. Over 1.5 million persons were employed as natural scientists and engineers. Some $30 billion were being spent annually for scientific or technological research and development. And Americans were expending in excess of $52 billion for public primary and secondary schools, along with about $25 billion for higher education.[1]

[1]These data are from *Statistical Abstract of the United States* (1973, pp. 128, 131, 135, 523).

This depiction could be enlarged and refined. But what we are point-
ing to is an elemental fact of life in advanced industrial society: that activities and functions centering around the intellectual community are
enormously extended. From this, the conclusion that this stratum—
diverse though it may be internally—merits serious attention as a
sociopolitical interest collectivity follows naturally.

No study of American politics in 1900 can legitimately overlook the
position of entrepreneurial business. And in much the same way, no
examination of American politics in the mid-1970s can properly ignore
the place of those groups in the population located around the application of trained intelligence.

The specific concerns of this study of college and university faculty
will be developed in the sections which follow. We are attending here to
only the most general conceptual underpinnings of the inquiry. And
these involve the view that academics, part of a broader intellectual
stratum, merit investigation of their social and political orientation as
much, say, as business and labor, in view of their assumption of a central place in postindustrial America. The orientations of faculty
"count" in the context of operation of their "home" institution, the university. But they matter, as well, in the context of the national polity.

A book such as this, based in large part on the analysis of two surveys
of the American professoriate, requires considerable funding and cooperation of many people and research organizations. The organizations
included the Carnegie Commission on Higher Education, which sponsored and substantially funded the 1969 survey of student and faculty
opinion; the American Council on Education, which joined in the sponsorship of that survey; and the U.S. Office of Education, which shared
in the basic funding of the survey. Other organizations that provided
support for this project are the American Enterprise Institute for Public
Policy Research, which supported our follow-up 1972 survey; the
Social Science Data Center of the University of Connecticut, which administered the 1972 study and which also provided technical personnel facilities and funds for data analysis; the American Jewish Committee, which funded a special study of Jewish academics; the Center
for Advanced Study in the Behavioral Sciences, which furnished Lipset with a Fellowship and with research support in 1972–73; and the
Guggenheim Foundation, which awarded each of us a fellowship.

On the personal level we are particularly grateful to Clark Kerr of the
Carnegie Commission and William Baroody of the American Enterprise
Institute for having confidence in the projects which went into this

book. Martin Trow of the University of California at Berkeley was particularly helpful in the early stages of the study when he and Lipset collaborated in designing the basic questionnaire for the 1969 survey. That questionnaire was intended to provide data for two related but separate projects: an analysis of the academic profession by Trow, and our study of the politics of academia. Alexander Astin, then of the American Council on Education, contributed much to the final shape of the questionnaire. Various of our colleagues, students, and research associates were helpful at different stages of our work. It would be impossible to name all of them, but particularly noteworthy are Gary Orren, David Riesman, William Schneider and Lloyd Blankfein of Harvard; Peter Natchez of Brandeis; Charles Hadley of the University of New Orleans; Lauriston King of the National Science Foundation; and Peter Hooper of the University of Connecticut. Anne-Marie Mercure, William Gammell, Margaret Pyne, Michael Gold, Gary Grandon, Joffre Levesque and William Howard, all staff members of the Social Science Data Center at Connecticut, contributed significantly throughout the demanding enterprise of data analysis. Special thanks are due Eleanor Wilcox, who typed the several drafts of the manuscript with expert care, and Diane Reed, who served as the principal research associate to the project.

Finally, it should be noted that much of our work appeared in various articles and two monographs. Since we have necessarily drawn heavily on these earlier publications in writing this book, we would like to express our acknowledgments to those who published the earlier products of this study. The articles and monographs are listed in the reference section at the back of the book. Although the contents of many of these earlier publications and this book overlap, there is much in them which has not been included here because of considerations of relevance and space. Conversely, this work contains a great deal not previously presented in article or monograph form.

Everett Carll Ladd, Jr.
Storrs, Connecticut

Seymour Martin Lipset
Belmont, Massachusetts

May 1975

The Divided Academy

Introduction

Interest in the politics of college faculty and students surged upward in the 1960s with the renewal of a vigorous campus political activism. Protests and demonstrations seemingly enveloped American higher education in the late sixties—spurred on notably by reactions to the growing United States involvement in the Vietnam War, even though not exclusively attributable to anguish brought on by the war. The protests of the 1960s were important not only in their own right, but also because they called attention to a development of more fundamental significance: the increased prominence of universities in American social life. Campus protests had the impact they did because academia had expanded so dramatically and had assumed a central position.

In 1920, just 48,000 people were employed as faculty members in America's colleges and universities; a half century later, in 1972, there were more than 600,000. The most dramatic increases came between 1965 and 1970, when the professorial ranks were swelled by 150,000, with the number of *new* positions created and filled exceeding *the entire number* of faculty slots that existed in 1940 (Table 1). There were 238,000 students at all levels of college training at the turn of the century. The numbers grew steadily, exceeding 1 million in 1930 and 2.5 million in 1950. But in the 1960s, the college student population took an extraordinary jump, increasing by 4 million.

Achievement of a central place by universities in American society has occurred partly through the sheer growth to which the above data attest. But the growth only reflects the increased requirement of postindustrial society for university-trained people and continuing high levels of innovative research.

Among the many functions which have fallen to the university in a society highly dependent upon trained intelligence, none is more important than that involving *certification*. Academics occupy a unique position among occupational groups since they alone serve to certify

TABLE 1 *Numbers of faculty and students in American colleges and universities, 1900–1972*

Year	Faculty (number in thousands)	Students (number in thousands)
1900	24	238
1910	36	355
1920	48	598
1930	82	1,101
1940	147	1,494
1950	247	2,659
1960	381	3,446
1965	404	5,226
1970	551	7,484
1972	603	8,116

SOURCES: *Historical Statistics of the United States* (1960, p. 210) and *Statistical Abstract of the United States* (1973, p. 131).

other elites as technically competent through the steps of formal education and produce the scientific and cultural resources which the various other collectivities need. The university has become the great legitimizing and certifying institution of contemporary secular societies. This means not only that lawyers must go through university law schools and social workers through schools of social work or that persons not armed with a bachelor's degree need not bother to apply for executive positions in private industry or government, but also that other elites, especially those associated with intellectual functions, look increasingly to the university for approbation. We see this in the case of churches, whose leaders appear to seek the approval of the intellectual community located principally around the universities.[1]

Another sphere of activity in which the elite show clear signs of being influenced by ties to the university world is the mass media: the people who write for major newspapers, magazines, and news services, and who direct network broadcasting, have values and political orientations

[1]Lipset and Dobson (1972, p. 179) have noted that this reference group phenomenon finds symbolic reflection in the location of major seminaries in the United States around university centers: for example, Union Theological Seminary and the Jewish Theological Seminary are adjacent to Columbia; Pacific School of Religion is up the hill from the University of California; the Episcopal Theological Seminary is near Harvard. Catholic seminaries such as Woodstock have recently moved to secular academic communities. It is not by chance that those in university climes carry the highest prestige and are considered the most innovative.

similar to academics. It may be argued that those who have risen to prominent positions in the media seek acceptance as intellectuals and along with theologians look to faculty as a primary reference group. A. James Reichley of *Fortune* has described this development in the outlook of journalists (1971, p. 93):

Since World War II the old reporters of the *Front Page* school, whose attitudes were at least as much anti-intellectual as anti-government, have gradually disappeared. The new journalists have tended to be better educated and more professional—and strongly influenced by prevailing currents of opinion in the academic community. The part played by the Ivy League in the intellectual establishment has no doubt been exaggerated, but it is worthy of note that almost one third of the nation's most influential journalists . . . turn out to be graduates of Ivy League schools. Even the top journalists who are not college graduates . . . operate in a milieu in which liberal intellectual attitudes are pervasive. The suggestion of one critic that many national journalists now function as a kind of "lesser clergy" for the academic elite is not far from correct.

In sum, the greatest source of influence of academics may stem from their control of the process of certification as to competence for virtually the entire range of elite occupations, and in particular their position as key reference group for the larger community who live by the manipulation of ideas.

Within postindustrial America, the intellectual stratum and its associated cohorts have acquired a position of particular prominence, and in this larger context the university has come to play a pivotal role. We investigate the politics of faculty, then, as a strategically placed subgroup in the American population.

This inquiry draws upon a variety of sources of information. One massive survey of the professoriate, however, unique in its size and scope, has been of special importance in providing relevant data. The general dimensions of this major survey investigation should be pointed out here.

THE CARNEGIE SURVEY OF THE AMERICAN PROFESSORIATE

In 1969, the Carnegie Commission on Higher Education sponsored a series of large scale, parallel national surveys of undergraduate and graduate students, faculty, and administrators. The faculty study, on which we draw most heavily, employed a questionnaire that was mailed to approximately 100,000 full-time college and university professors located at 303 schools around the country.[2] The questionnaire solicited more than 300 items of information from each respondent, including social background, professional activities and achievements, and opinions on a broad range of political issues and controversies, from those largely restricted to the campus to matters of national and international affairs.[3]

A disproportionate random sampling procedure was used to select colleges and universities in order to obtain adequate numbers of institutions of various types and characteristics. The 303 schools thus chosen include 57 junior colleges, 168 four-year colleges, and 78 universities. Next, a six-in-seven random sample of faculty was drawn from the rosters of the included institutions, yielding a sample of 100,290.[4] A very high return of completed questionnaires—60 percent—was achieved as a result of the standing of the sponsors (the Carnegie Commission on Higher Education and the American Council on Education), careful survey administration, and systematic follow-ups with faculty not initially responding. The returned questionnaires were differentially weighted, adjusting the data for the disproportionate sampling of institutions and for the unequal rates of response. Tabulations from the weighted data of this survey ($n = 445{,}115$), then, may be taken as reasonably representative of the entire population of teaching faculty at colleges and universities in the United States.

Our working sample in the Carnegie study, 60,028 unweighted cases, is exceptionally large, and this has allowed us to perform detailed analysis of field (and other) subgroups which appear too few in numbers in national surveys of a conventional size. Included, for example, are 1,707 physicists, 2,916 mathematicians, 3,402 faculty in English, 1,036 in sociology, and 2,243 full-time academics in schools of business administration. There are 5,907 professors of Jewish background, 9,096 of Catholic parentage. The sample includes 837 black faculty, 9,316 women, 1,061 academics under 30 years of age, 2,070 who could claim more than 10 professional publications in the two years preceding the

---

[2]These surveys were conducted with the financial support of the Carnegie Commission and the United States Office of Education, Department of Health, Education and Welfare. They were administered by the Survey Research Center of the University of California, Berkeley, with advice and technical assistance from the Office of Research of the American Council on Education.

[3]The Carnegie faculty study questionnaire is reproduced in Appendix A.

[4]Various aspects of the methodology employed in the survey are described in detail in "Technical Report..." (1971) and Bayer (1971).

survey, 9,660 who voted for Barry Goldwater in the 1964 presidential election, 3,176 professors at Ivy League schools, and so on.

In the summer of 1972, recognizing that important changes had occurred in the political agenda of American higher education, we saw merit in the updating that a new faculty survey would make possible; so we initiated a small follow-up to the massive 1969 study. A telephone survey of a national sample of professors was conducted in late August and early September; in November (following the presidential election, which served as a focal point in the inquiry) we again questioned these respondents through a mailed questionnaire.

Our approach was to build these surveys into the structure of the much larger 1969 Carnegie investigation. All the four-year colleges and universities included in the 1969 study were assigned to a series of categories defined by essential institutional characteristics; then a subset of institutions was randomly selected from each stratum. Rosters of all full-time faculty members at these schools were obtained, from which a random sample was drawn. A ratio was instituted providing that the number selected from a given stratum should constitute the same percentage in the sample as in the entire professoriate.

Between August 29 and September 13, 1972, our staff attempted to interview by telephone each of the 523 academics thus selected for inclusion in the survey. A total of 472 interviews was completed (90 percent). In November 1972, this panel was queried again, using mailed questionnaires, and a response rate of 86 percent was achieved.[5] While the much smaller 1972 study was, naturally, of much less analytic value than the "parent" survey, it did in fact serve to provide some useful updating, and in that context we draw upon it here.

THE PLAN OF THE BOOK

Three immediate sets of concerns have occupied us in this study, and each serves to define a principal section of the book. First, we attend to general characteristics of the "academic mind," to the way professors conceptualize political life, and the relationship of their perspectives to broad currents within the intellectual stratum. College and university professors are part of the intellectual community, and their political re-

---

[5]The 1972 surveys were conducted with the financial support of the American Enterprise Institute for Public Policy Research. The text of the questionnaire is presented in Appendix B.

sponses cannot be understood separated from orientations which have distinguished secular intellectuals throughout the modern era.

In Part II, we explore sources of divisions within the professoriate. Academics display distinctive political orientations which set them apart as a stratum, but individually they are hardly of one mind. The intense, and remarkably predictable, divisions within the faculty are laid out and explained (we trust, with clarity). Attention is directed to basic structural determinants of professorial opinion.

Finally, in Part III, we attend to some specific issues which reflect both the underlying dimensions of conflict in faculty politics and the rapidly shifting context in which academic politics is acted out. American life generally is enveloped in social change extraordinary in its scope, extent, and rapidity–and universities are hardly untouched by such transitions. The 1960s began as an "era of growth," with expansion setting the predominant tone in academia. Then, while growth by no means ended, higher education entered "the era of campus confrontation." Protests and demonstrations—initiating them, resisting them, trying in some measure to cope with them—became the preoccupation of academics. In the 1970s, the academy entered yet another era, with a distinctive "political agenda." Austerity in its many forms commands attention now much as protests did a half decade ago.

Chapter 8 discusses the "protests" era and the kinds of conflict it engendered on American college campuses. In Chapter 9, then, we examine faculty responses to the choices offered by the 1972 presidential election, especially as the division among academics reflects the persisting effects of the struggles of the 1960s. Chapter 10 picks up a new issue not on the agenda of the sixties that is indicative of strains which are emphasized by a time of austerity. The growing acceptance of unions and collective bargaining by faculty—traditionally unreceptive even to the suggestion that such practices are appropriate to the university—carries profound consequences for the future of higher education in the United States, and points to some of the major changes intruding upon the character of professorial life.

Part One

Intellectuals, Academics, and Political Life

1. The Politics of Intellectuals

Gradually the diffusion of intelligence caused learning and talent to become a means of government; mental ability led to social power, and the men of letters took a part in the affairs of the state.

TOCQUEVILLE
Democracy in America

Secular intellectuals, as a distinct occupational stratum, are creatures of societal abundance. Before the first stirrings of the Industrial Revolution in the seventeenth century, there were, of course, various clerical intelligentsias devoted to revealing, interpreting, and communicating the word of God. Art, architecture, and letters—sometimes lofty— followed from these pursuits. A few "unattached intellectuals" functioned under the patronage of church or aristocracy. But preindustrial society simply was not able to support a large cadre of men and women devoting themselves to symbolic formulations. Those few it could underwrite were necessarily required to explain and to sustain the existing order, "to stabilize custom and validate social authority by perpetuating the tradition and interpreting it in a manner conformable to the understanding of common man" (Becker, 1936, p. 93).

In contrast, the growing affluence provided by industrialism has supported an ever-larger secular intelligentsia, one component of which occupies itself with the creation of knowledge. The relationship of creative intellectuals to industrial and now postindustrial society is symbiotic. The latter needs the inputs of the former for development. Science and technology, which have imposed the essential features of present society, are obviously creations of intellectuals. But secular intellectuals, as a large occupational stratum, are dependent upon the largess of advanced industrial orders. If the latter cannot exist without the performance of the former, it is also true that the intellectual stratum of the contemporary United States, for example, is a luxury which only an extraordinarily affluent society can afford and includes many persons who are not performing essential services—essential here defined by the needs of technology.

Postindustrial society offers more than the wherewithal for a large secular intelligentsia. The same affluence which permits extraordinary consumer indulgence contributes to an atmosphere profoundly indulgent with regard to expression. Restraints and restrictions are seen as functional necessities when a society is bent upon harnessing its limited resources for the great enterprise of industrial development. This is why, of course, both the United States of the late nineteenth century and the Soviet Union of the 1950s—different in so many regards— are appropriately described as "puritanical." Freedom of expression—sexual, artistic, political—has been circumscribed as individuals are required to subordinate themselves to compelling national objectives. The affluent society, of which the United States is now the prime example, has in contrast "arrived." It not only supports a massive intellectual stratum, but extends to that stratum a measure of openness and influence without parallel in history.

It is appropriate, then, that this study of the politics of American academics begin by surveying the broader context in which faculty as a part of the intellectual stratum have operated, and the social needs they satisfy. Much that is distinctive in university political life is so because universities share in the developmental dynamics and political currents which have enveloped secular intellectuals as this stratum has developed over the past 200 years.

ACADEMIC FUNCTIONS AND POLITICAL CONSEQUENCES

The politics of the university world may be derived in part from a consideration of three functions which institutions of higher education have fulfilled, particularly in modern times: socialization, in the sense of the transmission of traditional values, whether secular or religious; innovation and scholarship, the support for creative intellectuals in the sciences, humanities, and social sciences who are concerned with advancing the frontiers of knowledge and artistic work; and community service, the application of the knowledge and skills concentrated in the university to achieve objectives set by lay powers, including both government and private institutions. The first task, to the extent it is performed, may be identified today largely with the professor's role as

teacher. The second may be seen in the academic's role as scholar, scientist, or creative artist; and the third, in his role as consultant or as applied researcher.

While all three roles have probably existed within most Western institutions defined or described as universities since they first arose in the Middle Ages, there is a clear temporal sequence in their development. The earliest universities in Europe, and colleges in English North America, were primarily teaching institutions, almost invariably linked to religion, with a clerical faculty. Their basic tasks were to train the clergy and to serve as centers of theological scholarship. To the Faculty of Theology were often added those of Law and Medicine to help provide society with members of these professions. Scientific research first emerged outside colleges and universities, often in academies. In colonial America, out of 18 members elected to the Royal Society in London, only one, John Winthrop of Harvard, was a college professor. The emphasis on original scholarship began to penetrate the higher education world in the eighteenth century, but almost all *American* colleges and universities remained teaching institutions until the last quarter of the nineteenth century, when the efforts to create major research centers and graduate schools on the model of the German universities finally took hold in schools such as Johns Hopkins, Harvard, Chicago, Michigan, Wisconsin, and Stanford. Up to this point, American higher education was generally apolitical or conservative, for as long as the college was controlled by the churches, as most of the predominantly private American institutions were, instruction by the faculty did not stray far from revealed, traditional truth. Professors sought to socialize new generations in the accepted system of values. Colleges were largely centers of conventional thought. The secularization of the university, then, with the attendant emphasis on original research and creativity, is a major factor associated with the American university becoming an important center of political activity in modern times.

The emergence of a focus on original scholarship produced tension between higher education and the religious and secular powers, as leading scholars published articles and voiced opinions which were at odds with the interests and values of various extramural establishments. As the nineteenth century drew to a close, academic freedom *causes célèbres* grew in number (Metzger, 1961, pp. 139–193). Professors received notoriety for their involvement in various forms of protest politics, including activity of the "mugwumps" and opposition to the Spanish-American War as the most significant instances. The growth of scholarship also brought increasing emphasis on applied science and scholarship, notably among the faculties of agricultural and engineering schools, but in many other professorial fields as well. Both public and private financial supporters sought assistance from the university and were prepared to pay for it. And the university began to come under attack from radicals as a handmaiden of the established order (Veblen, 1918).

The differences in political predispositions inherent in the diverse roles of higher education as a transmission agent of the culture and knowledge of a society and as the principal source of intellectual innovation were anticipated in the 1870s by a major figure in the international history of education, Arinori Mori, the minister of education in Meiji Japan. Addressing his cabinet colleagues, engaged with him in the great task of transforming the country into a strong, modern industrial society, Mori distinguished sharply between those components of the modernized education system which would teach needed skills, including fundamental literacy, and the role of major universities, which would be assigned the task of supporting and training scholars to be in the forefront of research. In identifying the political dimensions of the system, he noted that the lower segments, up to and including teachers colleges, would "help teach people to be loyal to the state." As he indicated, teachers are "transmitters of knowledge rather than free seekers after truth. . . ." The universities, however, as centers of the innovative scholarship which a modern society requires, had to "be allowed sufficient freedom in the conduct of research to assure academic progress." And given his assumption that research-oriented universities, necessarily centers of original and free thought, might upset the basis for loyalty to the state, Mori proposed that these institutions should be physically separated as much as possible, preventing contact with the general population, and that they should not be allowed to train teachers for the rest of the system (Nagai, 1964, pp. 29–30). More succinctly, Mori anticipated that the conditions which would foster creative scholarship would also breed disloyalty, while teaching, separated from research, could be relied on to support the state and emperor.

The recognition by policy makers of a linkage between an emphasis on scholarship and disloyalty was, of course, not limited to Japan. As early as 1798, President John Adams, observing the role of intellectuals in the French Revolution, recommended against admitting a party of French scientists to the United States, observing: "I really begin to think, or rather to suspect, that learned academies, not under the immediate inspection and control of government, have disorganized the world, and are incompatible with social order" (Adams, 1853, p. 596). Three-quarters of a century later, Mori's contemporary, New York

Tribune editor Whitelaw Reid, noted from an approving perspective: "As for the scholar, the laws of his intellectual development may be trusted to fix his place. Free thought is necessarily aggressive and critical. . . . And so we may set down, as a . . . function of the American scholar in politics, *an intellectual leadership of the radicals*" (Reid, 1873, pp. 613–614).

Such commentary forms part of what has become a well-developed theme—that the intellectual community, of which faculty are a part, is inherently questioning, critical, socially disruptive. This commitment to an antiestablishment position has been deduced by many writers from factors inherent in the very concept of the intellectual and scholar. Intellectuals, as distinct from professionals, are concerned with *creation* of knowledge, art, or literature. In awarding status within the occupation, the emphasis is on creation, innovation, *avant-gardism*. Professionals are the *users* of knowledge. And many writers such as Thorstein Veblen, Joseph Schumpeter, and C. P. Snow have pointed out that inherent in the obligation to create, to innovate, has been the tendency to reject the status quo, to oppose the existing or the old as philistine. Intellectuals, as Tocqueville noted, are also more likely than those in other occupations to be partisans of the ideal, of the theoretical, and thus to criticize reality from this standpoint. The need to express the inner logic of their discipline, of their art form, also presses them to oppose the powers, the patrons, who seemingly are philistines, who prefer continuity rather than change.

In repeating these analyses which link creative scholarship to critical or even radical and seditious social thought, we do not mean to imply that university faculty as a stratum are necessarily sympathetic to such politics. Although a visible cadre has played significant roles in leading and supporting protest movements of both the left and the right at different times in history, most have accepted the status quo. Universities remain primarily educational institutions, which implies that they are part of the social apparatus designed to transmit the existing culture, including the beliefs that help to legitimate the authority system of the society. In spite of the changes noted earlier, involving a shift from institutions expounding the doctrines of the church to centers of free thought and scholarship, the vast majority of contemporary institutions of higher education, while called colleges and universities, are essentially schools. They are not, that is, knowledge-creating centers. The school requires the faculty to be primarily involved in the transmission of useful skills and indoctrination of accepted values, in preparation for life, and in the development of total personality and character. In essence, therefore, the "school" components of higher education are conservative aspects (Lipset, 1972*a*, pp. 273–277).

The third major function of the contemporary university—service to the community, in the form of consultation, applied research, external lecturing, and the like—not only may provide outside income and thus enhance the position of the professoriate as part of the privileged strata, but also links it to the external establishments. Both higher income and such extramural ties have been frequently cited as further sources of conservative views within academe. From this perspective, professional schools, which are usually closely related to professions or the business world in their teaching, applied research, and consultation functions, are often perceived as centers of "establishment" influence within the university.

The current debates concerning the multiversity, which involve criticism of the university and faculty for serving mammon rather than scholarship, are not new. At the beginning of the twentieth century a budding young radical intellectual, Van Wyck Brooks, complained as a Harvard undergraduate that the growing emphasis on the graduate professional schools would "make of Harvard the factory of American imperialism," that "the old fashioned humanist fades away, with the [growth of the] University the efficient practitioner of the future emerges" (Brooks, 1908, pp. 643–649). Another Harvard humanist, Bliss Perry, also criticized the involvement of many professors in nonscholarly activities.

[A] newer type of college professor is . . . everywhere in evidence: the expert who knows all about railroads and bridges and subways; about gas commissions and electrical supplies; about currency and banking, Philippine tariffs, Venezuelan boundary lines, the industries of Puerto Rico, the classification of the civil service, the control of trusts. . . . The professor's photograph . . . assaults your eye in the marketplace. The college press club and the university's bureau of publicity gives his lecture dates in advance (B. P., 1902, pp. 284–285).

THE POLITICAL VIEWS OF ACADEMICS BEFORE WORLD WAR II

The basic record would seem to sustain Richard Hofstadter's (1963, p. 39) generalization that for almost all of the past century, the political weight of American intellectuals, including leading academics, has been disproportionately on the progressive, liberal, and leftist side. Quantitative data derived from post-World War II attitude surveys, plus assorted other earlier reports of the political orientations of the American professoriate, strongly indicate that academics have consistently leaned to the left.[1] This bias, to a considerable extent, reflects the absence or weakness of a legitimate national conservative tradition in America. National identity and national ideology are linked to a value system, stemming from an elaboration of those principles enunciated in the Declaration of Independence, that emphasizes egalitarianism and populism. Thus, when American intellectuals are moved to point up the gap between the real and the ideal, whether represented by what was (a bygone Jeffersonian laissez-faire utopia of equal yeoman farmers) or what should be (a classless participatory future), they challenge the system for not fulfilling the ideals implicit in the American Creed.[2]

In spite of Whitelaw Reid's description of the political role of the nineteenth century scholar as foe of the "established" and leader of the "radicals," there is little in the historical record to suggest that many professors were active in fostering major social change following the victory of the antislavery cause which had brought the large majority in the North to the Republican party. The available reports suggest, however, that the visible links between Republican administrations and aggressive industrial capital, plus concern over the need for civil service reform, weakened the allegiance of academics to the GOP. Many became "mugwumps": they "supported the Republicans through 1880, then voted for Grover Cleveland, then returned to the Republican fold in 1896 (though unenthusiastically, regarding McKinley as a lesser evil), and (commonly though not always) adopted some form of Progressivism after 1900." Laurence Veysey (1962, pp. 160–161) notes that at the time "academic mugwumpery symbolized the professor's

---

[1]For a report of various studies bearing on this point see Lipset (1963, pp. 332–371). A more recent comprehensive survey of analyses of the political attitudes and behavior of American academics is Lipset (1972a, pp. 211–289).

There is little quantitatively reliable material dealing with faculty opinions prior to the 1950s. Historians and other observers have, however, sought to generalize about the academic role in earlier eras, largely from examination of the behavior of the most prominent among American faculty, those at the leading universities. As we shall have occasion to note at length in subsequent chapters, there are considerable differences between faculty at the more prestigious universities and the lesser institutions. Yet as historian of academia Laurence Veysey indicates, "there is a strong argument for examining any articulate, self-chosen group . . . —whether lawyers, artists, professors—primarily in terms of its leadership. For lawyers, this would mean the Wall Street firm rather than the small-town practitioners, for professors, this means primarily those at leading universities" (Veysey, 1969, p. 2).

[2]Lipset (1967a) has elaborated on these themes in the American value system with reference to the work of analysts such as Tocqueville, Martineau, Bryce, Hartz, Riesman, and others.

relationship to all institutions, including his own: uneasy discontent, yet an unwillingness to 'throw his vote away.' He far preferred to purify one of the major political parties. . . ." To a considerable extent, inspiration for the anticorruption, clean-government ideals of the mugwumps stemmed from the colleges.

More significant, perhaps, in attesting to professorial "idealism" is the fact that "faculty opposition to imperialism during the 1890s was observed as general all over the country" (Veysey, 1962, p. 160). At Harvard, which dominated the "public image of higher education" at the time, considerable opposition developed to the aggressive American foreign policy actions of both the Cleveland and McKinley administrations (Lipset, 1975). A week before President McKinley went to Congress for a declaration of war against Spain, "eighty-six members of the Harvard faculty led by President Eliot . . . [declared] against war and for peace" (Schirmer, 1972, p. 53).

Leading academics continued to engage in antiwar agitation during the Spanish-American War, and they urged independence for the Philippines during the Filipino insurrection. While the war was still on, Oliver Wendell Holmes, Jr., commented to a friend: "I confess to pleasure in hearing some rattling jingo talk after the self-righteous and preaching discourse which has prevailed to some extent at Harvard College and elsewhere" (Freidel, 1970, p. 77). An article in the *Atlantic Monthly* in 1902 reported that college professors had acquired a reputation for taking obstructionist political positions. "Within a twelve-month college teachers have been openly denounced as 'traitors' for advocating self-government for Filipinos. In many a pulpit and newspaper office, last September, it was declared that the utterances of college professors were largely responsible for the assassination of President McKinley" (B. P., 1902, p. 286). Whitelaw Reid (1913, pp. 241–242), who in 1873 had praised the antiestablishment role of American scholars, complained in a speech at Stanford in 1901 that it was a misfortune for the country that its college "instructors are out of sympathy with its history, with its development, and with the men who made the one and are guiding the other."

In the next decade, observers, both foreign and domestic, commented on the strength of socialism among the faculty members of leading American universities.[3] The most influential young socialist intellectual of pre-World War I days, Randolph Bourne (1913, p. 295), while still an undergraduate at Columbia in 1912, explained the spread of socialism

[3]For references, see Lipset (1972b, pp. 148–151).

in the colleges as reflecting the fact that for a typical undergraduate, "his education, if it has been in one of the advanced universities, will only have tended to confirm his radicalism." John Reed (1939, p. 22), active in the Harvard Socialist Club, reported that it was supported by many professors. Although we have no quantitative measures to validate these impressions, a highly sophisticated survey of the religious opinions of academics in 1913–1914, a period in which most adult Americans belonged to churches, indicated that the large majority did not believe in God or immortality. And reinforcing the generalizations that faculty liberalism and radicalism were strongest in the leading schools, this survey found that the more distinguished faculty were much more irreligious than their less eminent colleagues (Leuba, 1921, pp. 219–287).

Large numbers of socialist and progressive intellectuals were swept away by the Wilsonian crusade to make the world safe for democracy. Yet by "1918–20 the doubts of many intellectuals about both the war and Wilsonian idealism turned to violent and bitter revulsion" (May, 1963, p. 19). Considerable enthusiasm was expressed in many intellectual circles for the Bolsheviks and the Russian Revolution. The growing discontent on the campuses led many in business and politics, including the then Vice-President-elect, Calvin Coolidge, to denounce the radicalism of college faculties.[4] Granville Hicks, perhaps the foremost Communist literary intellectual of the 1930s, saw the twenties as preparing the way for the Communist gains in the next decade.

There was in that decade [the twenties] a loose kind of united front against the *status quo*. The intellectuals were almost unanimous in their distaste for a business civilization and in their willingness to accept as allies all enemies of the existing order. Russia, with all its faults, was regarded as being on "our" side because it represented something new in the world and because it was hated and feared by the proponents and beneficiaries of the status quo.[5]

The propensity to reject the status quo is, of course, as compatible with taking a conservative or right-wing position as with a liberal or left-wing radical one. In the nineteenth century, when one found in the United States the two often antagonistic emphases on populist egalitarianism and business growth, the intellectual elite, linked to the declining values of New England and the Southern aristocracy, tended

---

[4]For references, see Lipset (1972*b*, p. 162).

[5]Hicks (1954, p. 165). For a more recent analysis by a Marxist of the revived radicalism of the intellectuals of the 1920s, see Sklar (1969, pp. 23–36).

to oppose both these emphases. Richard Hofstadter (1965, pp. 111–112), described this stance of alienation as "historical and traditional," and pointed out that "even the genteel, established intellectuals of the mid-nineteenth century were in effect patrician rebels against the increasing industrialization and the philistinism of the country."

This orientation continued as a minority emphasis within American intellectualdom in the early decades of the twentieth century, centering often in literary and humanistic academic circles such as the Southern Agrarian school of literature. Humanistic, antibourgeois, and elitist sentiments took a nasty form in the 1920s in support for restrictions on the admission of Jews and other "unassimilables" to universities as students and faculty members (Steinberg, 1974). On the political level, rightist resentment against American materialism and populism even led a small minority of leading American professors and other intellectuals to find reason to praise Italian fascism in the 1920s. Among the prominent Americans who dealt favorably with fascism were such writers as Wallace Stevens and Henry Miller, and a variety of humanistic scholars, including Irving Babbit, Charles Beard, Shephard Clough, Carlton J. Hayes, Horace Kallen, William Lyon Phelps, George Santayana, and Herbert Schneider.

Most of the renewed "alienation of intellectuals" in this period took on a nonpolitical, strongly antimaterialistic, and antibourgeois orientation, but the protests against the conviction of Sacco and Vanzetti for murder, which grew gradually through the decade and reached a crescendo in 1927, the year of their execution, eventually mobilized and radicalized a substantial number of intellectuals both on and off the campuses. As David Felix (1965, p. 16) said: "The Sacco-Vanzetti case belonged to the intellectuals." The large-scale protest movement only magnified the conflict between the intellectuals and the powers.

Thus when writers and professors began to voice . . . doubts, it seemed to many conservatives only another proof of dangerous radicalism among the intellectuals. And the writers and the professors, bringing out fact after fact which showed the prejudice and perjury involved in the conviction, came increasingly to feel that the leaders of business and government were not interested in evidence but only in teaching the radicals the brutal lesson that there was no room for dissent in America (Earnest, 1953, p. 279).

The explicit involvement of large numbers of prominent intellectuals in various forms of left-wing politics, particularly Communist and Communist-front groups, during the 1930s resulted in extravagant evaluations of the strength of communism among scholars (Lyons, 1941,

p. 129). In 1932 a significant number of the more prominent intellectuals of the country endorsed the Communist presidential ticket (Aaron, 1961, pp. 196–198). However one estimates the actual proportion of scholars who went so far as to back the party, no one seriously doubts that the Communists' most obvious success during the 1930s was among the intellectuals and their "apprentices," the college students. As Daniel Bell has written:

Except for its success in attracting an important section of the intellectual fringe and the student youth, the Communist party never achieved a wide mass following in America during the depression years. . . . It did have for many years a disproportionate influence in the cultural field. At one time, from 1936 to 1939, through the fellow travelers in the publishing houses, radio, Hollywood, the magazines, and other mass media, it exercized influence on public opinion far beyond the mere number of party members.[6]

The one serious attempt at a quantitative evaluation of the backgrounds of members of the Communist party supports these impressions. Ernst and Loth (1952, pp. 3–4) reported that

. . . the proportion of party members who have been to college is very high. Even more striking is the great number of graduate degrees among them. . . . In fact, the Communist party in America seems to be such a highly educated, nonmanual laboring group that at times there would be more rejoicing in its headquarters over the recruiting of one common laborer than over ten Ph.D.'s.

Given the paucity of data, it is difficult to form any conclusive statistical judgment about the distribution of opinion among academics and intellectuals in this period. It is possible, of course, that although the Communist party and other left-of-center groups drew the bulk of their support from intellectuals, as well as from their fellow travelers among the well-educated, most intellectuals were in fact unaffected, as the limited membership of such groups suggests. Certain data imply, however, a predominant academic and intellectual commitment to at least liberal views. A repeat in 1933 of the 1913 survey of religious orientations of academics, to which samples of writers and business and professional people listed in *Who's Who* were added, indicated that irreligion had grown among the professors during the 20-year interval. The more distinguished academics were again shown to have a greater propensity to be irreligious than their less eminent peers. Writers were also heavily

---

[6]Bell (1952, pp. 353–354). See also Howe and Coser (1957, pp. 273–318).

atheistic (62 percent), while substantial majorities among the business and professional communities were found to be believers. Although attitudes toward religion are not flawless indicators of political preferences, many studies indicate high correlations between being irreligious and having left views, at least in the United States. A 1937 survey of opinion in Chicago found academics to be much more liberal or radical on various socioeconomic issues than those in all other occupational groups (Kornhauser, 1938, p. 264). The one national survey of college student opinion in the 1930s, conducted by the Roper Poll, saw 24 percent express sympathy for "socialism," 6 percent for "communism," and 45 percent for "liberalism," but just 15 percent for "conservatism" and 2 percent for "fascism."[7]

A contemporary (1938) effort to account for the leftist views of the more intellectually oriented undergraduates of the 1930s by two psychologists, Gardner Murphy and Rensis Likert (1938, pp. 107–108), suggested that to be "bookish" meant to be exposed to radical thought.

To be bookish in this era has meant to steep oneself in the disillusioned gropings of postwar thinkers, most of whom, from philosophers to lyricists, are clearly "radical." . . . The literary groups to which these men belong, the day-by-day conversations in which they train one another to think and to feel, are full of the modern doubt and disquietude, and even more frequently, of the modern challenge and rebellion. To be bookish today is to be radical.[8]

The support given by many intellectuals to organized leftist groups, particularly the Communists, was highly unstable. The dramatic shifts in the party line, along with events in the Soviet Union—from the famines imposed by enforced collectivization to the purges of the Soviet leadership and the Moscow trials of 1936 and 1938—leading finally to the Hitler-Stalin pact of 1939, which enabled the Germans to go to war, served to alienate almost all the intellectuals from the party. (Ironically, just before the Hitler-Stalin pact was approved, over 400 intellectuals, including many professors, signed a manifesto published in *The Nation*

---

[7]For a report on this study and other surveys conducted during the 1930s, see Lipset (1972b, pp. 178–182, 184).

[8]Writing of the literature of the post-World War II decades, Lionel Trilling reached similar conclusions as of 1965. "Any historian of the literature of the modern age will take virtually for granted the adversary intention, the actual subversive intention, that characterizes modern writing—he will perceive its clear purpose of detaching the reader from the habits of thought and feeling that the larger culture imposes, of giving him a ground and a vantage point from which to judge and condemn, and perhaps revise, the culture that has produced him" (Trilling, 1965, pp. xii–xiii).

[August 10, 1939] testifying to their faith in the *bona fides* of the Soviet Union.) Except during the period of the Hitler-Stalin pact (1939–1941), the Communist party from 1936 on had strongly urged all leftists to adopt a "defensist" posture, to support the United States and the other Western democracies. The Communists, joined by many socialists and liberals, argued that fascist totalitarianism was so dangerous that intellectuals and other critics of Western democratic systems had an obligation to restrain themselves and to defend their very imperfect societies against an attack from a much worse system. The Popular Front tactic, uniting all antifascist forces, pushed intellectuals to become supporters of the domestic status quo.

POLITICS IN THE POSTWAR ERA

The end of the antifascist war was followed by a renewed concern for Western democracy, again under totalitarian attack. This time, ironically, the threat was thought to come from an aggressive Stalinist totalitarianism. Open anti-Semitism in Russia, the Czech coup, the Berlin blockade of 1948—these and other developments served to undermine any lingering faith in a Communist utopia. Many intellectuals, including most avowed socialists among them, were led to continue or to revive the policy previously urged on them by the Communists—to defend the existing society against an external threat. Philip Rahv, Brandeis English professor who had been an editor of *Partisan Review*, the principal radical literary-political magazine of the 1930s (pro-Communist in the beginning, later sympathetic to Trotskyism), pointed to these shifts in orientation in 1952.

Among the factors entering into the change, the principal one, to my mind, is the exposure of the Soviet myth and the consequent resolve (shared by nearly all but the few remaining fellow travelers) to be done with utopian illusions and heady expectations. In their chastened mood American democracy looks like the real thing to the intellectuals. . . . Whether capitalist or not, it has so far sustained that freedom of expression and experiment without which the survival of the intelligence is inconceivable in a modern society. . . . In the palmy days when it was possible to take democracy for granted—that is, before the rise to global power of Hitlerism and then of Stalinism—the intellectuals were hardly aware of the very tangible benefits they derived from it. Now, however, only the most doctrinaire types would be disposed to trade in those benefits for some imaginary perfection of good in the remote future (Rahv, 1969, pp. 176–177).

Yet even during this period in which American academics and intellectuals accommodated to the system, the quiescence was only relative. Reacting to the attacks on academe by Senator Joseph McCarthy and other right-wing leaders, many became heavily involved in the beginnings of the "New Politics" of the intelligentsia, the Adlai Stevenson presidential campaigns, and the "reform Democratic" club movement (Wilson, 1962). Surveys taken of national samples of professorial opinion reported that in the 1948 presidential election, faculty were much more likely to have voted for the Progressive party candidate, Henry Wallace, or the Socialist nominee, Norman Thomas, than were the general electorate. In each of the three presidential elections from 1948 through 1956, the Republican nominees, Thomas Dewey and Dwight Eisenhower, received a considerably smaller percentage of the votes among academics than among any other distinguishable professional or middle-class group, and even less than among manual workers (Howard, 1958). A survey of the effect of McCarthyism on the beliefs and behavior of American social scientists concluded that they were relatively unintimidated; their heads were "bloody but unbowed." Paul Lazarsfeld and Wagner Thielens, Jr. (1958, pp. 95, 104) suggest that it was more dangerous for the career of an academic to be a public supporter of McCarthy on a college campus than to be a bitter opponent. Robert Nisbet (1971, p. 143) has credited the McCarthy period with helping to legitimate and thereby stimulate campus political activism. The activism of the 1960s drew support from the politicized university faculties which had resisted McCarthyite pressure during the 1950s.

No single figure, no single issue ... had ever seized the minds of faculty members as did the person of Senator Joseph McCarthy and the cause he represented in the 1950's. . . . For McCarthy's enemy, his declared enemy, was not labor, not labor unions, not the people—in the Populist sense—but almost strictly and exclusively the intellectuals in this country, academic intellectuals especially.

Given his assaults in so many intellectual areas, his challenging of the loyalty of intellectuals, his threats to "get" Harvard and other universities, it would be extraordinary if the mind of the American faculty had *not* become visibly radicalized in the 1950's.[9]

Faculty politics in the decade and a half immediately following World War II did not involve a rupture of the historic alignment. There was, nonetheless, temporarily a lesser inclination to challenge institutions and practices of the society, as these were seen as operating in a state of

---

[9]See also Ulam (1972, pp. 57–58) for a similar analysis.

siege. One of us (Lipset, 1963, pp. 369–371) noted at the end of the 1950s that

> the political issue of the 1950's has become freedom versus Communism, and in that struggle many socialist and liberal intellectuals find themselves identifying with established institutions. This identification comes hard to intellectuals who feel called upon to reject conventional stupidities, and results in a feeling of malaise which takes the form of complaining that everyone, including the intellectuals, is too conformist. . . . Their solution to this dilemma is to continue to feel allied with the left, but to vote Democratic; to think of themselves as liberals—and often even as socialists—but to withdraw from active involvement or interest in politics and to concentrate on their work, whether it be writing poetry or scholarly articles.
>
> . . . In spite of the powerful conservatizing forces, the inherent tendency to oppose the *status quo* will still remain. . . . Any *status quo* embodies rigidities and dogmatisms which it is the inalienable right of intellectuals to attack, whether from the standpoint of moving back to traditional values or forward toward the achievement of the equalitarian dream.

This period came to an end with the breakdown of one of the principal ideological justifications for the cold war—the threat of a monolithic Communist movement. De-Stalinization in the Soviet Union set a dynamic process in motion within the Communist world which made conflict inside various countries and among the bloc nations very visible. Protest was more common; the Sino-Soviet split gave the final lie to the idea of Communist unity. Many of the pressures which had prevented intellectuals in the West from attacking their own societies ceased to operate. As ideological anti-Communism lost its strength, some of the older, once-leftist intellectuals turned back to elements of earlier beliefs. More significant, perhaps, was the emergence among younger academics and students of widespread social criticism. This began in the civil rights area, expanded substantially because of the Vietnam War, and ultimately came to touch a host of issues that affected almost all major American institutions. The new generations who knew neither Hitler nor Stalin, and had no firsthand experience of the 1948 Czech coup or the Hungarian revolution, found no reason to hold back in their criticisms.

Many now forget that an early target of the revived critical stance of intellectualdom in the 1960s was the man who in death was to become the cultural folk-hero of the decade, John F. Kennedy. In spite of his valiant efforts to win their support, he was not popular among non-policy-involved intellectuals during his lifetime. Adlai Stevenson and to a lesser extent Hubert Humphrey were the preferred candidates of politicized intellectuals. This group despaired of Kennedy, whose record revealed no great political passions and who had sat out the fight against McCarthy while other members of his family, including his brother Robert, had actively supported the Wisconsin Senator. For many, the choice between Kennedy and Nixon meant no choice. "In looking over the now-ancient journals of 1960 we can see how bitter the intellectuals were over the choice of candidates and philosophies, how sure they were that the ages of McKinley, Coolidge, and Eisenhower had put their unequivocal stamp on the American culture" (Berman, 1968, p. 4).

Recognizing his difficulties with this constituency, Kennedy deliberately emphasized the "public role of the intellectual" during and after his inauguration. And as Joseph Kraft indicated, this emphasis had "a political purpose—as plain as the appointment of a Negro judge or a Polish Postmaster General. It is aimed, to be specific, at the egghead liberals within the Democratic party ... " (Kraft, 1963, p. 112). But during the thousand days of the administration, Kennedy continued to meet with considerable rebuffs. Nine months after the young President took office, James Reston wrote a column in the New York *Times* discussing the "discontented intellectuals." He noted that the new regime was being described as "the third Eisenhower administration," that the intellectuals were "disenchanted by the absence of new policies, the preoccupation with political results, the compromises over education and the techniques of appointing conservatives to put over liberal policies and liberals to carry out conservative policies" (Reston, 1961, p. 10E). And in an article published in November 1963, just before the assassination, Kraft reported that in spite of the large number of academics who held important governmental posts as "technical bureaucrats" and the use of cultural awards as "a form of patronage," there was considerable tension between the administration and the intellectuals. "Harsh criticisms have come from the novelists Norman Mailer and James Baldwin, the playwright Gore Vidal, and the political scientists Sidney Hyman and Louis Halle. 'Where,' the critic Alfred Kazin asked in a notable essay, 'is the meaningful relation of intellectuals to power' " (Kraft, 1963, p. 112).

Ironically, the tragic death of the young President and the succession of Lyndon Johnson, who appeared to typify the "wheeler and dealer" politician, accomplished what Kennedy had been unable to do in life. This change was curiously prophesied before the 1960 election by James MacGregor Burns, who, after noting the lack of appeal of Kennedy's nonemotional pragmatic orientation, stated: "If he should die tomorrow in a plane crash, he would become at once a liberal martyr, for the liberal publicists of the land would rush to construct a hero" (Burns, 1960, p. 16).

During the mid-1960s, American intellectuals once again appeared to take over the role of polemical "moralists" with respect to political criticism, denouncing the system for betraying its own basic democratic and anti-imperialist beliefs. Beginning with the faculty-initiated teach-ins against the Vietnam War in 1965, academics played a major role in sustaining a mass antiwar movement out of which a number of radicals emerged.

The movement of the late 1960s differed substantially from that of the 1930s, notably in the absence of a single radical group or coalition around which activity was centered. Many hundreds of thousands of persons—possibly millions—identified with the various militant protests. A sense of alienation was widely diffused; there seemed to be a rejection of authority; many spoke of the need for a new noncapitalist social order. Yet, with the exception of the short-lived conglomerative antiwar organizations, no national group recruited more than a few thousand members. No new radical political party of any substance emerged. At the heart of the movement, perhaps, were the many hundreds of New Left or "underground" papers, of which the most influential was the "aboveground" *New York Review of Books*.

In spite of its loose level of organization, the different elements of the movement succeeded in challenging the system on a number of issues. Universities became staging areas. Liberal and left faculty, along with student activists, looked for a mass response. There were over 500,000 professors and 7 million students in the colleges and universities of the country. Ideas originating in these communities circulated quickly, and new forms of student activism and confrontation became common. As John Kenneth Galbraith (1971, p. 52) noted:

It was the universities—not the trade unions, nor the free-lance intellectuals, nor the press, nor the businessmen . . . —which led the opposition to the Vietnam war, which forced the retirement of President Johnson, which are forcing the pace of our present withdrawal from Vietnam, which are leading the battle against the great corporations on the issue of pollution, and which at the last Congressional elections retired a score or more of the more egregious time-servers, military sycophants and hawks.

NATIONAL SURVEYS OF PROFESSORIAL OPINION

Evidence that the dominant mood on the American campus is liberal to left and hence predisposed to favor politics dedicated to egalitarian social changes is clear and decisive, even though the first detailed national survey of faculty political opinion, other than presidential choice, in all disciplines did not occur until 1966 (an interesting fact in itself). A National Opinion Research Center (NORC) survey found in 1966 that 61 percent of the respondents described themselves as "liberals," as contrasted with 28 percent "conservative," (11 percent "neither") (Noll & Rossi, 1966, p. 17).

The most comprehensive data demonstrating the extent to which American academics stand to the left of other strata come from the largest extant national survey of the professoriate, which was conducted in 1969 for the Carnegie Commission on Higher Education, with assistance from the American Council on Education. Described in the introduction to this volume, this survey is intensively analyzed in the following chapters. Here we need only note that it shows faculty contributing disproportionate support to liberal and egalitarian positions. Some of these findings, together with the results of studies of American students and of the general public in the United States, are presented in Table 2. Both faculty and students gave comparable distributions of responses. Each was much more inclined to locate its politics on the left than was the American public at large.[10] Three years later, in the late summer of 1972, a national sample of American professors was again

TABLE 2 *Political ideology of academics and general public in the United States, 1969–1970 (column percentages)*

Political ideology	Under-graduates*	Graduate students*	Faculty*	U. S. public†
Left	5	5	5	4
Liberal	40	37	41	16
Middle-of-the-road	36	28	27	38
Moderately conservative	17	26	25	32
Strongly conservative	2	4	3	10

*Response to the question "How would you characterize yourself politically at the present time?" (Left, liberal, middle-of-the-road, moderately conservative, or strongly conservative.) Data from 1969 Carnegie Commission surveys.

†Response to the question "How would you describe yourself?" (Very liberal, fairly liberal, middle-of-the-road, fairly conservative, or very conservative.) Data from *Gallup Opinion Index*, Report No. 65 (November 1970), p. 17.

[10]Interestingly, A. H. Halsey and Martin Trow, in their 1966 survey of British academics, located a pattern of ideological self-identification strikingly similar to what we found in the United States. Of British college and university teachers, 5 percent described themselves as "far left," 48 percent "moderate left," and 28 percent "center," as against only 18 percent "moderate right" and 1 percent "far right" (Halsey & Trow, 1971, p. 403).

TABLE 3 Political ideology of academics and general public in the United States, 1972 (column percentages)

Political ideology	College students*	Faculty†	U. S. public‡
Left	9	9	3
Liberal	43	40	21
Middle-of-the-road	31	26	37
Moderately conservative	15	23	
Strongly conservative	1	2	38

*Gilbert Youth Survey (1972).
†1972 Ladd and Lipset faculty survey (1972).
‡Louis Harris Survey (1972).

queried as to their political views. Once more the faculty proved to be considerably to the left of the general public and showed a distribution similar to the student population (Table 3).

From the 1930s on, there are varieties of data dealing with party and candidate choice which reveal the relative liberalism of college professors, decisively when compared with other segments of the middle class but also to a lesser extent in comparison with manual workers and low-income groups generally. In 1937, a Chicago survey reported pro-New Deal sentiments among 84 percent of professors of social science and 65 percent of natural science faculty members, as contrasted with 56 percent among manual workers, and only about 15 percent in the ranks of lawyers, physicians, dentists, and engineers (Kornhauser, 1938, p. 264). A 1947 survey of 9,000 university graduates (*Time*, 1947) indicated large Democratic majorities in the 1944 election among teachers, scientists, and people in the arts. It is interesting that while 60 percent of those who reported their occupation as "scientists" voted for Franklin Roosevelt, 80 percent of those who listed themselves as engineers opted for his Republican opponent, Thomas Dewey. A questionnaire administered to 1,300 professors in 15 colleges and universities in October 1956 revealed disproportionate backing for the Democratic and leftist third-party candidates in the 1948 and 1952 elections, and a heavy Democratic preference in 1956 vote intent. Harry Truman received 50 percent of faculty votes in 1948, while Progressive party candidate Henry Wallace and Socialist Norman Thomas took about 10 percent. (The Democratic and left third-party candidates were backed by just over 50 percent of all voters, about 10 percent less than in the academic community.) Dwight Eisenhower swept the country in 1952 with 55 percent of the vote, but Adlai Stevenson was supported by 54 percent of academics. Various third parties on the left collected just over 2 percent of the academic vote, while garnering under one half of one percent among the electorate. In 1956, Stevenson's backing among professors rose to 60 percent (Howard, 1958, pp. 415–419).

The voting behavior of academic social scientists in the postwar elections was examined in a survey conducted by Paul F. Lazarsfeld and Wagner Thielens, Jr., in 1955. Although confined to a single discipline group—and that known to be the most liberal and Democratic within the faculty—the Lazarsfeld-Thielens investigation is nonetheless especially interesting because it is the first national survey of the politics of academics to apply fully the methods of systematic sampling. Lazarsfeld and Thielens (1958, p. 402) found that in 1948, 63 percent of social scientists voted for Harry Truman, 8 percent for Henry Wallace or Norman Thomas, and only 28 percent for Republican Thomas Dewey. Four years later, Stevenson took 65 percent of the social scientists' vote, as contrasted with 34 percent for Eisenhower.

Comparing the presidential voting of faculty with that of the general population over the last quarter century (Table 4), we find not only that professors have been more Democratic but also that their electoral distributions have borne a notably consistent relationship to the national vote. In 1956, professors gave Stevenson a proportion of their vote 18 percentage points higher than he received from the entire electorate; in 1972, McGovern's faculty total exceeded his nationwide percentage by 17 points.[11] Professors have been much more supportive of Democratic and, especially in 1948, left third-party candidates than have voters generally, and no significant change has occurred over the past five elections.

As far as we know, there was no national survey of faculty choice in the 1960 election, but the 1969 and 1972 faculty surveys provide unusually comprehensive data on the 1964, 1968, and 1972 presidential preferences of professors, along with other aspects of their political orientations. Lyndon Johnson was backed by 77 percent of professors, compared with 52 percent of the college-educated population generally and 54 percent of persons in professional and managerial occupations (Table 4). The faculty was then 20 to 25 percentage points more Democratic than groups of comparable socioeconomic status in the population at large. In fact, academics gave Johnson a higher proportion of their votes than any other distinguishable occupational or class stratum. The rela-

[11]In Table 4, Democratic and left third-party votes are combined. Here, the Democratic percentages only are reported, accounting for a slight variation from the table figures.

TABLE 4 *Democratic and left third-party Presidential vote among faculty and other population groups, 1944–1972 (row percentages)*

	1944		1948	
	Democratic vote as percent of total vote	Group Democratic proportion compared with national Democratic proportion	Democratic vote as percent of total vote	Group Democratic proportion compared with national Democratic proportion
ALL VOTERS	54		52	
Occupation				
Professors	57	+ 3	61	+ 9
Professional/managerial	39	−15	31	−21
Clerical/sales	49	− 5	41	−11
Manual	60	+ 6	66	+14
Education				
College	39	−15	32	−20
High school	47	− 7	47	− 5
Grade school	61	+ 7	62	+10

*Vote for left third-party candidates is included with the Democratic party vote. Except for 1948, the "minor party of the left" support was negligible among the general public. Among faculty, however, it was significant, totaling 2 percent in 1944, 11 percent in 1948, 2 percent in 1952, 2 percent in 1956, 1 percent in 1964, 3 percent in 1968, and 1 percent in 1972.

SOURCES: Data bearing on the vote choices of professors in 1944 are from a secondary analysis of a national survey of college graduates conducted by *Time* in 1947; for the years 1948, 1952, and 1956, they are from a study by Howard (1958); for the years 1964, 1968, and 1972, they are from surveys conducted by us and reported in detail in our various publications included in the references. The findings for other strata are based on secondary analyses of cumulated Gallup surveys for election years. We have not included 1960 since we do not know of any national survey of professional opinion in that year.

tive distributions in the 1968 contest between Hubert Humphrey and Richard Nixon were essentially the same. Of professors, 58 percent voted for Humphrey (and 4 percent for left third-party candidates), according to the Carnegie survey, in comparison with 43 percent of the electorate, 50 percent of manual workers, and just 37 percent of the college educated. Again in the 1972 balloting, academics showed up as decisively more Democratic than voters generally, of either high or low socioeconomic standing.

American college professors, though they are one of the most prestigious professions in the country and are paid salaries comparable to those of other upper-middle-class professionals, have recently been

TABLE 4   *(continued)*

	1952		1956	
	Democratic vote as percent of total vote	*Group Democratic proportion compared with national Democratic proportion*	*Democratic vote as percent of total vote*	*Group Democratic proportion compared with national Democratic proportion*
ALL VOTERS	44		42	
Occupation				
Professors	56	+12	62	+20
Professional/managerial	36	− 8	32	−10
Clerical/sales	40	− 4	37	− 5
Manual	55	+11	50	+ 8
Education				
College	34	−10	31	−11
High school	45	+ 1	42	0
Grade school	52	+ 8	50	+ 8

more heavily Democratic than other broad occupational strata. Similar findings are reported in various surveys of the British academic profession completed since the early sixties. The first such study, made in 1964, found Labour in the lead with just over 40 percent, ahead of the Tories' 35 percent and the Liberals' 14 percent. Labour retained their position in 1970, while the Conservatives experienced a 12 percent drop, and the Liberals moved up six points (Williams et al., 1974, p. 405). And in October 1974, just before the General Election, Labour was backed by 43 percent of academics, the Liberals by 32 percent, while the Tories brought up the rear at 24 percent (Kaufman, 1974, p. 1). In Britain, "university teachers look very much more like the working class in their political affiliations than like the upper middle class, to which they belong in respect to their incomes, status, education, styles of life, and other objective indicators of social class" (Halsey & Trow, 1971, p. 401).

Voting behavior and ideological self-identification may appear to be limited measures of the political posture of individuals or groups. An examination of the views of faculty on a range of issues indicates, however, that the commitment to a relatively liberal-left politics is general,

1964		1968		1972	
Democratic vote as percent of total vote	Group Democratic proportion compared with national Democratic proportion	Democratic vote as percent of total vote	Group Democratic proportion compared with national Democratic proportion	Democratic vote as percent of total vote	Group Democratic proportion compared with national Democratic proportion
61		43		39	
78	+17	61	+18	57	+18
54	− 7	34	− 9	31	− 8
57	− 4	41	− 2	36	− 3
71	+10	50	+ 7	43	+ 4
52	− 9	37	− 6	37	− 2
62	+ 1	42	− 1	34	− 5
66	+ 5	52	+ 9	49	+10

and applies with reference not only to the population as a whole but to other occupational strata, including all college graduates and frequently college students. This is clearly evident with respect to opposition to the Vietnam War.

There can be little doubt that academics turned against the war earlier than other strata. The national survey of professors taken by the National Opinion Research Center in 1966 found over half opposed to the government's Vietnam policy. As the NORC authors pointed out in comparing academics with the general public, a higher proportion of the former were critical, and the overwhelming majority of the critical faculty wanted to get out or to reduce American military involvement (Noll & Rossi, 1966, pp. 52–54). Among the general public, less than one-third thought American intervention in Vietnam was a mistake, according to Gallup surveys during that year. Not until the summer of 1968 did a majority of those interviewed by Gallup report that they considered the intervention wrong (Erskine, 1970, p. 134).

A variety of surveys of student opinion suggest that, in spite of the many well-publicized demonstrations against the war, the majority of the collegians supported it during the early years of American participation. In 1965, for example, the Harris survey reported that only 24 percent of a national student sample favored American withdrawal ("Campus '65," 1965, p. 53). Samuel Lubell (1966) concluded in the spring of 1966 that two-thirds of the students interviewed continued to back U.S. Vietnam policy, which was about the same proportion of support one found in the country as a whole. A Gallup survey of college students taken in May and June 1966 found that 47 percent of them endorsed the way "Johnson is handling the situation in Vietnam," while 23 percent disagreed because they thought the United States should be more aggressive, and an additional 16 percent opposed the President's policies for being "indecisive" or "inconsistent." A Gallup poll of student opinion a year later "showed 49 percent of students in favor of a policy of escalation compared to 35 percent who wanted military activity to be reduced." Not until the spring of 1968 did the proportion of students who thought the United States had made a mistake in getting involved in Vietnam reach 50 percent ("Gallup Poll release," 1968).

Yet though most students and the public at large were against the war from 1968 on, a majority of both accepted the new Nixon Administration's policy of gradual troop withdrawal and Vietnamization as the way to get out. In October 1969, more students (50 percent) told Gilbert Youth Research interviewers that they approved "the way President Nixon is handling the situation in Vietnam," than disapproved (44 percent).

College faculty continued their record of opposition. In the Carnegie survey, taken in the spring of 1969, a substantial majority favored getting out by either withdrawing all troops immediately (19 percent) or encouraging "the emergence of a coalition government in South Vietnam" (41 percent) as contrasted with 33 percent who backed withdrawal in the context of Vietnamization and 7 percent who supported committing "whatever forces are necessary to defeat the Communists." An almost identical question on Vietnam was presented to the general public through a Gallup survey eight months later (*The Gallup Poll*, 1972, p. 2031). Of those interviewed, 56 percent endorsed either Vietnamization or "more military force," alternatives which were backed by only 40 percent of the professoriate in the preceding spring.[12]

Similar evidence concerning the greater liberalism of college faculty

---

[12]In this Gallup survey, the "Vietnamization" alternative was phrased as "withdraw troops but take as many years to do this as are needed to turn the war over to the South Vietnamese," while the "more force" choice was framed as "send more troops to Vietnam and step up the fighting." The former was endorsed by 44 percent of the population, the latter by 12 percent.

as compared with other occupational strata, high and low, well-educated or not, may be adduced for a variety of other issues ranging from black rights to legalization of marijuana. Close to half the faculty interviewed (45 percent) agreed with the statement that "the main cause of Negro riots in the cities is white racism." Only 20 percent strongly disagreed with this interpretation. On the other hand, a Gallup survey of the general public in May 1968 found that 73 percent of the whites believed that in their community, Negroes are treated "the same as whites are," a position taken by 54 percent of those who had gone to college. Over half (54 percent) of those interviewed by Gallup in this survey also said that "Negroes themselves . . . [are] MORE to blame for the present conditions in which Negroes find themselves . . . [than] white people" (Erskine, 1968–1969, pp. 699–700).

The faculty also appear significantly more liberal on an issue which touches an especially raw nerve in contemporary American politics—school busing to achieve racial integration. A Gallup survey (*Gallup Opinion Index*, 1970, p. 9) taken early in 1970 indicated that only 14 percent of the public favored "the busing of Negro and white school children," on behalf of integration, while 81 percent opposed it. No predominantly white stratum or educational group gave more than 20 percent backing for the proposal. A March 1970 Harris survey (*Harris Survey Yearbook*, 1971, p. 229) found a similar distribution: Just 19 percent responding favored busing for integration, even if "it could be worked out so that there was no more busing of school children than there is now," while 73 percent were opposed and 8 percent unsure. Among the respondents to the 1969 faculty survey, however, 46 percent backed busing to achieve "racial integration of the public elementary schools," while 54 percent opposed it.

Some who recognize that academics are more inclined to favor liberal or radical social change than other strata argue, however, that such support ends at the borders of the campus, that faculty are conservative with respect to their own institution, the university. Clark Kerr (1966, p. 99) was making this point when he wrote that "few institutions are so conservative as the universities about their own affairs while their members are so liberal about the affairs of others. . . ."[13] This observation has considerable validity. As we shall see, many academics who are liberal or even leftist on larger social issues are relatively conservative in their reactions to campus events, particularly in recent years with re-

[13]For a similar statement by Charles Eliot of Harvard, made 100 years earlier, see Lipset (1975).

spect to issues stemming from student demonstrations and demands that they share "power" with students. Yet insofar as it has been possible to compare the attitudes of professors on such matters with those of the general public, once again the former appear more supportive of what might be described as the liberal or "permissive" positions.

At the outset, it may be noted that the faculty and the general public reacted in sharply different ways to what was perhaps the event of the 1960s in which campus-based activism most significantly affected the larger political process—the demonstrations and riots which emerged during the 1968 Democratic Convention in Chicago. Three-fifths of the faculty sampled by the Carnegie Commission disagreed with the statement that the "police acted reasonably in curbing demonstrations at the Democratic convention." When a comparable question was asked of the general public by the Survey Research Center of the University of Michigan, only 25 percent indicated they thought "that police had 'used too much force' " in dealing with demonstrators in Chicago. Responses to this question varied significantly with education, with the highly educated more likely to be critical of the police actions. Still, only 37 percent of college graduates and 52 percent of those with graduate degrees—compared with 59 percent of professors—were generally critical of the Chicago police (Robinson, 1970, p. 7). Strikingly, only 36 percent of those in the general public who supported Eugene McCarthy for the nomination believed that the police were overzealous. Even among supporters of the antiwar candidate who were under 30, the proportion saying "too much force" had been used came to only 50 percent.

American faculty have been both ambivalent and sharply divided in their reaction to the campus activism of the second half of the 1960s. In 1969, 42 percent stated that they approved "of the emergence of radical student activism in recent years," while 58 percent disapproved. Three years later, in 1972, the division was comparable, 44 percent in favor and 56 percent against (with 14 percent of uncertain or conflicting interpretations excluded from the computations for the sake of comparability). It is clear from their answers to a variety of questions that most faculty were bothered by the recourse in some demonstrations to illegal methods, particularly the seizure of buildings and efforts to prevent classes from being held. A substantial majority, 77 percent, felt in 1969 that "students who disrupt the functioning of a college should be expelled or suspended." Yet at the same time, only one-quarter of the professors queried thought that student demonstrations "have no place on a college campus." And over two-fifths of them (43 percent) were willing to agree that there are circumstances in which a strike by their teaching assistants (graduate students) "would be a legitimate means of action."

Support for certain forms of student activism actually increased among the professoriate when the questions were made concrete to specific situations, for example, when they dealt with the sit-ins and strike at Columbia University in the spring of 1968, or the most recent demonstrations on the respondents' own campuses. Almost all the faculty (95 percent) who indicated knowledge of the Columbia situation disapproved of the "methods" of the student militants. But close to two-thirds (64 percent) indicated approval of the "aims" of the Columbia protestors, which involved opposition to alleged links of the University to the war effort and the building of a gymnasium in a public park located on the borders of Harlem.

Two-thirds of the academics stated that their own campus had experienced protests or demonstrations during the current (1968–69) academic year. And half (51 percent) of these indicated that they approved of the aims of the student protestors. Less than a third (29 percent) were opposed, while the remaining fifth expressed uncertain or mixed feelings about the demonstrations.

There are no precisely comparable questions which have been asked of the general population. In general, however, the national polls taken during the era of frequent student demonstrations suggest overwhelming public hostility. Thus, in the spring of 1969, 94 percent of a Gallup sample said that they would "like to see college administrators take a stronger stand on student disorders" (*Gallup Opinion Index*, 1969, p. 26). A year later, during the wave of protests against the Cambodian incursion which swept academe, 82 percent said that they disagreed with "college students going on strike to protest the way things are run in our country" (*The Gallup Poll*, 1972, p. 2250). Asked during the Cambodian events to list the most important problem facing the country, a national Gallup sample (*The Gallup Poll*, 1972, p. 2252) put "campus unrest" at the head of the list.

A series of proposals to "democratize" the university by involving students in various institutional decisions was offered as an accompaniment to the political unrest of the 1960s. For the most part, such proposals called for students to share power with the faculty in decisions on curriculum, admissions policy, discipline, and academic appointments. When queried about matters such as these in 1969, the faculty naturally was most resistant to change involving its own immediate position. A slight majority (55 percent), for example, thought that students should have little or no role in evaluating faculty for appointment and promotion. Only 21 percent would give students a *formal role* in the process. Even here, however, the fact that almost half maintained students should have *some involvement* testifies to considerable liberalism with regard to "their own turf." Large, though varying, majorities of faculty favored students taking part in decisions concerning the "provision and content of courses," "undergraduate admissions policy," "bachelor's degree requirements," and "student discipline."

Again, it is difficult to find precisely similar questions addressed by pollsters to the general public. Two Gallup surveys come close. In December 1968, Gallup asked a national sample whether they thought "students should or should not have a greater say concerning the academic side of the college—that is, the courses, examinations, and so forth." Only one-third replied they should. Among those who had been to college, the level of support rose to 39 percent, but 58 percent of this group opposed any further student involvement (*The Gallup Poll*, 1972, p. 2178). Four months later, in April 1969, Gallup inquired whether "you think college students should or should not have a greater say in the running of colleges." Support (only 17 percent) for "a greater say," put in general terms, was even less than in the previous poll.

It would seem apparent from these data that the "upper class" of the university is more "liberal" with respect to proposed limitations on their intramural authority than the public at large.

It may be argued that the record cited here does no more than document the fact that American academics have been more *liberal* than other strata, and that only a small minority of them ever show up as *radical*, or as supportive of causes which might undermine their own high-status position. While there can be little doubt that a majority of those associated with universities and other intellectually linked occupations have been liberals or progressives rather than supporters of the extreme left, it is also true that no other stratum has approached the intellectuals in support for leftist third-party, socialist, and Communist activities. One would hardly anticipate, in a country where left-of-center movements have never secured more than a fraction of the national vote and where the proportion of the electorate who in 1972 identified themselves as radicals was 1 to 2 percent, that a very large segment of professors would occupy the political extreme. Yet whenever the choice available to Americans has been widened, as in the case of the Henry Wallace movement in 1948 or the McCarthy and McGovern candidacies in 1968 and 1972, the record shows faculty to be far more supportive of the liberal-left candidate than are those in any other occupational category. This privileged stratum manifests a relatively greater inclination than any other to oppose existing authorities "from the left"—both in the society and "at home" in the university.

2. The Ideology of Academics: Intersections of National and Campus Affairs

To observe that, *as a group*, professors have been more supportive of both liberal national programs and student protests than the public at large is to say little about the structure of their political mind-sets. The most obvious question here involves the intersection of national and campus controversies. What relationships do we find between orientations toward such broad concerns of society as race relations and foreign policy, and toward such intramural issues as how academic governance structures should be changed and the degree to which student views should be considered in university decision making? Are national and campus "liberals" essentially one and the same, or is the composition of these groups sharply different? Answers to such questions require that we consider the concept of *ideology*, for we are inquiring in the first instance about the ideological character of faculty opinion.

IDEOLOGY AND THE ACADEMIC MIND

Few concepts widely used in social science have been more variously construed than *ideology*.[1] It is important, therefore, to specify how we understand this concept and will apply it here. Central to an ideology or "ideological thinking" is a property which Philip Converse (1964) called "constraint." Anyone viewing the flow of public life encounters a diverse array of issues. These he may respond to "one at a time" or may order by imposing some integrative conceptual dimension. To the extent that he perceives an interconnection among issues and organizes his responses in terms of a larger "package" or system of policy preferences, his thinking manifests constraint. An ideology is a constrained

[1]For a review of these varied usages, see Minar (1961) and Ladd (1972, pp. 6–8).

set of political positions prescribing the "appropriate" responses to matters of government and public policy. It functions as a logically or quasilogically interrelated system of ideas which treats an area of political life that is both broad and significant. An ideology is like a patchwork quilt in which individual policy items are the patches. Like a quilt, an ideology is more than the sum of its patches; it is the patches bound together—"constrained"—in a specified and ordered arrangement. A person sees politics ideologically when he applies some overarching conceptual dimension to myriad policy choices, when he organizes remote and abstract matters into what, for him, is a logical or quasilogical system.

Different groups in the population may be compared as to the level of constraint in the political thinking of their members. A decade ago, Converse (1964, p. 218) reported that not more than 10 to 15 percent of the American public manifested enough constraint to justify describing their orientations as ideological. While later work of Field and Anderson (1969) suggests that a higher proportion of the population has come to show ideological awareness in response to generally sharper lines of cleavage in the polity, most observers agree that a decisive majority of Americans do not employ ideological criteria in assessing political events. It is also commonly acknowledged that there is a strong link between exposure to formal higher education and an inclination to evaluate politics in terms of systematic issue concerns. Lester Milbraith (1965, pp. 39–40) has observed that persons who have experienced higher education are less likely to shut out political stimuli, and that "exposure to stimuli about politics increases the quantity and sharpness of political knowledge, stimulates interest, contributes to the decisiveness of political choices. . . ." And Converse (1964, p. 213) noted that "the contextual grasp of 'standard' political belief systems [ideologies] fades out very rapidly, almost before one has passed beyond the ten percent of the American population that in the 1950s had completed standard college training. Increasingly, simpler forms of information about 'what goes with what' (or even information about the simple identity of objects) turn up missing. The next result, as one moves downward [in education], is that constraint declines across the universe of idea-elements. . . ."

If education promotes an ideological construction of political life, faculty should manifest unusually ideological politics. They are a community of professional intellectuals whose very "business" requires them to maintain a basic consistency of ideas. Professors' opinions should be more highly structured and interrelated than those of most groups outside the university. The high level of constraint which we in fact encountered in faculty opinion is not surprising, then, but it is nonetheless impressive. This ideological character comprises a primary dimension of faculty thinking, and as such presents a theme to which we will return throughout this volume. It is reflected in exceptionally high correlations among opinions across a broad array of issues, and in the unusually sharp or clear ideological differentiation of academics by such variables as academic status, social background and age.

One of the primary analytic tasks in working with the Carnegie data involved a search for potential underlying dimensions of faculty political opinion. Along with questions of national and international affairs, the survey probed faculty opinion on a wide range of issues and controversies largely internal to academe, many of which had become prominent only since the middle of the 1960s. Given the prevailing climate at universities, it was very difficult to specify, on an *a priori* basis, which of these were properly considered *political*. Even the most commonplace judgments, such as the basis for faculty promotion, had often been linked up in a larger pattern of conflict and dissension, which is what we mean when we refer to the "politicization" of academic life. We chose, finally, to work with all national issues and with all questions regarding decision making in the university, what goals and purposes the academy should serve, the distribution of institutional resources, and the relationship of higher education to components of the larger society, *which in fact had become major points of contention in schools around the country.*

It proved difficult to reduce the complex interrelations which we found among faculty opinions (that is, their correlations) to a small number of neat and distinct categories. The mass of opinions did coalesce, however, around five primary dimensions.[2] One of these contained broad societal issues. Responses to five questions were combined to construct a general Liberalism-Conservatism Scale. Four of the questions were equally weighted: positions on the Vietnam War, the legalization of marijuana, the causes of Negro riots, and busing as a means for school integration. One question was double-weighted—the

[2]A factor analysis and orthogonal rotation were performed.

faculty member's own self-categorization of his political ideology.[3] In working with this scale, we computed the raw scores for all respondents to the survey, and then collapsed these scores into five approximately equal categories, ranging from that fifth of the faculty with the most left or liberal orientations to the fifth of the professoriate with the most conservative scores.

Opinions on matters as diverse as Vietnam, race, and the legalization of marijuana probably could not be organized into a single liberal-conservative dimension for the American general public. That these opinions did consistently represent a single dimension in our factor analysis of the Carnegie faculty data indicates the presence of an underlying ideological perspective among academics which allows them to organize a diverse set of issues.

The other four dimensions identified in the factor analysis all fall in the realm of intrauniversity politics, and scales were constructed from the items included in each: a four-item Campus Activism Scale, including questions calling both for a general evaluation of "the emergence of radical student activism" and for prescribing the appropriate university response to protests and demonstrations;[4] a five-item index measuring

---

[3]The text of the questionnaire items is as follows: (1) "The main cause of Negro riots in the cities is white racism." (Strongly agree; agree with reservations; disagree with reservations; strongly disagree.) (2) "Marijuana should be legalized." (3) "Racial integration of the public elementary schools should be achieved even if it requires busing." (4) "Which of these positions on Vietnam is closest to your own?" (The United States should withdraw from Vietnam immediately; the United States should reduce its involvement and encourage the emergence of a coalition government in South Vietnam; the United States should try to reduce its involvement, while being sure to prevent a Communist takeover in the South; the United States should commit whatever forces are necessary to defeat the Communists.) (5) "How would you characterize yourself politically at the present time?" (Left; liberal; middle-of-the-road; moderately conservative; strongly conservative.)

[4]The items comprising the Campus Activism Scale, equally weighted, are:
1. "What do you think of the emergence of radical student activism in recent years?" (Unreservedly approve; approve with reservations; disapprove with reservations; unreservedly disapprove.)
2. "Student demonstrations have no place on a college campus." (Strongly agree; agree with reservations; disagree with reservations; strongly disagree.)
3. "Students who disrupt the functioning of a college should be expelled or suspended."
4. "Most campus demonstrations are created by far left groups trying to cause trouble."

faculty judgments as to *university policy toward blacks* (Black Support Scale), whether "normal academic standards" should be relaxed in recruiting black undergraduates and faculty, whether black studies programs should be established upon the demand of black students and controlled by blacks, and whether the overall response of American colleges and universities should be considered "racist";[5] a Student Role Scale composed of five questions asking what role undergraduates should play in faculty appointment and promotion, undergraduate admissions policy, the provision and content of courses, and student discipline, with the alternatives ranging from "control" to "little or no role";[6] and finally an index measuring positions on faculty role in university governance, including questions on whether the professor considers his department's administration autocratic, whether junior faculty have too small a voice in decision making, and whether the faculty should play a larger role in setting university policy at the expense of

[5]The items comprising the Black Support Scale, equally weighted, are:
1. "More minority group undergraduates should be admitted here even if it means relaxing normal academic standards of admission." (Strongly agree; agree with reservations; disagree with reservations; strongly disagree.)
2. "Any institution with a substantial number of black students should offer a program of Black Studies if they wish it."
3. "Any special academic program for black students should be administered and controlled by black people."
4. "The normal academic requirements should be relaxed in appointing members of minority groups to faculty here."
5. "Most American colleges and universities are racist whether they mean to be or not."

[6]The items comprising the Student Role Scale, equally weighted, are:
1. "Faculty promotions should be based in part on formal student evaluations of their teachers." (Strongly agree; agree with reservations; disagree with reservations; strongly disagree.)
2. "What role do you believe undergraduates should play in faculty appointment and promotion?" (Control; voting power on committees; formal consultation; informal consultation; little or no role.)
3. "What role do you believe undergraduates should play in decisions on undergraduate admissions policy?"
4. "What role do you believe undergraduates should play in decisions on provision and content of courses?"
5. "What role do you believe undergraduates should play in decisions on student discipline?"

trustees and administrators.[7] Despite the absence of complete independence among these factors—a number of individual questions appeared
to cut across several categories—it seemed appropriate to construct a
separate measure for each and to explore their empirical relationships.

OVERLAY OF NATIONAL AND CAMPUS POSITIONS

Analysis of the Carnegie data reveals to a striking extent the presence of
an underlying ideological dimension which is felt across a range of intramural, as well as national, issues. In general, the national liberals are
the campus liberals, and national conservatives the campus conservatives.

Before exploring and explaining this broad subject further, two important caveats are in order. First, the above generalization applies in
the context of *relative*, not *absolute*, positions. Those most liberal in national affairs are on the whole relatively the most supportive of change
in liberal or equalitarian directions on campus matters. But this observation says nothing about absolute response patterns in either sector.
Second, we do not intend to suggest that the extension of a common
ideological dimension across responses to national and campus controversies occurs to the exclusion of cross-cutting interests. There are
striking and important instances in which groups of faculty who are the
most liberal in national affairs are particularly resistant to certain pressures for liberal change within the university. This is a matter to which

---

[7]The items comprising the Faculty Role Scale, equally weighted, are:
1. "Do you feel the administration of your department is:" (Very autocratic; somewhat
autocratic; somewhat democratic; very democratic.)
2. "Junior faculty members have too little say in the running of my department."
(Strongly agree; agree with reservations; disagree with reservations; strongly disagree.)
3. "A small group of senior professors has disproportionate power in decision-making
in this institution."
4. "This institution would be better off with fewer administrators."
5. "There should be faculty representation on the governing board of this institution."
6. "Trustees' only responsibilities should be to raise money and gain community support."

Scales were constructed from questions comprising each factor, and the procedure and
general structure are in each case the same. Frequently, the alternative answers presented
respondents were a five-point variety, from "strongly agree" to "strongly disagree." Responses to all items in each scale were then coded positive for liberal (or variously supportive of student activism, of a broadened student role in decision making, etc.) positions
(+2,+1), negative for "conservative" positions (−1,−2), and 0 for positions ("middle of
the road," etc.) in between. The raw scores for each respondent on each scale were computed in a straight additive fashion. These raw scores were then collapsed into five approximately equal categories, from that fifth of the faculty with the most liberal or supportive responses on down to the fifth which was most "conservative."

we will return at length in Chapters 8 and 10. There is an impressive linkage, then, involving the way academics order their positions on a disparate array of issues running from the society to the campus, but in calling attention to the linkage we do not intend to overlook important cross-cutting interests and perspectives.

We found a generally high association between positions on the Liberalism-Conservatism Scale and on the indices of response to campus politics. Those faculty most liberal-left in national affairs tend on the whole to be the most supportive of student protests and demonstrations, the most willing to bend traditional university practices in such areas as admissions and faculty hiring in the interest of racial equity, the most in favor of giving students a bigger role in decisions affecting the academic community, and the most inclined to change other features of university governance in the direction of greater faculty (as opposed to administration) control, and toward junior in contrast to senior faculty. But as Table 5, which reports correlations among the five scales, makes clear, the strength of the scales' interrelationships, and in particular the link between views on external and internal political disputes, is by no means uniform. The correlations among the Liberalism-Conservatism, Campus Activism, and Black Support Scales are exceptionally high. Bringing in the Student Role Scale, we find a slightly diminished but still strong association. On the other hand, position on the Liberalism-Conservatism and Governance indices are not highly correlated, and in fact the latter measure seems to tap a dimension of political ideology substantially different from the other four.

Bivariate tables give us further insight into the associations revealed by Table 5. In Table 6 we compare the positions of faculty, differentiated by their views on national and international affairs, on each of the campus politics scales. As noted above, the association between a left-

TABLE 5 *Interscale correlations (gammas),* faculty opinion on national and campus issues*

	Scales			
Scales	*Campus Activism*	*Black Support*	*Student Role*	*Faculty Governance*
Liberalism-Conservatism	.69	.56	.46	.25
Campus Activism		.53	.50	.23
Black Support			.50	.22
Student Role				.19

*The "five quintile" versions of all five scales, not the raw scores, were used in these computations.
SOURCE: 1969 Carnegie Commission Survey of Student and Faculty Opinion.

TABLE 6 *Positions of faculty, by liberalism-conservatism in national affairs, on four scales measuring responses to campus politics (percentages of n)*

	Liberalism-Conservatism		
	Very liberal (n = 12,294)	*Liberal* (n = 13,758)	*Middle-of-the-road* (n = 10,278)
Campus Activism Scale			
Strongly supportive	58	25	9
Moderately supportive	29	35	24
Middle-of-the-road	10	27	33
Moderately opposed	2	8	18
Strongly opposed	1	5	16
Black Support Scale			
Strongly supportive	53	23	11
Moderately supportive	21	24	19
Middle-of-the-road	16	28	28
Moderately opposed	8	18	26
Strongly opposed	3	7	16
Student Role Scale			
Strongly supportive	51	27	14
Moderately supportive	26	31	30
Middle-of-the-road	11	20	23
Moderately opposed	8	13	19
Strongly opposed	4	9	14
Faculty Governance Scale			
Strongly supportive	33	20	14
Moderately supportive	20	17	16
Middle-of-the-road	21	22	22
Moderately opposed	16	23	22
Strongly opposed	11	19	26

SOURCE: 1969 Carnegie Commission Survey of Student and Faculty Opinion.

of-center posture in the national arena and relatively high support for the student protests of the late 1960s is extremely close. Of academics classified "very liberal" on the Liberalism-Conservatism measure, 87 percent score in the two most supportive categories of the Activism index, while 80 percent of those "very conservative" are located in the two quintiles most opposed to the student protests and demonstrations.

Scale	
Moderately conservative (n = 13,011)	*Strongly conservative* (n = 10,683)
3	1
13	4
30	16
25	25
30	55
5	1
13	5
28	17
31	33
23	44
9	4
23	14
24	21
24	24
21	36
12	10
14	13
21	18
25	23
28	36

Liberals in the national arena are significantly (although not dramatically) less likely to be the most in favor of extending student participation in such areas as admissions, discipline, and courses and curricula. On the Student Role Scale, 77 percent of left faculty are recorded in the two most supportive categories, compaed with 87 percent in comparable positions on the Activism measure. On the other hand, 39 percent of very conservative academics show up relatively supportive or as centrists on questions of student role, as against just 21 percent in such categories on the index measuring opinion on campus protests and demonstrations. Responses to compensatory university programs in admitting black students and hiring black faculty, and more generally to the level of condemnation of past academic efforts in the area of race, show a closeness to orientations on national matters somewhere between the Activism and Student Role Scales.

The Faculty Governance Scale, as noted above, does not correlate at all highly with general liberalism-conservatism. Only 53 percent of "left" academics and 37 percent of "liberals" are found in the two quintiles of this governance measure most critical and change-oriented with reference to present practice, as compared with 26 percent of "moderate conservatives" and 23 percent of "very conservative" faculty.[8]

These data further support the conclusion that academics are distinguished by the intensely ideological character of their thinking. They "tie things together," see order in a diverse assortment of abstract political questions. Specifically, they perceive an underlying ideological dimension—involving general liberalism-conservatism—suffused through a range of campus controversies. In 1969, when the Carnegie survey was conducted, "protests and demonstrations" was the intrauniversity issue area with the closest connection to national politics. While student activism had a number of quite different sources, its immediate precipitant and most visible target was American involvement in Vietnam. It is not surprising, then, that most faculty perceived a link, and that positions on the Liberalism and Activism Scales were the most highly correlated. The Black Support Scale, touching matters of racial equity, albeit in a campus context, also had a close connection with general liberal and conservative impulses. The argument that students should play a bigger role in determining what courses are to be offered, in decisions on student discipline, in evaluating faculty, and the like, can be seen to touch the egalitarian strain which is an important part of liberalism, along with receptivity to "progressive" change; but at the same time, it clashes with faculty prerogatives and lacks any immediate tie to issues in the broader society. We are not prepared to say that endorsement of more student power in deciding course and curriculum questions is *liberal*, because there are obviously other cross-cutting and conflicting components to the matter, but the student role area does tap the liberalism dimension significantly.

---

[8]These terms—from "left" to "very conservative"—are merely our descriptive labels for the five quintile groupings on the Liberalism-Conservatism Scale.

The Faculty Governance Scale touches a dimension with a far more ambiguous link to general liberalism-conservatism. It differs from the other indices first in that, to a degree, it is university and department specific. Instead of posing general questions of academic policy, it requires evaluation of administrative experience and practice in the specific departmental and college context in which the respondent moves: for example, "Junior faculty members have too little say in the running of *my department*," and so on. It does, of course, go beyond the immediate setting in which the professor is operating to solicit a set of opinions on two contrasting views of academic governance: one which is somewhat hostile to "administrators" and favors more influence in decision making for the faculty and especially its junior members, and one which endorses a more hierarchial pattern with greater authority for officials and senior faculty. While these two views of faculty role are linked in obvious fashion to different interests and perceptions of groups in the professoriate, they appear little related to the general dimension of political liberalism and conservatism—and the markedly weaker correlations which we get with the Governance Scale seem to confirm this interpretation.

NATIONAL AND CAMPUS POLITICS: A LOOK AT SPECIFIC ISSUES

Useful as the scales are in revealing broad patterns of association, their abstractness cuts us off from the actual distributions of opinion on specific national and campus issues, and their relationships. In concluding this chapter, some attention to the link between positions on concrete societal and intramural controversies may be useful. To simplify presentation, a single national question, involving United States policy in Vietnam, serves as the independent variable in Table 7. The dependent variables are various campus issues. Together, these relationships both illustrate specifically the thrust of a clear underlying ideological dimension, and at the same time convey something of the variation in response structures called forth by different intramural controversies.

The faculty in 1969 was roughly evenly divided in its overall assessment of the "pluses and minuses" of campus activism. Those academics who favored immediate United States withdrawal from Vietnam, however, endorsed student protests by a majority which exceeded 70 percent, while just 20 percent of their colleagues who backed the Administration Vietnam policies ("reduce American involvement but prevent a Communist victory") took this favorable position. A large majority (80 percent) of the professoriate, at the same time, took the position that students who actually disrupt the functioning of a college should be ex-

TABLE 7 Faculty positions on selected campus issues, by policy preferences with regard to United States involvement in Vietnam (percentages of n)

		"Which of these positions
	All faculty (n = 60,028)	Faculty favoring immediate withdrawal (n = 11,439)
"What do you think of the emergence of radical student activism in recent years?"		
Unreservedly approve	3	11
Approve with reservations	40	60
Disapprove with reservations	42	22
Unreservedly disapprove	16	7
"Students who disrupt the functioning of a college should be expelled or suspended."		
Strongly agree	51	27
Agree with reservations	29	29
Disagree with reservations	14	27
Strongly disagree	6	17
"More minority group undergraduates should be admitted here even if it means relaxing normal academic standards of admission."		
Strongly agree	12	26
Agree with reservations	27	31
Disagree with reservations	28	20
Strongly disagree	32	23
"The normal academic requirements should be relaxed in appointing members of minority groups to faculty here."		
Strongly agree	4	11
Agree with reservations	17	27
Disagree with reservations	28	26
Strongly disagree	51	37
"What role do you believe undergraduates should play in decisions on the provision and content of courses?"		
Control	—	1
Voting power on committees	14	27
Formal consultation	35	36
Informal consultation	37	27
Little or no role	14	9

*Full text of responses appears in note 3 of this chapter.

SOURCE: 1969 Carnegie Commission Survey of Student and Faculty Opinion.

Faculty favoring reduced involvement, coalition government (n = 25,524)	Faculty favoring reduced involvement, but prevent Communist takeover* (n = 17,745)	Faculty favoring all-out military victory (n = 3,507)
2	—	1
52	20	12
39	55	41
7	25	46
39	70	84
38	23	11
18	5	3
5	2	2
14	5	4
34	20	9
28	34	24
24	41	64
4	2	2
22	9	4
32	26	17
42	63	77
—	—	—
17	7	4
40	31	22
34	45	44
9	17	32

pelled or suspended. On this issue, the most strongly antiwar faculty were fairly evenly split, whereas those who supported the Vietnam policy of the United States government or wanted even more of a military commitment were nearly unanimous in backing sanctions for disruptive students.

Nearly three-fifths (57 percent) of antiwar professors maintained that "more minority undergraduates should be admitted . . . even if it means relaxing normal academic standards of admission," the judgment of only 39 percent of all professors, of 25 percent of those who backed "Vietnamization," and of just 13 percent of academics who wanted a military victory. Faculty who were willing to relax regular hiring standards to increase minority representation in the professoriate itself were a small minority (21 percent of the total), but the range—from 38 percent of the most antiwar academics taking the position to just 6 percent of the "hawks"—again is very substantial. Especially striking is the variation, by views on the war, in the proportion *"strongly* disagreeing" that hiring standards should be altered to get more black representation: from 37 percent of those in favor of immediate unilateral withdrawal to 77 percent among the "military victory" faculty.

It is a long way substantively from views on the war to assessments of the appropriate student role "in decisions on the provision and content of courses." But as Table 7 shows, the relationship between these two sets of views is nonetheless impressive. Among the most hawkish faculty, 73 percent wanted student involvement in this area limited to—at most—informal consultation, the position of 62 percent of the "Vietnamization" group, 43 percent of academics who preferred a reduction of American Vietnam involvement coupled with support for a coalition government, and only 36 percent of the "unilateral withdrawal" group.

Our 1972 survey showed the persistence of these same strong relationships. For example, 79 percent of faculty then backing "Vietnamization" indicated general disapproval of the student activism of recent years, compared with 29 percent of academics who were in favor of immediate unilateral withdrawal.

CONCLUSION

The constraint in faculty opinion is notable, manifesting itself in strong and remarkably consistent relationships among positions on a broad range of national and campus concerns. Because academics form a community who attend rather persistently to ideas, their views on diverse issues are unusually ordered—and thereby predictable.

This ideological character of professorial thinking is of considerable conceptual importance to an effort to understand academic political life, particularly the bitterness expressed against those of differing orientations. It also carries immediate implications for analysis and presentation of findings in the chapters which follow, where we explore the sources of divisions within the professoriate. Specifically, since national and campus orientations are so highly intercorrelated, we can concentrate on locating factors which differentiate faculty along a basic liberal-conservative continuum. There is, in fact, an underlying ideological dimension, rather than a series of essentially distinct or lightly linked opinions across a range of issues.

Part Two
The Divided Academy: Differences in Professorial Politics and Their Sources

3. Academic Discipline and Politics

American academics have stood further left politically than any other major occupational group for a long time. It should be evident, however, that there are deep divisions within the faculty. Large numbers of professors have backed almost every variety of opinion and political action that secured support among the general public—with the important exceptions of explicitly racist and extreme rightist positions. (Many academics in Europe have stood with the extreme right as well.) In the 1972 Presidential election, an overwhelming Republican triumph in the electorate at large contrasted with a modest Democratic lead among the faculty. But 45 percent of professors voted for Richard Nixon. Even in 1964, a year of unprecedented Republican weakness, close to a fifth of academics opted for Barry Goldwater.

An exploration of the scope and sources of political divisions within the professoriate, then, is called for. As we will see, the origins of these ideological differences are quite distinct from those applying to the public at large.

For one thing, they involve the long and intense processes of professional socialization experienced by academics—and the immense differences in these processes among the various disciplines. The prominence of departments and fields of study in the organizational structure of universities extends as well to the political differentiation of faculty. This chapter begins our exploration of the sources of political divisions in academe with discipline subcultures.

DISCIPLINES IN THE MULTIVERSITY

The professoriate has come to be deeply divided because in the age of the multiversity it has become extraordinarily disparate in its range of fields, substantive interests and outside associations, career lines and expectations, and social backgrounds. No longer does "college" refer primarily to a small cluster of liberal arts faculty all performing more or less the same task. " 'The Idea of a Multiversity,' " Clark Kerr wrote in *The Uses of the University* (1966, pp. 41, 1), "is a city of infinite variety. . . . The university started as a single community—a community of masters and students. It may even be said to have had a soul in the sense of a central animating principle. Today the large American university is, rather, a whole series of communities and activities held together by a common name. . . ."

The principal neighborhoods in this "city of infinite variety" are the departments or fields. With the tremendous expansion of higher education during the last quarter century—from 165,000 faculty members and 1,675,000 students in 1945 to over 600,000 faculty and more than 8 million students in 1975—the fields have become at once larger and far more self-contained and disparate. To a pronounced degree, what Robert Oppenheimer (1959, pp. 56, 58) called "a thinning of common knowledge" among the various disciplines has occurred. In 1963, just before student activism entered the university, Clark Kerr (1966, p. 101) could note that "it is a sad commentary on the 'community of masters' [that] its elements come together in interchange only when they coalesce feverishly over a grievance about some episode related to a change of the calendar or a parking fee."

The fields are units of association in which faculty members spend large portions of their professional lives. These associations are personal. A professor will often know members of his field at universities across the country better than he will know most people in other departments at his own university. But his associations within his field are with bodies of ideas, interests, norms and values, and professional styles as well. From the days of his undergraduate major, through graduate school, and into his career as a member of the profession, the professor is pervasively exposed to the distinctive academic subculture which is his subject.

The degree to which disciplines are separated in the multiversity, and the pervasiveness of the professional socialization each entails, would lead us to expect some field-related variations in political attitudes. But the degree of this differentiation is really quite extraordinary. For example, 81 percent of clinical psychologists described their politics as "left" or "liberal" in the Carnegie survey, as compared with 61 percent of professors of English, 39 percent of chemists, 25 percent of mechanical engineers, and just 17 percent of faculty in colleges of agriculture. We find further (Tables 8 and 9) that basic population groups in the larger society—the young and the old; Protestants, Catholics, and Jews;

TABLE 8 *Nixon support, 1968 Presidential election, by disciplines within the faculty, and by religious, educational, and income groups in the general population (percentages of n)*

Faculty	Nixon support	General population	Nixon support
Field of study		*Religion*	
Social sciences (n = 7,160)	20	Jewish (n = 42)	11
Humanities (n = 10,333)	23	Catholic (n = 295)	37
Law (n = 611)	35	Protestant (n = 758)	51
Fine arts (n = 3,475)	35	*Education*	
Physical sciences (n = 8,064)	39	Through 8th grade (n = 198)	33
ALL FACULTY (n = 60,028)	37	Through 12th grade (n = 552)	44
Education (n = 3,401)	39	Some college (n = 275)	53
Biological sciences (n = 4,567)	41	College graduate (n = 117)	51
Medicine (n = 2,395)	45	*Income*	
Business (n = 2,338)	55	Up to $4,999 (n = 290)	41
Engineering (n = 4,373)	60	$5,000–$9,999 (n = 449)	44
Agriculture (n = 1,398)	62	$10,000–$14,999 (n = 225)	48
		$15,000 + (n = 157)	56

SOURCES: The general population data are from AIPO (Gallup) survey #771, November 7, 1968; those on the faculty, from the 1969 Carnegie Commission Survey of Student and Faculty Opinion.

whites and blacks; the prosperous and the poor—appear less sharply distinguished on important questions like Vietnam and who should be President than professors in the various academic departments. Such comparisons should not be carried too far: one important reason why general population subgroups are not more clearly set apart in political opinions is precisely because they are general, because they contain collections of people who are different in so many ways, even though they all possess the designated characteristic. *Protestants* encompasses a group which is much more heterogeneous than, say, *economists*. Still, the fact that the faculty in social science and their engineering col-

TABLE 9 *Percentage critical of American policy in Vietnam, by disciplines within the faculty, and by religious, racial, age, and income groups in the general population (row percentages)*

	Faculty	
	Unilateral withdrawal	*Coalition government with Communists*
Field of study		
Social sciences	27	50
Humanities	25	47
Law	18	49
Medicine	17	49
ALL FACULTY	19	42
Fine arts	20	43
Physical sciences	17	43
Biological sciences	17	41
Education	15	39
Engineering	12	33
Business	10	34
Agriculture	5	31

SOURCES: The general population data are from AIPO (Gallup) survey # 795, December 8, 1969; those on the faculty, from the 1969 Carnegie Commission Survey of Student and Faculty Opinion.

leagues are more dissimilar in some basic political commitments than are members of such grossly differentiated groups as the affluent and the poor is striking testimony to the prominence of disciplines in university life. Our understanding of faculty politics requires some attention to the general mechanism through which professors in the various fields come to hold such widely differing views. The remarkable uniformity of distributions by discipline across a varied set of political questions attests to the highly ideological character of the thinking of academics, noted in Chapter 2. In contrast to much of the general public, professors apply what Converse (1964, p. 215) described as "an overarching conceptual dimension" to order a disparate array of policy choices.

Table 10 compares the responses of faculty in various academic fields to the five items of the Liberalism-Conservatism Scale for national

	General population	
	Immediate withdrawal	*Withdrawal by end of 1970*
Religion		
Protestant	18	24
Catholic	18	24
Jewish	36	28
Race		
White	17	23
Black	40	30
Age		
Under 30	22	28
30–49	19	24
50 +	17	22
Income		
Up to $4,999	24	25
$5,000–$9,999	17	24
$10,000–$14,999	16	23
$15,000 +	15	26

issues. In working with this scale, we computed the raw scores for all respondents to the Carnegie survey, from +12 (the most liberal) to −12 (the most conservative), and then collapsed the raw scores into five approximately equal categories: from that fifth of the faculty with the most liberal responses to that fifth with the most conservative responses. If more than 20 percent of the faculty in any given field is classified as "very liberal," then the proportion of very liberal faculty in that field is larger than it is in the entire professoriate.

POLITICAL CHARACTERISTICS OF FACULTY BY FIELD

Apart from the sheer magnitude of the variations, the most striking discovery bearing on faculty political attitudes by discipline is the rather neat progression from the most left-of-center subject to the most conser-

TABLE 10 *Faculty positions on the Liberalism-Conservatism Scale,* by discipline (row percentages)*

Field of study	Very liberal	Liberal	Middle-of-the-road	Conservative	Very conservative	Percentage liberal minus percentage conservative
Social sciences	35	29	16	14	6	44
Humanities	28	26	17	17	12	25
Law	24	28	19	17	11	24
Fine arts	21	24	17	21	17	7
ALL FACULTY	19	22	17	23	20	−2
Medicine	13	24	19	24	21	−8
Physical sciences	16	21	18	24	22	−9
Biological sciences	14	21	20	26	19	−10
Education	12	22	16	30	20	−16
Business	8	15	18	27	32	−36
Engineering	10	14	17	27	33	−36
Other applied fields	4	14	16	34	32	−48
Agriculture	4	10	13	30	44	−60

*Opinions on five questions were combined to construct a general Liberalism-Conservatism Scale for national issues. Four of these were equally weighted: position on Vietnam War, the legalization of marijuana, the causes of Negro riots, and busing as a means for school integration. One question was double weighted, the faculty members' self-characterization of their political views. The text of the questionnaire items was as follows: (1) "The main cause of Negro riots in the cities is white racism." (Strongly agree, agree with reservations, disagree with reservations, strongly disagree.) (2) "Marijuana should be legalized." (3) "Racial integration of the public elementary schools should be achieved even if it requires busing." (4) "Which of these positions on Vietnam is closest to your own?" (The U.S. should withdraw from Vietnam immediately; the U.S. should reduce its involvement and encourage the emergence of a coalition government in South Vietnam; the U.S. should try to reduce its involvement, while being sure to prevent a Communist takeover in the South; the U.S. should commit whatever forces are necessary to defeat the Communists.) (5) "How would you characterize yourself politically at the present time?" (Left, liberal, middle-of-the-road, moderately conservative, strongly conservative.)

SOURCE: 1969 Carnegie Commission Survey of Student and Faculty Opinion.

vative, running from the social sciences to the humanities, law, and the fine arts, through the physical and biological sciences, education, and medicine, on to business, engineering, the smaller applied professional schools such as nursing and home economics, and finally agriculture, the most conservative discipline group. Social scientists are decisively the most liberal by this measure, with 64 percent in the two furthest left quintiles, compared with 41 percent among the faculty at large, and just 14 percent among college of agriculture professors. The range in political liberalism-conservatism is immense. Social scientists and engineers are separated by a full 80 points—computed in terms of the percentage in the two most liberal minus the percentage in the two most conservative quintiles.

In the 1968 Presidential election, Richard Nixon received the votes of about 37 percent of the faculty who went to the polls, as against 43 percent of the electorate generally. These distributions (Table 11) understate the liberalism of the academic vote, however, because George Wallace, who picked up more than 13 percent of the total popular vote, received only negligible backing in academe. The discipline array remains the one which has become familiar: social scientists and humanists were the most overwhelmingly Democratic, while faculty in colleges of business, engineering, and agriculture were decisively Republican.[1]

Our 1972 faculty survey contained too few cases to permit attention to the more specific discipline clusters, but Table 12 makes it clear that the same general pattern prevailed. Thus, the Democratic nominee was backed by 76 percent of academics in the liberal social sciences, by 71 percent of the humanists, by just 53 percent of the natural scientists, and by only 30 percent of professors in the conservative, business-related applied fields (engineering, business administration, departments or colleges of agriculture). Differences in voting patterns between professors in the social sciences and those in the business-related applied fields vastly exceeded those separating such grossly differentiated groups in the larger society as businessmen and manual workers, or the young and the old. Returning to a comparison made earlier, it is interesting to note that the difference in the margin of McGovern support between social scientists and engineers in the academic world (approximately 50 percentage points) was about as great as that between blacks and whites in the society at large.

There are a variety of consistent and fascinating differences among individual fields, each of which would require a detailed treatise for adequate explanation and hence are beyond the scope of our inquiry here. This is a good place, however, to call attention to the general dimensions of such specific discipline configurations. And the natural sciences are a case in point.

Only physics and biochemistry, among the natural science and engi-

[1]To avoid undue complexity, data in this chapter are presented, for the most part, by basic field groups: for example, social science, the humanities, the physical sciences. Readers interested in background characteristics and attitudinal orientations of specific subjects are directed to the tabulations contained in Appendix C.

TABLE 11 *Electoral preferences of American academics in the 1968 and 1964 Presidential elections, by discipline (row percentages)*

	1968 vote†				1968 Democratic Convention choice	
Field of study	*Humphrey*	*Nixon*	*Wallace*	*"Third party left"‡*	*McCarthy*	*Humphrey*
ALL FACULTY	59	37	1	3	55	45
Social sciences	75	20	*	5	59	41
Humanities	72	23	1	4	63	37
Fine arts	62	35	2	2	63	37
Law	65	35	*	*	51	49
Physical sciences	57	39	2	2	57	43
Biological sciences	56	41	1	2	55	45
Medicine	54	45	*	1	53	47
Education	59	39	1	1	45	55
Business	40	55	4	1	48	53
Engineering	37	60	2	1	48	52
Other applied fields	44	54	1	1	44	56
Agriculture	36	62	2	*	31	69
Popular vote for President	42.7	43.4	13.5	0.2		

*Less than 1 percent.

†Nonvoters are excluded from the computation.

‡Includes those voting for Eldridge Cleaver, Dick Gregory, and the "regular" minor left parties—Socialist Labor, Socialist Workers, and Communist.

§Includes Socialist Labor and Socialist Workers parties.

SOURCE: 1969 Carnegie Commission Survey of Student and Faculty Opinion.

neering fields, gave Nixon less support than the faculty average in 1968, while mathematics and physiology followed the average exactly. All the other hard sciences were more Republican than the professoriate as a whole. Civil engineers, 68 percent of whom backed Nixon, were the most heavily Republican group in academe. In the 1964 Presidential election, the natural sciences, along with universities generally and indeed the rest of the country, were overwhelmingly Democratic. Among the hard sciences, biochemistry and physics produced the strongest support for Johnson (83 and 81 percent), although they were

1968 Republican Convention choice		1964 vote†		
Rockefeller	Nixon	Johnson	Goldwater	"Third party left"§
70	30	78	21	1
86	14	89	10	2
80	20	86	13	1
73	28	79	20	1
80	20	87	12	1
68	32	76	23	1
71	29	79	20	1
70	30	74	26	1
68	32	82	17	1
56	44	64	36	*
57	43	62	38	1
51	49	65	34	1
52	48	60	40	*
		61.1	38.4	0.1

somewhat less Democratic than the social sciences (89 percent) or social work (95 percent)—the field that gave Johnson his biggest margin. Only civil and mechanical engineering were more Republican than the national electorate. Physicists were the strongest McCarthy backers in the natural sciences, 61 percent preferring him to Humphrey as the Democratic nominee in 1968. This is 10 percent higher than McCarthy's support in chemistry, 20 percent higher than his support in chemical engineering, and it exceeded even the 54 percent for McCarthy in the entire professoriate and the 58 percent among social scientists. All the

TABLE 12 *Electoral preferences of American academics in the 1972 Presidential election, by discipline group (row percentages)*

Field of study	McGovern	Nixon	Other
Social sciences	76	22	2
Humanities	71	29	*
Natural sciences	53	47	*
Business-related applied fields	30	70	*

*Less than 1 percent.
SOURCE: 1972 Ladd-Lipset Survey.

disciplines in the hard sciences except civil engineering preferred Rockefeller to Nixon as the Republican nominee; and here again, physicists and biochemists gave the strongest backing to the candidate perceived as the more liberal.

Within the "hard" sciences generally, the most liberal faculty members are in physics; the range from liberal to conservative then continues from biochemistry, molecular biology, medicine, and mathematics, on to physiology and chemistry, then to general biology (zoology and botany) and geology, and finally to the engineering fields, in which electrical engineering is the least and civil and mechanical engineering are the most conservative.

In Table 13, we extend the comparison of discipline politics to campus issues. The three scales reported here are, as described in Chapter 2, a four-item measure of responses to campus activism, a Student Role Scale of five items dealing with the appropriate position of undergraduates in university decision making, and a five-item scale measuring faculty judgments on university policy toward blacks.

With only minor changes, the pattern of field relationships in Tables 10, 11, and 12 holds for campus controversies. The social sciences maintain their position as the most liberal (or, if one prefers, least conservative) set of subjects, giving much more backing for the campus protests of the late 1960s, for demands that students have more say in university affairs, and for change in campus policies affecting blacks. At the other end of the field continuum, again, are the business-related applied fields, the least supportive of all such liberal or equalitarian intramural actions.

On campus questions with the closest link to national affairs—those involving protests and demonstrations—the range of field differences is almost identical to what we have seen on the Liberalism-Conservatism Scale. Sixty-six points—again measured in terms of the percentage op-

TABLE 13 Faculty positions on the Campus Activism, Black Support, and Student Role Scales, by discipline (row percentages)

Field of study	Campus Activism Scale			Black Support Scale			Student Role Scale		
	Percentage supportive (a)	Percentage opposed (b)	Column (a) minus column (b)	Percentage supportive (a)	Percentage opposed (b)	Column (a) minus column (b)	Percentage supportive (a)	Percentage opposed (b)	Column (a) minus column (b)
Social sciences	61	18	43	49	30	19	61	24	37
Humanities	50	30	20	40	37	3	50	31	19
Fine arts	42	36	6	39	37	2	44	35	9
Education	41	35	6	40	37	3	52	32	20
Law	42	38	4	39	37	2	41	38	3
ALL FACULTY	40	37	3	34	43	−9	46	35	11
Biological sciences	37	39	−2	29	46	−17	44	36	8
Medicine	34	37	−3	28	46	−18	40	40	0
Physical sciences	35	39	−4	28	47	−19	41	40	1
Business	26	49	−23	20	55	−35	37	43	−6
Engineering	25	48	−23	21	59	−38	30	46	−16
Other applied fields	22	56	−34	23	51	−28	43	35	8
Agriculture	16	63	−47	19	59	−40	32	41	−9

SOURCE: 1969 Carnegie Commission Survey of Student and Faculty Opinion.

posed—separate social scientists and engineers on the Activism Scale. When the issue, however, has no direct connection with national affairs, the extent of discipline dissimilarity narrows appreciably. We see this in the notably more compressed distributions on the Student Role Scale.

While the relative positions of the various disciplines remain essentially the same across these three scales, then, the *strength of the association weakens as the connection between the issue and general liberalism-conservatism becomes more attenuated.* The pattern of field positions which we have identified is a function of the commitments of the faculty on policy matters which are essentially of the society rather than of the academy. In the politically charged climate around universities in the past decade, some components of campus politics have been suffused with broad societal concerns, that is, linked to a liberal orientation, but the correlation is somewhat reduced for those touching closest to issues of intramural governance.

Some may question how reliably opinion data represent actual political behavior. Behavioral (social) scientists were criticized by some radicals, such as Noam Chomsky, for supposed heavy involvement in support of the Vietnam War, while natural scientists were seen as being at the heart of the antiwar movement. These images may have been derived from the well-publicized role of a handful of social scientists as national security advisers and as consultants on Vietnam matters, on the one hand, and of Nobel Prize–winning scientists as the most frequently mentioned opponents in news stories about protests, on the other. Fortunately, one form of actual public behavior as distinct from sampled opinion—protest statements—may be analyzed. One of us (Ladd, 1969) examined the characteristics of academics who signed eight anti-Vietnam War statements which were published as advertisements in the Sunday *New York Times* between October 1964 and June 1968. The measurement that was devised is explained in the note to Table 14, which reports the results by academic categories and disciplines. Once again the liberal arts faculty were more likely to actively oppose the war than those in other schools, and within the liberal arts the social scientists were more involved than the humanists, who in turn rank higher in these terms than the natural scientists. Business-linked professional fields were notably underrepresented in the petition protests. Those on the staffs of colleges of agriculture were least likely to sign an antiwar advertisement, while sociologists and anthropologists stood out as the most involved opponents of the war. *Overall, the variation in behavior among individual fields was almost identical to the variation found in the attitude surveys.*

TABLE 14 *Distribution of faculty signers of protest statements among academic fields and selected subjects*

Field and subject	Number of signers (3,037)	Percentage of all faculty signers	Profession Representation Index*
Social sciences	747	24.6	251
Sociology and anthropology	171	5.9	304
Political science	146	5.0	284
Psychology	213	7.3	281
Economics	110	3.8	211
Humanities	844	27.8	132
Philosophy	124	4.3	287
History	184	6.3	166
English	264	9.1	110
Languages	138	4.8	89
Physical sciences	489	16.1	122
Physics	231	7.6	253
Mathematics	185	6.1	127
Chemistry	61	2.0	54
Life sciences	556	18.3	117
Health fields	337	11.1	137
Biology	207	6.8	85
Fine arts	149	4.9	60
Engineering	140	4.6	60
Education	94	3.1	18
Business	12	0.4	10
Agriculture	6	0.2	6

*This Profession Representation Index was computed by dividing the percentage of all full-time faculty employed in a given field by the percentage of all faculty signers who are in that subject. A score of more than 100 means that the field is represented among the petition signers in a higher proportion than among the faculty at large.

SOURCE: Ladd (1969, pp. 1425–1430; 1970a, pp. 542–556).

THE SOURCES OF DISCIPLINE DIFFERENCES

We have described the sharp differences in ideological orientation which exist among academic disciplines—the pronounced increase in support for conservative positions which occurs with movement from the social sciences to the humanities, on to the natural sciences, and finally to applied professional fields like business administration, engineering, and agriculture. This naturally invites the question of why discipline is so important in faculty political differentiation. What are the mechanisms through which a field comes to be associated with such substantial and patterned variations in political outlook?

The administrative importance of fields of study in the college or university is apparent. They are the principal organizational entities. University decision making revolves around them. While the central administration retains substantial formal authority, in most four-year institutions the school or department hires and fires, determines what is taught and how it is presented, and is the principal claimant in the distribution of institutional resources. Since the department looms so large in the organization of professors' work lives, it naturally plays a big part in shaping informal associations and friendships.

In this structural regard, however, university departments are not very different from the divisions of other complex organizations. Groups of men may be set off administratively and yet not be differentiated politically in any significant way. The importance of academic disciplines as units of differentiation results from subject matter and the concerns, orientations, identifications, and associations which the subject nourishes.

The fields of the contemporary university cover an exceptionally wide range of social experience. From improved crop techniques to literary criticism, from race relations in American cities to the reproduction processes of the mosquito, from bridge construction to fifteenth century French drama, the subjects which academics work with involve them in enormously disparate mental worlds. The subject defines the problems which occupy their work life. It carries with it a distinctive way of approaching matters, a conceptual frame which is developed in response to the materials and concerns of the discipline, but which is obviously applied beyond the boundaries of the discipline.

The subject matter of a field also influences the associations and identifications an academic is likely to have outside the university. A professor of engineering, for example, typically has a lot more contact with the personnel of business enterprises than does a professor of English literature. A faculty member in a college of agriculture is frequently in contact with farmers, agricultural interest groups, food processors, and the problems and concerns generally of agriculture; the professor of drama associates with writers and actors, and is concerned with the problems and achievements of the performing arts. Even more generally, the subject brings the faculty member into contact with the distinctive concerns, values, and commitments of his external peer group.

It has been argued that these features of subject matter—the areas of activity it encompasses, the problems and concerns with which its practitioners are involved, its distinctive styles and modes of thought, and the interests and groups outside the university which it defines—together influence the type of person recruited into the field. That is to say, a given discipline, occupied with special problems and having specific kinds of associations and references outside academe, *selectively recruits* people with consistent interests and values. In a panel study of student field and career choices involving repeat interviews over a two-year interval, Morris Rosenberg found that the predominant values, including political orientations, characterizing those concentrating in particular disciplines helped to explain changes. Thus conservative students who had chosen to concentrate in a liberal field tended to shift out of it to one more attractive to conservatives or, in some cases, to change their beliefs to adapt to those dominant in their fields. Liberal students initially in conservative disciplines shifted the other way (Rosenberg, 1957, pp. 81–83). Selvin and Hagstrom (1965, pp. 511–513) found at the end of the 1950s that freshmen and sophomores at Berkeley who strongly opposed restrictions on the political freedoms of people touched with the brush of "Communist" were much more likely to major in the social sciences than in more conservative business-oriented fields such as engineering and business administration. And from a cross-national perspective, Donald Emmerson (1968, p. 403) reports that "evidence from 19 countries shows, on the whole, students in the social sciences, law, and the humanities are more likely to be politicized and leftist than their colleagues in the natural and applied sciences."

Within the university, a discipline's subject matter requires a bundle of professional work experience, defines the groups and interests which serve as points of reference and association, and seems to attract people of a particular value orientation; together these factors contribute to the formation of distinctive discipline subcultures. And once formed, such subcultures apparently become more than the sum of their contributing parts. A set of characteristic styles, concerns, values, traditions, and general orientation to the social and political world takes shape, and members of the discipline are in intellectual contact with it throughout their professional lives.

We cannot sort out precisely the relative importance of discipline socialization on the one hand and selective recruitment on the other.

Nor can we treat in depth the subcultures of the entire range of academic subjects. But we can begin to untangle, expand upon, and explain some basic factors which bear on the political differences among disciplines described above.

ACADEMIC SUBCULTURES: BASIC VERSUS APPLIED SCIENCES

That substantial "political distance" separates faculty in the liberal arts and sciences from their colleagues in the applied fields is evident from the data thus far presented. And the "liberal versus applied" distinction is probably the most commonly encountered means of differentiating academic subcultures. The distinction is useful in a general way if the notion of a dichotomy is replaced with that of a continuum, with the liberal arts and sciences in a loose cluster at one end and the applied disciplines at the other, with but a few "deviant" fields. What characteristics define this continuum and determine the place of a discipline on it?

One element is intellectuality. If, as we argued in Chapter 1 and will again try to demonstrate in Chapters 5 and 6, intellectual pursuits predispose one to a critical position, such an orientation should be found most heavily among the faculty of the more "intellectual" fields. This was implied over 50 years ago by Thorstein Veblen (1934, pp. 226–227), who observed that "the first requisite for constructive work in modern science . . . is a skeptical frame of mind." He went on to argue that, for the gifted scientist, "the skepticism that goes to make him an effectual factor in the increase and diffusion of knowledge among men involves the loss of that peace of mind that is the birthright of the safe and sane quietist. He becomes a disturber of the intellectual peace. . . ." Individuals in the liberal arts and sciences, on the whole, appear to be somewhat more engaged in academic activity corresponding to the historic function of the general intellectual, involving a creative, innovative, and critical orientation, while work in the vocationally oriented fields is closer to that of the professional—the use of knowledge to solve immediate problems. C. P. Snow (1954, p. 176) has stressed the importance of the dimension of intellectuality in differentiating the natural sciences and engineering.

The engineers . . . the people who made the hardware, *who used existing knowledge to make something go,* were in nine cases out of ten, conservatives in politics . . . interested in making their machine work, indifferent to long term social guesses. . . .Whereas physicists, *whose whole intellectual life was spent in seeking new truths, found it uncongenial to stop seeking when they had a look at society.* They were rebellious, protestant, curious for the future and unable to resist shaping it. The engineers buckled to their jobs and gave no trouble, in America, in Russia, in Germany; it was not from them but from the scientists, that came heretics, forerunners, martyrs, traitors [italics added].

The second related factor defining the continuum involves the *uses* to which knowledge in a given discipline is put and the resultant contacts with groups and interests outside academe. A large segment of the faculty in the applied subjects subsumed by "technology and business" is in close association with private business corporations. This is the case with engineers, whom Herbert Shepard (1952, p. 211) described as marginal men between science and business. The faculty in the arts and sciences, on the other hand, as seekers "for truth aside from any consideration of practicality or usefulness," have lacked outside associates organized around economic interests. The more closely a discipline is linked to the business world, the more conservative—in the context of academe—it is likely to be.

If the argument is valid that engineering fields are more conservative than basic sciences partly because they are less intellectual, we should expect the most intellectual engineering field to be the least conservative. This, in fact, appears to be the case. Electrical engineers are significantly more liberal than their mechanical and civil colleagues, and electrical engineering, through the innovations in computer science and artificial intelligence, seems now to be the most intellectually creative of the engineering disciplines.

Something of this same distinction between the basic and applied fields can be seen in the liberal arts and sciences, partially accounting, to take one example, for the greater liberalism of physicists in comparison with chemists.[2] J. P. Nettl (1969, pp. 67–70, 80–82) argued that the differentiation of scholarship within a field into a variety of highly particularistic specialties reduces the potential for the type of behavior associated with intellectuality—which he saw as including a concern for broad structural rearrangements according to universal principles. If this view is accepted, physicists, whom Wright (1964, p. 294) has described as "the generalists among physical scientists (if not among all scientists)," should approximate the archetypal intellectual more closely than do chemists or geologists. Meier (1951, p. 170) has maintained that physicists are relatively more left-of-center politically because:

---

[2]The relative liberalism of physicists, evident from our survey data, manifests itself in a high level of political activism in the American Physical Society. For a discussion of recent activity in the APS from the perspective of a critical physicist, see Schwartz (1971, pp. 19–34).

[They have been] schooled in the proposition that progress is made by discarding various assumptions and premises and thereby making it possible to create a more powerful theory upon a simpler underpinning. The physicist, more than any scientist, deals with abstractions which make nonsense out of observations based upon the commonplace; he is educated in doubt and can disregard evidence which to the ordinary observer is both convincing and conclusive.

Chemistry, as a more "practical" field, is in closer contact with private industry. Relatively more chemists than physicists are employed in industrial positions. And 10 percent of the academic chemists, compared with just 2 percent of the physicists, reported that they had received research support from private industry during the year prior to the Carnegie survey. As a result, the faculty in chemistry are closer in their outlook to the conservative engineers, while physicists are more disposed to view social problems in liberal terms and not to identify with the problems of "establishment" institutions.

ACADEMIC SUBCULTURES: NATURAL VERSUS SOCIAL SCIENCES

All the natural sciences, we have seen, are significantly more conservative politically than the social sciences. One might expect the professional subculture of the latter fields to be more politicized because social and political problems are vastly more central to their subject matter. But this does not in itself explain why their faculties are more oriented toward critical, left-of-center politics than are faculties in the natural sciences. Two factors seem to be the most important here—one relating to recruitment, the other to professional socialization.

Selective recruitment of ideological types by the various disciplines is discussed in the following section, and hence can be passed over lightly here. It is enough to note that the social sciences, given their subject matter, appeal far more than the natural sciences (more, in fact, than any other group of disciplines) to those who would combine an academic career with a concern for social problems.

Another element in the political differentiation of social and natural scientists arises from the fact that the former are uniquely drawn by their expertise to cast a critical eye on the social norms and political practices of societies, often the one in which they live. Lazarsfeld and Thielens (1958, p. 149) made this point when they observed that "the intellectual task involved in these and many similar endeavors of the social scientist are contingent on his ability to visualize a state of human affairs radically different from that of today. . . .[F]or him ultimate scholarly accomplishment must depend upon a kind of imagination which has initially to be akin to criticism. . . ."

Our findings that natural scientists and engineers are more conservative than their academic colleagues in the social sciences speak to the position of the natural sciences in an open and democratic society today. At other times in history, and in other societies today, the natural sciences have occupied very different political positions, and in some instances have been the principal centers for social criticism and dissent. A field of study becomes highly ideological when, under a given set of circumstances, it offers a fulcrum for the rejection of established social arrangements; and from the seventeenth through the nineteenth centuries, natural science occupied this position in different countries at varying times. Feuer (1969a, p. 146) notes, for example, that in late nineteenth-century Russia "the students of natural science and medicine were the most active in the student disorders" and that "Russian students long regarded chemistry as the most ideological science and expected from it the solution of the social question." In nineteenth-century Germany, the humanities and subjects now in the jurisdiction of the social sciences were strongly linked to the national ethos, were perceived as being at the heart of the *Volkswesen,* the national essence. As such, they were the particularistic and conservative fields. Jews and radicals were barred from them, since such people were *wesenfremd,* alien to the national essence. The natural sciences, in contrast, were freer and more open, more universalistic.

The first Minister of Education in Meiji Japan, Arinori Mori, argued that a modern technological society must have scientists in the forefront of research and, consequently, that the natural sciences must be allowed much more freedom than other fields (Nagai, 1964, p. 29). This freedom of inquiry would inevitably produce some persons who were disloyal, yet it was a price that the country would have to pay if it were to become "modern." The social sciences, in contrast, were to be given only "limited freedom." They were not expected to train "free seekers after truth." And in authoritarian societies such as the Soviet Union, the social sciences have been committed to a conservative, regime-sustaining function; academics in these fields could not hope to report findings that clashed with party dogma, a factor which presumably discouraged critical and imaginative students from going into them. Parry (1966, p. 280), for example, cites reports that students in the natural sciences in Russia are the most active and dissenting politically. According to one, "the physical-science majors ... were by far more alert and critical of the regime than social-science students. ... Physical-science students were aware of the difference and proud of their own critical attitude." Students inclined to question and criticize have gone into the natural sciences at points in the history of nations when those fields offered

TABLE 15 *Political positions of upper-class and under-class students (the former in parentheses), by actual or intended major (as percentages of n)**

			Political self-
Field of study	*Left*	*Liberal*	*Middle-of-the-road*
Sociology (n = 1,084; 1,383)	(16) 14	(54) 50	(21) 25
Anthropology (n = 169; 212)	(24) 20	(55) 55	(15) 18
Psychology (n = 1,908; 2,048)	(14) 11	(53) 54	(24) 26
All social sciences (n = 5,875; 7,191)	(15) 12	(52) 51	(22) 25
Political science (n = 1,285; 1,732)	(18) 15	(53) 50	(18) 21
Economics (n = 604; 901)	(9) 7	(49) 40	(26) 32
Humanities (n = 8,283; 9,610)	(13) 9	(49) 46	(25) 29
Biological sciences (n = 1,991; 2,015)	(7) 5	(47) 43	(29) 33
Physical sciences (n = 3,284; 3,116)	(7) 6	(44) 40	(30) 34
Education (n = 1,971; 2,176)	(2) 2	(36) 33	(43) 46
Engineering (n = 1,715; 1,896)	(3) 2	(35) 36	(33) 38
Business (n = 841; 1,003)	(3) 1	(37) 36	(34) 41
Agriculture (n = 250; 255)	(3) 2	(27) 27	(35) 47

*Under-class students here are those in semesters 1 through 4; upper-class, in semesters 5 through 8.
SOURCE: 1969 Carnegie Commission Survey of Student and Faculty Opinion.

them greater freedom. In short, the natural and social sciences have changed positions over time and have occupied contrasting positions in democratic and authoritarian societies.

SELECTIVE RECRUITMENT OF IDEOLOGICAL TYPES

Earlier studies have found clear relationships between the political orientations of undergraduates and their choice of discipline. For example,

identification		Vietnam position
Conservative	Strongly conservative	For immediate U.S. withdrawal
(8) 10	(–) –	(78) 72
(5) 5	(–) 1	(83) 83
(9) 8	(1) 1	(79) 74
(10) 10	(1) 1	(76) 70
(10) 12	(2) 1	(75) 66
(14) 19	(2) 2	(70) 58
(12) 14	(1) 2	(75) 66
(15) 16	(1) 3	(66) 60
(17) 18	(2) 2	(64) 56
(19) 18	(1) 1	(60) 56
(26) 21	(3) 4	(51) 44
(23) 20	(3) 2	(54) 52
(32) 21	(3) 3	(42) 54

the studies by Selvin and Hagstrom (1965) and that by Emmerson (1968), cited earlier, showed a propensity toward the social sciences among the most left-of-center students. But perhaps the most impressive evidence of the attractiveness of these fields for left-inclined students is provided by the major national survey of undergraduates conducted in late 1969 under the auspices of the Carnegie Commission. As Table 15 shows, freshmen and sophomores—students at the beginning of their collegiate experience and presumably not yet greatly influenced by exposure to the ideas and orientations of faculty in the respective disciplines—who planned to concentrate in the social sciences were to the left politically of their counterparts in all other discipline groups. For example, only 38 percent of the prospective concentrators in engineering described their views as left or liberal, compared with 47 percent in the natural sciences. The proportion was somewhat higher among humanities majors (55 percent), and decidedly the highest for concentrators in social science (63 percent). Differences among undergraduate majors in the respective social science fields generally were modest, although economics majors showed up as markedly more conservative. Upper-class students were to the left of freshmen and sophomores by a slight but consistent margin.

The Carnegie faculty study permits a direct if limited test of the hypothesis that the political stance of faculty in the various fields results from recruitment. Respondents to the survey were asked to locate their "politics as . . . college senior[s]" along a "left" to "strongly conservative" continuum. The results, as given in Table 16, indicate a general confirmation of the "selective ideological recruitment" hypothesis. Undergraduate, preprofessional politics are remembered as left or liberal by 56 percent of social scientists compared with 47 percent of humanists, 39 percent of the faculty at large, 26 percent of the engineers, and only 17 percent of professors in colleges of agriculture. Analysis to be presented in Chapter 7 shows further that undergraduate commitments, thus measured, have a powerful *independent* effect upon the current political orientations of faculty. In other words, if the respondents' memories of their student-days views can be accepted as generally accurate, then the selective recruitment of more left to liberal persons into the social sciences contributes significantly to the (relatively) highly liberal position of these fields in the array of academic disciplines.

We get an additional indication of this by looking at the current politics of faculty in the various subjects, holding constant their preprofessional political positions. The discipline arrangement remains essentially the same when we confine our analysis to faculty who remember their college-days politics as left or liberal as when we deal with the entire professoriate (Table 17). But in the former case, discipline differentiation is much less pronounced. For instance, among all faculty, 46 points separate social scientists and the sample at large, and there are 80 points between social scientists and engineers—measured in terms of the proportion in a field scoring in the two most liberal quintiles of the Liberalism Scale minus the percentage recorded in the two most conservative quintiles. In contrast, among liberal-background professors only,

TABLE 16 *Politics of faculty as college seniors, by discipline (row percentages)*

			Politics as college seniors		
Field of study	*Left*	*Liberal*	*Middle-of-the-road*	*Moderately conservative*	*Strongly conservative*
Social work (n = 510)	15	51	20	12	2
Social sciences (n = 7,160)	10	46	23	18	3
Humanities (n = 10,333)	6	41	25	22	5
Law (n = 611)	6	41	26	20	7
Fine arts (n = 3,475)	3	38	27	23	8
Medicine (n = 2,395)	5	35	26	28	6
ALL FIELDS (n = 60,028)	5	34	29	27	6
Biological sciences (n = 4,567)	4	32	30	29	6
Physical sciences (n = 8,064)	4	31	30	30	6
Education (n = 3,401)	3	32	31	28	6
Business (n = 2,338)	2	26	30	34	9
Engineering (n = 4,373)	2	24	33	33	8
Agriculture (n = 1,398)	1	16	33	41	9

SOURCE: 1969 Carnegie Commission Survey of Student and Faculty Opinion.

the difference between social scientists and all faculty is just 21 points. As another example, 76 percent of social and 61 percent of natural scientists with a common ideological background (left-liberal) were recorded as very liberal or liberal, whereas when background is not held constant, 64 percent and 37 percent, respectively, score in these two quintiles.

Faculty in the various academic disciplines do not appear to be distinguished significantly by the political leanings of their parental families. The proportion in social science who remember their fathers to have held left to liberal views is not substantially greater than the pro-

TABLE 17   *Faculty positions on the Liberalism-Conservatism Scale, by discipline; all respondents and those indicating left or liberal politics as college students (row percentages)*

| | Faculty left or liberal as college seniors | | |
| | Liberalism-Conservatism Scale | | |
Field of study	Percentage very liberal and liberal (a)	Percentage conservative and very conservative (b)	Column (a) minus column (b)
Social work	77	11	66
Social sciences	76	12	64
Humanities	71	15	56
Law	70	13	57
Fine arts	66	17	49
ALL FIELDS	63	20	43
Medicine	59	21	38
Physical sciences	61	23	38
Biological sciences	60	23	37
Education	51	27	24
Engineering	49	31	18
Business	39	39	0
Agriculture	37	40	−3

SOURCE: 1969 Carnegie Commission Survey of Student and Faculty Opinion.

portion among professors in the conservative business-related fields (Table 18). The big divide, in terms of ideological background, occurs with political views held in college student days. Some academics-to-be were pushed by experiences in their student years far to the left of their parents' views, and these chose the liberal arts, and especially the social sciences, in a proportion far in excess of their peers who were not similarly liberalized. Social scientists see themselves as having moved very far from their fathers' positions by the time they were college seniors, on the verge of selecting their field of graduate study. On the other hand, academics who selected business-related applied disciplines recall only a slight movement to the left from their parental political leanings to their own as undergraduates.

Then, as Table 18 shows, those who entered the social sciences and humanities continued to move left after graduation, while faculty in the more conservative fields remained much closer to the politics of their parents. For the latter, the ideological climate of their discipline was far

	All faculty	
Liberalism-Conservatism Scale		
Percentage very liberal and liberal (a)	*Percentage conservative and very conservative* (b)	*Column (a) minus column (b)*
70	13	57
64	20	44
54	29	25
52	28	24
45	38	7
41	43	−2
37	45	−8
37	46	−9
35	45	−10
34	50	−16
24	60	−36
23	59	−36
14	74	−60

closer to that of the middle-class world outside. For social scientists, discipline experiences continued a drift to the left apparently started in student days.

SOCIAL SCIENCE LIBERALISM: RECOGNITION AND REWARD

A very different approach to explaining political variations by discipline emphasizes the question of how satisfied or dissatisfied members feel regarding the place of their calling in the society. Since the argument has been developed primarily as a way of accounting for the critical posture of social scientists, we will concentrate on this group here even though, if valid, it would presumably have wider applicability.

Paul Lazarsfeld and Wagner Thielens, Jr. (1958) developed this interpretation at some length in *The Academic Mind*. They found faculty in the social sciences in the mid-1950s somewhat depressed, feeling that

TABLE 18   *Political characterizations by faculty of their own and their fathers' politics, by discipline (row percentages)*

Field of study	Father's politics		Politics as college senior		Present politics	
	Left-liberal	Conservative	Left-liberal	Conservative	Left-liberal	Conservative
Social work	28	49	66	14	79	7
Social sciences	23	50	56	21	69	12
Humanities	20	55	47	27	60	18
Law	21	47	49	29	55	17
Fine arts	17	59	42	31	49	29
ALL FIELDS	19	56	39	33	47	27
Biological sciences	19	53	36	35	44	26
Education	18	58	37	33	43	27
Physical sciences	19	55	35	36	42	29
Medicine	21	58	40	34	42	29
Business	14	59	28	43	31	40
Engineering	19	54	26	41	29	41
Agriculture	8	70	17	50	17	53

SOURCE: 1969 Carnegie Commission Survey of Student and Faculty Opinion.

TABLE 19 *Assessments by social scientists of how their profession is ranked or valued by businessmen, congressmen, and college trustees (row percentages)*

Presumed judge	Presumed rank of social scientists among four sets of occupations				
	1st	2d	3d	4th	Don't know
Businessman	8	12	18	54	8
Congressman	4	19	19	48	10
Trustee	20	23	15	25	17

SOURCE: 1955 Lazarsfeld-Thielens survey.

they were being put upon. One indication of this was derived from a question in which respondents were asked to compare the standing of their occupation with that of three others: the manager of a branch bank, an account executive of an advertising agency, and a lawyer. "Suppose a typical businessman were to rank these four occupations by the esteem he holds for each—in which order do you think he would rank each?" This same question was asked two additional times, substituting for the businessman as judge a "typical congressman" and a "typical trustee of your college."[3] The results of this inquiry are presented in Table 19. About half of the respondents felt that businessmen and congressmen would rank their field at the bottom of the pile, below bankers, advertising executives, and lawyers. Fewer than one in ten thought their profession would be assigned the first rank in esteem. And even trustees, presumably sympathetic to higher education, were believed to hold professors in low regard. A large majority of social scientists thought their trustees would rank lawyers ahead of them, and they saw their profession in a close race for trustee esteem with managers of branch banks.

Lazarsfeld and Thielens (1958, pp. 13–14) found, interestingly enough, that the higher the academic status of the social scientist, the more likely he was to feel his profession underappreciated by the world outside. They interpreted this finding as reflecting the fact that as aca-

---

[3]In the occupational recognition question, the term college *professor* was used rather than *social scientist*. We assume, however, that the social scientists in *The Academic Mind* survey were thinking primarily of the standing of their own pursuits in the eyes of outside judges. In other words, what we have is an assessment of the status of college professors from the perspectives of a group whose experience is limited to the social science fields.

demics moved up in professional standing, they came to expect a greater measure of prestige than they found accorded them. Supporting this was the fact that only 22 percent of instructors, compared with 29 percent of assistant professors, 31 percent in the associate rank, and 34 percent of full professors, said that trustees would rank academics last among the four reference occupations.

The authors of *The Academic Mind* linked this sense of insufficient recognition to an inclination toward protest politics, including, for example, heavily Democratic voting patterns. "Here we wish to submit that in part they are voting for the party which is traditionally the rallying place for protesting minorities" (1958, p. 14).

There is no congruence between the perceptions of status which Lazarsfeld and Thielens encountered among social scientists in the mid-1950s and the actual standing of college professors in the eyes of the American public. As Lipset (1963, pp. 347–350) has shown in his review of relevant studies, academics may well *feel* rejected, but the community in fact accords their profession a high status. One NORC survey of 96 occupations, for instance, showed college professors ranking above persons in every nonpolitical position except medical doctor. In general, this study found that intellectual pursuits have prestige comparable to that of the upper echelons of the business world (Hodge, Siegel, & Rossi, 1966, pp. 324–325). A principal source of this contradiction between "inside" views of what the "outside" thinks, and what the latter actually thinks about the professorial calling, seems to be comparisons of the status of American academics with the glorified image of the position of their European counterparts.

... the very intellectuals who completely accept the egalitarian implications of the American Creed have felt themselves underprivileged, as a group, because they have not been accorded the symbols of high status which their counterparts in Europe receive. Ironically some of the reasons why American intellectuals do not get the signs of respect which they crave spring from the strength of the egalitarian standards which they espouse (Lipset, 1963, p. 344).

The fact that highly achieving college professors, especially in the 1950s, have been paid less than their counterparts in other professions such as medicine and law is presumably another, quite different, source of their low self-image.

Yet another argument along this theme that dissatisfactions surrounding their professional status contribute to the receptivity of social scientists to a critical and change-oriented politics has been presented by Charles Page and by Robert Bohlke with specific reference to sociology, the most left-of-center field. Page (1959, pp. 587–590) sees sociology as occupying a marginal position, uneasily located on the border between humanism and science, between commitment to normative concerns and a desire to be perceived as a science which involves a large measure of quantitative rigor and formal theory. The result is a sense of marginality among sociologists, a feeling that they possess a low level of "legitimacy," low prestige within the academy. Discussing this thesis, Bohlke (1968, p. 4) argues that their position as "outsiders" presses sociologists toward a set of political actions that only increase further their marginality:

In terms of the scientific establishment as a whole, sociologists would appear to occupy a position of marginality. They have turned their back on the status of humanist or social philosopher, but they are still not fully accepted within the scientific fraternity. Thus, we are suggesting that their recent deviant behavior is a function of increased marginality, particularly in as much as sociologists seem to be increasingly concerned about being viewed as scientists. If this analysis has any validity the response to marginality—that is, an increased activist orientation as sociologists—will, if anything, increase . . . their marginal position.

The Carnegie survey was not designed to examine the thesis that anxieties and dissatisfactions surrounding professional status, and specifically the feeling that their work is undervalued by the society, partially accounts for the left, antiestablishment politics of social scientists. But some of the data bear on this matter, and these raise questions about the validity of the thesis. For one thing, the Carnegie survey posed a number of questions designed to assess how satisfied respondents were with their job, the school at which they were teaching, and the academic profession generally. Uniformly, *those who are the most satisfied show up as the most liberal and critical in political orientations.* As an example, on the question "If you were to begin your career again, would you still want to be a college professor?" we find 65 percent of social scientists who answered "definitely yes" scoring in the two most liberal quintiles of the Liberalism-Conservatism Scale, compared with just 45 percent of those responding "definitely no." For social scientists at major colleges and universities, the greater liberalism of the most satisfied is even more pronounced (Table 20). Only 11 percent who said that they would definitely elect a professorial career if they were starting again are recorded in the most conservative quintiles of the Liberalism-Conservatism Scale, as against 51 percent of those who indicated they definitely would choose another calling. There is no suggestion, of

TABLE 20 **Politics of social scientists at major colleges and universities, by degree of professional satisfaction (as percentages of n)**

"If you were to begin your career again, would you still want to be a college professor?"	Very liberal (a)	Liberal (b)	Middle-of-the-road (c)	Conservative (d)	Very conservative (e)	Columns (a) & (b) minus columns (d) & (e)
Definitely yes (n = 2,176)	44	32	13	8	3	65
Probably yes (n = 1,418)	38	32	14	10	5	55
Probably no (n = 258)	38	25	14	14	9	40
Definitely no (n = 37)	24	21	4	25	26	−6

SOURCE: 1969 Carnegie Commission Survey of Student and Faculty Opinion.

course, that professional satisfaction breeds liberalism! What we have here is another case of the phenomenon, discussed in Chapter 5, whereby the most highly achieving academics, as creative intellectuals, give more support than colleagues of lesser attainment to a politics of social criticism. Our measures of career satisfaction are significantly correlated with indicators of academic achievement. Still, if the liberalism of faculty generally and of social scientists in particular stems partly from a sense of being undervalued by the society, one would not expect that those most satisfied with their choice of careers would be the most liberal.

Reanalysis of the original Lazarsfeld-Thielens data raises further doubts. As was reported in *The Academic Mind,* faculty who saw their profession as of low value in the eyes of businessmen, trustees, and the like were somewhat more supportive of the Democratic party in the 1948 and 1952 Presidential elections than were their associates who considered academe's status high. But looking at other measures of political orientation, we frequently encounter different results. For example, social scientists who felt the typical businessman would rank the professorial calling highest proved slightly *more supportive* of the rights of Communists and other political minorities than their colleagues who felt businessmen would rank professors lowest in the occupational hierarchy (Table 21). In all cases, the association between sense of professional status and political position was weak. A thorough examination of the data supports only one conclusion: that there is *no consistent or clear link between the perception by social scientists of the standing of their occupation in the community outside and their political stance on a general left-right continuum.* In view of this, we must question the broader

TABLE 21   *Political positions of social scientists, by their assessments of the standing of their profession in the eyes of businessmen (as percentages of n)*

A "typical businessman" would rank professors in the four-occupation array	Civil Liberties Scale				
	Highly libertarian	*Moderately libertarian*	*Middle-of-the-road*	*Moderately restrictive*	*Highly restrictive*
1st (n = 192)	28	18	28	8	17
2d (n = 283)	19	21	28	16	16
3d (n = 438)	24	20	28	14	15
4th (n = 1,330)	21	21	29	15	14

SOURCE: 1955 Lazarsfeld-Thielens survey.

thesis—that academics are led to a critical politics by a sense of being "deprived" or "cheated."

Furthermore, there is no indication that social scientists, relative to faculty in other fields, either are or feel they are badly treated. Analysis of the Carnegie data does not yield a picture of the social science contingent as "marginal men." For one thing, social scientists are, in the academic context, well paid. At elite colleges and universities, 19 percent of social scientists reported their current (1969) institutional salary as over $20,000 a year and only 11 percent as under $10,000, compared with 18 and 18 percent, respectively, for the much more politically conservative and supposedly more highly appreciated physical scientists at these same institutions. Humanists were much less well paid, with only 14 percent over $20,000 and 30 percent under $10,000. (All these data are based only on regular full-time faculty.) The median salary for sociologists in the 35 to 49 age stratum at elite institutions—to take the most productive and highly achieving group—was $16,000, exactly the same as that of their counterparts in physics, $4,000 higher than the median for like-positioned professors of English; and, interestingly enough, about $1,500 higher than the median for political scientists, who in the context of the social sciences are much more conservative. Taking into account the fact that some faculty reported an eleven-month and others a nine-month institutional salary, we find that only professors of medicine and law surpassed social scientists in the level of remuneration provided by the school which employed them.

Social scientists also do well in securing outside funds. For example, among faculty in major colleges in the 35–49 age bracket, 22 percent in social science reported earning 30 percent or more above their base salary from outside sources, as against 21 percent in the physical sciences and just 8 percent in the biological sciences. In the social fields 24 percent listed consulting as their principal outside source of money, in comparison with 4 percent of humanists, 18 percent of physical and 16 percent of biological scientists, 44 percent in business, and 36 percent in engineering. In this elite-school, middle-aged group, 19 percent of the social scientists found research grants the largest external source, and this compares with 39 percent of physical scientists, 18 percent in the life sciences, 5 percent in education, and 4 percent in business administration. Only engineers, business school faculty, medical scientists, and law school professors do better in outside remuneration. In other words, with the exception of the professional schools, social scientists prove to be among the most able to augment basic income from outside sources.

In other areas of academic life, our data present a picture of social scientists operating from a position of relative efficacy, satisfaction, and strength, not from marginality. For example, 25 percent of political scientists, 21 percent of sociologists, and 20 percent of economists described their opportunity "to influence the policies of [their] institution" as "a great deal" or "quite a bit," as against 17 percent among physicists, 15 percent of biochemists, 14 percent in math and history, 13 percent of faculty in foreign languages, 12 percent of engineers, and 17 percent of the faculty at large. Of the "marginal" sociologists, supposedly unappreciated by the public and hanging perilously between science and humanism, 65 percent said that if they were starting over again in selecting a career they "definitely" would choose the same calling, as compared with 57 percent of the more secure and revered physicists, 59 percent of chemists, 55 percent of mathematicians, 59 percent of professors of English, 47 percent of medical school professors, 41 percent of electrical engineers, and 41 percent of faculty in colleges of engineering.

What all this seems to say to us, and we present further data on the same theme in Chapter 5, is that application of the "class theory of politics" to academe is often ill-advised. This variant of the class theory, of course, would have it that a left and critical politics is a response to a sense of being put upon and deprived, of sharing inequitably in financial and status rewards. Social scientists are the most left-of-center academicians, and hence, it is argued, this must be partly due to strains and dissatisfactions in their position. In fact, we find that the better satisfied and rewarded professors are generally to the left of the faculty as a whole, and that social scientists are better paid, feel more secure in their choice of careers, and display a greater sense of efficacy within their institutions than do academics in most other fields.

SELECTIVE RECRUITMENT OF SOCIAL GROUPS

Some commentary on variations in political orientation by discipline has dealt with selective recruitment from social groups, maintaining that the collective backgrounds of faculty in the several field groups differ significantly.[4] In Table 22, we present data on basic background characteristics for the principal subject areas; in the following text dis-

---

[4]See, for example, Meier (1951, p. 170), the Editors of *Fortune* (1948, p. 106), and Helson and Crutchfield (1970, p. 255).

TABLE 22 *Social background of faculty, by field*

Field of study	Religious background (percentage Jewish)	Race (percentage black)	Sex (percentage female)	Father's occupation (percentage manual)
Social sciences	15	3	15	22
Humanities	8	2	23	21
Law	25	*	3	14
Fine arts	7	3	24	23
Education	6	5	29	32
Biological sciences	10	3	16	23
Medicine	22	1	6	10
Physical sciences	8	2	9	26
Engineering	9	*	*	26
Business	8	3	16	27
Agriculture	1	5	*	21
ALL FIELDS	10	3	19	24

*Less than 1 percent.

†Working with the Duncan occupational prestige scale, occupations were classified as "high status," "middle status," and "low status."

SOURCE: 1969 Carnegie Commission Survey of Student and Faculty Opinion.

cussion we attend as well to social group characteristics of individual fields, some of which are even more strikingly disparate.

The academic disciplines present widely differing "mixes" in terms of the social origins of their members. For example, 24 percent of law school faculty and 21 percent in medicine and in biochemistry are of Jewish background. At the other end of the continuum are civil engineering (4 percent Jewish), geology (3 percent), and agriculture (a fraction of 1 percent). Clearly, the early penchant of Jews for medicine and law, which have been both prestigious and least subject to the prejudices and whims of employers, has carried over into teaching and research. Not surprisingly, in view of the historic limitations on Jews in agriculture in Christian Europe, they are largely absent from the faculties of agricultural schools and are heavily underrepresented in fields linked to the soil or agriculture, for example, earth sciences, botany, and zoology. The considerable numbers of Jews in social science departments (and schools of social work), in comparison with most of the humanities and the natural sciences, may be related to the disposition

Father's education (percentage having attended college)	Father's occupation (percentage high status)†
42	21
43	24
50	32
42	23
30	14
43	22
59	39
40	21
39	19
32	13
22	9
39	20

of secularized Western Jews toward reform-oriented politics.[5] And as the newest group of disciplines, the social sciences have been less discriminatory and more committed to universalistic principles than the humanities. The latter, as the oldest and least "practical" fields, have tended to be identified with high socioeconomic status, and hence more restrictive in their admissions policies.

In class background, professors of medicine and agriculture again occupy opposite poles; 59 percent of the former, as against just 22 percent of the latter, come from families in which the father had attended college. The fathers of just 9 percent of academics in colleges of agriculture held occupations which we have classified as "high status," in contrast to 39 percent of fathers of medical school professors.

Certain disciplines stand out rather dramatically as "women's fields." Nursing school faculty are overwhelmingly female, of course, but the

[5]For further discussion of this, see Lipset and Ladd (1971a, pp. 93–96).

representation of women among the faculties of social work (40 percent), literature (30 percent), and education (29 percent) is also well above that in the faculty at large (19 percent). On the other hand, there are staunch male bastions, such as economics, where only 4 percent of all academics are female, law (3 percent), physics (3 percent), and engineering and agriculture, where women comprise less than 1 percent of the faculty.

Interesting as these background differences are, most are inconsequential in terms of interfield political variations. Analysis of the faculty survey data (reviewed in detail in Chapter 7) makes clear that whether the faculty member was brought up in a working-class family, had parents who had not completed the twelfth grade, or was the child of a university-trained professional is of little importance to his present political opinions. Neither parental occupation nor parental education is significantly correlated with any political opinion item in the surveys. Similarly, male and female faculty show no important differences in general political ideology. Black faculty are too few in numbers (at just 3 percent of the professoriate) to influence the pattern of field distributions by their relative presence or absence in specific subject areas.

Religious background is another matter. Faculty members of Protestant and Catholic parentage do not, as groups, differ much in their politics, but as we have demonstrated elsewhere, Jewish faculty (who make up 10 percent of academics) are much more liberal-left than their Gentile colleagues.[6] Compare, for example, the political orientations of Jews and Gentiles in medicine, as measured by their position on the Liberalism-Conservatism Scale:

	Percentage "very liberal" and "liberal"	Percentage "conservative" and "very conservative"
Jews	58	21
Gentiles	31	50

Disciplines which have attracted an exceptionally high proportion of Jews, especially medicine, as a result show a somewhat more left-of-center distribution. For example, medical school professors appear slightly more liberal than mathematics faculty, but Protestants and Catholics in math are somewhat to the left of their co-religionists in

[6]Lipset and Ladd (1970, 1971a, 1971b, 1972a); Ladd and Lipset (1971a). See, too, Chapter 6 of this volume.

medicine. Jews in these two fields, however, show almost exactly the same political orientations, and it is their far higher representation in medicine which gives that discipline its overall more liberal posture.

DISCIPLINE POLITICS: THE IMPACT OF INSTITUTIONAL BASE

Just as disciplines have their distinctive subcultures, so do institutions. Specifically, faculty at the elite, cosmopolitan, research-oriented schools are significantly more liberal-left than are their colleagues at lesser institutions (Chapter 5). The relatively liberal subcultures prevailing at the major institutions pull their faculty members in a liberal-left direction. This fact is important to our discussion of variations in the political views of faculty when their disciplines are differentially located in terms of major research centers and less prestigious teaching colleges. And there are sharp differences in field locations by type of institution. Two-thirds of the medical school professors, for example, are at schools we have classified as elite, and all are at universities rather than at four- or two-year colleges. Colleges of medicine, of course, are exclusively university enterprises, and the lesser (and therefore more conservative) institutions do not, for the most part, have them. Of the faculty in general zoology and general botany, 50 percent are at institutions without graduate programs, compared with just 13 percent of biochemists, indicating that general zoology and general botany are more strictly teaching fields. Among the general biologists, only 26 percent professed to be primarily interested in research, as contrasted with 76 percent in biochemistry.

The relative liberalism of medical science results from a kind of homogeneity in the field: most of its full-time faculty are scientists engaged in creative research; as a result, they are disproportionately located at and exposed to the liberal subcultures of elite universities. Actually, medical school professors at elite institutions are more conservative than most of their fellow natural scientists and are about as conservative as the engineers. Similarly, when the type of school is held constant, biochemists and faculty in general zoology and botany show comparable distributions of political opinion, although overall the former appear significantly more liberal than the latter. Mathematicians at elite universities are more liberal than their counterparts in any other natural science discipline, indicating that the relatively less liberal position of the entire mathematics faculty results from the field's heavy mix of teachers rather than research-oriented scholars. In fact, 58 percent of mathematicians, compared with 40 percent of physicists and 35 percent of molecular biologists, are at four- and two-year colleges rather than at universities.

CONCLUSIONS

Discipline differentiates faculty political orientations to such a high degree as to make questionable the wisdom of references to the politics of *academics*. Between social science and engineering there is a gulf in political opinion and behavior of the magnitude we would expect only between the most grossly dissimilar social groups in the larger society.

To understand the impact of discipline lines upon faculty opinion, we must appreciate how multipurposed an institution the contemporary American university has become and, in this context, how strong the discipline walls are. The subject matter of the various fields attracts persons of very disparate political orientations. And once within a field, faculty members become subject to powerful professional socialization impulses. Discipline subcultures reach far beyond the political dimension, but they are linked up to proclivities toward sharply contrasting political stances.

Once these phenomena bred of recruitment and subject matters are under way, an elaborate process of reinforcement comes into play. Paul Lazarsfeld and Wagner Thielens, Jr., (1958, p. 150) described this aptly a decade and a half ago, and while they were referring primarily to the social sciences, their argument seems generally applicable:

Any group which inclines to a professional ethos—doctors or businessmen or civil servants—will tend to reinforce it by mutual interaction. There is no conspiracy by which faculties exclude candidates with a conservative bent from appointment. . . . What actually is likely to happen is this: when people drift into occupational pursuits without any clear ideological commitment, as many do, they can develop either conservative or permissive [liberal] tendencies in their thinking. But two factors crystallize and reinforce the nonconservative component [in the social sciences]. For one, young teachers see that professional success is attained more often by permissive [liberal] seniors. Furthermore, once permissive colleagues are in the majority, even a slight numerical differential may build up to a considerable effect on the uncommitted man. By mere chance he is likely to find friendships among the less conservative; the result will be a slow atrophy of conservative potentials unless they were very strong to begin with. This is a process to which we have referred before: the development of norms by mutual interaction. And it applies to faculties as well as it does to any other group.

The ideological bent of a discipline subculture thus is not a casual thing. It possesses "staying power." The array of fields, in terms of the political outlook of their members, described here appears as a persisting feature of academic life.

4. Discipline and Politics: The Case of the Social Sciences

We have noted that by all measures of political orientation, faculty in the social sciences[1] are more liberal or left of center than their colleagues in any of the other principal academic disciplines. Their polar position is not the only reason, however, that we will examine their political position in a separate chapter. As subjects directly concerned with matters of polity and society, the social sciences at once possess a greater potential for political influence and a larger measure of political vulnerability. They are the "political sciences."[2] On the one hand, the political orientations of social scientists are of greater moment because their disciplines are directly involved, in both teaching and research, with broad questions of public policy. And on the other hand, divisions over policy, both intramural policies and policies of the larger society, intimately affect the internal operations of the social fields.

POLITICAL INFLUENCE

The interest of both conservatives and leftists in the political stance of social scientists has grown since the 1930s, in part because of the view

[1] *Social and behavioral sciences* is a fairly long and cumbersome phrase, and although it is the most exact one, we will usually substitute the simpler term *social sciences*, with apologies to clinical and experimental psychologists who would accept the designation *behavioral* but not *social*. In any event, we include in this category full-time faculty of colleges and universities who give as their principal teaching field one of the following disciplines: anthropology, economics, political science, psychology, and sociology.

[2] Columbia University formally acknowledges this central focus. Its Graduate School of Arts and Sciences has three divisions: the Faculty of Pure Science, the Faculty of Philosophy, and the Faculty of Political Science, the latter including anthropology, economics, geography, history, sociology, and political science.

that social scientists have an impact upon the political leanings of their students. There is little available information which indicates with any precision the contributions of faculty in the social sciences to the shaping of the long-term political outlook of their youthful charges. Most of the commentary resembles the observations of the youthful William Buckley (1951) writing on his experiences as an undergraduate at Yale in the post-World War II era, exposed to a predominantly liberal group of teachers, or Ronald Reagan (Lipset, 1972*b*, p. 209) seeking to account for the militancy of Berkeley students in the 1960s and crediting it substantially to a left-disposed social science faculty. What we do know with certainty is that academics in the social sciences are a principal source of information about things social and political for millions of students each year, and that this exposure is considerable, extending to a number of course offerings over the students' undergraduate years. Students in turn graduate, take up other positions and roles in the society, and carry with them orientations and conceptual pictures bearing on sociopolitical matters which in some way—not readily delimited—reflect their training in the political disciplines (Spaeth & Greeley, 1970, p. 108).

Important as teaching would seem to be, the influence of social scientists on public policy is not restricted to the classroom relationship. Increasingly over the last several decades, academics have become involved in the formulation of policy—serving as consultants to those charged with making public decisions, as authors of studies purporting to analyze the sources of social ills and to prescribe solutions, and generally (and probably most importantly) as architects of the "scientific" construction of social issues.

Surely the most visible example here is the gradual suffusion of Keynesian economics into government policy and the institutionalization of input from academic economics through the Council of Economic Advisers. It is not a typical case, of course, because there is no sector of public policy where sociologists, psychologists, or political scientists shape decisions in so direct and sustained a way, or play an institutionalized role comparable to that played by economists through such mechanisms as the CEA.[3] But a large part of the social science

---

[3]The various proposals to set up a Council of Social Advisers which would perform the equivalent of the economists' role—one of which was introduced in 1967 by Senator Walter Mondale of Minnesota in the Full Opportunity and Social Accounting Act—have not yet been translated into law.

community has been involved to some extent. A number of important areas of American policy have been influenced by social scientists since World War I—for example, race relations, beginning with the heavy reliance on social science evidence by the Warren Court in the *Brown v. Board of Education* decision (1954). The involvement of social scientists in policy-relevant research has become institutionalized in an enormous array of institutes and centers for policy research. These range from nationally known off-campus facilities like the government-oriented Rand Corporation and the Brookings Institution to the left-wing Institute for Policy Analysis. In addition, countless campus centers are studying military strategy, foreign policy, urban problems, environmental questions, and relationships of law and society. Social scientists are active in project research for virtually the entire range of government units, from the Department of Defense (DOD) and the Department of Health, Education and Welfare (HEW), at the national level to state departments of welfare and mental health, to municipal school systems and law enforcement agencies.

In the early 1970s, that primary center for the support of basic research, the National Science Foundation, inaugurated a major new applied research program (Research Applicable to National Needs or RANN) with a large social science component. Faculty in the political sciences have in recent years been engaged, both as staff and as consultants, by the wave of Presidential commissions charged with investigating central political issues: the President's Committee on Juvenile Delinquency and Youth Crime ("Crime Commission"), the National Advisory Commission on Civil Disorders ("Kerner Commission"), the National Commission on the Causes and Prevention of Violence ("Violence Commission"), and the President's Commission on Campus Unrest ("Scranton Commission"). Congressional actions have served to broaden the involvement of social scientists in policy matters by extending the techniques of social accounting to new areas, as through Section 402 of the Civil Rights Act of 1964, which instructed the Commissioner of Education to conduct a survey "concerning the lack of availability of equal educational opportunities for individuals by reason of race, color, religion, or national origin in public educational institutions. . . ." The study which resulted, identified by the name of its principal author, sociologist James S. Coleman (1966), quickly became a storm center in the continuing controversy over school integration policy. Perhaps the most vivid testimony to the extent of the intrusion of social science into public policy is the appearance of a new professional subfield devoted to this subject, one already nourished by a staggering body of reports, scholarly studies, and polemics.[4]

There is no question that academics in the social sciences are much caught up in the process through which public policy is formulated, but there is great disagreement as to precisely what their role is or should be. Do political leaders really take social science research seriously, or do they simply use it on those occasions when it serves to legitimate the positions they wish to take on issues? Does the emphasis on applied social research often entail a pursuit of the "fast buck" which takes social scientists away from the basic problems they should be studying? How much does the involvement of social science with government and public policy rob it of the autonomy it requires? Does social science in fact have its greatest impact when it eschews "policy research" in the sense of "issues of the day" and concentrates instead upon the development of broad social theory and discipline-oriented empirical research? Should links between research and government be promoted in order to contribute to intelligent public policy, or should research be dissociated from public authority so as to foster social criticism? Should the resources of the social disciplines be marshaled to *influence the formulation of policy*, or is their greatest contribution likely to result from *precise measurement of the results of programs initiated by government*? What, in other words, is the most appropriate institutional role for the social sciences in public affairs—policy direction or policy evaluation?

When the overall record of social scientists in the area of public policy is assessed, vastly different conclusions are drawn. At one end of the continuum, surely among the most optimistic, are the judgments of Ithiel Pool. Pool (1967, pp. 267–268) maintains that social science should lend its talents not only to agencies with obviously liberal and humane missions, such as the Agency for International Development (AID) and HEW, but also to the Federal Bureau of Investigation (FBI), the Central

[4]In the past several years, three substantial reports have appeared on the role of the social sciences in American society: *The Behavioral Sciences and the Federal Government* (1968), *Knowledge into Action: Increasing the Nation's Use of the Social Sciences* (1969), and *The Behavioral and Social Sciences: Outlook and Needs* (1969). As Lyons (1971, p. 133) has noted, these reports came out at the close of a decade in which governmental sponsorship and use of social science research had increased to a massive extent, one measure of which is the federal dollar contribution, where the jump was from $73 million in 1960 to $345 million in 1970. As Horowitz remarks in the introduction to *The Use and Abuse of Social Science* (1971, p. 1): "The history of social science, like most other history, tends to be carved up into decades, with each decade tidily labeled according to its dominant principle. . . .For the 1970s the dominant organizing principle seems to be policy making."

Intelligence Agency (CIA), and DOD, because the social disciplines can play a humanizing and civilizing role. In the past, he argues, public leaders ("mandarins") were trained in the humanities to provide them with a broader, richer understanding of the human condition. Now, exposure to social science better serves this end:

The day of philosophy, literature, etc., is not over. They have their value. But there are a great many things that we have learned to understand better through psychology, sociology, systems analysis, political science. Such knowledge is important to the mandarins of the future for it is by knowledge that men of power are humanized and civilized. They need a way of perceiving the consequences of what they do if their actions are not to be brutal, stupid, bureaucratic, but rather intelligent and humane. The only hope for humane government in the future is through the extensive use of the social sciences by government.

Pool insists that the involvement of social scientists with the Defense Department has had beneficial results:

The McNamara revolution is a star example of how the introduction of social science systems analysis and other relevant kinds of knowledge has had the effect of taming what would otherwise be a terrifying institution. . . . We are all aware of the expansionist, mission-justifying character of any bureaucracy. A 50-billion-dollar bureaucracy justifying its nuclear mission is frightening to contemplate. What has tamed it? The McNamara revolution is essentially the bringing of social science analysis into the operation of the Department of Defense. It has remade American defense policy in accordance with a series of ideas that germinated in the late 1950's in the RAND Corporation among people like Schelling, Wohlstetter, Kahn and Kaufmann. These were academic people playing their role as social scientists. . . . While one might argue with their conclusions at any given point, it seems to me that it is the process that has been important. The result has been the humanization of the Department of Defense. That is a terribly important contribution to the quality of American life (1967, pp. 268–269).

Pool's MIT colleague Noam Chomsky (1967, pp. 9, 26) stands about as far from this optimistic reading as it is possible to be. Finding the Vietnam War "simply an obscenity, a depraved act by weak and miserable men," he concludes that it was "designed and executed by [Pool's] new mandarins, and it testifies to the concept of humanity and civilization they are likely to bring to the exercise of power." While the indictment of social science scholarship which Chomsky advances centers upon foreign policy and specifically Vietnam, it extends to the whole range of involvement with government and public policy. As any group gains access to power and wealth, it develops an ideological frame to defend and justify its position. The absorption of social scientists into the decision-making structure leads naturally to a growing willingness to endorse reactionary, change-resisting social policies:

That is, one might anticipate that as power becomes more accessible, the inequities of the society will recede from vision, the status quo will seem less flawed, and the preservation of order will become a matter of transcendent importance (Chomsky, 1967, p. 28).

Such differences of opinion naturally lead to conflicting evaluations of the actual values of social scientists as their disciplines become increasingly important to the polity. There seems to be widespread agreement that, despite some commitment to the goal of "value freeness" or political neutrality in the discipline, social science is in fact heavily imbued with a distinctive ideological coloration. But there is total disagreement over what this coloration is and where the prevailing political biases lead in policy terms. This should not surprise anyone. We are not, after all, dealing with a spade which should be recognized as such by people of different political values, but with political values themselves. Still, the range of interpretations from eminent academic observers is striking.

Maximum Feasible Misunderstanding by Daniel Patrick Moynihan, while primarily a study of the evolution of the "community action" component of the War on Poverty, is one extensive commentary on the prevailing ideological commitments in social science. During the 1960s, in Moynihan's (1969, p. 177) view, social scientists gained "quite extraordinary access to power" which they employed for intellectually partisan objectives, "to promote social change in directions *they* deem[ed] necessary and desirable." He sees the social scientist as suffering from a kind of split personality, on the one hand as a scholar genuinely committed to an objective pursuit of truth, but at the same time as a "passionate partisan of social justice and social change to bring it about." The dominant ideological posture among social scientists is liberal-left, a kind of upper middle-class leftism which involves strong sympathy for the disadvantaged—"social scientists love poor people"—but a total lack of appreciation for the needs and interests of people in the middle, of values like stability and order. And he argues:

In particular, they would appear to have but little sympathy with the desire for order, and anxiety about change, that are commonly enough encountered among working-class and lower middle-class persons. . . . The presumption of superior empathy with the problems of the outcast is surely a characteristic, and a failing, of this liberal mindset (Moynihan, 1969, pp. 178–179).

Their commitment to social change and to advancing the interests of the disadvantaged led social scientists, together with other well-provided liberals and radicals, to induce or sanction various forms of public disorder, disregarding the effects upon the public at large. Anxieties over violence were dismissed "on grounds that those who [expressed them] either were not intelligent enough to comprehend fully any complex issue or else had something other in mind than their putative concern for the public safety" (Moynihan, 1969, p. 181). Moreover, Moynihan (1969, pp. 179, 181–182) argues that activist social scientists "had acquired an interest in the political turmoil of the moment and came very near to misusing [their] position to advance that interest. . . . The reaction . . . was not to be appalled by disorder, *but almost to welcome it.* How grand to live in interesting times!" Moynihan's (1969, pp. 190–191) overall assessment of the ideological directions of social scientists is clear enough; they are "a teeming and irrepressible group . . . on hand proffering proposals for universal improvement doubtless for all time to come."

There are plenty of opposing statements, such as that of Chomsky cited earlier, but one of the most interesting and comprehensive has been developed by Alvin Gouldner in *The Coming Crisis of Western Sociology.* Although written primarily with reference to just one of the social sciences, the argument seems generally applicable and has, in fact, been made by left-oriented observers in the other disciplines.

Gouldner's main point is that the sociologist confronts a basic tension. He is a relatively successful and comfortable person, having "moved onward and upward, with increasing access to the corridors of power, with growing public acknowledgment and respect, and with an income and a style of life increasingly like that of comfortably privileged strata . . . " (Gouldner, 1970, p. 58). At the same time, his professional work makes him especially aware of inequities, of failures in the society. The tension resulting from this combination of personal comfort and perception of deep problems finds resolution in an ideology which permits him to seek remedies without challenging any of the "essential premises," that lets him endorse social change while working within and for the existing society. Gouldner sees an element of hypocrisy here, for, fundamentally, sociologists are "successful men comfortable with the status quo . . . " (1970, p. 59).

According to Gouldner's (1970, pp. 335–336) critique, the supposedly dominant theoretical orientation of American sociology, functionalism, is positionally conservative, in that

its fundamental posture toward its surrounding society entails an accept-ance of its master institutions. . . . Committed as it is to the value of order, it can do no other than accept the kind of order in which it finds itself. This commit-ment to order has two sides, which taken together, spell out what I believe to be the core of Functionalism's conservatism. On the one side, it is disposed to place itself and its technical skills at the service of the status quo, and to help maintain it in all the practical ways that a sociology can. . . . On the other side, it is not disposed to a public criticism of the master institutions of the larger soci-ety. Functionalism's conservatism is expressed, then, in both its reluctance to engage in social dissent or criticism and its simultaneous willingness to help solve social problems within the context of the status quo.

There is a lot of distance between Moynihan's dominant social scien-tists, "a teeming and irrepressible group . . . proffering proposals for universal improvement," and Gouldner's visions of a social science "disposed to place itself and its technical skills at the service of the status quo, and to help maintain it in all practical ways. . . ." Putting aside all the rhetorical subtleties, Moynihan is saying that American social scientists have been serving as a socially disruptive, change-directed force, while Gouldner sees them fundamentally as defenders of the status quo.

When the point is made that social scientists are now intensely in-volved in the process of forming public policy, it is certainly not being suggested, then, that their new association with government and decision making is simple and unambiguous as to form, consequences, or the desired state of affairs. The point is, regardless of the difficulty in measuring their influence on policy questions, whatever the disagree-ment over whether social science is being beneficently used or seriously abused, and however much dominant value premises are in dispute, developments since World War II have enormously expanded the social science community and linked it closely to the process through which the great public issues are analyzed and responded to. In a society at the stage of advanced industrialism, social problems do take on formidable complexity. The existence of greater resources for their resolution often only adds to the difficulty in determining what the response should be, because the range of responses available is so vastly enlarged. The public leaders of an affluent social order, having been exposed as students to the abstract thinking of higher education, are far more receptive to academic analysis than earlier generations of decision makers. And the productive capacities of the economy are sufficient to underwrite a large cadre of men of ideas whose primary task is to think about social problems, a cadre which is part of a yet larger body of men and women comprising what is too cutely called the "knowledge industry." There is nothing mysterious about the prominence of academic social science in the formulation of political ideas and responses in the contemporary United States; it is a natural product of the kind of society we occupy, one which is variously labeled postindustrial, knowledgeable, a *civilisation technicienne*.

POLITICAL DISSENSUS

Looking closely at the political views of faculty in social science can be justified on the grounds that this occupational group has disproportionate political influence, or at the very least that there is a good prima facie case for its ability to exert influence. There is, however, another reason for our interest in the politics of the political sciences. As we have seen, these disciplines are political not only in the sense that they deal with public policy, but also because divisions over policy intimately affect their internal operations. The last decade has seen a new measure of politicization of academe, and the social sciences, more than any other fields, have been the center for political "dissensus."

Paul F. Lazarsfeld and Wagner Thielens, Jr. (1958) studied the opinions and responses of a group of American academics in a period when political divisions of the larger society intruded massively upon the campus. The country had emerged from its historic insulation to lead a great war effort against Germany and Japan and, victory won, found that it could not recover the insulated tranquility of former days. It at once entered a cold war, constantly threatening to become hot, with a formidable ideological opponent. As one of the two "superpowers" and the unquestioned leader of the West, it seemingly could not avoid worldwide defense responsibilities. And new weapons technologies had suddenly removed the protection which geography had previously provided. In this setting, widespread anxiety over national security appeared, which became manifest in a search for signs of domestic disloyalty—a hunt to which a junior senator from Wisconsin was to give his name. University professors, whose business was ideas and whose teaching and research often involved them in areas of controversy and dissent, became a principal target.

When Lazarsfeld and Thielens, under sponsorship of the Fund for the Republic, sought to examine "some ramifications of this spotlight on college teachers," they elected to focus on faculty in social science. Their reason was straightforward: " . . . it was they who dealt directly in the classroom with the very issues over which the larger community was concerned" (1958, p. 4). Since social scientists deal professionally with the whole range of public issues and controversies, they are uniquely exposed to all the effects of political conflict. Humanists, natural scientists, and professors in engineering, business, education, and medicine, as well as social scientists, are of course interested in the resolution of various social problems, do work which often has important political implications, may be attacked from without for political stances they take, and themselves may be divided by political disputations. But in all these other fields, the political dimension is largely peripheral to immediate professional activities.

The contemporary context obviously differs in many ways from that which prompted *The Academic Mind*. In the McCarthy era, for one thing, internal divisions in social science were not prominent as they now are. It was much more simply a case of hostile intrusions from without. The one parallel between the McCarthy and the Vietnam years—but an important one in terms of our analysis here—is the presence in both periods of deep tensions and conflicts in the polity which necessarily made both eras particularly stressful for the political sciences.

A variety of issues and developments, among which the war in Southeast Asia was certainly primary, produced a dramatic growth in campus political activism after the middle of the 1960s. The whole university community was affected, but no fields were touched as profoundly as the social sciences. The concerns of the activists, after all, had fallen largely in the intellectual domain of social science. And because of the close link between the sources of dissensus and the subject matters of the political disciplines, a disproportionate number of students with a politically activist orientation came to major in these subjects, thereby carrying the struggle more directly to them.

The activist-oriented social science student has often asked his professor to join him in his effort to achieve social change by immediate political activities. The demand for academic "relevance" in many cases has been a demand for courses which involve advocacy of particular sorts, or which see faculty members serving as political advisers. Efforts by professors to be "objective" in courses which treat social and political issues have been regarded as merely a flight from an obligation to combat inequities, as support for "the system."

Sharp political divisions developed among social scientists themselves. The professional meetings of sociology, political science, economics, anthropology, and psychology, in the past usually rather tranquil affairs, became, after 1965, settings for acrimonious debate. Between 1965 and 1972, the main precipitating issue was the Vietnam War. There was never any disagreement over whether an academic who objected to American policies in Vietnam should speak out, but a real split developed over defining the *professional responsibilities* of social scientists. Should the discipline, through its association, intervene directly, formally against the war? In the case of sociology, the battle began in earnest at the August 1967 annual meeting in San Francisco. A Member's Resolution to record the Association as condemning the war and demanding an "immediate end to the bombing of Vietnam and the immediate withdrawal of American troops from South Vietnam" was submitted to the Executive Council of the ASA. The Council unanimously rejected the resolution, maintaining that "the ASA as a scientific and professional organization should not express an official position on political issues."[5]

These were opening shots in a heated and persisting battle over the proper response of sociologists as sociologists to the great issues of the day. The battle has been fought out in the pages of *American Sociologist* and other journals, in books, at business meetings of subsequent conventions, and in sociology departments around the country. While Vietnam was the first great national issue of this period to thus intrude upon professional debates, others followed quickly: The question became whether academic sociology, in the name of "science" and "objectivity," had sold out the interests of the poor and blacks, the deprived and powerless of the United States, and indeed the world. A radical caucus of the discipline, the Sociology Liberation Movement, put the charge bluntly:

. . . we have abstained from our moral duty to speak out against the forces of repression in our society. The reactionary nature of our government becomes "beyond the scope of our field." . . . We have placed our expertise at the disposal of the establishment, letting the development of our field be guided by the needs of those who can pay for our time. . . . In the name of value-neutrality, we have failed [to help] the poor, the powerless or the unorganized. . . .[6]

While the division has perhaps been deeper in sociology, it extends throughout the social science fields. The same general lines of dispute

[5]American Sociological Association (1967, p. 223). See also Walum (1970, pp. 161–164).

[6]From a broadsheet, "Knowledge for Whom?" of the Sociology Liberation Movement, quoted by Brown (1970, p. 29).

can be found in all the sister disciplines, with embellishments peculiar to the subject matter of each. In 1970 and 1971, to take an example, anthropologists were exercised by charges that some of their colleagues had engaged in research involving complicity with United States counterinsurgency activity in Thailand. Had American anthropologists who conducted studies of a sort common to their profession among Thai tribesmen provided the governments of the United States and Thailand with information potentially useful to campaigns against Communist guerrillas, and if so, did that constitute reprehensible professional behavior?[7]

In a period, then, in which Americans have been intensely divided over the actions of their government and the course of public policy generally, the social sciences as fields directly concerned with matters of polity and society have, unavoidably, been fractured in their internal (professional) work by issues which have external (societal) origins.

Other disciplines are not totally immune to this. For instance, the debate among natural scientists over what constitutes a proper concern for the social consequences of their work, and especially over the use of science for military purposes, has heated appreciably in recent years.[8] But important as such matters are, they do not involve the professional fabric of the "hard" sciences to anything approaching the degree that the social science disciplines have been affected by national controversies. There is nothing in natural science today comparable to the debate which has engulfed social science: in which one side argues that the proper role of the social disciplines is to subject societies and their processes to as careful, objective, dispassionate, and scientific an analysis as is possible, to explain rather than to exhort; while the other maintains that any explanation of a set of social facts should be viewed primarily as upholding or undermining various political interests and the societal "reality" in which these interests are rooted, and that social scientists should, as professionals, be "involved," should make conscious moral commitments in their work and strive for political relevance.

An unusually complete documentation of this point, that the social sciences have manifested far more internal political dissensus in recent years than most other disciplines, has been provided by Ira Wessler (1973) in his study of political resolutions brought before the entire range of American learned societies.[9] Wessler shows that between 1965

---

[7]For a brief report on this controversy, see Shenker (1971, p. 79). See also Wessler (1973).

[8]For discussion of this, see Ladd and Lipset (1971*b*); (1972, pp. 1091–1100).

[9]For a more limited study of political dissent in American learned societies, see Bloland and Bloland (1974).

and 1971 (as earlier) almost no political resolutions were passed by the various natural science associations. Such resolutions and constitutional amendments seeking to involve a learned society in broad social controversies were in fact seriously debated in the meetings of only three natural science associations—the American Mathematical Society, the American Physical Society, and the American Mathematical Association—and in most cases "these proposed resolutions and amendments were overwhelmingly defeated" (p. 236). Similarly, radical caucuses and other dissident groups were largely absent from the professional associations of the "hard sciences." He "was unable to locate a single Black Caucus or Women's Caucus within the twenty-nine natural science societies studied. Only in the American Physical Society were groups of radical dissident members found to be in existence. These scientists belong either to Scientists for Social and Political Action, the American Physicists Association or Scientists, Engineers and Students for Political Action. These groups, however, have been completely ineffective in getting their resolutions and constitutional amendments accepted by the entire membership" (p. 238).

The level of internal political dissensus and interest in intervening in societal disputes has been somewhat higher, Wessler found, in the humanities associations. The American Philosophical Association (APA) and the Modern Language Association (MLA) have been notably engaged. During the APA annual meetings in 1969, resolutions on the Vietnam War were hotly debated. And in the 1969 session of the MLA, there were activists' demonstrations and caucuses centering around opposition to the Vietnam War and racial injustice. However, "at the annual meetings of no other humanistic learned societies has this type of activity taken place" (p. 241). Only the MLA and the APA have nurtured "well-organized groups of dissident radicals . . . blacks, women and graduate students" (p. 242).

By comparison, the social science professional associations have been by far the most politically engaged. Wessler reports that "every social science learned society . . . passed resolutions following the violence at the 1968 Democratic Convention in Chicago requesting that the site of future annual meetings be moved from Chicago to some other city," with the American Sociological Association also condemning the "gestapo-like suppression and brutalization" of the demonstrators (p. 243). "Radical" caucuses have been organized to do battle with "conservative" establishments represented by the leadership of the regular associations: The Sociology Liberation Movement and the Union of Radical Sociologists, Anthropologists for Radical Political Action, the Caucus for a New Political Science, the Union of Radical Economists, and, weaker and less active, Psychologists for Social Action. Other politically directed caucuses such as, in sociology, the Caucus of Black Sociologists, the Women's Caucus, and the Chicano Caucus have also been active, introducing resolutions and holding public demonstrations.

Wessler accounts for the high measure of political dissensus in the social sciences by the presence of "two distinct and opposing value orientations" among the faculty and student membership. "Ever since the founding of the social sciences, its members have been unable to agree whether they should remain aloof and clinically detached or should become actively involved" (p. 412). The strong commitment to political activism, as Wessler sees it, follows from the influence of three basic and widely noted factors: "[that] their subject matter is basically connected with values . . . , [that] social scientists constantly participate in value laden situations and . . . [that] social scientists are essentially motivated to contribute to human welfare" (p. 412).

These manifestations of active concern with external political developments and consequent political dissensus within the social science fields long antedated the 1960s. Wessler, for example, notes the much higher level of debate over controversies of the larger society in the learned associations of the social sciences—compared with the humanities and the natural sciences—throughout the time span he covers, that is, since 1920. As a related matter, we should note that the formal birth of the social science disciplines in the latter part of the nineteenth century resulted in the first large and highly publicized academic freedom cases. Both leftists and rightists (liberals and conservatives in modern parlance) found the teachings of assorted social scientists alien to their interests or beliefs (Thelen, 1972). Most of the cases that arose in the nineties involved the firing of liberals or radicals whose views were offensive to conservatives. As Walter Metzger, the preeminent historian of academic freedom, put it, "the decade of the nineties—so curiously and inappropriately called 'gay'—had seen the rise of a new kind of heresy defined as economic nonconformity" (1961, p. 149). The much weaker left, in the form of Populist politicians and university presidents in a few Western state institutions, was equally partisan in its criteria for social science appointments and dismissals.

Although there was a sharp decline in the number of academic freedom cases after the turn of the century, in part, perhaps, because of the vigorous, well-publicized resistance by leading academics and opinion journals, the problem continued. Not surprisingly, most of the activity dedicated to institutionalizing the rights of faculty was conducted by social scientists. Thus in 1913, a joint committee established by the American Economic Association, the American Sociological Society, and the American Political Science Association attempted to draw up a statement of principles (Metzger, 1961, p. 200). A year later a national conference was held which resulted in the formation of the American Association of University Professors (AAUP), which thereafter assumed the main burden of evaluating charges of academic freedom violations, and of organizing the defense of scholars judged as having been unfairly treated. The Association's first Committee on Academic Freedom and Academic Tenure, which formulated its basic statement of principles and procedures, was composed of 15 prominent scholars—10 social scientists, 3 humanists, 1 lawyer, and 1 natural scientist (Joughlin, 1967, p. 155).

Since its formation, the AAUP has received notice of more than 3,000 alleged violations of academic freedom. Although there is no breakdown of the fields involved, examination of published reports of firings reinforces the impression that social scientists were disproportionately represented among them. Given the subject matter of these fields, which involves social, political, and economic values and interests, heterodox or innovative views clearly can run afoul of assorted interest groups. More importantly, however, since society and politics constitute the basic substance of the various social science fields, practitioners in such fields are perforce political actors. Thus, when extramural authorities in the United States have expressed concern over the political impact of academe, they usually have meant the activities, scholarly and other, of social scientists.

Political involvement and political dissensus, then, have cut through the social sciences as a two-edged sword. On the one hand, social science faculty have been internally divided on the subject of what their response should be—which is to say, what their role should be—when confronting *as professionals* the great public disputes of the day. On the other hand, the subject matter of the social fields has required that they address broad matters of political controversy so as to invite, necessarily, attempts at retaliation from "offended" groups outside the academy.

POLITICAL ORIENTATIONS OF SOCIAL SCIENTISTS

Our discussion thus far has treated the social scientists as one unit. In fact, there are a number of discrete social fields with political dissimilarities which deserve attention. A substantial body of survey data permits attention to these variations.

TABLE 23 *Political positions of social scientists in the 1950s, by field (percentages of n)*

Field of study	Self-identification as "more liberal" or "more conservative" than most of the faculty		Disagrees that a social scientist who is an admitted Communist is not fit to be a teacher
	More liberal	More conservative	
Sociology (n = 405)	53	7	48
Social psychology (n = 141)	47	11	56
Political science (n = 384)	47	17	32
Economics (n = 565)	40	15	42
All social sciences (n = 2,451)	43	14	39

SOURCE: 1955 Lazarsfeld-Thielens survey.

Two basic observations should be made. First, the differences within the social sciences are relatively slight compared with those between them as a group and the other major discipline categories. Clearly, the fields in the group called the social sciences have much in common when judged by the political views of their members. But although the intragroup differences are relatively modest, they are sufficiently clear to be described, and, most importantly, perhaps, they follow a distinct pattern. Sociology, often in tandem with anthropology, is the most liberal or left field, followed generally but less consistently by psychology, with political science and economics located on the conservative side of the human behavior disciplines.

In studying reactions to the repressive pressures of the McCarthy era, Lazarsfeld and Thielens found that sociologists, and the closely related group of social psychologists, stood out as the most left-of-center group. Over 10 percent of the sociologists and 14 percent of the social psychologists (the only category of psychologists interviewed in the 1955 survey) reported voting for left third-party candidates in 1948; this was notably more than the percentage of economists and political scientists voting for such candidates (Table 23). Sociologists and social psychologists also were more prone to describe their political views as to the left of faculty generally than were professors in political science and economics. On the more salient matters of civil and academic

Opposes the firing of an admitted Communist from college teaching	Voted for Henry Wallace or Norman Thomas in 1948
52	10
56	14
42	6
48	7
44	8

rights for Communists, the field variations were even more distinct and in the same direction.

Studies conducted by a group of Santa Barbara sociologists and political scientists generally support the Lazarsfeld-Thielens findings. Among the three social science fields which were investigated, sociologists were again found to be the most liberal. Only 10 percent described themselves as Republicans. Similarly, sociology faculty reported the highest backing for Truman and Stevenson, the Democratic presidential nominees in 1948, 1952, and 1956. In 1948, when academe gave a substantial vote to left third-party candidates, 17 percent of sociologists in these surveys opted for Henry Wallace or Norman Thomas, as contrasted with 14 percent of the psychologists and 11 percent of the political scientists.[10]

Earlier, we noted that a 1968 study of the discipline backgrounds of those who had signed seven anti–Vietnam War advertisements appearing in *The New York Times* reported that social scientists as a group were much more likely to have identified publicly with the antiwar movement than humanists or natural scientists. Looking more closely at variations within the social fields, we find once again the familiar pattern of

[10]Turner, Spaulding, and McClintock (1962–1963a, p. 275; 1963b, p. 653); McClintock, Spaulding, and Turner (1965, p. 213).

differentiation. Sociologists and anthropologists, considered as one field, were more than three times as prone to have signed such statements as were academics generally. Political scientists and psychologists were next, with about the same rate of participation, while economists participated the least within the group.

Sociologists initiated the most substantial petition protest against the war of any academic discipline. About 1,300 "individual fellows and active members of the ASA" signed an "open letter" to President Johnson and the Congress on November 1, 1967 deploring "the conduct of the Vietnam War and its effects upon our society," and urging "an immediate and unconditional cessation of the bombing . . . [and] a genuine attempt to seek negotiations for peace with representation of all parties concerned . . . [and] orderly, phased withdrawal of American forces from Vietnam."[11]

In a follow-up study to his analysis of the characteristics of the antiwar petition signers, Ladd (1970*a*, p. 552) sent questionnaires to a sample of the participating social scientists. He found that the sociologists among them were decisively the most inclined to attack the war as immoral, as an aggressive act of an imperialist power (the United States) against a militarily weak people, whereas the political scientist protesters referred largely to national interests and to strategic and tactical mistakes in describing their reasons for opposing American involvement (Table 24). In a similar fashion, the sociology petitioners gave the greatest support to the student protests of the late 1960s, which, while having sources quite removed from the war, frequently had war-related activities as their immediate targets. Among the social

TABLE 24 *Profession Representation Index, signers of anti—Vietnam War petitions, by discipline*

Field of study	PRI*
All social science	251
Sociology and anthropology	304
Political science	284
Psychology	281
Economics	211

*Refer to Table 14, Chapter 3, for an explanation of the construction of the Profession Representation Index.

SOURCE: Ladd (1969; 1970*a*)

[11]Ad Hoc Committee of Sociologists for Peace in Vietnam (1967). For a discussion of the signers of this petition, see Walum (1970, pp. 161–164).

TABLE 25 *Political identification of American sociologists (1964)*

Party identification	Number of respondents	Percentage of total
Conservative Republican	45	1
Moderate Republican	127	4
Liberal Republican	287	8
Conservative Democrat	46	1
Moderate Democrat	517	15
Liberal Democrat	1,808	53
Socialist	244	7
Independent	214	6

SOURCE: Gouldner and Sprehe (1965).

scientists who signed a petition against the war, those least in favor of the student protests were the political scientists and economists (p. 554).

The image conveyed here, of sociology as the most liberal or politically critical discipline in academe, runs sharply counter to the considerable literature in books and articles by left-oriented scholars, and the many pamphlets and other political documents by representatives of "radical" caucuses and related groups in the discipline, which allege that sociology has been the "handmaiden" of the Establishment. Therefore, before turning to a more intensive analysis of the variations among social scientists as reflected in the data of the 1969 Carnegie investigation, it would seem worthwhile to note the results of the largest single opinion survey ever made of an individual academic discipline, that conducted in 1964 by Alvin Gouldner and his then assistant and doctoral student, J. Timothy Sprehe.[12] This study is especially interesting because Gouldner, notably through his book *The Coming Crisis of Western Sociology* (1970), has established himself as one of the foremost critics of the allegedly conservative posture of the discipline.

In fact, the largely unpublished data from the Gouldner-Sprehe survey reveal a discipline disproportionately left-of-center in its politics, socially critical, highly activist, convinced its role involves action to promote social change. In partisan politics, sociologists were concentrated on the left wing of the Democratic party (Table 25). The percent-

---

[12]For a brief published report on the survey, with marginals, see Gouldner and Sprehe (1965, pp. 42–44). A detailed report of the study may be found in the dissertation by Sprehe (1967).

age describing themselves as socialists (7 percent) in 1964 exceeded that in the conservative and moderate Republican and conservative Democrat categories combined. Respondents to the survey were asked to list the three most pressing social problems facing the United States, and whether "the solution would require basic change in American social structure and values." As of 1964, race relations was perceived as the most pressing issue, followed in order by unemployment, mental health, and urban problems. Sprehe constructed an Index of Radicalism from the question of whether solution to these problems required fundamental social change:

A response of "Basic Change in Structure and Values" was considered a radical diagnosis; "No Change in Structure and Values" was taken as a conservative diagnosis. The sample as a whole scored towards the radical side on the Index of Conservatism-Radicalism. . . . [O]nly 13.3% felt little change in basic structure or values would be necessary to solve these problems; 10% were at the midpoint; 76.7% scored on the side of "Basic Change in Structure and Values" (Sprehe, 1967, pp. 321, 264–265).

In 1964, before the rise of student activism and antiwar protest, sociologists were found to be strongly committed to solving social problems. Seventy-one percent agreed that one component of the sociologist's role "is to be a critic of contemporary society" (Table 26). More than 60 percent maintained that the model of "sociology for its own sake" was inadequate, that the field needed to apply its expertise to pressing problems. Seventy-seven percent insisted that sociologists were responsible for the way their findings were used. More than six in ten were critical of the emphasis on methodology which "too often diverts sociologists from a study of society to the problem of how to study society."

The Gouldner-Sprehe survey showed that most sociologists perceived major social institutions as caught up in tension-producing conflict and hence unstable. They saw the social order as so complex that only "planned change" could be expected to bring solutions to problems. Only 8 percent accepted the premise that "social problems tend to correct themselves without planned intervention."

Gouldner and Sprehe did not find the profession attached to a "scientistic" perspective. Far from retreating into methodology and "pure sociology," the respondents were occupied by social problems, and their perspective on change was heavily reformist. Interestingly, although most believed other sociologists paid lip service to the idea of being "value-free" in their work, they themselves did not think value

TABLE 26 *"Domain assumptions" of American sociologists (1964) (as percentages)*

Item	Agree	Uncertain	Disagree
The sociologist, like any other intellectual, has the right and duty to criticize contemporary society.	91	4	5
One part of the sociologist's role is to be a critic of contemporary society.	71	10	19
Sociology for its own sake is good enough; it need not be applied.	32	7	61
Sociologists must take some responsibility for how their findings are used by others.	77	6	17
Emphasis on methodology too often diverts sociologists from a study of society to the problem of how to study society.	61	10	29
The problems of modern society are so complex that only planned change can be expected to solve them.	62	11	26
By and large, social problems tend to correct themselves without planned intervention.	8	6	86
Many modern social institutions are deeply unstable and tensionful.	61	15	24
Most sociologists pay lip service to the idea of being value-free in their work and are really not value-free.	73	10	17
Sociologists do not really keep separate their personal experiences and their professional work.	59	14	27
Active involvement in efforts to remedy social problems need not seriously bias a sociologist.	77	5	18

SOURCE: Sprehe (1967, pp. 221–229).

freeness was possible. At the same time, they were not of the opinion that "active involvement in efforts to remedy social problems" necessarily will "seriously bias" a sociologist (Table 26).

The survey Gouldner and Sprehe conducted in 1964 demonstrated clearly, then, that a majority of sociologists neither identified with a highly abstract, scientific view of their discipline nor accepted the system-maintenance, conservative implications Gouldner personally perceived in Parsonian functional analysis (which he identified as sociology's dominant theoretical orientation). Rather, sociologists held to the view that basic changes in the structure and values of American society were needed to solve the major social problems, that many modern institutions were "deeply unstable and tensionful," and that the sociologist should be a "critic of contemporary society." This major survey, while contradicting Gouldner's own premises, sustains and extends an interpretation of the politics of sociologists as disproportionately left and critical.

The basic pattern of differentiation among the social sciences indicated by the various surveys conducted since 1955 is reaffirmed by the results of the 1969 Carnegie Commission investigation. Here, the attitudes of 7,160 social scientists in the five major disciplines can be analyzed on close to 100 attitude items pertaining to national politics and campus affairs.

Once again the three "behavioral" fields, sociology, anthropology, and psychology,[13] appear to the left of the two "institutional" fields, economics and political science. And on many of the questions, sociologists were much more liberal than their fellows in anthropology and psychology. Sociologists gave the most support (28 percent) for the position that a "Communist regime is probably necessary for progress in underdeveloped countries"; whereas, at the other pole, 17 percent of the political scientists took this stance. Nearly a third (31 percent) of the faculty in sociology strongly agreed that "white racism is the cause of Negro riots," compared with less than a fifth (19 percent) of political science and economics professors. In 1968, over three-fifths of the faculty in the three behavioral groups backed Senator McCarthy over Senator Humphrey for the Democratic nomination, with the sociologists again in the lead (64 percent). On the other hand, less than half of the political scientists and economists were for McCarthy.

Not surprisingly, the disciplines revealed the same relative distributions of political inclinations with respect to campus matters as to external affairs. Thus, 70 percent of the sociologists approved "the emergence of radical student activism," as against 55 percent of economists; and while 43 percent of those in sociology took issue with the statement that "students who disrupt the functioning of a college should be expelled or suspended," just 32 percent of political scientists and 28 percent of economists took this position. A clear majority of sociologists (56 percent) agreed that "most American colleges and universities are racist whether they mean to be or not," although only 44 percent in political science and 41 percent in economics approved the statement.

We find a comparable array of answers to questions involving the ap-

[13]Differences in substantive focus, and in political orientations, are especially pronounced among the three principal subspecialties of psychology—social, clinical, and experimental—as we show later in this chapter. Psychology does not fit neatly, then, into the rough dichotomy we are developing. What is clear is that social psychologists closely resemble their colleagues in sociology and anthropology in general political orientation.

propriate student role in university decision making. As would be expected, professors are most willing to give undergraduates a bigger say in questions of student discipline, and most opposed to a substantial student voice in the faculty's immediate area of concern, professional appointments and promotions. Only 13 percent of the professoriate wanted to limit the role of undergraduates to, at most, polite consultation ("informal consultation" or "little or no role") in the area of student discipline, as against 51 percent opting for this limitation of involvement in curriculum decisions, 63 percent in undergraduate admissions policy, and 80 percent in faculty personnel decisions. In all these sectors of university decision making social scientists gave more backing to an increase in undergraduate involvement, with sociologists and economists occupying opposite poles among the social scientists. Thus, 15 percent of sociologists, compared with less than 7 percent of economists, wanted to give students a formal vote in faculty hiring. In the case of undergraduate admissions policy, the figures are, respectively, 27 and 16 percent; and 80 percent in sociology, as against 69 percent in economics, maintained that students should have a formal vote in the enforcement of rules and regulations affecting students.

The variations between sociologists, anthropologists, and psychologists at one pole, and political scientists and economists at the other, are not only related to attitudes, but are reflected as well in behavior in campus controversies. Faculty in the behavioral fields have been more highly participant in campus protests than their associates in other social sciences, and much more, of course, than the professoriate at large. Of sociologists, 5 percent said that they had actively joined in demonstrations on their home campus, while more than one-fourth (27 percent) indicated that they had openly endorsed these protests. By comparison, just 3 percent of economists and 1 percent of the entire faculty engaged in acts of campus protest, and only 15 and 11 percent, respectively, openly supported the local demonstrations.

These contrasting sympathies seemingly carried over to the children of academics. Thus, 47 percent of anthropologists and 46 percent of sociologists (among those with children of the appropriate age) replied that their offspring had been active in demonstrations, as against 37 percent of economists and political scientists, and only one-quarter (26 percent) of all faculty members.

WHY THE DIFFERENCES AMONG THE SOCIAL SCIENCES?

In the previous chapter, we sought to account, in part, for the greater propensity of social scientists as a group to favor liberal-to-left positions and to be active in various forms of protest. But as we have seen here, the social sciences vary among themselves in a fairly consistent fashion. Discussion of some of the factors that promote these internal differences may contribute to a further understanding of the contrasting political pressures within academe.

The five major social science fields considered here appear to fall into two groups, those which primarily analyze the behavior of individuals and groups—sociology, anthropology, and psychology—and those which deal with institutional systems—economics and political science. The first group stands consistently to the left of the second. In accounting for this split, a series of considerations stemming from general substantive orientations seem most important.

The behavioral group deals particularly with topics which inherently remain a focus for discontent—race, stratification, urbanism, power, crime, mental illness, delinquency, and the like. They differ from the two social sciences of direct policy relevance—political science and economics—in their preoccupation with social and personal breakdowns, and with "outsiders" rather than "insiders." More than in their sister disciplines, much of the grand (and petty) tradition in the behavioral fields has fostered the "distrust of reason" through the effort to explain opinion and behavior as motivated by hidden private drives, by concealed self-interest, and by the system needs of societies (Bendix, 1970, pp. 831–843). Methodologically their members are cautioned against accepting rational, manifest explanations for human activity. Robert Merton (1968, pp. 66–94) has effectively pointed out that functionalism, the major approach in sociology and anthropology, does not differ from Marxism in this respect. As an example, he outlined the similarities between the functionalist and Marxist analyses of religion—both see it "as a *social mechanism* for 'reinforcing the sentiments most essential to the institutional integration of the society'." Elsewhere, Lipset has pointed out that the three major approaches to social stratification—those of Marx, Weber, and Durkheim (functionalism)—each assumed a form of alienation, of self-estrangement, as a consequence of inequality. Thus no "school" of sociology believes that social hierarchy can constitute a stable system accepted fully by the lowly. He observes that

functionalist sociology . . . like the Marxist and Weberian forms of analysis . . . points to ways in which the demands of a stratification system press men to act against their own interests, and alienate them from autonomous choice. . . . [T]he focus in functionalism on means-ends relationships reveals the conflict-generating potential of stratification systems, in which goals are inherently scarce resources. Hence, functional analysis, like the other two, locates sources of consensus and cleavage in the hierarchial structures of society (1970*a*, p. 184).

Anthropologist Stanley Diamond (1964, pp. 432–437) reminded his colleagues some time ago that one of the field's founding father figures, E. T. Tylor, concluded that it "is essentially a reformer's science." Diamond went on to argue that the nature of the field has an even more radical potential than Tylor realized.

Although careerism and slick professionalism have made their inroads among us, we are largely self-selected to study people off the mainstream of contemporary civilization.... We come close to being real citizens of the world ... [and] such an adherence can be a dangerous frame of mind. We are, in other words, marginal in temperament....

The concern for living among and analyzing primitive communities, in part, reflects some dissociation from one's society and points out alternative ways, which often seem morally superior, of handling the problems of human existence. Anthropologists are led to question the myths that societies erect about their own progress and superiority. Somewhat earlier, Ralph Linton (1936, p. 490) argued that "for men to take an interest in ... the study of culture and society ... is in itself a criticism of the existing order, an indication that they doubt its perfection."

Lazarsfeld and Thielens, in *The Academic Mind,* presented yet another variant of this argument:

The social scientist faces an additional situation deriving from the nature of his work, which is likely to strengthen a basically permissive [liberal] attitude. A great discovery of anthropology was that there are social systems completely different from ours and yet viable. A major contribution of historians is the idea that in other periods the modes of thinking and the forms of social relations were different from ours, and require reconstruction for contemporary understanding. The intellectual task involved in these and many similar endeavors of the social scientist are contingent on his ability to visualize a state of human affairs radically different from that of today. It is true that as a scientist he is subject to the same laws of evidence as are his colleagues in all other realms of knowledge. Yet for him ultimate scholarly accomplishment must depend upon a kind of imagination which has initially to be akin to criticism and is not, therefore, consonant with the intellectual mood of the conservative (1958, p. 149).

The behavioral fields also have a "debunking" effect on belief in the basic assumptions of given societies through their production of empirical data which frequently "disprove" the validity of desired national self-images. Research on social stratification conclusively indicates the existence of sharp inequities with respect not only to income, status, and power, but also to education, health, housing, treatment before the law, and many other values. Whether resulting from research on the destructive impacts of colonialism and other efforts to incorporate "simpler" cultures into more complex ones, from studies of social mobility and education in the Soviet Union and Poland, or from work on such disparate subjects as infant mortality and job possibilities in the United States, the evidence all points to the punitive character of social systems' impact on the personalities and life chances of the offspring of the low-valued. It may be argued, then, that the behavioral social scientists, more than their "system-concerned" associates, are recurrently exposed to the "contradictions" of their society.

To turn to the sources of the relative conservatism of political scientists and economists, the factor that strikes us as particularly relevant is their disciplines' preoccupation with analysis of the way in which the ongoing system works. Although their research necessarily points out gaps between actual performance and the ideals of the political or economic system, almost inherent in their approach is an emphasis on reforms, on moderate changes which will make the system work. In the case of political science, stress on law and order, legitimacy, and constitutionality are often component parts of a "world view." And where they are not engaged in advanced professional training, political scientists are preparing students to become civil servants, administrators of the polity. Similarly, economists prepare people to operate the economy through government or business.

In Ladd's study of professors who signed advertisements against the Vietnam War, the underpinnings of these discipline variations are further revealed. The basis for the opposition of sociologists and psychologists differed sharply from that of political scientists and economists. The latter were more likely to indicate "realist" reasons for opposing the war—that is, the belief that we had erred in intervening without viable South Vietnamese allies, that we had miscalculated our chances to win, that we lacked *vital interests* in Vietnam. In other words, the errors of American policy were political, not moral. Over half the political scientists (57 percent) took this position. Conversely, the majority of the sociologists and anthropologists gave a variety of "moralist" objections to the war, opposing United States intervention because it inflicted uncalled-for sufferings on the Vietnamese or involved support of a corrupt and unrepresentative regime in South Vietnam. Thus, sociologists, anthropologists, and to a lesser extent psychologists

TABLE 27 *Principal objections to United States Vietnam policies of social science petitioners, by subject (in percentages)*

	Economics (n= 82)	Political science (n = 144)	Psychology (n = 170)	Sociology and anthropology (n = 131)	All (n = 497)
Types of response					
1. Moralist	18	15	28	40	26
2. Undemocratic	18	4	11	9	10
3. Internationalist	2	7	3	5	4
4. Democratic	1	5	8	5	6
5. Realist	28	57	21	14	29
Combinations of types of response					
6. Moralist-democratic	10	5	12	7	9
7. Moralist-undemocratic	11	3	10	8	8
8. Undemocratic-democratic	2	0	3	2	2
9. Realist-democratic	4	1	2	2	2
10. Undemocratic-internationalist	4	1	1	1	1
Unclassifiable because of insufficient response	2	2	1	7	3
TOTAL	100	100	100	100	100

SOURCE: Ladd (1970a).

described their objections primarily in terms of American immorality. Political scientists, and to a lesser degree economists, were much more inclined to talk of American interests, of strategic and tactical mistakes.

Table 27 summarizes the field distribution of principal objections to United States Vietnam involvement, among antiwar social scientists. Two sets of objections—represented here by the terms *moralist* and *realist*—account for more than half the respondents; or if the combinations of types in which these appear are included, nearly three-quarters.[14]

Similar differences appeared, too, with regard to which presidential candidate was preferred in 1968 by the various antiwar social scientists.

[14]For a full description of the categories contained in Table 27, see Ladd (1970a, pp. 551–553).

Choosing between support for the "hard-headed" and "realistic" Robert Kennedy and the "romantic" and "soft-headed" Eugene McCarthy, political scientists among the petition signers chose Kennedy by a margin of 6 to 1, while a clear majority of the sociologists backed McCarthy. Here, economics and psychology were in the middle, the former more favorable to Kennedy than the latter (Ladd, 1970a, p. 549).

It seems clear from these data, as from those of the larger Carnegie survey, that political science and economics have emphasized a more pragmatic approach to power and its uses, in contrast to an orientation in sociology, anthropology, and the more sociological parts of psychology favoring social reform and social action. Political scientists have occupied themselves with problems of government and governing, and so have tended to be more exposed to, and hence sympathetic with, the problems and perspective of politicians who must make hard, pragmatic, expedient, "half-a-loaf" decisions. In contrast, sociologists, dealing with topics like race, urbanism, poverty, crime, and delinquency (inherently foci for dissent) have identified more with outsiders, the critics of society, and have been partisans of the ideal in place of the practical.

SPECIALTIES IN PSYCHOLOGY

In analyzing differences among the social sciences, each field has been treated as a discrete entity, as though all salient characteristics apply uniformly across it. In fact, of course, academic disciplines subsume enormous internal differences. Within sociology, for example, there are those primarily concerned with general theories of social system, those engaged in historical and comparative "macro" analysis of differences and changes among societies, and, in sharp contrast, scholars involved in small group experiments, as well as those seeking to apply rigorous mathematical analysis to social behavior. Political science is even more internally disparate, comprising theorists who are primarily political philosophers dealing with the history of ideas, those in public administration occupied with the training of civil servants, historians of politics, area specialists analyzing developments in particular countries, students of electoral behavior utilizing survey methods, and many others. We would expect scholars working in such contrasting subfields to differ in their exposure to various aspects of society, and hence in the configurations of their political concerns.

For the most part, the Carnegie faculty survey did not identify subdisciplines. There are a few exceptions, however, in the case of fields where subspecialty differentiations had been clearly formalized. One such case involves psychology, whose members were invited to locate themselves in the social, clinical, or experimental component of the field.

In the external and intramural political controversies investigated by the Carnegie survey, these three subdivisions of psychology were aligned in a consistent order. Social psychology was the most left specialty, followed by clinical, with experimental psychology faculty relatively the most conservative. For example, 60 percent of social psychologists agreed that "most American colleges are racist," a position accepted by 52 percent of the clinician colleagues and 44 percent of the experimentalists. The student protests of the late 1960s were broadly endorsed by 79 percent of professors in social psychology as contrasted with 62 percent in the experimental branch.

Such differences among the three psychology subdisciplines would seem to correspond to variations of content and method in these specialties. Social psychology, which is most like sociology and often deals with the same substantive topics, seemingly attracts people with similar political predispositions. Clinical psychology, an individual treatment—oriented field whose techniques are an art, falls somewhere in between social and experimental psychology, resembling the humanities in this respect. Experimental psychology, the most hard-data oriented of the three, presumably attracts people who, like the natural scientists, are less socially concerned.

SOCIAL SCIENTISTS: CONSERVATIVES, LIBERALS, OR RADICALS?

We observed earlier in this chapter that critics have come to widely different conclusions about the dominant political orientations of contemporary social scientists. Conservatives, within and without academe, bemoan an overwhelmingly left-of-center commitment among faculty of the social disciplines, wish they could somehow get "equal time," and fear that the strategically placed social science community is pulling the national polity dangerously left. The critics on the left within the social sciences attack their professions for being fundamentally conservative. While it is inevitable that people with different political perspectives will arrive at conflicting evaluations, we can still ask how closely these competing descriptions conform to the actual state of affairs.

Lackies of men of power   Critics of the left who find social science essentially conservative typically have strayed across three quite different meanings of the term *conservative*. Many radicals have argued that social scientists work as lackies of men of power, as defenders of the status quo endorsing only as much change as "society's managers" favor, devoting themselves to social order rather than to social change. Two decades of survey research decisively refute any depiction of the social sciences as conservative by this construction. Members of these professions, and most notably those in the "social problems" fields, have operated in disproportionate numbers as critics of the political establishment, frequently in policy matters of the greatest importance, such as United States involvement in Vietnam. They have been consistent advocates of social change, supporting political candidates most committed to left reform. As the Gouldner-Sprehe survey showed, they have insisted that fundamental restructuring is necessary to solve key social problems. Even in the campus context, they have been remarkably sympathetic to pressures for change.

Opposed to truly radical change   A second and quite different construction of *conservative* is invoked when social scientists are taken to task for their commitment to what Gouldner calls "master institutions." Sociology and the other social sciences are criticized by radicals within them for failing to advocate truly radical change, for seeking to conserve the basic constitutional or constituent arrangements of American society and polity. There can be no doubt that the radical perception here is valid. Most academic social scientists are not radicals, and do not seek or support radical change in the polity or in the academy. While far from being apologists for all or most major policy initiatives of the ruling elites of the country, the vast majority of social scientists are also far from being advocates of a fundamentally new constitutional order. They are critics *within* the system. They vote for liberal Democrats, not for socialist or radical left parties. Probably no occupational group—certainly no other discipline group in academe—came so quickly or so massively into opposition to the Vietnam War, or as strongly supports changes to achieve racial equity, as social scientists, but the vast majority do not actively pursue visions of a radically different society. Any social scientist who holds radical commitments has sufficient reason, then, to fault a majority of his colleagues.

Still, it should be noted that *there is a much higher proportion of radicals among social scientists than among any other group in American society that may be defined by occupational criteria.* In 1948, 11 percent of the sociologists interviewed by Lazarsfeld and Thielens were for the left third-party candidates Henry Wallace and Norman Thomas, as were 8 percent of social scientists generally, in contrast to only 2 percent of the entire American electorate. More strikingly, in 1968, when left-wing third-party candidates were on the ballot in considerably less than half the states and were largely ignored, 7 percent of the sociologists reported having voted for them, along with 4 percent of other social scientists, compared with 2 percent of professors generally and well under 0.50 percent of the electorate. While most American social scientists have supported liberal Democrats rather than radical socialists, this must be understood in the context of choices as they are offered by the American political system. Whenever the range of viable choices is extended (as in a number of other Western democracies and Japan), social scientists give heavy backing to the most left-of-center alternatives, typically to Socialists and Communists.

The inherent conservatism of scholarship   The final construction of *conservative* often encountered in the radical critique appears when social science is faulted for being insufficiently activist. The charge is made that a majority in the profession opt for a relatively detached, scholarly role instead of committing themselves as activists, and thereby assume a fundamentally conservative posture. The survey data show that social scientists have given much more support than the faculty at large to campus activism in the contemporary period, but these data also indicate a substantial base for the above-mentioned critique. Social science, like scholarship generally, appears to have a built-in gradualist bias, by stressing the need to consider all hypotheses and possible evidence before coming to definitive conclusions. Scholarship and politics are different areas of human activity, even though some individuals are active in both. A scholar is expected to report all evidence that challenges his basic assumptions, and to stress the limitations of his results and their tentative and uncertain character. A politician, on the other hand, is an advocate and an organizer. He is expected to make the best possible case for his point of view, to ignore contradictory materials, to decide on the basis of what limited information he can secure before the deadlines imposed on him by his role, and then to act in a self-assured fashion. One of the worst things that can be said about a politician is that he is as "indecisive" as an intellectual, an unfortunate labeling Adlai Stevenson experienced. Conversely, an academic will be subjected to criticism for publishing too quickly before all the evidence is in, or for oversimplifying what is inherently a complicated phenomenon.[15]

[15]For a more detailed elaboration of this point, see Lipset (1972b, pp. 202–206).

In the stress-filled and conflict-laden environment of the last decade, social scientists, probably more than professors in any other set of disciplines, have felt a tension resulting from their simultaneous attachment to the canons of scholarship and relatively high commitment to social change. It is not surprising that the various attempts to resolve this tension have proved generally unsatisfactory. From our perspective here, however, the very presence of the tension provides the strongest testimony to the predominant left-liberal and change-directed orientations of social science faculty.

5. Class, Intellectuality, and Academic Politics

Since the emergence of the university as a base from which radical critics of social policy have pressed their views, there has been considerable discussion of the internal dynamics of university politics, relating differences to status variations. Two diametrically opposed theories regarding academic status have been advanced. Some radical critics have applied an economic self-interest or "class" theory to account for the views of the relatively conservative portion of academe. They have contended that those who consult for government and business, who receive large research grants, who hold tenured and high-salaried positions, who publish extensively, and who dominate the professional activities of their disciplines have been co-opted into "the system." Successful academics, along with other members of society's "establishment," have the most to lose from any significant change and uphold a conservative stance.

Another body of sociological analysis, which can be traced back to the French Revolution, has contended that the posture of academics as social critics derives in some large part from the nature of the intellectual role, from its emphasis on innovation, on creativity, on rejection of the traditional and the established within given fields of inquiry.[1] The argument that intellectuals, including academic scholars, are rewarded for being original suggests that the "achievers" within the academy will be more socially critical than those who are less involved in, or less successful at, research and scholarly tasks. Evidence in assorted studies of academe is relevant to evaluating both sets of interpretations.

THE CLASS THEORY OF INTELLECTUAL RADICALISM

Conservative polemicists have frequently explained the anti-Establishment or radical politics of certain intellectuals as a product of frustra-

[1] Parts of this larger argument were discussed in Chapter 1, especially pp. 9–14.

tions resulting from failure to achieve what society values. But the founding fathers of revolutionary socialism, Marx and Engels, are also among those who have related propensity to support a given variant of political protest with failure within the intellectual stratum. To be sure, they identified progressive social views with the deprived industrial working class and argued that any protest movement composed of or led in significant measure by intellectual or other middle-class elements was politically unreliable. It should be noted, however, that in line with their emphasis on materialistic as distinct from idealistic explanations of behavior, Marx and Engels described intellectual and student radicals as drawn from the deprived or unsuccessful members of their stratum, suggesting that their support for protest politics reflected discontent with an inferior social position. This assumption produced invidious explanations, such as that suggested by Engels (1967, p. 134) to account for the intellectual opposition paving the way for the Revolution of 1848 in Germany: "It became more and more the habit, particularly of the inferior sorts of literati, to make up for the want of cleverness in their production by [anti-governmental] political allusions which were sure to attract attention."

Responding to Bakunin's report in 1870 of 40,000 revolutionary students in Russia, Engels exclaimed, in a letter to Marx (cited in Avineri, 1967, p. 154): "How awful for the world. . . . If there is anything which might ruin the western European movement, then it would have been this import of 40,000 more or less educated, ambitious, hungry Russian Nihilists; all of them officer candidates without an army." A similar line of reasoning appeared in Engels' writing on the socialist student movement in Germany in 1890, which he saw as the activity of declassed bourgeois elements—including those who did not achieve expected goals (Feuer, 1969*b*, p. 55). Marx wrote more negatively of anarchist intellectuals, labeling them "a bunch of *déclassés*, the dregs of the bourgeoisie . . . lawyers without clients, doctors without patients and without knowledge, pool-room students . . . and particularly journalists of the small press . . . " (cited in Nomad, 1961, p. 132).

The Dutch social-democratic academic Henri de Man (1927, p. 226), writing in the late 1920s, believed that successful high-status intellectuals could be found to some extent in the social-democratic movements, but that extremist movements drew their intellectual support from "pseudo-scientists . . . unsuccessful inventors; unpublished poets; painters overburdened with originality. . . . " He argued that radical movements should be "more congenial to the destructive nihilism of these thwarted individualists."

Since the rise of the student-based New Left movement in the 1960s, Marxist comment on the nature and sources of intellectual radicalism has lost much of its invidious character. But some Marxist writers have continued to explain intellectual radicalism in "materialist" terms. Thus, the Belgian Trotskyist Ernest Mandel (1969, pp. 47–53) has argued that the protest of intellectuals is related to "profound changes in intellectual employment," that is, to the downgrading in status, opportunity, freedom of work, and reward inherent in the mass growth and consequent bureaucratization of the occupations subsumed in the stratum. In seeking to explain why 1968 was a year of widespread student and intellectual revolt through much of Europe, an article in the *World Marxist Review* ("Upsurge of the Youth Movement . . . ," 1968, pp. 6–7), the organ of international (pro-Russian) Communism, stressed that the time was "marked by the rise of mass unemployment," that jobs were not available in sufficient quantity to keep up with the wave of expansion of universities. "These contradictions affect the intellectual community in the same way as they affect workers. After all, are not 80 to 90 percent of the intellectuals in the big capitalist countries wage-earners?" An analysis by a Chilean Communist of the prevalence of radical anti-imperialism among Latin American intellectuals suggests that this outlook reflects excessive exploitation inherent in the fact that few intellectuals can earn a living from creative activity, and hence that "most of them can devote only their spare time for their vocation." Engaged in nonscholarly work, the Latin American intellectual

has to spend the best part of his time and energy in activity distasteful to him . . . and, although realization of this wounds his pride, he is a semi-proletarian because of the way in which he earns his livelihood. He fully fits Engels' definition of the proletariat . . . "reduced to selling their labor power in order to live" (Teitelboim, 1968, pp. 73–74).

The thesis that political views among intellectuals, especially college faculty, are correlated with status, that the more successful are the more conservative, has been reiterated frequently since the mid-1960s by spokesmen for radical tendencies within American higher education. Books and articles dealing with a variety of specific disciplines—mainly the social sciences, but the humanities and natural sciences as well—have described the academic political situation in these terms.

One of the most persuasive formulations was presented by Alvin Gouldner (1970), whose work was discussed earlier. Some of the flavor of his analysis may be seen in the following statements:

After World War II and under the stimulus of the Welfare State, American sociology grew at a more rapid rate than ever before. As it grew, sociology increasingly lost its academic isolation, and sociologists were exposed to new pressures, temptations, and opportunities. . . . Sociologists, then, grew more numerous, more worldly, more experienced, more affluent, more powerful, and more academically secure. They have, especially since World War II, gone up in the world. Often, all too often, this has meant a smug complacency . . . (p. 23).

As such [outside research] funding becomes increasingly available, the emphasis on rigorous methodologies assumes a very special rhetorical function. . . . Positivism's social impact is not random or neutral in regard to competing social mappings; because of its emphasis on the problem of social order, because of the social origins, education, and character of its own personnel, and because of the dependencies generated by its own funding requirements, it persistently tends to lend support to the *status quo* . . . (p. 105).

Functionalists [the dominant and controlling tendency in sociology under the leadership of Talcott Parsons], then, constitute the sociological conservation corps of industrial society. They are conscientious "guardians" devoted to the maintenance of the social machinery of whatever industrial society they are called upon to serve. They pray to the gods of the city—whoever they may be and wherever they may be . . . (p. 332).

For tenured faculty, the university is a realm of congenial and leisured servitude. It is a realm in which the academician is esteemed for his learning but castrated as a political being . . . (p. 441).

As we noted in Chapter 4, Gouldner attempted over a decade ago to validate his assumptions through an empirical study of the attitudes and behavior of sociologists, touching on both societal and discipline concerns. In a doctoral dissertation drawing upon this survey, Gouldner's research assistant and collaborator, J. Timothy Sprehe (1967, p. 150), reports that the project was premised on the assumption that "there [is] a group of persons who informally dominate any social system," and the analytic objective "was to seek out dominant groupings within sociology and to examine their ideological leaning." Gouldner and Sprehe defined the sociology Establishment to include those coming from prestigious graduate departments, who were employed in large secular universities, were tenured, had significant sums of research money, published at a relatively high level in professional journals, and had actively participated in the professional associations (Sprehe, 1967, pp. 151–152).

Following the general assumption that the most privileged academics hold the most conservative views, this Gouldner-Sprehe inquiry hypothesized initially that "dominant" sociologists would show positive orientations toward an emphasis on "Scientific Method," "Value Freeness" in social research, "Professionalization," and "Self-Image." Conversely, the hypothesis was advanced that the "dominants" would tend "to score low on Optimism and Radicalism" (Sprehe, 1967, p. 152). That is, the more prestigious and highly rewarded sociologists should be more conservative, less optimistic about the possibilities of social reform, more supportive of a scientistic view of the discipline, in greater favor of the idea that social science research can and should be value-free, and more inclined toward formal professional standards for membership in the discipline. The "dominants" also "were expected to score low on Societal Roles" (involvement in action groups), because "those espousing the ideology of dominant sociology [should] engage principally in the work of sociology itself and not personally concern themselves with political or social action" (pp. 153–154).

A radical philosopher, Richard Lichtman, also has argued the case that federal support for academic activities is one of the principal ways through "which the pattern of society is impressed on higher education." He concludes that "the immediate result is that the University is more and more manipulated by scholar-researchers who more resemble idiot-savants than men of wisdom. . . . " Lichtman echoes a familiar theme among radical critics of the university—that research and teaching are in conflict, and that teaching represents a morally superior activity, while success in research often implies a careerist orientation and adaptation to the values of those who control access to research funds.

In the University the teacher retreats before the onslaught of the research technologists and knowledge diffusers. Every university maintains a house Negro or two—a professor whose advancement has been based predominantly upon his power as a teacher and who is dragged out on ceremonial occasions to silence the critic. But for every such anachronism there are one hundred practitioners of the conventions who have scrambled to respectability over a mass of journals and anthologies. The teacher who embodies a vision, whose life manifests in its own activity the content of his teaching art, is vanishing from sight (Lichtman, 1971, pp. 27, 29, 30–31).

A pamphlet composed by a group of literature professors contends that the conservative emphasis in their discipline is determined by a small elite located in the major universities. They object to the emphasis on "notions of professional integrity, pure scholarship and academic integrity" pressed by those who control the Modern Language Association. And they note that:

Over the past 37 years, moreover, above half of the governing officers of the MLA were on the faculties of America's most prestigious universities—Harvard, Yale, Princeton, Chicago, Johns Hopkins, Cornell. This in itself may seem to express only coincidence, but the fact that departmental standards at Harvard-Yale-Etcetera guide policy at Pecan State makes the affiliation seem more like an interlocking directorate than a coincidental affiliation. . . .

It's in the graduate school that we find ourselves being what William Arrowsmith called "'conscript scholars'—people by and large of admirable sensibility who went into the field because they liked literature and wanted to teach young people, and who found that the way to convert these commendable tastes into an adequate living and the respect of others was to write what the profession seemed to want—but what it rarely read" (Richard Ohmann, "An Informal and Perhaps Unreliable Account of the Modern Language Association of America," *Antioch Review*, Fall 1969). Our graduate training turns us into research specialists, not teachers (Cantarrow et al., *n.d.*, pp. 7–8).

A similar analysis and complaint about the situation in political science has been voiced by Alan Wolfe (1971, p. 402), who finds the American Political Science Association dominated by a conservative, research-minded group supportive of "a system which punishes people who take too great an interest in their own teaching and service to the college and the surrounding community, who thereby have no time to be 'successful' within the discipline. . . ."

The argument that teaching is an activity morally superior to research, that those who are successful in the latter are largely and necessarily collaborators with the status quo, is less frequently encountered among natural scientists. Yet there too, radical critics, while usually not rejecting research, do argue that the "dominants" who receive large government research grants and who consult for government and business are the main opponents of efforts to make scientists concerned political actors.[2]

The identification of research with careerism and support for Establishment policies has gone so far in some academic circles that one scholar could publish an article entitled "Is Research Counterrevolutionary?" and answer his rhetorical question with a definite "yes." Bert Meyers insisted "that the scientist's research may well be not merely

---

[2]For example, see Charles Schwartz (1970, p. 747) and Marc Lappé (1971, pp. 96–118).

split off from his political activism but actually at odds with it," asserting that even most "pure" scientific research inevitably can and will be misused:

For example, while bright microbiologists decode the DNA and RNA molecules, hack technicians apply their findings, to breed mutant strains of virulent microbes resistent to treatment and capable of incorporation in aerosols for germ warfare. Similar applications have been made or are planned (or can be anticipated by anyone familiar with the dynamics of technology) for findings in the physics of optics, in psychopharmacology, in the social psychology of attitude change, in ecology, in fact, in virtually all branches of science (Meyers, n.d., pp. 10–11).

Critiques of the system-supporting role of academe, such as those cited above, may be found in practically every field. Inevitably, scholars are involved as consultants or researchers in almost every governmental policy. From this fact, assorted critics have drawn the conclusion that an academic Establishment increasingly functions as a major force upholding the status quo, and conversely that the ready availability of governmental largesse is a corrupting and conservatizing factor. During the Vietnam years, Senator J. William Fulbright often articulated the latter concern:

Among the baneful effects of the Government-university contract system the most damaging and corrupting are the neglect of the university's most important purpose, which is the education of its students, and the taking into the Government camp of scholars, especially in the social sciences, who ought to be acting as responsible and independent critics of their Government's policies. The corrupting process is a subtle one: no one needs to censor, threaten, or give orders to contract scholars; without a word of warning or advice being uttered, it is simply understood that lucrative contracts are awarded not to those who question their Government's policies but to those who provide the Government with the tools and techniques it desires. . . . This betrayal is most keenly felt by the students . . . [who] having seen their country's traditional values degraded in the effort to attribute moral purpose to an immoral war . . . now see their universities—the last citadels of moral and intellectual integrity—lending themselves to ulterior and expedient ends, and betraying their own fundamental purpose . . . (Fulbright, 1967, p. 36182).

Viewed broadly, the "class theory" of politics, as applied to academe, finds the most highly achieving and professionally successful faculty in the position of having the most to lose from any significant changes, either in the university or in the larger society, and hence the most supportive of the status quo. In particular, contact with the federal government (receipt of grants, work as a consultant, etc.) is seen to have a conservatizing "taint." Challenge to this conservative establishment comes, as it must, from the "backbenchers," especially younger members who reject "professionalism and prefer to emphasize teaching."

INTELLECTUALITY AS A SOURCE OF CRITICAL POLITICS

There is an alternative to the class theory model which leads to very different assumptions about the dynamics of academic politics, and specifically about the political orientations of dominants and backbenchers. An extensive literature, spanning centuries, has stressed the general tendency of achieving intellectuals to support a politics of social criticism.

This second model, as we have seen, is based on the argument that there are factors inherent in the social role of intellectuals which result in their persistent position as social critics. Thus, the great nineteenth century French social commentator Alexis de Tocqueville (1955, pp. 146–147) attributed to intellectuals, to the *philosophes,* a potent role in the French Revolution, asserting that they

built up in men's minds an imaginary ideal society in which all was simple, uniform, coherent, equitable, and rational in the full sense of the term. It was this vision of the perfect State that fired the imagination of the masses and little by little estranged them from the here-and-now.

In his study of the 1848 revolutionary eruption, the British historian Lewis Namier (1964, p. 2) described it as "primarily the revolution of the intellectuals—*la révolution des clercs.*" He saw the 1848 events as the "outcome of thirty-three creative years," in which intellectuals across Europe fostered, in Lamartine's words, "a moral idea, of reason, logic sentiment . . . a desire . . . for a better order of government and society." Raymond Aron (1962, p. 210) has written generally of "the tendency to criticize the established order [as], so to speak, the occupational disease of the intellectuals."

The capacity for criticism, for rejection of the status quo, is not simply a matter of preference by some intellectuals for this quality of mind. For the intellectual is one whose activities involve the creation of *new* knowledge, *new* ideas, *new* art. Reality is held up to the test of the ideal, the theoretical. There are very few "pure" intellectuals—people who expend their entire vocational energies in efforts at creation or innovation—but it is some "critical mass" of this commitment which defines the intellectual role.

Emphasis upon creativity and innovation has its beginning in the work of specific disciplines, but the thrusts of this approach, this mindset, often carry beyond to perspectives on the range of social institutions and processes. It was this jump which Joseph Schumpeter (1962, p. 148) had in mind when he called attention to the fact that the "humanists [of the Renaissance] were primarily philologists but...they quickly expanded into the fields of manners, politics, religion and philosophy ... from criticism of a text to criticism of a society, the way is shorter than it seems."

Full appreciation of the sources of an oppositionist stance among intellectuals requires attention to the creation of a new social role in response to the massive social changes of the last two and a half centuries.[3] A set of social and economic transformations began in the seventeenth and eighteenth centuries in Western Europe, the various dimensions of which have received different names: *industrial,* if we look at economic life; *scientific* and *technological,* if attention is drawn to the explosion of knowledge; and *egalitarian,* if the focus is on participation or involvement in the making of decisions for the system, the overturning of societies based upon the aristocratic principle. Ascriptive class societies have not been rare historically. In their various forms, in fact, they represent the principal type of postprimitive social organization. Egalitarian societies are historically exceptional. The massive repudiation of aristocratic arrangements in Western Europe after the seventeenth century, and since then throughout the world, is thus among that handful of fundamental political events.

With the transition from agricultural to industrial systems, resources enormously expanded. Under what conditions is it possible that the millions will readily agree to extensive privileges for the few from which they and their children are formally and permanently excluded? It would only happen when there is no possibility of most men living beyond bare subsistence, no matter what the manner of distribution. In societies of gross scarcity, if any culture is to flourish, it is only through the arbitrary extension of privilege to a few. Aristocracy offers a morally tenable standard for parceling out values only in scarcity-bound societies. Let the pie dramatically expand—and that is what the economic-technological developments began to achieve in the seventeenth and

[3]Ladd (1972, pp. 17–52; 1970, pp. 15–27) has dealt with this subject at some length in other publications.

eighteenth centuries—and groups of men outside the hereditary privileged class will come forward to claim their share, will come to believe that life owes them something more than perpetual wretchedness.

These egalitarian-industrial-technological changes can properly be described as a revolution, and from its beginnings in seventeenth-century Europe this revolution has progressed through a number of stages and has expanded and become global. From our perspective, the most important feature of this massive revolutionary surge is that major change became a constant: all manner of social and political institutions were forced into a process of continuing adaptation. In this context, the need arose for a category of people who could explain and chart and direct the flow of societal response "to help society adjust to novel conditions while discarding outmoded patterns" (Lazarsfeld & Thielens, 1958, p. 151). The historian Carl Becker (1936, p. 93) has nicely described the emergence of this new social role:

Until recently the chief function of the sophisticated, the priests and scribes, has been to stabilize custom and validate social authority by perpetuating the tradition and interpreting it in a manner conformable to the understanding of common man. During the last three hundred years ... there has emerged a new class of learned men, successors to the priests and scribes, whose function is to increase rather than to preserve knowledge, to undermine rather than to stabilize custom and social authority.

An interpretation which gives intellectuality a primary place in the larger dynamic of faculty politics naturally leads to expectations about the orientations of the dominants which are diametrically opposed to those postulated by the class theory. For if the "natural" posture of the intellectual is critic, and currently that of the intellectual in the United States is critic from a liberal-left perspective, then the most intellectual among academics might be expected to display the most left-of-center commitments. The "top" should be more critical than the "bottom."[4]

INTELLECTUALITY AND POLITICAL CRITICISM: THE TEST OF A HYPOTHESIS

The assumption that the most intellectual scholars are likely to be the most socially critical, it must be recognized, is a hard one to test. How

---

[4]Large numbers of faculty, we know, are not primarily involved in what, by the above construction, could be termed intellectual activities. Many are teachers, not scholars, and as such are engaged in passing on the existing tradition rather than in enlarging or critically rejecting it (Merton, 1968, pp. 263–264; Geiger, 1949, pp. 2–3).

does one go about assessing and measuring intellectuality when dealing with a large population group like the academic community? There appear, still, to be ample grounds, from both sense impressions and systematic studies, for maintaining that academic achievement is a good general indicator of intellectual bent. A position at a major institution, a high level of scholarly publication, the ability to secure research support, general recognition from one's colleagues—such measures of intellectuality are the best we can expect to obtain for a large collection of faculty. These characteristics, of course, identify the dominants of the academic community. If the assumptions we have been making are valid—that in a scholarly discipline those who are the most intellectual tend to be the most critical, and that academic achievement is a reflection of intellectuality—the faculty Establishment should not be the center for conservatism, for defense of the social and political status quo, but rather should be to the left of the rank and file.

Survey data spanning a half century allow us to test the competing hypotheses concerning the politics of the "notables" in the university. Are they more conservative or more liberal than the backbenchers? Are researchers who are closely linked to agencies of the federal government through grants and consulting arrangements to the right or the left of their colleagues not so connected or co-opted? What, in sum, can be said of the politics of the most highly achieving and influential professors in relation to the general membership of their professions?

The Leuba surveys   The earliest studies of faculty attitudes—analyses of variation in religious beliefs conducted by James Leuba, a psychologist, in 1913–1914 and again in 1933—revealed that the more distinguished professors among both natural and social scientists, were *much more irreligious* than their less eminent colleagues. Leuba (1921, 1934, 1950) sampled members of the American Sociological Society and the American Psychological Association along with physicists and biologists in 1914 and again in 1933. Table 28 shows the marked differences in religious views between the "greater" and "lesser" scientists in each field, with inclusion in the former category determined by panels of experts judging on the basis of professional standing. Thus, in 1933, 31 percent of the "lesser" sociologists professed a belief in immortality, more than twice the percentage among the "greater" members of the field. Only 2 percent of the most highly achieving psychologists expressed a belief in God in the 1933 survey, as contrasted with 13 percent of the rank and file of that discipline. Leuba found, furthermore, that the higher the standard of eminence, the greater the degree of disbelief. He asked his panel of evaluators in sociology to break the

TABLE 28   *Religious beliefs of scientists, by field and scholarly attainment; Leuba surveys, 1914 and 1933 (row percentages)*

	Believers in God		Believers in immortality	
	1914	*1933*	*1914*	*1933*
Sociologists				
Lesser	29	30	52	31
Greater	19	13	27	10
Psychologists				
Lesser	32	13	27	12
Greater	13	2	9	2
Physicists				
Lesser	50	43	57	46
Greater	34	17	40	20
Biologists				
Lesser	39	31	45	32
Greater	17	12	25	15

SOURCE: Leuba (1934, p. 297).

"greater" group into two parts, "*eminent* and *most eminent.*" In 1933, 20 percent of the former were believers, but only 5 percent of the latter. Although religious and political beliefs are clearly quite different, many investigations have shown that they are highly correlated; that is, religious unbelief is associated with liberal to left political values among Americans.

The Lazarsfeld-Thielens survey   In 1955, Paul Lazarsfeld and Wagner Thielens, Jr., conducted their survey of the political orientations of social scientists, and found a clear relationship between high scholarly achievement and propensity to a more liberal-left viewpoint and to a more activist politics. For example, only 11 percent of social scientists with three or more professional publications scored in the "highly restrictive [opposed]" category of the Civil Liberties Permissiveness Scale constructed by the original investigators, a proportion just half that among faculty who had not published at all (Table 29). Professors who had published, had been officers of professional associations, and had served as consultants to government or business gave more backing to liberal nominees in the 1948 and 1952 Presidential elections and were more supportive of the civil liberties of Communists and other political minorities than were their less highly achieving colleagues. And by all measures of academic standing or attainment, the "dominants"

TABLE 29 Political orientations of social scientists, by scholarly attainment (percentages of n)

Attainment	Civil Liberties Permissiveness Scale*		1952 vote for Stevenson	Activism Scale†	
	Highly libertarian	Highly restrictive		Highly activist	Nonactivist
Number of publications					
None (n = 693)	17	22	59	10	38
Three or more (n = 1,378)	24	11	68	17	28
Index of personal academic status‡					
Lowest (n = 303)	15	23	58	12	38
Highest (n = 358)	25	7	70	19	26
Served as consultant?§					
Yes (n = 854)	26	11	67	17	26
No (n = 1,583)	20	16	64	13	33

*A six-item scale based upon whether a faculty member endorsed the right of persons accused of Communist ties to speak on campus, favored the right of students to organize Young Socialist or Young Communist Leagues, considered it desirable for his institution to employ radical professors, and opposed the firing of admitted Communists from positions such as college teaching.

†A three-item scale based upon whether the respondent would "vigorously protest" decisions by his college administration to (a) prevent the school debating team from debating the admission of Red China, (b) ban Owen Lattimore from speaking on campus; and whether he would (c) speak publicly on a controversial issue despite the consequences involved.

‡The index is based upon highest degree held, whether dissertation was published, whether the respondent had held office in a professional society, and whether he had served as a consultant to industry or other organizations.

§Respondents were asked whether they had served as consultants to "industry or other organizations."

SOURCE: 1955 Lazarsfeld-Thielens survey.

showed themselves more inclined to an activist political style and were more willing to publicly defend controversial positions. Looking at sociologists alone, we find that the same relationships hold. Thus 33 percent of the nonpublishers *disagreed* with the position that an admitted Communist should as such be fired from a college teaching position, compared with 46 percent of those who had published three or more professional works. Among sociologists scoring lowest on the Lazarsfeld and Thielens "index of personal academic status," 39 percent described themselves as more liberal than most of their academic colleagues, as contrasted with 57 percent among those in the highest status category.

Lazarsfeld and Thielens found a consistent relationship between age and political views, with the younger the more supportive of the rights of Communists and generally the more liberal-left. Because the type of indicator of academic attainment cited in Table 29 has a strong age bias—in that, for example, a faculty member who has been in his profession 25 years has had far more opportunity to build a record of scholarly publications than a colleague at the start of his career—controlling for age should enhance the relationship between the achievement indicators and measures of liberalism. This is in fact the case. The simple (Pearsonian) correlation between the personal academic status variable and the Civil Liberties Permissiveness Scale is .10, while the partial correlation coefficient, holding age constant, is .17. Table 30 shows a set of bivariate relationships involving scholarly attainment and political orientations within three age strata: under 40 years of age, 40 to 50, and over 50. Differences between achievers and nonachievers are especially sharp among faculty over 50 years of age. In this category,

TABLE 30   *Political orientations of social scientists, by age and scholarly attainment (percentages of n)*

Age and attainment	Civil Liberties Permissiveness Scale		1952 vote for Stevenson	Activism Scale	
	Highly libertarian	Highly restrictive		Highly activist	Nonactivist
Under 40 years					
Index of personal academic status					
Lowest (n = 218)	20	18	65	15	30
Highest (n = 105)	36	6	75	24	19
40 to 50 years					
Status index					
Lowest (n = 43)	5	37	39	7	51
Highest (n = 128)	23	9	75	20	22
Over 50 years					
Status index					
Lowest (n = 42)	2	31	34	0	67
Highest (n = 125)	19	8	55	13	35
All age strata					
Status index					
Lowest (n = 303)	15	23	58	12	38
Highest (n = 358)	25	7	70	19	26

SOURCE: 1955 Lazarsfeld-Thielens survey.

only 2 percent of social scientists of low academic attainment scored in the "highly libertarian" category of the Civil Liberties Permissiveness Scale, compared with 19 percent of their highly achieving colleagues. Stevenson was backed in 1952 by just one-third of the former group, as contrasted with 55 percent of the latter.

Another indicator of the relationship between "intellectuality" and political orientation is the predominant political outlook at institutions which emphasize scholarship. Those schools whose faculty rank among the more prominent scholars in their fields; which devote a considerable portion of their resources to support of scholarly endeavors in the form of good libraries, laboratories, and research budgets; which have relatively high admission standards; and which are heavily involved in graduate education tend to have both faculty and student bodies who are disproportionately liberal or left. In 1955, Lazarsfeld and Thielens found a strong correlation between the academic quality of institutions and the willingness of their faculty to be "permissive" (liberal) with respect to various forms of political and personal nonconformity and dissent. Being "permissive" was strongly associated with the conventional left-right distinction.

The Gouldner-Sprehe survey   We noted earlier in this chapter that Alvin Gouldner and Timothy Sprehe approached their study of the "domain assumptions" of American sociologists from a hypothesis that the most eminent and established members of the field would hold the most conservative academic and political views. The results of their analysis, however, *decisively disconfirmed this hypothesis.* Typically, the precise opposite of what the investigators predicted occurred: The "dominants" held the more left-of-center positions. Some sense of this may be obtained from various of Sprehe's (1967, pp. 301–303) conclusions:

Respondents from smaller schools tended to hold the concept of applied sociology in disfavor while those from larger schools scored higher on Societal Role [activist]. . . . In general, it appeared that the more research funds a respondent claimed to be responsible for, the higher he scored on Societal Role. . . . Those who participated heavily in professional associations tended to score high on Societal Role . . . .

The higher the score on Societal Role, the lower the predicted score on dominance measures. For the variables, Prestige School of Origin, Size of School, Research Funds Responsible for, and the Indexes of Periodical Publication and Professional Participation, the . . . hypothesis appears disconfirmed. For the first three variables named immediately above, the relationship is apparently opposite to that predicted. . . .

In summary, as regards general, diffuse beliefs concerning the role of sociology in solving society's problems, the over-all relationships seem to be: the higher the score on dominance measures the . . . higher the factor score.

The factors of "Value Freeness" and "Pure Sociology" (support for general social theory and sociology for its scientific worth) were related inconsistently or inconclusively to the indicators of dominance. Moreover, Sprehe reported (1967, p. 305) that "the more research funds a respondent is responsible for, the more likely he was to score low on Value Freeness. The statistical relationship was the strongest for any considered of this factor."

The investigators had posited the hypothesis that "Professionalization"—that is, desire to limit membership in the ASA and set up formal requirements for defining who qualified as a sociologist— would be correlated with indicators of dominance. Again, however, "the . . . hypothesis . . . was largely disconfirmed." There was, in fact, some indication that low-status and aspiring sociologists ("respondents from non-prestige schools" and "non-tenured faculty") were "more in favor of professionalizing sociology," while curiously, "the greater the amount of research funds a respondent had, the more likely he was to score low on Professionalization" (p. 314).

"The . . . hypothesis for the Index of Radicalism stipulated that the dominant sociologists would be low scorers." Here again, the results indicated that the "hypothesis must be considered largely disconfirmed" (pp. 312–313). With respect to possession of research grants, "radicalism tended to increase . . . as the amount of research funds grew larger, except for the very highest category" (pp. 322–323). The only measure of dominance which correlated positively with the Radicalism Index was the age-related factor of academic rank.

As Sprehe recognized, many of the dominance indicators he utilized were inherently associated with age. And since increasing age was generally accompanied by a more conservative position on academic and political issues, controlling for age should reduce any association of the dominance indicators with a more conservative posture and enhance the relationships found with a more liberal, radical, or activist position. In the bulk of the dissertation analysis, Sprehe did not deal with the age variable. In a brief chapter toward the end of the study, however, some age-controlled relationships were presented, which, for the most part, did strengthen the associations between dominance and a more activist, reformist view of sociology and society, particularly among sociologists over forty. Some relevant statements may be cited:

Beginning with age forty, there seems to be a tendency to score in the following manner: the higher the age and the lower the research funds, the lower the score on Societal Role. . . . Older respondents who have little or no research money tend to oppose an activist conception of sociology. In other words, respondents who were least likely to affect their field in a productive manner through research and publication are the individuals who opposed a concept of applied sociology (pp. 446–447).

Interestingly, among the older respondents [over forty], those who have little or no research funds tended to score rather high on Value-Freeness. . . . Those with least ability to affect their field productively hold strongly to the belief that sociology is, will be, and should be a value-free science (pp. 449–450).

[Holding age constant] it seemed generally true that the greater the amount of research funds a respondent had, the more likely he was to score low on Professionalization (p. 451).

Studies of the 1960s A series of limited survey investigations conducted during the 1960s arrived at this same general conclusion, that the "top" of academe stands to the left of the "bottom." For example, a 1966 study by Edward Noll and Peter Rossi of the National Opinion Research Center found faculty at major schools more liberal than their counterparts at institutions of lower scholarly standing:

Roughly four out of five (79 percent) faculty members from high quality schools consider themselves liberal as compared to only 45 percent of those at low quality schools. On the other hand, there are only 16 percent of the individuals from high quality schools who claim to be conservative, but 40 percent from low quality schools say they are conservative. Surprisingly even the majority of Republicans [62 percent] say they are liberal at high quality schools, while only about a fourth of the Republicans at low quality schools say they are liberal (Noll & Rossi, 1966, p. 21).

Eitzen and Maranell (1968, p. 149), drawing upon a national survey of party affiliation of faculty, reported that "professors in large, public schools are the most predisposed toward the Democratic party and professors in small denominational schools are the most Republican." Ladd (1970a, p. 544) reported that most of the signers of anti-Vietnam War advertisements "came from the 100–150 institutions generally regarded as being in the higher or middle range. They were not all from the great universities, but most were from good ones." And a study of the characteristics of the 1,300 sociologists who signed the "Open Letter to President Johnson and Congress" in November 1967 opposing the Vietnam War showed that "the overrepresented signer is male, an ASA Fellow with a Ph.D., primarily engaged in research or teaching at an

TABLE 31 *Political orientations of academics, by scholarly standing and achievement (percentages of n)*

	Support busing for integration*	Support immediate United States withdrawal from Vietnam or coalition government with Communists†	1964 vote for Johnson
ALL FACULTY (n = 60,028)	46	59	78
School quality			
1. Elite (n = 19,089)	55	74	87
2. Middle tier (n = 30,042)	45	61	78
3. Lowest tier (n = 10,872)	42	51	73
Consultants-grantees (n = 3,570)	52	70	88
High achievers (n = 4,668)	54	76	89
Low achievers (n = 9,132)	41	50	73

*"Racial integration of the public elementary schools should be achieved even if it requires busing." [Strongly agree; agree with reservations; disagree with reservations; strongly disagree.]

†"Which of these positions on Vietnam is closest to your own?" [The United States should withdraw from Vietnam immediately; the United States should reduce its involvement and encourage the emergence of a coalition government in South Vietnam; the United States should try to reduce its involvement, while being sure to prevent a Communist takeover in the South; the United States should commit whatever forces are necessary to defeat the Communists.]

‡"What do you think of the emergence of radical student activism in recent years?" [Unreservedly approve; approve with reservations; disapprove with reservations; unreservedly disapprove.]

SOURCE: 1969 Carnegie Commission Survey of Student and Faculty Opinion.

academic institution located in the Northeast. These characteristics hardly describe the younger, less professionally socialized, and more alienated member of the profession. Rather, they point to a signer who is well integrated into the profession and who signs from at least an objective position of security and strength" (Walum, 1970, p. 163).

The Carnegie faculty survey The findings of previous investigations received impressive confirmation from our own 1969 survey of academics. The more scholarly and highly achieving faculty appear significantly more disposed to liberal-left views than the entire professoriate. Table 31 shows, for example, that 74 percent of faculty at elite colleges

| 1968 vote | | Support | Very liberal |
for Humphrey	for left third party	"radical student activism"‡	and liberal (Liberalism-Conservatism Scale)
58	2	43	39
71	3	50	55
59	2	44	40
52	2	38	31
70	2	46	50
71	3	48	55
52	2	38	31

and universities favored, in 1969, either an immediate unilateral withdrawal of American troops from Vietnam or a reduction of involvement coupled with support for a coalition government including the Viet Cong; these positions were taken by only 51 percent of faculty at schools of the lowest tier.[5] Hubert Humphrey received the votes of 71 percent of

[5]Institutions were ranked on the basis of a three-item index of academic standing, including SAT scores required for admission (selectivity), research expenditures adjusted for the number of students (research), and total institutional expenditures, also adjusted to a per student basis (affluence). All colleges and universities were arrayed on this index, with raw scores ranging from 3 (highest standing) to 27 (lowest). "Elite schools" here are those with index scores of 3 to 9; the "lowest tier" institutions scored in the 18 to 27 range.

elite school professors in 1968, but only 52 percent support at schools of the lowest range. Of academics at elite institutions, 55 percent were located in the two most liberal categories of the five-item Liberalism-Conservatism Scale, in comparison with 40 percent of their colleagues at middle-tier institutions and just 31 percent of those at schools of the lowest tier.

In comparing the orientations of the most successful and influential academics with those of the general membership of the profession, we worked with a number of other vehicles for defining the former. One of these was "high achievers"—faculty who have gained positions at major universities (elite schools as described in note 5) and have also maintained a high level of scholarly productivity (five or more professional publications in the two years preceding the survey). "Low achievers," in contrast, are faculty at institutions of the lowest quality who have contributed little to active scholarship (two publications or less in the preceding 24 months). We see in Table 31 a marked contrast between these two groups of faculty in all political measures, with the high achievers consistently to the left. For instance, 68 percent of those with high academic attainment, contrasted with just 41 percent of the low achievers, described their political views as left or liberal; 48 percent of the former, but only 38 percent of the latter, indicated general approval of "the emergence of radical student activism in recent years." The use of busing to achieve school integration was endorsed by more than half of the high achievers, in comparison with just two-fifths of the low achievers.

Because it has frequently been alleged that federal consulting and research grants tend to make the recipients more conservative, we examined the politics of consultants-grantees—faculty who in the 12 months preceding the survey had both served as paid consultants to some agency of the national government and held federal research grants. Some may have become more conservative as a result of these contacts, but professors who consulted for the government and drew on its largesse were still more liberal-left in general political orientation—for example, more critical of government policies in Vietnam and more supportive of the student protests of the late sixties—than were the rank and file of faculty.

A high level of professional publication, position at a major university, success in attracting external funding for one's scholarly activities—all these are indicators of intellectual attainment, as well as of participation in an academic culture which emphasizes original research and innovation. This "research culture" as an expression of intellectuality fosters a critical and, in the American context, a liberal politics, whereas the "teaching culture," associated with the transmission of knowledge rather than original inquiry, sustains a more conservative orientation. This is why, we must deduce, faculty at elite scholarly centers are consistently and markedly more liberal than their counterparts at "teaching" institutions of lower academic standing. Other variables contained in the Carnegie survey that tap this "research versus teaching culture" component all produce a comparable differentiation of faculty political opinion. For example, respondents were asked whether their "interests lie primarily in teaching or in research." Of those "very heavily" committed to research, 49 percent scored in the two most liberal quintiles of the Liberalism-Conservatism Scale, compared with just 31 percent of their colleagues "very heavily" oriented toward teaching. The persistence of this relationship in all types of college and university settings is even more revealing. For example, 55 percent of "research faculty" at elite schools are located in the two most liberal categories of the scale, as against 45 percent of the "teaching faculty" at these same institutions (as classified by the Index of School Quality). At colleges of the lowest academic standing, the percentages are, respectively, 41 and 29.

Data in Table 32 demonstrate that differences in political views between faculty of high and intermediate-to-low intellectual standing and attainments extend throughout the several age strata. Opposition to the prevailing United States position in Vietnam in 1969, for example, was expressed by 60 percent of professors of intermediate-to-low attainment in the under thirty-five age group, as contrasted with 81 percent of their age mates of high attainment; and 47 percent of the former, but 60 percent of the latter, indicated support for the busing of public school children to promote racial integration. In each age group, the high achievers are consistently more liberal than the low.[6]

The greater liberalism of eminent faculty persists across all disciplines in the contemporary university. For example, in the 1968 Presidential election, 61 percent of the "high achievers" in engineering voted for Hubert Humphrey, compared with 38 percent for all academic engineers. Within the biological sciences, the comparable per-

[6]In Table 32, we have applied "breaks" with regard to achievement somewhat different from those used in Table 31. To simplify matters in view of further controls for age, only two attainment categories were used: faculty at elite colleges and universities, and those at the top of the second tier, with five or more professional publications in the two years preceding the Carnegie survey; and all those with fewer than five publications at institutions of academic standing below the elite and upper-second-tier levels.

TABLE 32   *Political orientations of academics, by scholarly achievement and age (percentages of n)*

	Support busing for integration	*Support immediate United States withdrawal from Vietnam or coalition government with Communists*	*1964 vote for Johnson*
All faculty			
*Achievement dichotomized as:**			
High (n = 6,552)	54	74	88
Intermediate-to-low (n = 25,593)	42	54	75
Under 35			
High (n = 1,602)	60	81	87
Intermediate-to-low (n = 8,439)	47	60	74
35 to 49			
High (n = 3,510)	53	74	89
Intermediate-to-low (n = 10,953)	40	53	75
50 and over			
High (n = 1,425)	48	66	87
Intermediate-to-low (n = 6,075)	40	47	74

*The definitions employed here differ from those applied in Table 31. Footnote 6 explains both the reasons for and the substance of these contrasting definitions.

SOURCE: 1969 Carnegie Commission Survey of Student and Faculty Opinion.

centages are 72 and 55; for mathematics, 81 and 56. Also, 81 percent of the "high achievers" in physics and 76 percent of those in chemistry opposed Administration policies in Vietnam (as of mid-1969), in contrast with 67 and 56 percent, respectively, of the rank and file. Among the highly achieving sociologists, 85 percent scored in the two most liberal quintiles of the Liberalism-Conservatism Scale, as against 72 percent of all faculty in that discipline.

CLASS AND INTELLECTUALITY: SOME CONCLUSIONS

There seems to be little doubt that the model suggested by the literature on the socially critical posture of achieving intellectuals provides a far

1968 vote		Support	Very liberal and liberal
for Humphrey	for left third party	"radical student activism"	(Liberalism-Conservatism Scale)
69	3	48	52
55	2	40	34
72	6	54	63
56	4	50	44
70	2	50	52
56	1	37	33
64	2	36	42
50	1	32	24

more satisfactory guide to understanding political differences between the "top" and the "bottom" levels of the professoriate than does one stemming from application of the class theory of politics. Surveys of professors, from James Leuba's analysis of the factors associated with religious belief through the Carnegie data gathered in 1969, all agree that achievement in higher education, however measured, has been as-sociated with more liberal-to-left views on a wide array of social and political issues. Perhaps most startling of all is the conclusion first presented by Lazarsfeld and Thielens in *The Academic Mind* with re-spect to support for the rights of Communists and other minorities, and reiterated in our analysis of the Carnegie data with reference, for example, to opposition to the Vietnam War: That faculty consultants for the federal government have been more likely to align themselves against the government's position on crucial issues than colleagues not on the consulting payroll of the "political establishment" (Tables 29 and 31). These findings do not mean, of course, that consulting for the federal government or for business presses scholars to take a more critical position, but rather that consultants are generally recruited from the ranks of the more eminent in various fields, and hence, as we have seen, from the more liberally disposed members of academe. In a somewhat ironic twist, the political Establishment draws its advice from among those professors who are the most socially critical and questioning.

The "top" of the academic community is more liberal than the "bottom," not because its members are more advantaged in salary, research opportunities, and various perquisites of academic life, but seemingly because *within* the group role and orientations are closer to those of the ideal intellectual. The fact of greater liberalism among faculty of high attainment and recognition testifies to the essential inapplicability of the class theory in explaining dominant characteristics of professorial politics. The academy turns the class theory of politics on its head. A very different dynamic is at work.

6. Intellectuality and Social Background: The Liberalism of Jewish Academics

Discussion of the sources of divisions in academic politics has thus far been restricted to factors intrinsic to scholarly life itself—variations related to experiences in the discipline and to the roles and culture associated with intellectuality. Numerous external elements also normally differentiate political behavior among the general public. Among them are class, religious and ethnic background, sex, age, and generational experiences. Some of these intrude upon academic politics.

One of the sharpest breaks in faculty political opinion separates persons of Jewish and Christian background; it is especially interesting because it appears to result from an intersection of intellectuality and social background. The Carnegie data, as well as those from other surveys, show Jews, nearly one-tenth of the American professoriate, to be highly predisposed to a left-of-center politics. And Jewish faculty are disproportionately liberal, it seems, both as a group response to historic discrimination and as a result of cultural experiences which commit them heavily to the role and values associated with the intellectual. The former element seems to be a "direct" consequence of social background; the latter results from background through a process in a sense "once removed." There is a link between Jewishness and intellectuality and, as we have seen, between intellectuality and political liberalism. Jewish academics, then, belong to two groups which have been more liberal or leftist politically than other strata or ethnic-religious collectivities.

JEWISH ACADEMICS AND INTELLECTUAL ACHIEVEMENT

Over fifty years ago, Thorstein Veblen (1934, pp. 221, 223–224) addressed himself to the issue of the "intellectual pre-eminence of the Jews," describing their contribution, which he linked to discontent, in highly laudatory terms:

It is a fact which must strike any dispassionate observer that the Jewish people have contributed much more than an even share to the intellectual life of modern Europe. So also is it plain that the civilization of Christendom continues today to draw heavily on the Jews for men devoted to science and scholarly pursuits. It is not only that men of Jewish extraction continue to supply more than a proportionate quota to the rank and file engaged in scientific and scholarly work, but a disproportionate number of the men to whom modern science and scholarship look for guidance and leadership are of the same derivation. . . . They count particularly among the vanguard, the pioneers, the uneasy guild of pathfinders and iconoclasts, in science, scholarship, and institutional change and growth.

Evidence of this pattern has been gathered by students of intellectual and scientific behavior from the Middle Ages to the present in many different countries.[1]

There is probably no country in which Jews have been able to do as well intellectually as in the United States, given the extraordinary spread of higher education in this country in the post-World War II years. Studies of undergraduate enrollment indicate that about 80 percent of college-age Jews are enrolled in higher education, as compared with 40 percent of the population as a whole ("The American Jew . . . ," 1971, p. 63). And the Jewish students are heavily located in the more selective (higher academic standards) schools (Drew, 1970, pp. 11–12). A 1969 American Council on Education survey of college freshmen found that, as a group, those of Jewish parentage had higher secondary-school averages than their Gentile counterparts, in spite of the fact that a much larger proportion of Jews than of non-Jews go on to college (Drew, 1970, p. 35). Moreover, Jews seemingly perform better as students, once admitted to college; for example, they have been represented in the membership of Phi Beta Kappa at about twice their proportion of the undergraduate population (Weyl, 1966, p. 94).

The generalizations and findings concerning the propensity of Jews to achieve intellectually are reinforced by our data. By every criterion of academic accomplishment, Jewish faculty *as a group* have far surpassed their Gentile colleagues (Table 33). (There is, of course, a considerable range of variation among Jews, as among non-Jews.) Thus, Jews are more likely than Christians to be located at graduate student- and research-involved universities than in four- and two-year colleges. They are heavily represented on the faculties of Ivy League schools, other elite private universities, the "Big Ten," and the various cam-

[1]For a summary of such evidence, see Lipset and Ladd (1971*a*, pp. 96–99).

TABLE 33 *Respondent's school classified as university, four-year college, or two-year college (percentages of n)*

	University	Four-year institution	Two-year institution
Jewish faculty (n = 5,907)	70	24	6
Catholic faculty (n = 9,096)	37	46	17
Protestant faculty (n = 37,804)	45	39	16
ALL FACULTY (n = 60,028)	46	38	15

SOURCE: 1969 Carnegie Commission Survey of Student and Faculty Opinion.

puses of the University of California; they are considerably under-represented in the other, generally less prestigious, state universities. When the schools in the sample are rank-ordered according to the Index of Academic Quality (based on Scholastic Aptitude Test scores required for admission, research dollars per student, and revenue per student), 32 percent of the Jews are at schools which are in the highest-quality category, in contrast to 9 percent of the non-Jewish professors. Conversely, over 40 percent of the latter are at the lowest-quality category schools, as compared with 14 percent of the Jews (Table 34).

The same pattern of accomplishment is reflected in the data on publications. The Jewish faculty have published many more books and articles than their Gentile compeers (Table 35). To some degree, these variations in research accomplishments are linked to the fact that the Jews in the sample, on the average, spend more time "on professional

TABLE 34 *Respondent's school as classified by the Index of Academic Quality (row percentages)*

	(Highest quality) 1	2	3	4	(Lowest quality) 5
Jewish faculty	32	13	12	30	14
Catholic faculty	8	7	12	32	42
Protestant faculty	10	8	12	28	43
ALL FACULTY	12	9	12	29	39

SOURCE: 1969 Carnegie Commission Survey of Student and Faculty Opinion.

TABLE 35 *Number of articles published in academic or professional journals (row percentages)*

	None	1–2	3–4	5–10	11–20	More than 20
Jewish faculty	26	18	10	14	12	21
Catholic faculty	51	21	10	8	5	6
Protestant faculty	44	20	10	10	6	9
ALL FACULTY	43	20	10	10	7	10

SOURCE: 1969 Carnegie Commission Survey of Student and Faculty Opinion.

reading, writing or research" than do their non-Jewish colleagues. They also are much more likely than other professors to report themselves as primarily interested in research.

Not unexpectedly, these academic achievements of the Jewish faculty are reflected in their rank and financial status. Although Jews were slightly younger on the average than non-Jews (the median age for Jews was 38, as contrasted with 40 for Gentiles), a larger percentage of them were full professors. And the salaries of the Jewish professors were considerably higher than those of other faculty. Thus, in 1969, when these data were gathered, 16 percent of the Jews, but only 7 percent of the entire sample, had annual salaries of $20,000 or more.

The propensity of Jews for academic achievement would seem to be linked to their greater commitment to intellectual activities. They form a disproportionately large part of the market and audience for art and literature. Wealthy Jews are relatively more generous in their support for such endeavors than equivalent Gentiles. Alvin Toffler (1964, p. 34) described the extensive contribution of Jews to American cultural life:

... although there is no statistical data that even attempts to analyze the racial or religious background of the arts public, conversations with gallery directors, orchestra managers, and other art administrators in many cities lead one to conclude that the culture public contains a higher than proportionate number of Jewish people. Jews, of course, have always been prominent as artists. . . . The extension director of a university in California, in discussing the rising level of cultural activity in Los Angeles, cites the growth of the Jewish population as the causative agent. A museum director in San Antonio says: "The vast majority of collectors here are Jewish." In Dallas the arts attract considerable support from the Jewish community.

Sam Welles (1960, p. 166) stressed the contribution of the New York Jews to "the world of art, theatre, and music . . . sometimes strident, generally exciting, and often original and profound." He wrote:

An educated guess has it that perhaps a third of the city's art galleries are Jewish owned or managed. In the theatre, Jews are prominent as owners, directors, playwrights and actors. They have been leaders in radio and television from the earliest days of these media. In music they have enriched the city with special abundance.

Jews in academe reflect this group disposition by exhibiting a greater commitment to "intellectuality" than their non-Jewish fellow professionals. Previous studies of academe have indicated that Jewish professors are more likely to think of themselves as "intellectuals" than comparably located Gentiles (Anderson, 1967, p. 452). And this difference in self-perception is associated with a greater involvement in serious culture, as reflected by reading habits and other cultural tastes (Anderson, 1967, pp. 447–449). The much more extensive Carnegie sample validated these earlier findings. Twice as many Jews (36 percent) as Christians (17 percent) strongly agreed with the statement, "I consider myself an intellectual." This variation between the religious groups is linked to quite different tastes. More than half of the Jewish professors almost never attend an athletic event (53 percent) in contrast with only one-third (32 percent) of the Gentiles. The Jews, on the other hand, are more likely to attend concerts and plays regularly and to go to "art" films, as the data in Table 36 indicate.

The greater commitment of Jewish academics to the intellectual role and activities clearly has its roots in Jewish culture.[2] Many have sought to explain this trait as a secularization of the emphasis on religious study which characterized life in the ghetto for over a millenium. Pre-

TABLE 36 *Frequency of attending cultural events (row percentages)*

	Once a week or more	2 or 3 times a month	About once a month	A few times a year	Once a year or less
Jewish faculty	7	25	35	28	5
Catholic faculty	5	12	35	41	8
Protestant faculty	3	14	30	45	8
ALL FACULTY	4	15	31	43	8

SOURCE: 1969 Carnegie Commission Survey of Student and Faculty Opinion.

[2]For a description of the historic commitment to education among Jews, see Weyl (1966, pp. 151–168) and Aubery (1962, pp. 248–257, 265–275).

TABLE 37 *Amount of formal education attained by respondent's father (row percentages)*

	11 years or less	High school graduate	Some college/ college graduate	Graduate training
Jewish faculty	49	17	17	17
Catholic faculty	54	18	16	11
Protestant faculty	41	18	24	18
ALL FACULTY	44	17	22	17

SOURCE: 1969 Carnegie Commission Survey of Student and Faculty Opinion.

sumably, the status given to the religious scholar and the activities of the mind remains within secularized Jewish culture, transferred in large part to the intellectual and his work. The intellectual orientation of the current crop of Jewish faculty members is not due to the greater educational and intellectual achievements of their parents. They come from poorer, presumably more recent immigrant, and hence less educated families, which were less represented in the teaching professions and in other occupations requiring high levels of education than were the more well-to-do and better-educated families of the Gentile professors. A larger percentage of the Jews than of other academics had fathers who had not graduated from high school. More Protestants had fathers who had attended college (42 percent) than did the Jews (34 percent), as shown in Table 37. A similar pattern is reflected in family occupational background. Almost half (45 percent) of the Jews had fathers who were in business, typically small business, as contrasted with 16 percent of the others. Although 8 percent of the Protestants had fathers who had been employed in education at some level, only 3 percent of the Jews gave similar reports. Thus, though the Jewish professors must have absorbed their drive for intellectual accomplishment in their home environment, more of them than of their non-Jewish colleagues were the first generation of their often foreign-born families to attend college.

THE POLITICAL LIBERALISM OF AMERICAN JEWS

The general propensity of Jews to be located on the left has been discussed in a number of writings,[3] and the overwhelming supportive evi-

---

[3]These include the following works: Fuchs (1956); Cohn (1958, pp. 614–626); Weyl (1968); Glazer (1969, pp. 112–113, 126–129); Ruchames (1969, pp. 228–252); Liebman (1969, pp. 1034–1059); Glazer and Moynihan (1970, pp. 166–171); Lipset (1970a, pp. 376–400).

dence need not be reviewed in detail here. The source of this disproportionate liberalism is somewhat in dispute. Some find it primarily in aspects of Jewish religious teaching. Most, however, locate it in the historic pattern of discrimination which forced or disposed Jews to oppose European conservative parties, so often aligned against the claim of Jews for equal rights. Although discrimination was greater in much of Europe than in the United States at any time, American Jews did confront real barriers in employment, in admission to professions, and in access to leading private universities, and also faced sanctions against their participation, even if they were well-to-do and highly educated, in the social activities of the predominantly Protestant affluent strata (Broun and Britt, 1931).

In response to this condition, a striking proclivity for liberalism developed. The results are etched deeply in all facets of American political life over the past half century. Jews have, for instance, been much more supportive of Democratic presidential candidates than any other identifiable ethnocultural group since the New Deal years (Table 38). In 1936, when Franklin Roosevelt received 61 percent of the vote among the electorate at large, he was supported by 85 percent of Jews. The Democratic and left third-party candidates in 1948 were backed by just over half of all voters, but by three-fourths of Jews. Especially striking is

TABLE 38 *Democratic presidential vote, 1936–1972, Jews and all voters (as percentages)*

	Jews	All voters	Percentage difference, Jews and all voters
1936	85	61	+24
1940	84	55	+29
1944	91	54	+37
1948	73*	52	+21
1952	75	44	+31
1956	70	42	+28
1960	87	50	+37
1964	95	61	+34
1968	82	43	+39
1972	66	38	+28

*The 1948 figures include the Democratic (Harry S. Truman), Progressive (Henry Wallace), and Socialist (Norman Thomas) party votes.

SOURCE: The data on voting by Jews are drawn from the following American Institute of Public Opinion (Gallup) surveys: For 1936, nos. 150, 208, 209, 215, 219; 1940, nos. 215, 219, 248; 1944, nos. 336, 337; 1948, nos. 431, 432; 1952, nos. 507, 508, 509; 1956, nos. 573, 574, 576; 1960, nos. 637, 638, 640; 1964, nos. 699, 701, 702; 1968, nos. 769, 770, 771, 773, 774; and 1972, nos. 857, 858, 859, 860.

the fact that Progressive party candidate Henry Wallace and Socialist Norman Thomas, supported by only 2.6 percent of the entire voting public, were the choices of 19 percent of Jewish voters. Jews supported Adlai Stevenson in what were, for Democrats, the "lean" 1950s by a margin of roughly 3 to 1. In 1968, Hubert Humphrey was the choice of more than 80 percent of Jewish voters, as compared with just over 43 percent of all persons going to the polls. And in 1972, when the Democratic presidential vote was proportionately lower than it had been in any election since 1924, Jews backed McGovern by an overwhelming margin of 2 to 1. Throughout this 10-election sequence, Jewish voters were in every instance markedly more Democratic than the electorate at large—by margins of between 21 and 39 percentage points, averaging an exceptional 30 points.

Such findings bearing on political behavior are reflected, too, in political self-image. Between October 1970 and January 1973, Gallup on five separate occasions asked national samples of the public to locate their political orientations along a five-point scale from "very conservative" to "very liberal." The results are presented in Table 39 for respondents by their religious backgrounds. Only 5 and 6 percent of Protestants and Catholics described themselves as "very liberal," the position of 12 percent of Jews, while 51 percent of the Jews identified themselves as liberals and only 25 percent as conservatives, in contrast to a 23 percent/44 percent split among Christians.

When we look at subgroups in the population, we find this same sharp division in aggregate political distributions by religious background. Table 40, for example, reports on political views of college freshmen (in 1969), drawing on a national survey conducted by the American Council on Education. Since all the students were at the very beginning of their college experience, we can be confident that orientations drawn from the parental home, not the milieu of higher

TABLE 39   *Political self-identification of the general public (1970–1973), by religious background (row percentages)*

	Very liberal	Fairly liberal	Middle-of-the-road	Fairly conservative	Very conservative
Jews	12	39	25	19	6
Catholics	6	21	35	27	11
Protestants	5	17	33	32	14
ALL RESPONDENTS	6	19	33	29	12

SOURCE: These data are a composite drawn from the following American Institute of Public Opinion (Gallup) surveys: nos. 815, 828, 850, 856, and 863.

TABLE 40 *Political orientations of college freshmen in 1969, Jews and other religious backgrounds (column percentages)*

	Jewish	Other religions
Political self-identification		
Left	9	3
Liberal	46	29
Middle-of-the-road	34	45
Moderately conservative	11	21
Strongly conservative	1	2
Agree, capital punishment should be abolished	67	50
Agree, marijuana should be legalized	52	24
Agree, the federal government should be more involved in promoting school desegregation	73	53
Participated in protests against U.S. military policy in Vietnam	20	6

SOURCE: Drew (1970).

education, are decisive. Among Jewish freshmen, 55 percent located themselves on the liberal-to-left end of the political continuum, as against just 32 percent of the Protestants and Catholics. More than half of the former favored legalization of marijuana, twice the proportion among those of non-Jewish parentage. A full fifth of the Jewish freshmen indicated that they had personally participated in protests against American policies in Vietnam, a posture of only 6 percent of the Protestants and Catholics.

Such data only point up a conclusion already well sustained. Jewish faculty are part of an ethnocultural tradition strongly associated with backing for liberal programs and candidates, partaking of a "liberal tradition" which has deep roots outside academic life.

POLITICS OF JEWISH ACADEMICS

The extent to which the political background of Jewish academics differs from that of others may be seen in the responses to the Carnegie survey question: "What were your father's politics while you were growing up?" Fathers who were "left" or "liberal" in their views were reported by 46 percent of the Jews, as contrasted with 19 percent of the Catholics and but 14 percent of the Protestant majority. Conversely,

TABLE 41 *Respondent's memory of father's political orientation (percentages of n)*

	Left	Liberal	Middle-of-the-road	Moderately conservative	Strongly conservative
Jewish faculty (n = 5,907)	5	41	34	16	4
Catholic faculty (n = 9,096)	1	18	31	35	15
Protestant faculty (n = 37,804)	1	13	23	40	23
ALL FACULTY (n = 60,028)	2	17	25	37	19

SOURCE: 1969 Carnegie Commission Survey of Student and Faculty Opinion.

20 percent of the Jewish professors had "conservative" fathers, while 63 percent of the Protestant academics indicated such a background (Table 41).

The contribution of faculty of Jewish background to liberal and left political groups has been stressed in a number of surveys preceding our own. Thus, earlier studies showed that close to 90 percent of Jewish academics regularly voted Democratic in presidential elections back to 1944 (Lipset, 1970b, pp. 97–100). Jewish faculty have also been found to contribute heavily to the backing of leftist third parties. According to a 1948 study, fully 30 percent of the Jewish professors voted for Henry Wallace (Howard, 1958, p. 418). The same proclivity can be seen in Britain, where a faculty opinion study reported that the Jews were "the most Left-wing of all" (Halsey & Trow, 1971, p. 415). Recent studies of American college professors conclude that Jews have been much more heavily opposed to the Vietnam War, and stronger supporters of student activism, than their Gentile colleagues (Armor et al., 1967, p. 170).

The Carnegie Commission's survey yielded the same strong relationships. The Jewish faculty were much more inclined to identify their politics as "left" or "liberal" than Protestants and Catholics (Table 42).

TABLE 42 *Political self-characterization of faculty (row percentages)*

	Left	Liberal	Middle-of-the-road	Moderately conservative	Strongly conservative
Jewish faculty	12	62	18	7	1
Catholic faculty	4	40	30	23	2
Protestant faculty	4	37	28	28	3
ALL FACULTY	5	40	27	25	3

SOURCE: 1969 Carnegie Commission Survey of Student and Faculty Opinion.

TABLE 43 *Faculty support for the Democratic party presidential nominee, 1964–1972 (row percentages)*

	1964	*1968*	*1972*
Jewish faculty	97	87	88
Catholic faculty	81	68	54
Protestant faculty	74	52	51
ALL FACULTY	77	58	56

SOURCE: 1969 Carnegie Commission Survey of Student and Faculty Opinion, and 1972 Ladd-Lipset survey.

Jews contributed disproportionately to the small group who backed left-wing third-party presidential candidates in 1968. In 1964, only 2 percent of Jewish faculty voted for Barry Goldwater, compared with 26 percent among those of Protestant parentage (Table 43). Eight years later, McGovern was supported by 88 percent of Jewish faculty, as compared with 54 percent of those of Catholic and 51 percent of Protestant background.

The Jews, as a group, took much more liberal positions on such issues as the use of force at the Chicago Democratic Convention in 1968, the Vietnam War, student activism, the treatment of blacks in both the university and the larger society, and the legalization of marijuana. The gap between Jews and Christians on these issues is very large, while among Christians, Protestants are usually slightly more conservative than Catholics. For example, 59 percent of the Jews gave general approval to "the emergence of radical student activism in recent years," compared with 44 percent of the Catholics and 40 percent of the Protestants. The proportion of Jews favoring immediate United States withdrawal from Vietnam as of spring 1969 was twice that of non-Jews. Three-fifths of the Jews favored the legalization of marijuana (59 percent), compared with 33 percent of the Catholics and 29 percent of the Protestants.

Although Jews were invariably more liberal and change-oriented than Gentiles in their responses to all the politically relevant questions in the Carnegie questionnaire, it is striking that the gap between Jewish and non-Jewish faculty is smallest for items which pertain to changes in academic standards. Jews were only modestly more willing than others to waive academic standards in appointing members of minority groups to the faculty, or in admitting them to the student body (Table 44). Jewish faculty were only slightly more favorable than the faculty as a whole to offering a program of black studies. The same pattern of response occurred with respect to questions dealing with "student power." Though relatively sympathetic to campus activism, the Jewish scholars were not much more disposed to give students a

TABLE 44 *Faculty responses to questions involving the position of blacks in the university (column percentages)*

	Jewish faculty	Catholic faculty	Protestant faculty	All faculty
Agree, regular academic requirements should be "relaxed" in appointing minority group faculty	31	22	20	22
Agree, more minority undergraduates should be admitted even if a "relaxation" of regular academic standards is required	53	40	38	40
Agree, any college should offer a Black Studies program if substantial numbers of black students want it	73	71	67	69

SOURCE: 1969 Carnegie Commission Survey of Student and Faculty Opinion.

major share in important decisions within the university than their Gentile colleagues (Table 45).

This weakening of Jewish liberalism when academic standards are involved reflects a general phenomenon, that successful, creative, and research-oriented faculty are more liberal or left on general political questions, but are also heavily committed to the university and scholarship. This latter involvement reduces, though it does not eliminate, the impact of their general political ideology on matters internal to academe.

The reader will note that we have not much attended to political differences separating academics of Protestant and Catholic background. This "omission" has been dictated by the data. There simply is no

TABLE 45 *Faculty opinion on appropriate student role in questions of faculty appointments and promotion (row percentages)*

	Control	Voting power on committee	Formal consultation	Informal consultation	Little or no role
Jewish faculty	0.1	8	20	28	44
Catholic faculty	0.3	6	15	26	52
Protestant faculty	0.2	5	14	25	56
ALL FACULTY	0.2	6	15	25	54

SOURCE: 1969 Carnegie Commission Survey of Student and Faculty Opinion.

pattern of notable variations. There are some exceptions, to be sure. Catholic faculty do exhibit the traditional loyalties to the Democratic party associated with their coreligionists generally. Thus in 1968, only 25 percent of faculty of Catholic parentage voted for Nixon, as compared with 42 percent of the white Protestants. But on most matters, including the various attitude scales developed from the Carnegie questions, the two groups rarely varied by more than 3 to 5 percentage points.

It is clear that Jewish academics as a group are more likely than their non-Jewish peers to be located on the left in their opinions and political behavior and to exhibit a high level of scholarly achievement. In a real sense, it may be suggested that elements basic to the Jewish situation or culture contribute to the particular mix of critical social views and intellectuality, a relationship suggested by Thorstein Veblen over a half century ago when he argued that the social background which produced the creative scholar also nurtured "iconoclasts." In other words, *intellectual bent and political liberalism are both products of comparable social conditions.* Each is found where the other is present, as in the case of the better universities—and Jews as a collectivity.

At every level of academe, however, Jews exhibit higher commitments to intellectual values and activities. And the same pattern occurs with respect to political views. The differences in degree of liberalism are smaller among Jews than among Gentiles when the additional factors of school quality and/or discipline are introduced. Table 46 shows that Jews at major universities stand to the left of their coreligionists at lesser institutions, but by a modest degree, whereas elite-school Christians are vastly more liberal than their counterparts at places of lesser academic standing. Catholics and Protestants in the applied fields (professional schools) are *much more* conservative than their coreligionists in the liberal arts. Jews are only *somewhat more* conservative. Seemingly, the elements of a Jewish environment which dispose its products to left-

TABLE 46 *Degree of political liberalism* among faculty, by religious background and academic quality of institution*

Quality of school at which the faculty member teaches	Religious background	
	Jewish	*Christian*
Elite	72	54
Middle range	69	40
Lower tier	66	29

*Percentage located in the "very liberal" and "liberal" quintiles of the Liberalism-Conservatism Scale.
SOURCE: 1969 Carnegie Commission Survey of Student and Faculty Opinion.

ist views predominate over factors internal to the academic experience, such as institutional setting and discipline.

RELIGIOUS AND IRRELIGIOUS FACULTY: DIFFERENCES IN POLITICS AND SCHOLARSHIP

Before leaving this exploration of the relationship between religious background and political views within the professoriate, one additional dimension needs to be considered. Religion has thus far been invoked as an indicator of *ethnocultural* background and identification. Along a different dimension, it also comprises, of course, the element of degree of attachment to religious traditions, practices, and values.

We assumed that a faculty member's commitment to religious belief or his irreligion (1) is part of a much larger mindset which also includes his political perceptions, and (2) is related to intellectuality and to the niche he has found in academe. Political and religious conservatism are strongly associated.[4] And it seemed likely that professors who move in the highly secularized academic world of the major universities and who have committed themselves to the questioning and critical pursuit of scholarship would be much less likely than their less scholarly colleagues at lower-tier "teaching" colleges to find congenial the intellectual life of traditional religious pursuits.

The Carnegie data strongly support the first of these assumptions. The correlations between religiousness and political opinions are consistently among the highest encountered in the survey for the various biographical and personal characteristics of faculty, on the one hand, and their politics, on the other. The pattern for the Jewish faculty here is essentially the same as for Protestants and Catholics: those more deeply committed to, and involved in, religious practice are politically the most conservative. For example, only 48 percent of academics of Jewish background who consider themselves "deeply religious" score in the two most liberal quintiles of the Liberalism-Conservatism Scale, compared with 75 percent of those who are "largely indifferent to religion" and 82 percent who are "basically opposed to religion." For faculty of Protestant parentage, the comparable figures are 31, 50, and 71 percent (Table 47). Thus, 64 percent of those reared as Jews who identify their

---

[4]It is true, as Lenski has pointed out, that one cannot find in the general public a liberal-conservative dimension that encompasses both political and religious commitments, but that is, in significant measure, testimony to the fact that most people do not impose any ideological dimension on social and political events. College professors are a very special group whose "business" is ideas and whose social and political views are highly organized or ideological in the sense in which Converse uses the latter term. See Lenski (1963, pp. 208–211) and Converse (1964, pp. 206–261).

TABLE 47 *Percentage of faculty identified as most liberal (Liberalism-Conservatism Scale), by religious background and present religious practice (column percentages)*

	Religious background			
	Jewish	Catholic	Protestant	All faculty
Respondent's description of his religious commitment				
Deeply religious	48	33	31	33
Moderately religious	56	33	26	29
Largely indifferent to religion	75	56	50	56
Basically opposed to religion	82	73	71	75
Present religious association				
Same as that in which reared	64	34	27	31
None	82	69	65	67

SOURCE: 1969 Carnegie Commission Survey of Student and Faculty Opinion.

present religious attachments as Jewish are classified "liberal," in contrast to a much higher 82 percent among persons of Jewish background who claim no current religious ties. The variance here is even sharper for academics coming from Protestant and Catholic families. Just 34 percent of professors raised as Catholics who still consider themselves of that faith are in these liberal categories, while 69 percent who now claim no religious affiliation are so classified.

If the interrelation of religiousness and political opinion is close, as had been expected, the association of religious commitment and scholarly achievement has proved to be weaker than we had anticipated. We had looked for a powerful link going both ways, that is, as both cause and effect. It seemed likely that faculty members of a skeptical and questioning bent would be the most successful—for, as Veblen suggested, a restless and probing intellect is essential to any significant scholarly work—and that such academics would by this very same quality question all manner of regular religious beliefs and practices. Conversely, an intellectual approach that would leave an academic comfortable with organized religion should militate against his chances for scholarly achievement. At the same time, the major research universities are the most secular and irreligious, so that whatever his previous orientation to religion, the faculty member experiencing such an environment should be influenced by it in the direction of irreligion.

TABLE 48 *Frequency of attendance at religious services by number of publications in the past two years, Jewish and Christian faculty (column percentages are in parentheses)*

Faculty of Jewish background	None (n = 1,430)	1–2 (n = 1,577)	3–4 (n = 1,415)
Once a week or more (n = 287)	31 (5)	30 (6)	25 (6)
Two or three times a month (n = 284)	29 (5)	30 (6)	21 (5)
About once a month (n = 382)	32 (7)	28 (7)	19 (6)
A few times a year (n = 1,447)	34 (30)	24 (23)	20 (25)
Once a year or less (n = 3,521)	28 (54)	27 (59)	22 (59)

Faculty of Christian background	None (n = 19,215)	1–2 (n = 13,335)	3–4 (n = 7,815)
Once a week or more (n = 15,465)	63 (45)	22 (35)	8 (27)
Two or three times a month (n = 6,750)	51 (12)	27 (14)	12 (13)
About once a month (n = 3,345)	58 (7)	23 (6)	14 (8)
A few times a year (n = 6,990)	49 (12)	24 (12)	17 (18)
Once a year or less (n = 14,730)	46 (24)	29 (33)	14 (34)

SOURCE: 1969 Carnegie Commission Survey of Student and Faculty Opinion.

While the relationships we discovered are uniformly in the direction posited earlier, they appear weaker than our logic led us to anticipate. About 20 percent of the Jewish faculty who attend synagogue two or three times a month or more are among the more productive (five or more publications in the last two years), compared with 23 percent of the irreligious Jews (attendance of religious services a few times a year or less). About 8 percent of the most productive Jewish professors (more than 10 publications) attend services regularly, as do 10 percent of those not publishing at all. Among the Jewish faculty, 7 percent at elite colleges and 12 percent at the lower-tier schools frequently go to syna-

5–10 (n = 1,135)	More than 10 (n = 348)
13 (4)	2 (2)
15 (4)	5 (5)
16 (6)	5 (6)
16 (25)	6 (31)
18 (61)	5 (57) Gamma = 0.061

5–10 (n = 4,740)	More than 10 (n = 1,350)
5 (27)	2 (34)
9 (17)	2 (10)
4 (4)	2 (7)
8 (16)	2 (12)
9 (37)	3 (37) Gamma = 0.186

gogue, while 88 percent at the former and 81 percent at the latter attend only a few times a year or not at all. A higher percentage of the irreligious than of the religious Jews are teaching at the better schools, but again the difference is modest. Tables 48 and 49 show that the relationship between religiousness and academic achievement is somewhat stronger for Christian faculty. This is as expected, because support for intellectual activity has been stronger in Judaism than in the Christian denominations generally. Still, the most striking aspect of our findings is the relative weakness of the association between religious orientation and scholarship for Christians and Jews alike. The strength of the

TABLE 49 *Frequency of attendance at religious services, by quality of school at which the faculty member teaches, Jewish and Christian faculty (column percentages are in parentheses)*

Faculty of Jewish background	Lower-tier colleges and universities (n = 371)	Colleges and universities of the middle range (n = 2,568)	Elite colleges and universities (n = 3,104)
Once a week or more (n = 287)	25 (7)	41 (6)	34 (4)
Two or three times a month (n = 284)	19 (5)	44 (6)	37 (4)
About once a month (n = 382)	19 (7)	45 (8)	36 (5)
A few times a year (n = 1,447)	24 (35)	37 (25)	40 (24)
Once a year or less (n = 3,521)	15 (46)	37 (56)	49 (63)
			Gamma 0.174

Faculty of Christian background	Lower-tier colleges and universities (n = 9,525)	Colleges and universities of the middle range (n = 24,495)	Elite colleges and universities (n = 13,650)
Once a week or more (n = 15,465)	58 (46)	32 (36)	10 (23)
Two or three times a month (n = 6,750)	44 (12)	39 (15)	17 (13)
About once a month (n = 3,345)	43 (6)	41 (8)	16 (6)
A few times a year (n = 6,990)	37 (10)	42 (16)	21 (16)
Once a year or less (n = 14,730)	45 (26)	31 (26)	24 (41)
			Gamma = 0.205

SOURCE: 1969 Carnegie Commission Survey of Student and Faculty Opinion.

relationship is not altered by recourse to other measures of religiousness.

CONCLUDING COMMENT

Few variables differentiate faculty political opinion as sharply and consistently as religious background, structured in terms of Jewish and Christian. In all institutional and discipline contexts, Jews stand to the left politically of their Christian colleagues. The split between faculty of these two traditions is especially notable in those fields and college settings which are relatively most conservative, as the persisting impact of the Jewish cultural tradition in a sense overrides orientations linked to academic setting. At the other end of the continuum of academic environments—for example, social science departments of elite colleges and universities—the "political distance" between Christians and Jews is substantially less: The Jewish faculty are very liberal, but so, too, are the professors of Protestant and Catholic background therein represented.

Only one other ethnocultural collectivity in academe, black faculty (to whom we attend in the chapter which follows), rivals Jews in general sympathy for liberal causes. Thus far, however, the impact of the political views of black academics on university life has been far less substantial than that of Jews. While the Jews are located disproportionately at major colleges and universities, the blacks are clustered at schools of the lower range, with about half of them at predominantly black institutions. Jewish academics as a group are the most productive in scholarly terms and earn the highest salaries; by these standards, black faculty are unsuccessful. And the proportion of Jews in the professoriate is about three times that of Jews in the general public, while the percentage of blacks in the professoriate is only one-third of their proportion in the society.

7. The Demography of Academic Politics: Age and Social Background

Faculty, like other people, are distinguished by race and ethnicity, by religious background, sex, and the social class of their parents—factors which identify both *experiences* and *orientations* acquired prior to entering the professoriate and, in some cases, concrete *interests* of a persisting nature.

Another cluster of demographic factors includes age and academic generation. Age, and the changes in status and perspectives which accompany aging, have long been linked to variations in political behavior within the population. Young academics, specifically, are closer to the experiences of students than their older colleagues. And they are, typically, recent arrivals at the institutions where they are presently teaching, with looser ties to them. They have had less time than older faculty to move to positions of security and influence in their university and their profession. Faculty in the several age strata are also members of different academic generations, having arrived at different times in what has been the rapidly changing context of academic life. They are, potentially, of different "political generations," having come of age politically in varying climates and concerns.

SOCIAL BACKGROUND OF THE PROFESSORIATE

The professoriate in the United States has undergone an extraordinary expansion since World War II. In 1940, about 150,000 people were employed as faculty members in the country's colleges and universities; three decades later, in the 1970s, the number exceeded 600,000. The most dramatic increases came in the late 1960s, when the professorial ranks were swelled by 150,000 in one five-year span. The number of *new* positions created and filled in this half decade equaled *the entire number* of faculty slots in 1940.

With this growth have come important changes in social origins. The most substantial of these, by far, involves the increase in the proportion of academics of Catholic and Jewish parentage—which means, of course, from the ethnocultural groups these religious labels subsume.[1] Two sets of data comparisons demonstrate this development: One set compares the religious group identifications of social scientists in 1955, described by the Lazarsfeld-Thielens survey, with that in 1969, provided by our Carnegie survey; the other compares the parental religion of faculty in the several age strata, again working with Carnegie data.

When asked to identify their present religious preferences, slightly more than two-thirds of all social scientists (68 percent) interviewed by Lazarsfeld and Thielens described themselves as Protestant. Fourteen years later, the Carnegie survey found the proportion significantly reduced, to 51 percent.[2] The Catholic, Jewish, and "none" categories all showed increases. Parental religion, not asked about by Lazarsfeld and Thielens, is a better indicator of origins, of course, and was included in the Carnegie questionnaire. Table 50 shows the marked decline in the

TABLE 50   *Religious origins of faculty, by age (percentages of n)*

	Protestant	*Catholic*	*Jewish*	*Other*	*None*
60 and older (n = 4,398)	76	13	5	4	2
50–59 (n = 9,408)	73	16	7	2	2
40–49 (n = 16,113)	66	18	9	4	3
30–39 (n = 20,580)	63	19	9	5	4
Under 30 years (n = 8,607)	61	22	10	3	4
ALL AGES (n = 59,106)	66	18	9	4	3

SOURCE: 1969 Carnegie Commission Survey of Student and Faculty Opinion.

[1]Respondents to the Carnegie survey were asked to specify the religion in which they were raised, their present religion, and their race. They were not asked to provide any other information on their ethnic background. The questionnaire employed in the 1955 Lazarsfeld-Thielens survey did ask "country of origin" of grandparents, and we will make use of these data in exploring the relationship of ethnic origin to present politics, to enlarge the picture furnished by the Carnegie study.

[2]Lazarsfeld and Thielens put historians and geographers in social science, while we do not; and we include all psychologists, whereas they surveyed only social psychologists. For purposes of the comparison here, then, we have imposed a uniform definition on both surveys, including only sociologists, anthropologists, political scientists, economists, and social psychologists in the ranks of social scientists.

TABLE 51 *Race and sex of faculty, by age (row percentages)*

	Race			Sex	
	White	*Black*	*Oriental & other*	*Male*	*Female*
60 and older	93	5	2	79	21
50–59	95	4	1	77	23
40–49	96	3	1	80	20
30–39	94	3	2	85	15
Under 30 years	97	2	1	77	23
ALL AGES	95	3	2	81	19

SOURCE: 1969 Carnegie Commission Survey of Student and Faculty Opinion.

proportion of academics coming from Protestant families with movement from the oldest to the youngest stratum. About three-fourths of faculty 60 years of age and older, a generation which entered college teaching before World War I, were of Protestant parentage; in contrast, among those 35 and younger—entrants into teaching in the 1960s—only 62 percent were of Protestant stock. The proportion of Catholic background rises from just 13 percent among pre-World War II entrants to more than 20 percent of the "generation of the sixties." The jump in faculty of Jewish parentage is also large, from 5 percent of the oldest cohort to 10 percent of the youngest.

A big move toward opening the professoriate to Catholics and Jews occurred with World War II. The barriers that both groups encountered were largely dismantled in the postwar years, and general socioeconomic advances by the "newer" ethnic groups enabled their children to acquire the education necessary for college teaching.

In the case of some underrepresented groups, there has been no gain over the past four decades; there may even have been a relative decrease (Table 51). In 1969, blacks were only 3 percent of the faculty (while they were about 10 percent of the adult population). And they in fact accounted for a smaller proportion of academics under 35 (2.2 percent) than of the over 50 stratum (4 percent). The 1969 Carnegie survey of graduate students found that blacks made up just 2.7 percent of all students, and only 1.9 percent of doctoral candidates—while persons of Oriental background, less than 1 percent of the adult population, were 4.5 percent of the total enrolled in doctoral programs. The most recent survey data, from the 1972–73 American Council on Education faculty study, show blacks remaining at 3 percent of the professoriate, their relative position holding steady since 1969 (Bayer, 1973, p. 31). These data indicate conclusively that the representation of blacks on the faculty has not climbed substantially over the past two decades. The number of blacks in teaching positions rose, of course, but there was a struggle to keep pace with the tremendous growth of the entire professoriate.

In 1969, 19 percent of the faculty were women, ranging from highs of 98 percent in schools of nursing, 97 percent in home economics, and 55 percent in library science, to lows of well under 1 percent in the male bastions of engineering and agriculture.[3] The 1972–73 ACE survey found the proportion of women in professorial positions up ever so slightly, to 20 percent of the total (Bayer, 1973, p. 14). There does not appear to have been any significant secular change in the proportion of women in academe, with the very low percentage for the 30 to 39 age cohort possibly due to childbearing and child-rearing activities in these years.

As would be expected, there is still a strong middle-class bias to the professoriate. Children of the middle class are much more likely to pick up the training and intellectual orientations needed for academic pursuits. Thus, as Table 52 indicates, 57 percent of faculty in 1969 were sons or daughters of professionals, managers, or businessmen, occupa-

TABLE 52   *Occupations of fathers of faculty and of the male labor force in 1950*

	Fathers of faculty (percent of total)	*Male labor force, 1950* (percent of total)*
College or university teaching	4	0.3
Other teaching	3	0.7
Other professional work	14	5
Managerial and administrative	16	7
Business owner	20	5
Farm owner	10	10
Clerical and sales	8	13
Skilled wage worker	16	22
Semiskilled or unskilled wage worker	8	37

*These data are from U.S. Bureau of the Census (1968, pp. 232–235).

SOURCE: 1969 Carnegie Commission Survey of Student and Faculty Opinion.

[3] A 1963 study by the U. S. Office of Education found that 18 percent of the faculty in a large sample of four-year colleges and universities were women (U.S. Department of Health, Education and Welfare, 1966, p. 54).

TABLE 53 *Class background of faculty, by age (row percentages)*

	Father's education (percentage having attended college)	Father's occupation (percentage high status)*	Father's occupation (percentage manual)
60 and older	34	22	18
50–59	32	20	22
40–49	36	19	25
30–39	41	19	25
Under 30 years	52	23	21
ALL AGES	39	20	24

*Working with the Duncan occupation prestige scale, occupations were classified as high status, middle status, and low status.

SOURCE: 1969 Carnegie Commission Survey of Student and Faculty Opinion.

tions which accounted for just 18 percent of the male labor force in 1950 (chosen as more representative of the national occupational milieu that prevailed when the academics were growing up than later data). Only 24 percent of the academics had fathers who were blue-collar workers, although such occupations account for roughly three-fifths of the male work force.

Table 53 shows that there has been but a slight change over time in representation of the various socioeconomic strata, in the direction of a modest democratization. Less than 20 percent of those who entered college teaching before World War II, for example, were children of manual workers, with the proportion rising to about 25 percent among entrants in the 1950s and early 1960s. Then, however, without apparent reason, it drops off for the youngest, most recent entrants. One *might* expect this means only that persons of working-class background, on the whole, take a bit longer, partly because they must work more in outside jobs, to complete formal degree requirements, and hence that their true numbers are misrepresented in the ranks of faculty 29 years of age and younger. But this assumption is rejected by the Carnegie graduate student survey, which shows the percentage of doctoral candidates from working-class families to be exactly the same as that of faculty under 30 from similar socioeconomic backgrounds. The one really big change in occupational background is the marked decline in the number of professors coming from farm families, from the oldest to the youngest cohort, yet this only mirrors the sharp decrease of farmers in the general labor force. Similarly, the notable increase in the proportion from families where the father was college-educated appears

174 The divided academy

simply to reflect the big jump in the proportion of middle-class Americans attending college after World War II.

At the start of the 1970s, the American professoriate was composed very heavily of white males of middle-class parentage. The postwar years have seen substantial gains in the proportion coming from Jewish and Catholic European backgrounds, but the white, male, middle-class component of the base has not been altered substantially.

SOCIAL ORIGINS AND PRESENT POLITICS

As we have noted, a number of studies of faculty opinion have shown religious background to be influential, with Jews considerably more liberal than Gentiles. Class origins, on the other hand, with the single exception of a study by Charles Bidwell of professorial attitudes toward student political activism,[4] have been found to have little impact. What conclusions do the Carnegie data sustain?

Class background is most easily treated because our study so massively supports the predominant findings of earlier investigations: whether an academic is an offspring of university-trained professionals or was brought up in a working-class family by parents who had not completed the twelfth grade is of modest direct importance to his present political commitments in any of the areas covered by the survey. As an illustration of this point, Table 54 shows that faculty of the various groups defined by father's education and father's occupation manifest generally similar patterns of responses on the range of national and campus issues encompassed by four opinion scales—those measuring liberalism-conservatism on national issues, degree of support for student activism, backing for a broader student role in university decision making, and degree of acceptance of demands to change university practices in the interest of racial equity.[5]

On the whole, looking at Table 54, it does appear that we have another instance of "Marx turned upside down," with persons from high social backgrounds to the left of those from low SES families, especially on the national affairs issues. These variations, however, are entirely accounted for by subsequent career lines. That is, faculty from high SES backgrounds are more likely to be at major colleges and universities, where the subculture is more liberal, and less likely to be

---

[4]Bidwell (1970) found academics of high SES backgrounds to be decisively more supportive of campus activism than their colleagues of lower social-class origins.

[5]The construction and content of the scales included in Table 54 are described in Chapter 2, pp. 39–41.

TABLE 54 *Political opinions of faculty, by socioeconomic background (percentages of n)*

	Liberalism-Conservatism Scale (percentage "very liberal" and "liberal")	Campus Activism Scale (percentage "strongly supportive" and "supportive")	Student Role Scale (percentage "strongly supportive" and "supportive")	Black Support Scale (percentage "strongly supportive" and "supportive")
Father's education				
Less than 12 grades (n = 22,887)	35	35	42	31
High school graduate (n = 10,086)	39	38	44	33
Some college, college graduate (n = 13,932)	42	42	49	36
Advanced degree (n = 11,154)	49	45	48	37
Father's occupation				
Education (n = 4,641)	44	44	47	39
Other professional (n = 19,383)	45	43	48	35
Business (n = 17,472)	35	35	42	31
Clerical and sales (n = 4,632)	42	40	45	34
Manual (n = 12,183)	35	37	43	33

SOURCE: 1969 Carnegie Commission Survey of Student and Faculty Opinion.

in the relatively conservative applied fields. When field and type of institution are held constant, there are *no differences whatever* in the political orientations of academics by class background. Much the same thing applies to the finding that professors who are children of businessmen are somewhat more conservative. This is almost exclusively linked to their greater representation in business-related and more conservative disciplines. Within the social sciences, however, 63 percent of professors from business families are in the two most liberal quintiles of the Liberalism-Conservatism Scale, compared with 64 percent from homes where the father was in education and 63 percent of the offspring of working-class families.

We had not expected the class origins of professors to be very influential in shaping present politics. As he moves from his family class and ethnic situation to his career as an academic, the faculty member leaves one set of group interests and arrives at another, defined by his professional experience. Professors are members of a single, highly specialized professional cadre. They hold comparable class positions and have passed through a long internship socializing them to the norms and commitments of their respective professional disciplines. Only when the orientations and identifications attendant on a given social origin are particularly strong and coherent, or when they are continually reinforced by experiences after entry into the profession, should the association between origin and politics be strong. It would be expected, then, that being black or of Jewish parentage would distinguish the politics of a faculty member, while coming from a high-income as opposed to a low-income family would not.

If we expected that there would be only modest differences in general ideology by class background, we found it mildly surprising that there were no substantial class-related variations in electoral behavior. Socioeconomic groups in the United States are not clearly differentiated in terms of political ideology, but they surely are in electoral loyalties. In fact, however, Humphrey was backed in 1968 by 58 percent of faculty born of grammar school-educated parents and by 62 percent from families where the father held an advanced degree; by 54 percent whose fathers were business owners and by 59 percent from working-class families.

Two questions included in the Carnegie study differentiate faculty by racial and religious identification—one asking race, the other parental religion. White Protestants are by far the biggest group, just over 60 percent of all faculty. The differences in social background between professors of white Protestant and Catholic parentage are substantial, with the former of much higher socioeconomic status. But the political differences between these two groups are very modest. One exception, as we noted, involves electoral behavior, where Catholic academics are more Democratic. In the whole range of policy questions pursued in the Carnegie study, the ethnocultural groups identified loosely by "Protestant" and "Catholic" in no instance differ to any substantial degree. The Christian-Jewish division, of course, is another matter.

The position of blacks and Jews in the professoriate in many regards could scarcely be more dissimilar. While the latter, as noted, are located disproportionately at the major institutions and have enjoyed particular success in the academic milieu, the former are clustered at schools of the lower range, with about half at predominantly black institutions, and fall below the faculty average in salary and in various measures of academic attainment. Blacks and Jews agree, however, in their mutually high commitment to liberal policies.

Predictably, black faculty give more support than Jews, and certainly than white Protestants and Catholics, to proposed changes in university policy to promote racial equity, and are more critical of existing racial practice. But here the differences are largest on what are essentially symbolic commitments regarding race, rather than on concrete policy changes. For example, 34 percent of black academics "strongly agreed" that "most American colleges and universities are racist," in striking contrast to 13 percent of Jews and 10 percent of white Gentiles. However, on concrete policy issues the gap typically is much smaller. For example, just 53 percent of blacks as compared with 53 percent of Jews and 36 percent of white Gentiles favored relaxing normal admissions standards to increase the enrollment of black undergraduates.

In national politics, differences between black and Jewish faculty are generally modest. For example, 67 percent of the Jews, compared with 57 percent of blacks, scored in the two most liberal quintiles of the Liberalism-Conservatism Scale (Table 55), and 88 percent of the former and 96 percent of the latter voted Democratic in the 1968 presidential election. There are, however, a few issues which summon greatly different responses. Eugene McCarthy was preferred over Hubert Humphrey by 62 percent of Jewish academics and by 52 percent of white Gentiles, while Humphrey was the choice of 82 percent of blacks. Clearly, Humphrey's long-standing commitment to civil rights was the dominant factor for the latter, as McCarthy's stylish intellectualism and strong opposition to the war were for a majority of whites. On the issue of marijuana, only 22 percent of blacks in the professoriate favored its legalization, as contrasted with 59 percent of Jewish

TABLE 55 *Political opinions of faculty, by racial and religious background (percentages of n)*

	Liberalism-Conservatism Scale (percentage "very liberal" and "liberal")	Campus Activism Scale (percentage "very supportive" and "supportive")	Student Role Scale (percentage "very supportive" and "supportive")	Black Support Scale (percentage "very supportive" and "supportive")
Blacks (n = 860)	57	50	50	60
Jews (n = 5,907)	67	58	54	44
White Catholics (n = 9,051)	38	39	46	35
White Protestants (n = 37,002)	35	36	43	32

SOURCE: 1969 Carnegie Commission Survey of Student and Faculty Opinion.

academics, a difference which may reflect the widespread concern among middle-class blacks about the destructive effect of the increased use of drugs within the black community.

Sex discrimination in higher education has become a matter of hot contention in the 1970s. Women's groups operating within universities and women's caucuses within various disciplines have protested hiring practices, salary differentials, and generally what they allege to be the absence of equal professional opportunities for women. "Affirmative action" requirements have included stipulations about increased representation of women in faculty and related professional positions. There are many areas where variations in the opinions of male and female academics can be expected and deserve analytic attention.

When the Carnegie survey was administered in 1969, these sex discrimination issues had not attained much prominence, and none were included in the questionnaire. We are unable to treat here, then, that segment of faculty political opinion, by sex, which involves specific interests of the two groups. Where such "class interests" are present, men and women in the professoriate may differ greatly. We must conclude, however, that as of 1969 there were *no significant general ideological differences* separating male and female faculty. Examination of opinions on more than 100 diverse political controversies, from Vietnam to student role in university decision making, reveals a consistent absence of significant variations by sex. For example, 27 percent of women and 28 percent of men disagreed with the proposition that there can be no justification for the use of violence to achieve political objectives in the United States, and 60 percent of the former and 59 percent of the latter favored either immediate withdrawal of American troops from Vietnam or a reduction in involvement coupled with support for a coalition government. Humphrey was backed by 58 percent of male faculty, compared with 59 percent of women. Among female academics, 36 percent scored in the two most supportive quintiles of the Campus Activism Scale—virtually identical to the 39 percent for male faculty.

One item contained in our small national faculty survey, conducted in the fall of 1972, supports the expectation that male and female academics part company on some "class interest" matters even though they are not differentiated as groups in general ideological leanings. Respondents were asked whether they agreed or disagreed with the proposition that "groups which are underrepresented on the faculty—such as blacks, Chicanos and women—should be assigned a large share of future faculty vacancies until they are proportionately represented." Just

44 percent of the men concurred with the proposition, compared with 62 percent of the women surveyed.

IDEOLOGICAL BACKGROUND AND PRESENT POLITICS

Matters of origin and social background are looked upon as potentially important in determining a faculty member's present politics, to the extent that they lead to orientations which persist or connote continuing interests. At best, the relationship of background to political opinion, then, is once removed. Before leaving the matter of preprofessional influences on the commitments of faculty, we want to look at the way family background factors can most directly influence later attitudes—through ideological orientations of parents which may shape values in the years before the faculty member enters upon his career and other activities of adulthood.

The Carnegie survey asked a set of questions designed to determine ideological background. Respondents located their "father's politics while [they] were growing up" and their "politics as a college senior"—along with their present political views—on a continuum in which the categories presented were "left," "liberal," "middle-of-the-road," "moderately conservative," and "strongly conservative." The most serious problem in utilizing these data to assess persistence of orientations formed prior to entering the professoriate occurs in the need to rely on present-day reconstructions of past positions in general and ambiguous terms. We would like to know more. Were the faculty member's parents politically active or apathetic? Did they hold membership in political movements of the right or left? Was the academic himself politically active in his undergraduate days, and if so, precisely what sorts of organizational ties and policy commitments did he have? The questionnaire, however, contained only the two subjective political background questions.

There is no way to determine the nature of changes respondents may have made in the "frame" for their assessments of prior politics. For example, one professor who thinks of his present politics as strongly leftist might describe his father as a conservative, meaning by this latter depiction that the parent was conservative *in comparison with views the respondent presently holds*—even though the parent was *relatively* liberal in the context in which he operated. Another left-of-center academic, however, might classify his father's political stance in terms of the setting in which the latter lived. Such things simply cannot be untangled.

With these serious caveats before us, we should still give the data yielded by the questions on undergraduate and parental politics serious attention, and not just because they are all we have. College faculty are "idea people" whose judgments typically are far more precise and formal than are those of most groups in the society. Their belief systems are unusually elaborate and constrained. There is every reason to assume that the assessments offered of undergraduate and parental political views are serious and substantial, even though the frame is somewhat ambiguous.

We find a strong correlation between the politics to which professors remember being exposed in their parental family and the views they held in their undergraduate years. The gamma coefficient for these two variables is .49. Of faculty who remember their father's politics as "left," 81 percent classify themselves as "left" or "liberal" as college seniors, as against just 20 percent of those with strongly conservative fathers (Table 56). Of faculty from very conservative families, 63 percent remember their student position as either "moderately conservative" or "strongly conservative," as contrasted with just 8 percent of those from homes where the father's views were "left." For the majority of students over the last several decades, the college experience has been a liberalizing one, and it clearly was for those who went on to careers in teaching. But parental politics appears to have established the base upon which the liberalization has been effected.

The association between preprofessional political commitments and present politics is generally strong among academics. Since the rela-

TABLE 56 *Political positions of faculty when college seniors, by politics of their fathers when they were children (percentages of n)*

	Politics when college seniors				
Fathers' politics	*Left*	*Liberal*	*Middle-of-the-road*	*Moderately conservative*	*Strongly conservative*
Left (n = 1,095)	40	41	11	5	3
Liberal (n = 10,173)	6	65	18	10	2
Middle-of-the-road (n = 14,583)	4	39	38	15	3
Moderately conservative (n = 20,538)	3	25	33	36	4
Strongly conservative (n = 10,716)	2	18	17	44	19

SOURCE: 1969 Carnegie Commission Survey of Student and Faculty Opinion.

TABLE 57 *Present political positions of faculty, by their politics as college seniors (percentages of n)*

	Left (n = 2,964)	Liberal (n = 20,679)	College Middle-of-the-road (n = 15,942)
Present political self-characterization			
Left	37	6	2
Liberal	53	67	32
Middle-of-the-road	6	18	43
Moderately conservative	4	9	21
Strongly conservative	1	—	1
1968 vote			
Left third party	15	3	2
Humphrey	77	82	54
Nixon	7	15	43
Wallace	1	—	2
Vietnam position			
Immediate withdrawal	47	25	14
Reduce involvement, coalition government	42	48	38
Reduce involvement, but prevent Communist takeover	10	23	39
Win military victory	1	4	9
Liberalism-Conservatism Scale			
Very liberal	58	28	13
Liberal	24	32	18
Middle-of-the-road	9	17	19
Conservative	6	17	28
Very conservative	3	7	22
Campus Activism Scale			
Strongly supportive	47	25	15
Moderately supportive	28	27	19
Middle-of-the-road	14	24	24
Moderately opposed	6	12	17
Strongly opposed	6	12	25

SOURCE: 1969 Carnegie Commission Survey of Student and Faculty Opinion.

politics	
Moderately conservative (n = 15,015)	*Strongly conservative* (n = 3,291)
1	1
21	13
27	17
49	43
3	27
1	1
38	28
60	68
2	4
12	11
36	31
44	42
9	16
8	5
15	9
13	10
30	29
34	48
11	6
15	14
24	20
20	22
30	39

tionship naturally is greater with the more proximate of the two background indicators—position as a college senior—we will rely upon that measure in the analysis which follows. Among faculty who identified their undergraduate positions as "left" on the eve of choosing a career, 37 percent described their current views as "left," in comparison with just 1 percent of those who were conservatives in their student days. An extraordinary 15 percent of the old student leftists voted for the minor-party left candidates in 1968, as against less than 1 percent of their colleagues who were conservative students. On the other hand, Nixon was backed by a whopping 68 percent of the latter, and a decidedly less than overwhelming 7 percent of the former (Table 57). Among those who were leftist-inclined students, 47 percent favored an immediate unilateral withdrawal of American troops from Vietnam in the spring of 1969, as contrasted with 25 percent of student-day liberals, 14 percent of moderate conservatives, and 11 percent of those who had been strongly conservative. Among left-background faculty, 75 percent are in the supportive quintiles of the Campus Activism Scale, as against just 20 percent of their colleagues who were "very conservative" students.

Political orientation prior to entering the professoriate operates independently of other variables that differentiate the current commitments of faculty. For example, among academics of Jewish parentage, the differences by political background position are as great as among non-Jews. Table 58, which expresses the correlation between ideological background and present commitments in terms of the gamma coefficient, shows in a similar fashion that highly achieving faculty (with five or more professional publications in the two years prior to the survey and positions at major universities) differ as markedly by preprofessional political position as do their less eminent and less scholarly productive associates.

The extent to which views formed before entry into academe shape postprofessional opinions cannot be explored in a fully satisfactory manner through our data. The subjective assessment of prior political positions is far too imprecise. Still, there is a strong indication that early political socialization is very important. The consistency of the relationship, controlling for other factors which differentiate academics politically, is impressive.

AGE AND POLITICS

In discussions of the sources of varying political orientations, age is frequently cited as an important contributor. And presumably, in

TABLE 58 Correlations (gammas) between political position as undergraduates and present political orientations of faculty, by religious background, university association, and scholarly achievement

Politics as undergraduates of	Present politics			
	Liberalism-Conservatism Scale	Vietnam position	Political self-characterization	Campus Activism Scale
ALL FACULTY	.47	.33	.62	.34
Faculty of Christian parentage	.42	.27	.59	.31
Faculty of Jewish parentage	.44	.34	.63	.33
Faculty at elite schools	.46	.40	.62	.34
Faculty at middle-tier schools	.46	.33	.63	.34
Faculty at lower-tier schools	.45	.26	.61	.31
Faculty of high achievement*	.45	.39	.59	.31
Faculty of lesser achievement*	.46	.30	.62	.33

*Achievers are those with five or more scholarly publications in the two years prior to the survey and positions at elite universities; the "lesser achievement" category includes all other academics.

SOURCE: 1969 Carnegie Commission Survey of Student and Faculty Opinion.

TABLE 59 *Political positions of social scientists in the 1950s, by age (column percentages)*

Issue	Age strata					"Opinion distance" between the oldest and youngest strata
	60 years and older	50–59	40–49	30–39	Under 30 years	
Percentage agreeing that a social scientist who is an admitted Communist is not fit to be a teacher	70	69	66	55	43	27
Percentage agreeing that an admitted Communist social scientist is a dangerous influence on students	68	62	55	40	37	31
Percentage supporting the firing of an admitted Communist from college teaching	73	65	59	49	40	33
Percentage "restrictive" on Civil Liberties Permissiveness Scale*	43	38	30	23	19	24

*For explanation of construction, see note to Table 29, Chapter 5.
SOURCE: 1955 Lazarsfeld-Thielens survey.

periods of very rapid social change the differences between age cohorts are apt to be accentuated, as the current commentary on a pronounced "generation gap" suggests. Certainly our analysis of academics finds age a powerful factor differentiating political opinions.

The first comprehensive national survey of faculty political opinions, that of social scientists' reactions to academic freedom issues which became salient in the McCarthy era, found striking age-related differences, with the young notably more supportive of job and free speech rights of Communists and other radicals (Lazarsfeld & Thielens, 1958). Table 59 shows that in the "conservative" mid-1950s, the "opinion distance" between the youngest generation (those under 30) and the oldest (60 years and over) ranged between 25 and 30 percentage points on a variety of political questions. Whereas 37 percent of faculty under 30 agreed that an admitted Communist is "too dangerous to be exposed to students," the proportion jumped to 68 percent among those over 60. On a scale combining questions bearing on the academic rights of Communists and other radicals, over two-fifths of the oldest group fell in the "restrictive" or "opposed" category, compared with but 19 percent among the youngest cohort. Age was also strongly associated with voting choice. In 1952, a slight majority (51 percent) of the oldest social scientists voted for Eisenhower, the choice of only 26 percent of their colleagues under 40 years of age. Four years earlier, when 8 percent of social scientists had cast their ballots for left-wing third-party nominees—either Henry Wallace or Norman Thomas—fully 17 percent of those under 30 had backed these minority nominees, as contrasted with 3 percent among those over 60.

The Carnegie survey of the entire present-day professoriate reveals the same age progression. As Table 60 indicates, over half (51 percent) of faculty under 30 years of age scored in the most liberal quintiles of the Liberalism-Conservatism Scale, compared with just a quarter (24 percent) of those 60 and older. "The rise of radical student activism" received the general blessing of 53 percent of professors under 30 years old, 48 percent of those in their thirties, 39 percent of those 40 to 49 years old, 34 percent of faculty in their fifties, and just 29 percent of professors over 60. On all opinion variables, both those involving broad societal questions and those involving matters of purely campus concern, we find a neat progression (more liberal to more conservative) with movement from the youngest to the oldest cohort.

Our smaller survey of academics in 1972 also indicated the continued importance of the age variable. In an atmosphere of heightened ideological polarization between the two major-party candidates, the association between age and vote choice was especially sharp, with the young (under 35) faculty voting overwhelmingly for the Democratic nominee (71 percent) while their older (over 50) colleagues were solidly (58 percent) for Nixon.

INTERACTIVE EFFECT OF AGE AND OTHER VARIABLES

The striking relationship between age and political orientations and behavior must be explored with respect to other factors, particularly intellectual productivity and academic success, which have been found to be linked to political views. In general, increased age permits more success, greater access to research funds, and more opportunities to publish, although it also clearly separates those in a given generation who have "achieved" from those who have not. The evidence from all the extant surveys, including our own, is definite that age on the one hand, and academic success and creativity on the other, are genuinely independent correlates of contrasting political orientations.

In analyzing the relationship between age and opinion, Paul Lazars-

TABLE 60 *Political positions of faculty, by age (column percentages)*

Issue	Age strata					"Opinion distance" between the oldest and youngest strata
	60 years and older	50–59	40–49	30–39	Under 30 years	
Percentage "very liberal" and "liberal," Liberalism-Conservatism Scale	24	30	37	44	51	27
Percentage "left" and "liberal," political self-characterization	36	38	45	49	53	17
Percentage for immediate unilateral withdrawal from Vietnam or phased withdrawal coupled with support for coalition government, 1969	49	53	57	63	65	16
Percentage "strongly supportive" and "moderately supportive," Student Role Scale	30	36	44	49	55	25
Percentage "strongly supportive" and "moderately supportive," Campus Activism Scale	22	27	37	45	50	28
Percentage approving "the rise of radical student activism"	29	34	39	48	53	24

source: 1969 Carnegie Commission Survey of Student and Faculty Opinion.

feld and Wagner Thielens, Jr. (1958, pp. 248–250) found that the trend toward conservatism among the older faculty was greatest in the less prestigious schools, those which placed little or no emphasis on scholarly creativity, while the age gap was least in the "most prominent colleges." Opinion variations associated with age, that is, were lower within the more liberal social environments of elite institutions than in the more conservative lower-tier schools. Presumably, this might be due to environmental stimuli. The more liberal the general climate of opinion within which a person lives and works, the less likely it is that he will become more conservative as he grows older. Having a position at a major university should mean a greater chance of receiving liberal political stimuli from friends and associates.

The Lazarsfeld-Thielens finding is intriguing, but is *not* confirmed by analysis of the more extensive Carnegie data. Support for liberal programs and causes declines as much, if not more, with increasing age in liberal as in conservative academic environments. For example, Table 61 shows 35 percentage points separating the oldest and youngest cohorts (proportion in the most liberal quintiles of the Liberalism-Conservatism Scale) at elite colleges and universities, as against just 23 points between these cohorts at schools of the lowest scholarly standing.

What Table 61 suggests is reinforced by all our survey findings: age and such measures of academic standing and intellectuality as type of school in which the faculty member teaches and his participation (or nonparticipation) in research activity exert powerful and quite independent effects on political orientations. The most highly achieving are the most liberal, in each age cohort. And within each category of aca-

TABLE 61 **The effects of age on political opinion of faculty, by quality of school (all figures are percentage "very liberal" and "liberal," Liberalism-Conservatism Scale)**

	Age strata					"Opinion distance" between the oldest and youngest strata
Quality of school	60 years and older	50–59	40–49	30–39	Under 30 years	
1 (Elite)	35	45	52	62	70	35
2	27	30	40	46	52	25
3	19	27	30	38	46	27
4 (Lowest tier)	17	22	28	34	40	23

SOURCE: 1969 Carnegie Commission Survey of Student and Faculty Opinion.

demic attainment, the youngest faculty stand to the left of the oldest by decisive, and on the whole remarkably consistent, margins. The factors associated with age which make the older more conservative than the younger operate as strongly in liberal environments as in those which are relatively conservative. Older faculty in liberal climes such as major universities may well find their liberalism somewhat reinforced by environmental stimuli, *but relative to the milieu in which they move,* they are at least as much more conservative than younger colleagues as are their age counterparts in lesser academic institutions.

We find striking the uniformity of age-related variations in political opinion across different issue areas. Protests and demands for a bigger student voice in university decisions present issues on which younger faculty appear closer to the interests and perspectives of the initiators of change than are their senior colleagues. But the amount of opinion distance between young and old faculty on these questions is not appreciably greater than on broad societal disputes.

POLITICAL GENERATIONS AND AGING

The finding that there is a consistent relation between advanced age and more conservative views within academe bears on a topic which has been discussed since the time of the ancient Greeks—whether age differences are a consequence of the effects of aging itself or a function of the contrasting experiences of political generations.[6] Before turning to an examination of relevant data, it would seem appropriate to discuss the issues involved.

Analysis of "political generations" came to the fore in the 1930s in the work of such scholars as Karl Mannheim, Sigmund Neumann, and Rudolf Heberle.[7] They contended that individuals gain a frame of reference from the decisive events of the period when they first come to political consciousness—usually in their late teens or early twenties—which then shapes their subsequent values and actions. Thus the prevailing climate in which a cohort "comes of age politically" tends to frame its later political orientation.

Of course, those who speak of generations do not suggest that all or most people in the same age category react identically to key political events. Mannheim wrote of "generation-units," different groups

[6]Crittenden has informatively discussed this confusion (1962, p. 648).

[7]See Mannheim (1936, p. 270; 1952, pp. 276–322); Neumann (1939, pp. 623–628; 1942, pp. 234–244); Heberle (1951, pp. 118–127); Mentré (1920); Behrendt (1932, pp. 290–309); Ortega y Gasset (1958, pp. 50–84); Bettelheim (1963, pp. 64–92); and Eisenstadt (1956).

within the same age stratum who adhere to alternative, often conflict-ing, values. And more recently Bennett Berger (1971, p. 29) noted that "it is essential, when using the concept of the generation in a cultural sense, to specify generations of what, because it is only in a demogra-phic sense that people in the same age-group constitute a homogeneous unit." Obviously, the rich and the poor youth, factory workers and college students, blacks and whites do not experience events in the same way. But the general point holds that, whatever the specific gener-ational unit, early political values presumably persist through the years.[8] The "generation thesis" would lead us to expect age cohorts among faculty to differ in their politics in some measure, then, by the experiences of their formative student years. We would look for those who came of age politically in periods of liberal or radical politics, like the Depression decade, to reflect a more liberal-left and critical politics than those who were students in the conservative, "silent" 1950s. More generally, the opinions of the age strata should show irregularly dis-persed peaks and valleys associated with the political climate prevailing during their late teens.

The argument about the effects of aging has led to quite different conclusions. For both social and psychological reasons, it has been claimed, individuals, as they grow older, tend to move from the political extremes to a more "moderate" or centrist position. Those actions defined by society as "deviant"—for example, delinquent, bohemian, and radical—are largely youth phenomena (Matza, 1961, p. 106). Parties of the extreme left and right almost invariably draw disproportionate support from young voters. As they advance in age, the overwhelming majority of "deviants" will "settle down." They get "stakes in the sys-tem." This has meant that young people, as they grow older, tend to move toward the political center as it is defined at the time of their ma-ture years.

The moderating influence of aging has been stressed in a number of studies, but no one, perhaps, has made the argument as cogently as Aristotle in his *Rhetorica* (1941, pp. 1403–1406):

Young men have strong passions, and tend to gratify them indiscriminately....
They are hot tempered and quick tempered ... owing to their love of honor they cannot bear being slighted, and are indignant if they imagine themselves un-fairly treated.... They love ... money ... very little, not having yet learnt what it means to be without it.... They have exalted notions, because they have not

---

[8]Since people remain within many of the politically relevant social environments, such as religion or race, a "reinforcement" process is undoubtedly at work.

yet been humbled by life or learnt its necessary limitations.... They would rather do noble deeds than useful ones: their lives are regulated more by moral feeling than by reasoning.... They think they know everything and are always quite sure about it; this, in fact, is why they overdo everything.

The elderly, however, are characterized by quite opposite qualities:

They have lived many years; they have often been taken in, and often made mistakes; and life on the whole is a bad business. The result is that they are sure about nothing and *under-do* everything. They "think" but they never "know"; and perhaps because of their hesitation they always add a "possibly" or a "perhaps...." Further, their experience makes them distrustful and therefore suspicious of evil.... They guide their lives too much by considerations of what is useful and too little by what is noble—for the useful is what is good for oneself and the noble what is good absolutely.... They lack confidence in the future; partly through experience—for most things go wrong, or anyway worse than one expects.

As a middle-aged man, Aristotle saw virtue resting in the middle, "between that of the young and that of the old, free from the extremes of either." And these moderate views are held by "men in their prime," a period which occurs intellectually at age 49.

Max Weber reiterated an aspect of Aristotle's analysis when he suggested that the young are more disposed to adhere to the "ethic of ultimate ends," the older to the "ethic of responsibility." That is, the latter seek to accomplish what limited good is practically possible, even though to do so may mean to compromise with evil, while youth seek to protect their sense of virtue by refusing to compromise (Weber, 1946, pp. 120–128).

Neither the "generations" nor the "aging" thesis should provide a complete or fully satisfactory guide. And, of course, the two are not mutually exclusive: There could be both persistence of distinctive generational orientation and a moderating of views with age, for the general historical shift of political climate in the United States must be taken into account. The question remains as to the relative importance of these two contrasting processes to the politics of academics.

Table 62 shows the distribution of opinion of faculty in the 1955 Lazarsfeld-Thielens survey, by age cohorts expressed in terms of the years of college attendance. Our reanalysis of the data indicates a *steady* increase in conservatism with movement from the youngest to the oldest strata. Thus, the percentage of social scientists voting for Henry Wallace or one of the other left-wing candidates in 1948 (mainly Norman Thomas) was considerably higher among those who were in

TABLE 62 Political positions of social scientists, by years in which they were undergraduates (percentages of n)

Years in college as undergraduates	1948 vote				Civil Liberties Permissiveness Scale, percentage highly and moderately libertarian	Belonged to a controversial political group*
	Dewey	Truman	Wallace and other "left" candidates	Thurmond		
1944–1949 (n = 202)	25	59	17	—	55	30
1933–1943 (n = 936)	22	66	12	—	51	35
1923–1932 (n = 632)	25	69	6	—	41	29
1913–1922 (n = 465)	38	56	4	2	33	25
1912 and earlier (n = 202)	41	54	3	1	25	26
ALL COLLEGE-AGE COHORTS (n = 2,437)	23	63	8	—	43	30

*The question asked was: "Have you ever been a member of a political group which advocated a program or a cause which has been unpopular or controversial, or haven't you been a member of any such group?"

SOURCE: 1955, Lazarsfeld-Thielens survey.

TABLE 63 *Political positions of faculty, by years in which they were undergraduates (percentages of n)*

Years in college as undergraduates	Percentage "left" as undergraduates*	Percentage "left" today†	Percentage for immediate Vietnam withdrawal‡
During or before the early 1920s (n = 1,351)	2	1	9
1922–1926 (n = 2,932)	4	1	14
1927–1931 (n = 3,839)	4	2	15
1932–1936 (n = 5,431)	5	2	17
1937–1941 (n = 7,492)	6	3	17
1942–1948 (n = 8,503)	5	4	18
1947–1951 (n = 10,019)	4	5	18
1952–1956 (n = 10,503)	4	7	19
1957–1963 (n = 8,590)	4	9	24
ALL COLLEGE-AGE COHORTS (n = 58,660)	4	5	18

*Q: "What were your politics as a college senior?"
†Q: "How would you characterize yourself politically at this time?"
‡Q: "Which of these positions on Vietnam is closest to your own?"
SOURCE: 1969 Carnegie Commission Survey of Student and Faculty Opinion.

college between 1944 and 1948 than among the "generation of the 1930s," and there is a steady decline as one moves back through earlier college generations. The same pattern holds with respect to support for Stevenson against Eisenhower in the 1950s. Similarly, support for the rights of Communists and other unpopular minorities in the university during the (Joe) McCarthy era was greatest among the youngest, the postwar cohort who went to college in a supposedly apolitical period. Such support grew progressively weaker among each preceding cohort. This general relationship holds true even though those who were undergraduates in the 1930s reported having belonged to a greater

Percentage "very supportive" and "supportive," Campus Activism Scale	Percentage favoring Humphrey over McCarthy, 1968 Democratic Convention
16	64
21	57
25	57
30	55
34	53
39	50
43	47
48	39
51	32
39	47

number of "controversial political groups" while in college than those educated in subsequent decades. A larger proportion of faculty who were undergraduates in the 1930s had belonged to "controversial groups," but present political views followed a straight age progression.

The Carnegie survey of the entire present-day professoriate reveals the same age progression for the faculty as a whole. Those who were in college in the Depression and immediate post-Depression years report having been somewhat more "left" in their student days than any other college-age cohort, earlier or later (Table 63). But the proportion of those who attended college in the "conservative" atmosphere of the "silent" 1950s and who describe their *current* political orientation as "left" is roughly three or four times (7 to 9 percent) that among those who had completed their undergraduate studies in the "radical" climate of the 1930s (2 percent). Similarly the college generation of the 1930s was much less supportive of recent campus political activism than the generation of the 1950s, showed a markedly greater preference for Hubert Humphrey over Eugene McCarthy in their contest for the 1968 Democratic presidential nomination, and were less strongly opposed to American policies in Vietnam. The same pattern, support for a liberal-left and critical position increasing steadily as age decreases, holds for the entire professoriate just as it does for faculty in social science (Table 61).

Tables 62 and 63 provide strong preliminary testimony to the importance of age as a differentiating variable. Since the relationship shown involves *an essentially linear, age-related progression,* with none of those irregularly dispersed peaks and values which the "generations" thesis, if applicable, would produce, we may conclude that the decisive considerations are those social and psychological concomitants of growing older.[9]

The future views of today's faculty will, of course, reflect larger movements in American political culture, and aging will not necessarily be accompanied by "conservatizing" in any *fixed ideological sense* of the term. A variety of evidence drawn from national polls indicates that public opinion has generally moved to the left from the 1930s to the 1970s. Richard Nixon supported policies with respect to welfare, Keynesian economics, and state payment for medical care that Republicans denounced as outright socialism during the 1930s. Support for minority rights has grown steadily among the population. In a 1974 address to the influential Business Council, Paul McCracken, member of President Eisenhower's Council of Economic Advisers (1956–1959), chairman of the same body under President Nixon (1969–1972), and currently adviser to President Ford, points to the need for businessmen and conservatives to accept major aspects of the new emphasis on "equality of results." As he notes: "There is much in the new doctrine of equality of results that is solid. Equality of opportunity does turn out to be far more complex to implement than had been assumed, and there is some similarity between it and hereditary privilege" (Mc-

---

[9]We have discussed these matters for college cohorts in the society at large elsewhere (Lipset & Ladd, 1972*b*, pp. 63–84).

Cracken, 1974, p. 7). These arguments of a leading Republican economist reiterate a point of view found only among the socialist left just a
few years ago. Hence, even though older faculty may be much more
conservative *relative* to younger ones at any given present or future
time, they also may be more liberal in an *absolute* sense than when
they finished their student days. But whatever the political climate in
1980, those who entered the professoriate in the 1960s will be *relatively*
less receptive to the change-directed thrusts of future time than they
were at the start of their careers, and in that sense more moderate or
conservative than new cohorts of young academics.

AGE AND POLITICS IN ACADEME: THE IMPENDING PATTERN

Our findings that older cohorts in academe became more "moderate" or
"conservative," compared with an earlier position closer to the liberal
extreme, have an important relevance for an evaluation of the future political role of the American professoriate, as well as for the prospects for
educational innovation. The age structure within higher education is in
the process of moving consistently upward from a very low median
level of under 40 reached during the 1960s. As a result of the enormous
expansion which occurred in the last decade, the majority of those now
teaching entered the profession during the late fifties and the sixties.
This has meant that the young academics with their liberal views have
formed the majority of the faculty during the period of politicization of
the late sixties. As the following chapter will document, the frequent
votes of support for student activism which occurred in faculty meetings around the country often reflected the sentiments of the younger
academics. But the "golden age" of expansion is over, because of a
sharp decline in both the rate of increase in attendance at college and
financial support. The number of vacancies for new faculty will be
quite small between now and 1990. As a result, Allan Cartter (1972, p.
85), who has devoted considerable energy to analyzing the implications of these changes, suggests the median age, which was 39 in 1970,
"will rise to 42 by 1980 and may increase to 48 by 1990." As he points
out: "The dramatic change between today and 1990, under current
trends, would be the virtual disappearance of the under-35 age group
from the teaching ranks." Although assorted efforts to create vacancies, such as measures to encourage earlier retirement, will probably
avoid such a drastic outcome, there can be little doubt that faculty
opinion will increasingly represent the views of an aging population.
And as we have seen, this will probably mean *relatively* more conser-

vative sentiments than those held by the comparatively small proportion of young academics.

DIVISIONS IN FACULTY OPINION: SOME CONCLUSIONS IN OVERVIEW

We have noted that academics are entirely unlike mass publics in that they show a remarkable consistency of ideas across a wide range of issues. Dealing with ideas is their business, and maintaining consistency among them is their special skill. If we accept the notion that ideology can be described in terms of a high level of *constraint* among a range of issues, then academics can be seen as occupying a particularly ideological subculture in American life. This helps explain, of course, why we obtain such strong and consistent relationships between various characteristics of our respondents and their political opinions. Even so, the consistent interactive effects we encounter—for example, the effects of age, background, and intellectuality upon political opinions—are striking. Each cohort is more liberal than those its senior in age. Within the several cohorts, faculty of higher intellectual attainment are to the left of colleagues of lesser achievement. Within each group defined by age and intellectuality, those who remember their college politics as left or liberal give more support to liberal policies currently. Finally, Jews are more liberal than Gentiles, controlling for age, intellectual achievement, and political views prior to entering academic life.

We find, for example, that 48 percent of faculty under 35 years of age score in the two most liberal quintiles of the Liberalism-Conservatism Scale, as against 39 percent of the 35 to 49 stratum and 28 percent over 50. Among academics under 35, 65 percent at schools classified as elite (by the Index of School Quality) are recorded in these liberal quintiles. Of the young elite-school faculty whose politics as students were left-of-center, 81 percent are found in the most liberal categories of the Liberalism-Conservatism measure. Lastly, 86 percent of young, major university, liberal-background Jewish faculty are classified as "very liberal" or "liberal" by the scale we have been using—a status occupied by just 40 percent of the entire professoriate.

Table 64 carries this illustration further, showing the cumulative impact in terms of opinion differentiation of age, religious and ideological background, and intellectuality among American academics. The range between young, achieving Jews of liberal preprofessional politics and faculty of Gentile parentage, over 50 years of age, teaching at lesser schools, who brought a centrist to conservative orientation with them

TABLE 64 *The effects of age, religious and ideological background, and intellectuality upon opinion; figures are the percentages "very liberal" and "liberal" on the Liberalism-Conservatism Scale for, respectively, faculty over 50, 35 to 49, and under 35*

Ideological background	Major colleges and universities		All other colleges and universities	
	Jews	*Gentiles*	*Jews*	*Gentiles*
Left and liberal	65/76/86	59/71/79	60/72/83	44/53/61
Middle-of-the-road and conservative	46/53/60	24/35/51	31/39/52	14/23/32

SOURCE: 1969 Carnegie Commission Survey of Student and Faculty Opinion.

when they entered the professoriate—from 86 to 14 percent in the two most liberal quintiles of the Liberalism-Conservatism Scale—is extraordinarily large. It represents a magnitude of opinion difference we might at first brush expect to encounter among sharply polarized groups, such as blacks and whites, in the larger society, but not among fellow professionals in a related cluster of fields in one distinctive type of institution. Upon reflection, we recognize that sharp ideological differentiation has as a prior condition *the existence* of ideological constructions, and that the political thinking of academics is exceptionally ideological. Groups in the general society sufficiently at odds over a fundamental issue can, of course, be polarized on a series of specific questions and controversies which relate to that basic issue.[10] What we see among faculty, however, is not a deep conflict bred of vastly different stakes in the resolution of a major social problem, but rather the appearance of a multitude of distinctions following from an intensely ideological construction. Men of ideas develop interests in their ideologies, and the ideologies, beyond the interests and cognitions which nourish them, become sources of division. In this sense, ideological thinking produces "artificial" conflict. When you see politics ideologically, you become aware of distinctions most people do not attend to seriously.

[10]Philip Converse has discussed this in "The Nature of Belief Systems in Mass Publics" (1964, pp. 216–217). He pointed out that a large segment of the population approach politics with a "group interest" frame of reference. When people in this group "have been properly advised on where their own group interests lie, they are relatively likely to follow such advice. [But] unless an issue directly concerns their grouping in an obviously rewarding or punishing way . . . they lack the contextual grasp of the system to recognize how they should respond to it. . . ."

Part Three
Issues of Campus Politics:
From the 1960s to the 1970s

8. Issues of the 1960s: The Era of Campus Protests

The relatively strong commitment of college faculty to a politics shaped by liberal and egalitarian values, and receptivity to change, does not end with movement inward from the larger society to the campus. As we noted in Chapters 1 and 2, there has been a strong interrelation between positions on national and intramural issues; and the generally greater liberalism of academics—compared with most other subgroups in the population—is manifest in a higher measure of support for student protests and related aspects of an activist and change-diverted campus politics within the faculty than among the American public. This is an important part of the story of professorial reactions during the "era of campus protests." It is, however, only a part. The intramural response to university political activism of the late 1960s reflected the broad ideological predispositions of faculty and, at the same time, raised a bundle of other issues and concerns which produced a deep division among them that is far more complex than a neat "liberals vs. conservatives" dichotomy would suggest.

The student protests of the latter half of the 1960s drew from much of the professoriate a reaction which can only be described as ambivalent. A small minority, to be sure, were unequivocally supportive. In the Carnegie sample, 3 percent of the faculty said they "unreservedly approved of the emergence of radical student activism." A somewhat larger minority, 16 percent, "unreservedly disapproved" of the protests and demonstrations. But most of the faculty wrestled with at least contradictory reactions: 40 percent indicated that they "approved with reservations," while virtually the same proportion (42 percent) "disapproved with reservations."

The sources of this ambivalence are not hard to uncover. Many faculty members shared the concerns and objectives of the protesting students with regard to the need for changes in American society and in government policy. And specifically, a large majority disagreed with United

States policies in Vietnam. Still other professors who disagreed with the general objectives of student activists in national affairs were committed to the type of university in which dissent and criticism are freely expressed. At the same time, many academics found in the more extreme forms of student protests a threat to the relatively great autonomy the university has enjoyed, and to the atmosphere of free and open inquiry on which scholarship depends. Besides this, some of the challenges of the campus protesters were directed at academic procedures and privileges which many professors clearly value.

One way in which the faculty expressed its ambivalence about campus activism involved making an operational distinction between *demonstrations* and *disruption*. Thus, 70 percent disagreed with the proposition that "student demonstrations have no place on a college campus." Among those faculty members whose institutions had experienced recent demonstrations, 65 percent said they approved of the *aims* of the protesting students. But the faculty took a generally hard line on campus disruptions; 80 percent agreed that "students who disrupt the functioning of a college should be expelled or suspended," a proportion similar to that willing to *allow* student *demonstrations* on campus.

Whenever there was a suggestion of serious disruption of academic life, there was a marked lessening of faculty support. Thus, 63 percent endorsed the aims of the students in the Columbia revolt of 1968, but only 5 percent endorsed their methods as well. Disruptions by militant students were declared a threat to academic freedom by 83 percent of the faculty.

Such responses are subject to quite opposite evaluations. It is possible to conclude that academics strongly defended peaceful dissent on campus while they vigorously opposed acts which stop the university from going about its educational activity in a free and open way. On the other hand, one could conclude that a majority wanted to give verbal endorsement to vague "objectives," but became uneasy in the presence of acts which might upset their comfortable existence in the academy. Such judgments we leave to the reader. In this chapter, we propose to explore how the issues raised by the campus activism of the sixties affected the proverbial liberal reactions of the faculty.

THE DIVIDED PROFESSORIATE

As activism spread across the American campus from the Berkeley revolt of 1964 through the myriad sit-ins and other protests—marked particularly by the occupation of university buildings, followed by a calling in of the police and then a general student strike, as at Columbia in 1968 and Harvard in 1969—faculties met in recurrent, almost constant sessions, passed resolutions condemning use of the police, but also invariably condemned and sought to punish the most militant student radicals. Most descriptions of faculty reactions on specific campuses heavily affected by student activism have properly pointed to the tremendous divisions within the faculty, to the fact that only a part appeared sympathetic to the student demands or sought to protect protesting students from civil or university sanctions. Martin Trow (1968, p. 15), in discussing the role of faculty at Berkeley during the first four years of turmoil on that campus (1964–1968), emphasized this division:

> The faculty, during all this, has been rather sharply split along a number of lines. Some have quite consistently supported student demands and positions, some have done so with qualifications, others have supported the administration, while the great majority have tried to get on with their own work, returning to the political arena only at moments of great crisis, when ordinary work on campus was clearly disrupted; and when they did so, they tended to search for some reasonable compromise, some kind of broad consensus that would resolve the immediate conflict, allow the campus to "return to normal" and themselves to return to their unfinished manuscripts and experiments.
>
> ...[T]he faculty has uneasily and without enthusiasm continued from time to time to intervene in student affairs, while at the same time refusing to take a major role in day-to-day administration. It has thus allowed the students to see it as a part-time (and not wholly trustworthy) ally against the administration, encouraging actions designed to strengthen the alliance forged and reforged in moments of crisis.
>
> But while the faculty as a whole has by no means been hostile to the administration during this period, its support has been qualified and erratic. It has thus eroded the authority of the administration, whom it has in a sense been able to heckle and second guess between votes of confidence, even while it has disappointed the hopes of the activist students.

On almost every campus which faced a major crisis, the faculty split, sometimes formally, into two or three major factions or faculty political parties. At Berkeley, Columbia, Cornell, Harvard, and San Francisco State, to cite a few cases, these groups usually operated with elected executive committees, prepared strategies for dealing with faculty committees, and the like. The parties have been described as right, center, and left—hard, compromise-inclined, and soft—hawks, temporizers, and doves. In many schools, although three basic positions may be perceived, a two-party system emerged, with the leadership of each party tending to be chosen from the more moderate members, thus facilitating compromise and cooperation. Although the groups differed sharply in their fixing of responsibility for the campus crisis (the "hards" blamed the student activists, the "softs" held responsible the uncompromising stance of the administration), both groups as a whole sought a return to campus peace. Thus, the hards tended to become a vehicle for faculty communication with and pressure on the administration and trustees, while the softs tended to act as an intermediary with the radical students. From time to time, inevitably, these roles led critics from one party to see the other as a tool or stimulator of radical student or rigid administration policies.

A report on the conflict at Cornell during 1968–69 described the different ways in which the two main groupings of faculty saw that situation ("Cornell University Survey . . . ," 1969, p. 43):

The Concerned Faculty ("liberal leanings") are more likely to:

justify more disruptive forms of protest

be more approving of the Black Studies Program, and to believe in more autonomy for it

stress more the importance of social reform in education (while also insisting strongly on intellectual experience)

de-emphasize faculty rights in reference to academic freedom

and stress more a revision of the judicial system (including a multiple judicial procedure, which recognizes the special nature of dissent problems)

On the other hand, the "conservative" groupings . . . characteristically held attitudes which:

stress a lesser degree of autonomy in the Black Studies Program

stress the importance of career skills in education (while also insisting strongly on intellectual experience, as do the *Concerned Faculty*)

are more convinced that academic freedom is actually being threatened

are more disapproving of the Constituent Assembly [i.e., student participation in university governance]

are more strongly against change in the judicial system (except that the Administration should take a stronger hand); and insist more strongly on a single judicial system, be the problem one of individual misbehavior or politically initiated group dissent

The general pattern has been denoted by John Spiegel, whose Lemberg Center for the Study of Violence was engaged in analyses of various campus conflicts. He described three prime faculty positions as follows:

1) a desire to support the goals of the aggrieved students while minimizing any loss of face to the institution for what may be interpreted as surrender. This position is usually called the "soft line" advocated by the "doves"; 2) a desire to defeat and punish the students while minimizing any loss of face to the institution for what may be interpreted as callousness or cruelty. This policy is the "hard line" pursued by the hawks; 3) a middle ground, or temporizing position, which attempts to placate both the hawks and the doves, in part, while also partially satisfying the demands of the students—a balancing act which requires great skill, diplomacy, flexibility and inventiveness, plus some Machiavellian sleights of hand.

   ... the hawks can scarcely conceal their contempt for the doves—those "bleeding hearts," those "masochists" who, perhaps unconsciously, are out to wreck the university. On their side, the doves show a mild but persistent abhorrence of the wrath, and in their eyes, "sadism" of the hawks. Privately, they tend to believe, for the moment at least, that most of the hawks are paranoid personalities.

   ... The "temporizers" had been impressed by the amount of movement shown by the school prior to the outbreak of the initial disorder. They had shared, vicariously or actually, the "liberalization" of American life in recent decades. ... Accordingly, they feel offended by the ingratitude of the aggrieved students, who, in their perception, are "biting the hand that feeds them" (Spiegel, 1971, pp. 376–379).

These descriptions of factional division among professors ignore the dynamics of faculty opinion and roles during the intramural crises. Most participants and observers of major campus confrontations noted two types of changes among both faculty and students: initial radicalization, particularly after the police were called in, and a subsequent, much slower, process of disillusionment with the activists. The latter involved increased support for effective administrative measures to restore a normal state of teaching and research to a campus bedeviled by recurrent radical demands, confrontations, heated controversies, and frequent faculty meetings.

In the beginning stage of campus protest, nonpolitical and even conservative faculty often joined in the various meetings of ad hoc groups called to mediate the situation and prevent the police from being called in. Many professors and nonactivist students were initially inclined to consider the demands of the activists—involving campus political rules, outside recruiters, ROTC, community housing policy, and the like—at their face value. That is, many persons who were not involved in the protests assumed quite naturally that the only matter at issue was the one raised by the demonstrators. And the liberals among the university population more often than not concluded that the protesters had a good point, that the policies they were objecting to were wrong or that the reform they demanded would probably be a good thing. Consequently, they agreed that the university ought to negotiate, compromise if possible, give in if necessary. Since their major objection was to the tactics, not seemingly to the demands, they found it difficult to uphold strong action against the demonstrators. Others objected to repressive tactics, even against law violators, because they perceived the conflict as one between students (weak and politically inexperienced) and administrators (powerful and politically sophisticated). They, too, saw the situation as calling for compromise on the part of the university. Hence when the university or public authority sent in the police, much of the community was morally outraged. Many were "radicalized"—in the sense of accepting the view of the situation held by the more radical students—believing that they were the victims of the university's collaboration with reactionary social forces.

In this first stage, typically, the left faction among the faculty gained heavily. Many joined it who might have been expected to take a more conservative stance. Even those who felt that the protesters represented a dangerous, politically astute, radical grouping which had been able to outmaneuver a politically unsophisticated administration lacking experience in dealing with militants found it difficult to endorse the tactics of the administration. This group also included faculty who felt that the administration, by mishandling the situation, had lost its legitimacy—that part of its claim to authority which rested on the prestige, the personal reputation for competence, of a particular president, chancellor, provost, or dean. As a result, many academics who were sharply critical of the activists did not seek to defend the incumbent "regime," or if they did, because of personal loyalty or a desire to uphold authority, often failed to respond enthusiastically or effectively. The upshot of such a series of events, frequently, was the overthrow of the administration through the "resignation" of its most prominent officer(s).

The next stage usually involved a revival of conservative or moderate strength. One component of this comprised the intervention of senior faculty who had been consistently liberal in national politics through campus factions generally deemed conservative. This change occurred in part as a reaction to a continued state of disorder on campus. The student radicals had been both greatly strengthened and exhilarated by a sense of influence. Many then sought new issues around which they could organize new protest demands. These assumed a variety of forms, including efforts to revamp the internal operation of the school. And some of the more extreme elements among the students often initiated what appeared as provocative and disruptive activities, such as filthy speech campaigns, disruption of classes, and raids on the library or faculty club. As a result, many faculty who thought the settlement of the initial major confrontation, often through almost total acceptance of the demonstrators' demands, would end the period of disorder were brought to a position of support for more conservative policies and turned against the student movement and the faculty left. Thus, at Berkeley, the more conservative faculty faction began to win faculty elections after a relatively short period. At Columbia, close to 800 professors signed a public statement demanding that the administration bring more order to the campus during 1969–70, the years after the massive sit-ins. At San Francisco State, the moderate-conservative faction won the elections to the faculty executive committee after a year of police on campus and faculty and student strikes. Immediately following the sit-in, police action, and student strike at Harvard in the spring of 1969, the left or liberal caucus dominated faculty meetings and was able to elect a substantial majority among the professorial membership of the first committee chosen to deal with the crisis. In all subsequent elections to a newly created Faculty Council, established through pressure from the left group, the conservative or moderate caucus was able to win decisively down through 1974.[1]

Changes of the magnitude suggested by these events cannot be explained by any simple cross-sectional analysis of the sources of diversity in faculty attitudes as presented in opinion surveys. The survey vehicle provides only a static, time-bound examination. Specific events, the tactics followed by administrators or activist demonstrators, and the sophistication of the faculty leaders who rose to the forefront of the different groupings produced sharply different patterns of response. The "Chicago plan"—not calling the police, waiting out the demonstrators, and then enforcing university sanctions after order is restored—was effective on two separate occasions, in 1966 and again in 1969, in preventing the weakening of administrative authority

---

[1] Faculty caucuses had stopped meeting at Harvard by 1972, but their "former" steering committees continued to play a role, lobbying on questions of who should be appointed to key administrative posts and informally arranging competitive slates for Faculty Council elections (Lipset, 1975, Ch. 8).

and community radicalization at the University of Chicago. At San Francisco State and Cornell, John Summerskill and James Perkins, liberal presidents who sought to handle the crises by constantly negotiating, by repeatedly compromising with activist demands, found their campus support declining because those tactics did not prevent increased pressure and recurrent crises. They were both forced to resign. At Cornell, very liberal administrative policies eventually resulted in a more "conservatized" faculty who felt that academic freedom was being undermined by concessions to student agitators.

Clearly, our understanding of faculty reaction to the "crises of politicization" of the 1960s would have been advanced by panel studies (repeat interviews with the same people) or by a number of surveys conducted at the same institution to evaluate reactions to the flow of events. Such data are not available.

POLITICAL IDEOLOGY AND CAMPUS RESPONSE

The general ideological predispositions which faculty bring to campus issues and political crises have been major determinants of the way they have responded to these issues, both in specific universities and nationally (Chapter 2). But, as we have noted, intramural faculty conflicts over activism have not been simple, unambiguous left-right conflicts. In almost every well-known controversy, some prominent faculty liberals strongly opposed confrontationist tactics as destructive of the basic conditions for scholarship, as reducing academic freedom within the university. Conversely, some men of conservative values sharply opposed the policies of the administration in using force against student demonstrators on the grounds that administration and faculty, as the adult members of the university, had a greater moral obligation than students to restrain their use of sheer power; that in the given situation, they should have negotiated much longer than they did or have been willing to change outmoded policies, even under duress.

It is in this area of response to student activism that the extramural division of liberals and conservatives, radicals and reactionaries, partially broke down. The thrust of student activism in the 1960s contained a curious mixture of the external and the internal, of criticism of national policies and of the role of the university. Militant student activism was associated with sharp criticisms of the research culture of the university. Many activists who put political reform as primary saw the commitment of scholars to research and publication as self-serving careerism, leading those so engaged away from political involvement and away from devoting time to undergraduate education. For the activist, the university is or should be a "house of politics"; for the dedicated scholar, regardless of ideology, it is basically a "house of study." Thus the demands of the militants that faculty change their past style of occupational life became, in practice, insistence that professors abandon a portion of their academic life which many continued to value highly.

The politicization of academe also involved—indeed, continues to contain—demands that the university system give up its emphasis on meritocracy, on the judgment of both students and faculty according to canons of scholarship defined by practitioners in a given field. Intellectualdom, as we have seen, has stressed evidence of creativity as a basis for reward. Hence, the insistence of various activists that in appointments to the university the faculty and administration should respond positively to political considerations—that is, appoint more "radicals" or more members of groups which have been underrepresented on the faculty, such as blacks, women, and some other ethnic minorities—forms an explicit challenge to the historic emphasis on competitive merit.

The proposals for increasing "student power," providing student representation directly in the governance of the university, up to and including the appointment of faculty, also have constituted a challenge to the traditional assumption of intellectuals that they, rather than their patrons, employers, or customers, must be the arbiters of what is important in their area of work or inquiry. Particularly in major schools, few academics now question the right of students to influence their living environments, as in rules governing dormitory living and relations with other students. Many professors, however, not only oppose student participation in the choice of faculty, but also insist that curriculum decisions must remain primarily a professorial function, on the grounds that only those who are themselves fully engaged in a given field can understand what kinds of abilities and knowledge prospective new members must have.

Such issues most concern faculty at leading institutions which are both schools and research institutes. Insofar as a college or university places an emphasis on research, on creativity, it puts itself at odds with those who would seek to reform it by democratic methods of governance which give the less competent equal rights with the more highly trained, or which denigrate the emphasis on meritocracy.

These considerations point up factors that reduce the correlation between liberal social views generally and support for the demands of left-oriented students within the university. As we have seen, liberal-to-left social views and activity are associated with indicators of academic creativity and achievement. Faculty who publish more, who have research grants, who are at universities which are also great research institutes, who belong to groups which place a premium on intellectual accomplishment, such as the Jews, tend to be among the more liberal or left within academe. And a sizable portion of the scholarly, liberal faculty has been hostile to the student left's call for a downgrading of the research function.[2] Some left-of-center faculty have endorsed both the external and internal demands of the student activists, but many others, while supporting the former, have been troubled by part of the pressure for intramural change.

Only 3 percent of all the faculty in the Carnegie survey said they "unreservedly approve" the emergence of radical student activism, while just 7 percent of the liberal-left professors (here located by political self-description) gave complete endorsement. But the latter were abruptly separated from their more conservative colleagues by their willingness to give an ambivalent endorsement—"approve with reservations" in the language of the questionnaire (Table 65). The faculty liberals were attracted yet troubled. The extent of their malaise is revealed by their response to two additional items on student activism (Table 66). About six liberals in ten were sufficiently disturbed over implications of campus activism to favor the suspension of students disrupting the regular operations of the university, and seven in ten to declare such activity a threat to academic freedom.

Many left-of-center academics gave at best half-hearted support to student activism because they found in it a threat to the independence

TABLE 65 *Position on student activism of faculty, by political self-description (percentages of n)*

	*Response to student activism**		
	Unreservedly approve	*Approve with reservations*	*Disapprove*
All faculty (n = 60,028)	3	40	57
Liberal-left faculty† (n = 27,744)	6	64	30
Conservative faculty† (n = 13,938)	1	12	88

*The question was: "What do you think of the emergence of radical student activism in recent years?"
†The question was: "How would you characterize yourself politically at the present time (Left, liberal, middle-of-the-road, moderately conservative, strongly conservative)?"
SOURCE: 1969 Carnegie Commission Survey of Student and Faculty Opinion.

[2]For further discussion of this subject, see Lipset (1972b, pp. 197–235).

TABLE 66   *Response of liberal-left faculty to student protesters*

	Agree	*Disagree*
"Students who disrupt the functioning of a college should be expelled or suspended."	64	36
"Campus disruptions by militant students are a threat to academic freedom."	72	28

SOURCE: 1969 Carnegie Commission Survey of Student and Faculty Opinion.

and atmosphere of open inquiry necessary to nurture the various strains of the scholarly pursuit. The radical philosopher Robert Wolff points out in *The Ideal of the University* (1969, p. 75) that the myth of the "apolitical" university, though a myth, serves to protect such unpopular minorities as political radicals:

[T]he politicization of the university invites . . . the ever-present threat of pressure, censorship and witch-hunting by conservative forces in the society at large. The universities at present are sanctuaries for social critics who would find it very hard to gain a living elsewhere in society. Who but a university these days would hire Herbert Marcuse, Eugene Genovese, or Barrington Moore, Jr.? Where else are anarchists, socialists and followers of other unpopular persuasions accorded titles, honors, and the absolute security of academic tenure? Let the university once declare that it is a political actor, and its faculty will be investigated. . . . It is a bitter pill for the radicals to swallow, but the fact is that they benefit more than any other segment of the university from the fiction of institutional neutrality.

And Barrington Moore, Jr., one of the most radical American sociologists, has defended the open university not only on grounds of political utility but as a basic principle (1967):

Nevertheless the general situation does create a dilemma for those of us who find ourselves in passionate opposition to the general drift of American society—a position often reached with uneasy astonishment. As students and teachers we have no objective interest in kicking down the far from sturdy walls that still do protect us. For all their faults and inadequacies the universities . . . do constitute a moat behind which it is still possible to examine and indict the destructive trends in our society. . . . The faculty's overwhelming commitment to free speech in the university community is part of this moat, perhaps its most important part. To attack it heedlessly is irresponsible and self-defeating. That is so not merely because we who are vehemently opposed to many basic trends in American society may badly need its protection from time to time. The principle is important in its own right.

These prominent social critics are upholding the type of university slowly built in this century and the relatively free inquiry it has made possible. Tampering with this idea of the university—by anyone, including those with whom one sympathizes in terms of objections to government policy—is dangerous.

But even if some faculty members made this distinction between the external and internal demands of student activists with relative ease, for many others a serious problem was posed. It was, at the least, disconcerting for academics who had thought of themselves as left and progressive to be attacked as hypocrites by the student left and by some of their colleagues who variously led and followed the students in the call for a new "idea of the university." The net effect of the intense politicization of academe in the 1960s, involving as it did the conflict of two competing ideas of what a university should be and do among persons whose views on national issues were similar, served to further fragment the professoriate, to shatter any semblance of moral unity, to rob it of its capacity for decisive action before the troubles which beset it.

NATIONAL AND CAMPUS POLITICS: "CONSISTENT" IDEOLOGISTS AND "SPLITTERS"

We have pointed out the high measure of association between a liberal position in national affairs and *relatively* high support for campus activism, more student involvement in university decisions, and programs to meet the needs of minority groups in academe. There are, nonetheless, some faculty who combine notable noncongruent responses in these two sectors, who are among the most liberal-left in the disputes of the larger polity but are in the ranks of those most conservative in the politics of their own institutions. As one measure, 4 percent of academics in the Carnegie survey who score in the two most liberal quintiles of the Liberalism-Conservatism Scale are in the two most conservative categories of the Campus Activism index, while 5 percent of faculty who are national conservatives are "activism liberals." Substituting the Student Role Scale, we find an even higher proportion of "splitters," with 8 percent and 10 percent in the respective noncongruent categories. Table 67 shows a full distribution of faculty across the consistent ideologist and splitter groups as defined by the interaction of the Liberalism-Conservatism and campus politics scales. These divisions deserve some further attention. What characteristics distinguish faculty who display the various congruent and noncongruent response patterns?

TABLE 67 *Proportion of faculty classified as consistent ideologists and ideological splitters, national and campus politics (as percentages)**

	National liberals	National conservatives
Campus: (Student Activism)		
Liberals	32	5
Conservatives	4	26
Campus: (Student Role)		
Liberals	28	10
Conservatives	8	21

*A faculty member is classified as a "national liberal, activism liberal" if he scores in either of the two most liberal categories of both the Liberalism-Conservatism and Campus Activism Scales. Similarly, he is a "national conservative, activism liberal" if he is in the two most conservative quintiles of the Liberalism Scale but in one of the two most liberal quintiles of the Activism Scale. Comparable constructions are applied using the Liberalism-Conservatism and Student Role Scales.

SOURCE: 1969 Carnegie Commission Survey of Student and Faculty Opinion.

We expected age to be an important factor here: that a significant proportion of older national liberals would show up in the most conservative categories of the campus indexes. This proved to be the case. The consistent liberals are, of course, much younger as a group than the consistent conservatives; but the age profiles of those liberal on national affairs while among the most opposed to campus activism, and those of the consistent conservatives, are essentially the same. Of the former, 30 percent are over 50 years of age, compared with 31 percent of the consistent conservatives and just 14 percent of the consistent liberals (Table 68).

More interesting and revealing are the differences among our ideological cohorts on variables involving professional achievements and orientations. The consistent liberals are more likely to be at the better colleges and universities, to be oriented primarily toward research rather than teaching, and to be active publishers than are the consistent conservatives. All this was to be expected, in view of the analysis presented earlier. The fascinating variations involve the two groups of splitters.

Faculty who are national liberals but campus conservatives—only 4 to 8 percent of the total, it should be remembered—manifest a strikingly high level of scholarly achievement. They are disproportionately at the better schools, are more research-oriented, and publish *more* than any of the other groups. This is especially notable when the type of splitter is defined in terms of responses to demands to democratize the university. For example, 43 percent of this cohort described themselves as

TABLE 68 Distribution of faculty on selected career variables; consistent liberals, ideological splitters, and consistent conservatives (percentages of n)

	Liberalism-Conservatism and Campus Activism Scales			
	Consistent liberals (n = 19,020)	*Consistent conservatives* (n = 15,408)	*National liberals, campus conservatives* (n = 2,136)	*National conservatives, campus liberals* (n = 2,490)
Age				
Over 50	14	31	30	20
35–49	43	45	41	46
Under 35	43	24	29	35
Publications, last two years				
0–2	72	82	72	82
3–4	15	9	14	10
5 or more	13	9	14	8
Primary commitment to				
Teaching	69	84	72	81
Research	31	16	28	19
*School Quality**				
1. Lowest	13	23	14	21
2.	31	39	30	41
3.	28	26	25	24
4. Highest	28	13	31	14

*See note 5, Chapter 5, for a description of the construction of the Index of School Quality.

SOURCE: 1969 Carnegie Commission Survey of Student and Faculty Opinion.

primarily oriented toward research, compared with 27 percent of the consistent liberals, 20 percent of the consistent conservatives, and just 13 percent of faculty who are national conservatives but relatively sympathetic to demands for student power.

These findings are striking, but fully consistent with or supportive of analysis presented earlier in this chapter. A group of senior, research-directed, highly productive academics who endorse liberal programs in the national arena reacted negatively to many of the campus protests and student demands of the 1960s, which they saw threatening the more traditional scholarly function of the university and as threatening,

Liberalism-Conservatism and Student Role Scales			
Consistent liberals (n = 17,184)	Consistent conservatives (n = 12,159)	National liberals, campus conservatives (n = 4,674)	National conservatives, campus liberals (n = 6,147)
14	32	24	24
43	44	44	47
44	25	32	30
75	80	65	85
14	10	18	9
11	10	17	6
73	80	57	87
27	20	43	13
16	21	12	25
32	39	26	40
27	25	29	25
26	15	33	10

too, of course, their own positions as custodians and beneficiaries of this "idea of a university." This group, and its response set, is reflected by the "national liberals, campus conservatives" category.

In contrast, those academics conservative in national affairs but liberal in the campus conflicts come disproportionately from the teaching, nonscholarly culture of schools of lesser academic standing. They responded relatively favorably to student demands and demonstrations not because of an underlying commitment to ideological liberalism, but because the "idea of a university" which the protesting students brought under attack was one which they—although for different reasons—found profoundly unappealing. Here are conservative faculty in a sense "allied" with left-inclined students against a scholarly, research-directed conception of academic life.

CONCLUSIONS

Politics always makes strange bedfellows, and the campus politics of the late 1960s proved to be no exception. Looking at the professoriate at large, we find that the most liberally inclined were the most supportive of the demands of activist students for intramural change, while conservatives most strongly and consistently opposed these demands. But there were numerous exceptions. Most important was the negative reaction of a cadre of faculty at once research-committed and scholarly achieving, and liberals in the national arena, to campus activism and politicization. As the protests turned on the university role and atmosphere they valued, this group was brought into a de facto alliance, in the university arena, with academics of a consistently conservative ideological bent. And at the same time, the demands for campus change, initiated primarily by left-oriented faculty and students, found some support in the "teaching culture," which is generally linked to a more conservative and less socially critical politics.

9. Persisting Effects of the 1960s: The 1972 Presidential Election

In the summer of 1972, after the national nominating conventions of both major parties had completed their work, we became convinced of the desirability of surveying the electoral leanings of academics, and initiated the second survey described in the introduction to this volume. In particular, we were interested in the possible effects or spinoffs of the intense politicization and divisiveness which universities had experienced over the preceding half decade or so. Many academics who had been identified in the past as liberals and Democrats found themselves in alliance with conservatives to prevent actions they considered a threat to the integrity of the university and scholarship.

Opinion was divided about protests and demonstrations against the Vietnam War, some of which resulted in the seizure of buildings and similar confrontations, and about all the attendant arguments concerning the use of police, the proper role and responsibilities of the university, and the like. Demands for "affirmative action" or for quotas in hiring of blacks and women for professional positions and in admitting students were seen by some as appropriate university actions on behalf of equality and by others as assaults on meritocracy. Charges of racism within the academy and insistence upon vigorous steps to eradicate it were applauded by proponents of affirmative action as essential to full freedom for blacks, and rejected by opponents as inviting "smear tactics" and thus posing a threat to academic freedom. These and related conflicts over the last five years or so have produced sharp separations among faculty that divide opinion in a way which is very different from the conventional liberal-conservative axis.

Such intracampus controversies seem linked to a broader ideological division in the American intellectual community. It is far less meaning-

NOTE: The subject of this chapter has been examined at greater length in another of our publications: Ladd and Lipset (1973a).

ful to ask an American intellectual today, "Are you liberal or conservative?" than to ask, "Are you *Commentary* or *New York Review of Books?*" Some of the strains in this division are old, but others are very new, products of the massive changes which have occurred in the American political agenda in recent years. They show a change from intellectual residues of who bears responsibility for the cold wars to the intellectual boundaries of "equality"—for whom, through what channels, at what expense? On the whole, "*Commentary* intellectuals" rejected George McGovern, while those of the *New York Review of Books* embraced him.

For American college professors, then, as for the intellectual community at large, the 1972 presidential election, the issues it contained and the candidates representing those issues, promised to involve more than a simple liberal-conservative split. In particular, we expected among academics an interesting tension between disproportionately liberal inclinations of long standing and the "frontlash-backlash" generated by activism and the "new campus politics" of the preceding decade.

Some indication of this tension, and that it might actually be producing support for the GOP candidate, was suggested by two advertisements which the Committee to Re-elect the President ran in the Sunday *New York Times* (October 15 and 29). In them, about 100 leading academics, mainly in the social sciences, endorsed Nixon in the following terms: "Of the two major candidates for President . . . , we believe that Richard Nixon has demonstrated the superior capacity for prudent and responsible leadership." It is clear from the wording of the statement that it was carefully designed to gain the endorsement of traditionally liberal scholars who were anti-McGovern rather than favorable to the President or the Republican party. Although we have not systematically sought out comparable statements from preceding campaigns, we would greatly doubt that any previous *Republican* candidate had been publicly endorsed by as distinguished a group of scholars since the New Deal. Many of those who signed the advertisement had been active Democratic partisans; some had been Socialist supporters in earlier elections. One such signer, Sidney Hook, also published a statement explaining his support of Richard Nixon in *New America*, the organ of the Socialist party; he argued, "Nixon Is The Lesser Evil" (Hook, 1972, pp. 4–5, 7).

There was another, in a sense more obvious or direct, reason for our interest in the 1972 presidential politics of the professoriate. Along with its base among some depressed minorities, McGovern's activist strength appeared to rest heavily in the academic-intellectual community. The latter had been the major source of the antiwar movement which brought Lyndon Johnson down in 1968, and supplied both the ideological and the activist base for the Kennedy and McCarthy campaigns. How, in fact, was McGovern doing among college professors? Was his strength in the professorial ranks experiencing an erosion comparable with that among other traditionally Democratic groups? Or would professors (along with other segments of the intellectual community) move "against the grain," giving the embattled Democratic nominee perhaps even greater than normal support? Were those who signed the *Times*'s advertisements the top of a large "silent" group, more shame-faced about giving public expression to their support of an historic villain of liberaldom, Richard Nixon? How, in general, did academics see the choice between George McGovern and Richard Nixon? What issues moved them most strongly toward, or away from, the incumbent Republican President and his Democratic challenger? To what extent, in short, did the political battleground of 1972, as seen by academics, resemble that on which the presidential contest was being fought out in the larger society?

FACULTY VOTING IN 1972: THE BASIC RESULTS

Our survey found McGovern and Nixon running a virtual dead heat among professors in early September (Table 69). The Democratic nominee enjoyed, according to the survey, a scanty 3-percentage-point lead over his Republican opponent. But there was a modest shift toward McGovern between September and election day, one of about

TABLE 69 *Faculty presidential vote preferences, 1972; vote intent (preelection survey) and actual vote (postelection survey)*

	McGovern	Nixon	Other	Undecided
1972 vote intent (September), with those undecided included	48	45	1	6
1972 vote intent (September), with the "undecideds" excluded from the computations	51	48	1	—
1972 vote (postelection survey)	56	43	1	—

SOURCE: 1972 Ladd-Lipset survey.

5 percent.[1] Thus, Senator McGovern, backed by just under 38 percent of the national electorate and loser to Richard Nixon by a margin of 23 percentage points, was supported by 56 percent of the academics and carried this group by a 13-point margin.

Universities were popularly perceived to be islands of Democratic strength in a Republican presidential sea in 1972. There is ample basis for this view. McGovern's support in the professoriate was about 18 points higher than in the general public. Other surveys have shown a similarly high (if not what some had anticipated) performance by the Democratic nominee among college students.[2]

While McGovern's overall electoral performance among university voters was relatively strong, there were signs of weakness even on the surface. He ran behind Democratic candidates for Congress, although not by nearly so large a margin as in the electorate at large. Thus, 61 percent of professors cast their ballots for Democratic congressional can-

---

[1]While standard sampling procedures were observed in the small 1972 survey, and confidence in the reliability of the findings must be based on this, it is nonetheless informative to note the close parallels between distributions located by the small 1972 survey and those revealed by the exhaustive 1969 study. In all cases where such comparisons are possible, they show the highest consistency. For example, professors were asked in both the 1969 and 1972 surveys how they had voted in 1968:

	Humphrey	Nixon	Wallace	Other
1969 survey	58	39	—	4
1972 survey	56	40	—	4

Similarly, respondents in both studies were invited to locate their political views on a five-point scale, from "left" to "strongly conservative," and again the variations are insignificant.

	Left	Liberal	Middle-of-the-road	Moderately conservative	Strongly conservative
1969 survey	5	40	27	25	3
1972 survey	9	40	26	23	2

In objective personal characteristics—such as age, religious background, and academic discipline—the distributions contained in our 1972 survey match closely those known to exist among the faculty at large.

[2]An election day survey by CBS News found 54 percent of students between 18 and 24 years of age voting for McGovern, 45 percent for Nixon, with 1 percent for minor-party candidates ("Preliminary Tabulations, CBS News Election Day Survey," 1972).

didates, as compared with the 56 percent support McGovern received. Nixon was the choice of 43 percent of professors voting in the presidential election, but Republican congressional candidates received just 37 percent of faculty ballots. A liberal, antiwar Democratic presidential nominee who relied heavily upon a base of support in colleges and universities in fact ran less well among professors than did his party's congressional candidates.

Over the past decade, the proportion of the American electorate self-described as independents and engaging in independent electoral behavior has increased sharply, especially among those who have had formal higher education. Apart from the matter of how professorial votes were distributed in 1972, the extraordinary weakness of party ties and loyalties stands out as a notable finding of our survey. Gallup studies in 1972 showed independents to be the largest "party" among college-educated Americans, a status they held even more emphatically in the professoriate. Half of the faculty (49 percent) described themselves as independents, while 37 percent identified themselves as Democrats and just 13 percent as Republicans. The picture developed throughout this volume of the professoriate distinguished by a tendency to view politics in ideological or issue-oriented terms is dramatically reinforced here. Faculty members are disproportionately liberal or left of center in their political views, and, as such, disproportionately Democratic. Their consistently high support for Democratic nominees seems less a product of strong party loyalties than a product of issue commitments.

As Table 70 demonstrates, only 30 percent of our faculty sample both identified themselves as Democrats and voted for McGovern in 1972, while 12 percent of all respondents were Republican identifiers voting for Nixon. Thus, about three professors in five (58 percent) failed to meet what must be considered a minimal test of party regularity: profession of an identification with the party and support for its presidential nominee in a single election. Even more striking, perhaps, only one-fourth (26 percent) of Nixon's faculty support came from self-described Republicans, while Democrats furnished 17 percent and independents provided an extraordinary 57 percent of the total. McGovern, on the other hand, drew more heavily upon party identifiers, but even he received only half (52 percent) of his votes from self-identified Democrats, with another 4 percent coming from Republicans and 44 percent from independents. Among Democrats, 20 percent "defected" to vote for Nixon, while 14 percent of Republicans backed the Democratic presidential nominee. Independents split evenly, 50 percent for each of the major-party contenders. In short, a growing tendency toward inde-

TABLE 70 *Party identification and party voting by faculty in 1972*

Party identification	"Grand Total" percentages; each cell n divided by the total n	
	McGovern voters	Nixon voters
Democratic	30	7
Republican	2	12
Independent	25	25
	Row percentages	
Party identification	McGovern voters	Nixon voters
Democratic (n = 173)	80	20
Republican (n = 59)	14	86
Independent (n = 229)	50	50
	Column percentages	
Party identification	McGovern voters (n = 238)	Nixon voters (n = 184)
Democratic	52	17
Republican	4	26
Independent	44	57

SOURCE: 1972 Ladd-Lipset survey.

pendent electoral behavior, noteworthy among groups of high socio-economic status generally, is especially striking in the faculty.

Before we examine the sources of Nixon's and McGovern's support among faculty, what conclusions can we draw about the overall success, or the lack thereof, of the major parties in the 1972 elections? There are grounds for describing the election as a relatively successful one for both McGovern and Nixon within the universities. The Democratic nominee, so badly beaten in the national vote, won a solid majority among professors. And his faculty vote surpassed his national proportion by a margin (18 points) almost identical to that achieved by Democratic nominees over the past two decades. On the other hand, running as a liberal and antiwar nominee (in university circles where liberal and antiwar sentiments were predominant), with his candidacy heavily reliant upon university support, and contesting a Republican who had never been the darling of American intellectuals, McGovern gained a smaller proportion of the faculty vote in 1972 than did Democratic congressional candidates. At the same time, Nixon's academic vote in 1972 apparently was as high as any achieved by a Republican presidential nominee since the New Deal and, at 43 percent of the total, constituted a solid, if minority, position. Thus the presidential election as contested in the colleges and universities produced something of a mixed result. There was no Democratic erosion comparable with that in the public at large or among most population subgroups, but neither was there an especially strong McGovern performance. For more definite conclusions, we must begin to untangle the sources of Nixon and McGovern support in universities and how faculty saw the points at issue in this contest.

FACULTY VOTING IN 1972: A CASE OF FAMILIAR INTERNAL DIFFERENTIATION

In the earlier analysis of survey data on college and university professors taken primarily from our 1969 Carnegie survey, we identified a set of variables associated with especially sharp differences in faculty political orientations. The discipline in which the faculty member teaches, his age, and the type of school in which he is located, along with other measures of his scholarly or intellectual achievement, are linked causally to large, systematic differences in orientations across a broad range of social and political questions, both intramural and affecting the larger society. Support for Nixon and McGovern strongly reflected these basic underlying patterns in political commitments. Thus, as Table 71 shows, the Democratic nominee was backed by 76 percent of faculty in the liberal social sciences, by 71 percent of humanists, by 53 percent of the natural scientists, and by only 30 percent of professors in the conservative, business-related applied fields (engineering, business administration, departments or colleges of agriculture). Younger faculty have consistently been more liberal with respect to both societal and campus issues than their older colleagues. And not surprisingly, there was a high correlation between age and presidential choice in 1972, one much greater than in the electorate as a whole. Among professors under 35, 71 percent backed McGovern, as against only 42 percent of their colleagues 50 years and over. In the electorate at large, according to Gallup survey data, 42 percent of voters under 35 backed the Democratic nominee, compared with 36 percent in the 50 and over group, a margin of just 6 percent.

In Chapter 5 we discussed why the more eminent faculty have shown a greater proclivity than their less highly achieving colleagues for left-critical politics. This same relationship is evident in 1972 presidential voting. McGovern was the choice of more than 70 percent of faculty at institutions of high academic standing, but was supported by less than half of the professors at lower-tier schools. Noteworthy in the 1972 results, however, is a partial exception to the frequent finding in faculty

TABLE 71   Faculty presidential voting, by selected personal and professional characteristics (row percentages)

	1972			1968				1964		
	Democratic	Republican	Other	Democratic	Republican	American Independent Party	Other	Democratic	Republican	Other
Age										
Under 35	71	29	—	60	35	1	4	77	22	1
35–49	60	40	—	60	37	1	2	79	21	1
50 and older	42	58	—	53	44	2	1	76	23	1
Religious background										
Jewish	88	9	2	87	8	—	6	97	2	1
Catholic	54	46	—	68	27	2	3	81	18	1
Protestant	51	49	—	52	45	1	2	74	26	1
Field										
Social sciences	76	22	2	75	20	—	5	89	10	2
Humanities	71	29	—	72	23	1	4	86	13	1
Natural sciences	53	47	—	57	40	2	2	77	22	1
Business-related applied fields	30	70	—	38	58	3	1	62	37	—
Publications										
5 or more	54	44	1	65	31	1	3	84	15	1
1–4	66	34	—	62	35	1	2	81	18	1
None	43	57	—	54	42	2	2	74	26	1
School quality										
Upper tier	72	27	1	71	26	—	3	87	12	1
Lower tier	46	54	—	59	38	2	2	78	22	1

SOURCES: 1969 Carnegie Commission Survey of Student and Faculty Opinion; 1972 Ladd-Lipset survey.

studies of a strong relationship between intellectual accomplishment and political views. Looking at respondents in terms of personal accomplishments—for example, publication record over the last two years—we find McGovern weakest among those with no publications (43 percent support) and strongest among faculty with a moderate record of scholarly attainment (66 percent backed McGovern). Surprisingly, the Democratic nominee's strength dropped off considerably among the most highly productive scholars—he had 54 percent support among those who had published 5 or more items over the past 24 months. The reasons are discussed later in this chapter. It is enough to note here that this is an exception to the general rule of liberal strength increasing with the scholarly standing of the faculty. It may also indicate that the distinguished Democratic defectors who signed the *New York Times* advertisements for Nixon reflected the views of many in their circles.

Table 71 indicates that the falling off of Democratic presidential support (1972 compared with 1968) occurred disproportionately at the lesser rather than the better colleges and universities. Indeed, all the *net* decline was accounted for by faculty at the former places. The pronounced liberalism characteristic of elite institutions seems to be the decisive element in the above pattern. Currents producing a major Democratic defection nationally in 1972 seemingly were more influential in schools where the prevailing ideological—and hence partisan—balance was relatively even than where it was heavily tilted one way. The massive liberal and Democratic ascendancy at elite centers sustained an environment which discouraged defections to the Republicans. The country moved Republican in 1972, and many individual voters experienced interpersonal relations which encouraged them to move in this direction. No such pattern took shape in the heavily Democratic upper reaches of American higher education.

As Milton Himmelfarb (1973, p. 81) has pointed out, Jews among the public at large voted more heavily Democratic in 1972, as in 1968 and earlier, "than any other body of white voters—Protestants, Catholics, businessmen, farmers, workers; even professors; even students." But the dropoff in Democratic support between 1968 and 1972 was considerably greater for Jews generally (18 percent) than for Jewish academics (7 percent). Here is yet another indication of the importance of immediate social milieu for electoral decision making. The country swung massively from the Democrats in 1972, but academe did not. Especially at elite colleges and universities, where Jewish faculty are heavily represented, Republican voting remained, in the face of the Nixon landslide, the "deviant" case. Informal processes of social contact and

TABLE 72 *Comparison of faculty voting, 1968 and 1972 (percentages of n)*

| 1968 vote | Presidential choice in 1972, by 1968 vote | | | |
	McGovern	Nixon	Other	Nonvoters
Humphrey (n = 219)	78	17	1	5
Nixon (n = 155)	14	83	1	3
Other* (n = 15)	87	6	6	—
Nonvoters (n = 72)	44	18	1	36

| 1972 vote | Presidential choice in 1968, by 1972 vote | | | |
	Humphrey	Nixon	Other	Nonvoters
McGovern (n = 236)	72	9	6	14
Nixon (n = 181)	20	71	1	7
Other* (n = 5)	—	—	—	—
Nonvoters (n = 40)	25	10	—	65

*Exclusively for minor parties of the left.
SOURCE: 1972 Ladd-Lipset survey.

interaction continued to reinforce the tendency to vote Democratic in the many liberal enclaves of American higher education.

FACULTY VOTING, 1968 AND 1972: WHAT SHIFTS OCCURRED?

The modest gains in faculty votes made by the Republicans in 1972, compared with 1968, occurred in the face of a strong countercurrent which brought McGovern significant support that Humphrey had lost four years earlier. Table 72 shows that *a full fifth of 1972 McGovern supporters either backed third parties in 1968 (exclusively third parties of the left) or sat out the election* even though they were eligible to vote. In sharp contrast, Nixon received only 8 percent of his total faculty vote from those who either sat out the earlier presidential contest or cast ballots for a third-party candidate. Among professors who did not vote in the Humphrey-Nixon contest but did go to the polls in 1972, McGovern outdistanced Nixon by a margin of more than seven to three.

On the other hand, Nixon succeeded in 1972 in dislodging a substantial number of Humphrey adherents. Nearly a fifth of the academics who voted Democratic in 1968 supported Nixon four years later. And a full fifth of Nixon's faculty backers in 1972 had been in Humphrey's camp in the preceding election. By way of contrast, just 9 percent of McGovern's voters had favored Nixon in the 1968 balloting.

Two main currents are evident, then, in faculty presidential voting in 1972. One consists of 1968 nonvoters and third-party "defectors" enlisting as McGovern supporters by an overwhelming margin. The other, considerably stronger numerically, consists of Humphrey voters switching over to the Republican nominee whom they had rejected in the preceding election.

Thus far, some of the structural properties of the 1972 vote in universities have been identified, but little has been said about the source of the patterns, especially of the shifts from 1968. That subject, involving the ideological or issue base of the 1972 vote, deserves more extended analysis.

THE IDEOLOGICAL BASE OF THE 1972 VOTE

Ideology influences the electoral behavior of college and university professors to an unusually high degree. It comes as no surprise, then, to find Nixon and McGovern voters among the professoriate far more sharply and systematically differentiated in their policy preferences than the larger bodies of adherents of the Republican and Democratic nominees in the general public.

No issue of national or international affairs has occupied American academics as deeply since 1965 as America's involvement in Vietnam. Professors have been seen, and rightly, as a principal source of opposition to United States policies in the Indochina war and, along with their student apprentices, as the fulcrum of protest and dissent on such policies. The visibility of academic protests against the war has sometimes, however, served to obscure the existence of significant, if minority, support for Nixon administration policies. The 1969 Carnegie survey, as we have seen, found about three-fifths of all faculty favoring either an immediate unilateral United States withdrawal from Vietnam or an immediate reduction of American involvement coupled with encouragement of a coalition government in South Vietnam to include the Viet Cong. At the same time, however, a substantial minority supported what later came to be known as Vietnamization: "to reduce . . . [American] involvement, while being sure to prevent a Communist takeover in the South." And 8 percent of professors in 1969 actually endorsed a position more "hard line" than that of the administration, arguing that "the United States should commit whatever forces are necessary to defeat the Communists."

By the time of our 1972 survey, the dimensions of the Vietnam issue had changed somewhat. Desire to see the United States extricated immediately had spread much more widely through the population. But on the issue of how American extrication should be achieved, there was a sharp division rather neatly presented in the positions taken by the two 1972 presidential candidates. We asked our faculty respondents: "Which of these positions on Vietnam is closer to your own: That the United States should unilaterally withdraw from Vietnam at once; or that the United States should continue with the present 'Vietnamization' program?" The former alternative, clearly, was McGovern's, the latter Nixon's. A decisive majority (57 percent) of the faculty supported immediate withdrawal, but a strong minority (34 percent) favored Vietnamization, while 9 percent felt that their preferences were not adequately expressed by either alternative.

The position of professors on whether the unfolding of the Vietnamization program had been basically sound or unsound was associated to an exceptionally high degree with their preference for Nixon or McGovern. Thus, 87 percent of faculty who favored immediate unilateral withdrawal voted for the Democratic candidate, while the same proportion exactly (87 percent) who endorsed Vietnamization voted Republican. Table 73 shows that just 8 percent of McGovern voters

TABLE 73 *Position on Vietnam of faculty, by presidential vote choice (percentages of n)*

	Vietnam position		
	Withdrawal	*Vietnamization*	*Dissatisfaction with either approach as presented*
All McGovern voters (n = 219)	86	8	7
All Nixon voters (n = 155)	16	70	14
Switchers, Humphrey in 1968, Nixon in 1972 (n = 37)	32	42	26
Switchers, Nixon in 1968, McGovern in 1972 (n = 21)	85	10	5
All third-party voters and nonvoters in 1968 (n = 67)	69	24	7
Third-party voters and nonvoters in 1968, McGovern in 1972 (n = 45)	90	5	5

SOURCE: 1972 Ladd-Lipset survey.

supported Vietnamization, and only 16 percent of Nixon's backers were in favor of immediate unilateral withdrawal from Vietnam.

In 1968, when Hubert Humphrey secured 58 percent of faculty ballots, a significant minority of those who opposed him did so because of his identification with the Johnson war policies. Thus, almost 3 percent voted for leftist third-party candidates, men like Dick Gregory and Eldridge Cleaver, who were not even on the ballot in most states. More significantly, a proportion of Richard Nixon's 1968 vote came from professors who thought of themselves as liberals and were strongly antiwar. The 1969 Carnegie survey showed more than 7 percent of Nixon backers in favor of an immediate, unilateral United States withdrawal from Vietnam, while 9 percent described their political views as "left" or "liberal." They presumably saw their Nixon votes as a protest against the Democratic party establishment, or identified Nixon as more likely to end the war than Johnson's vice president. There is also evidence that a considerable segment of the 11 percent of faculty who did not vote in 1968 were liberals withholding their support from the Democratic nominee because of antiwar feelings.

Table 73 shows that faculty voting for Nixon in 1968 but for McGovern in 1972 were overwhelmingly antiwar and in favor of a unilateral United States withdrawal. From answers to open-ended questions in the survey, we are able to detect two principal groups among the Nixon-to-McGovern switchers. In one camp were faculty who voted Republican in 1968 purely as a means of protesting Democratic war policies. A philosopher at a leading private university, for example, said that he had "voted for Nixon four years earlier on the theory that you should vote the bastards out of office." McGovern was taking a position on the war which he favored, and naturally enough he was returning to the Democratic fold. The second group, in contrast, believed that Nixon really would extricate the United States from Vietnam quickly, and went against him in 1972 because he had not. We also see from the data in Table 73 that about two-thirds of all faculty who voted for third-party candidates in 1968 or who sat the election out were, in 1972, proponents of unilateral United States withdrawal from Vietnam. Those who came to support McGovern—a large majority of the third-party voters and the eligible nonvoters of four years earlier—were even more overwhelmingly antiwar than the rank and file of McGovern adherents. McGovern drew support from three groups who had not been Democratic in 1968—a segment of Nixon voters, third-party voters, and nonvoters—all of whom were strong opponents of American Vietnam policy and had been dissatisfied with Humphrey's candidacy mainly on the grounds of his association with the war.

TABLE 74 *Political self-description of faculty, by presidential vote choice (row percentages)*

	Left-liberal	Middle-of-the-road	Conservative
All McGovern voters	78	17	6
All Nixon voters	13	36	52
Switchers, Humphrey in 1968, Nixon in 1972	25	53	22
Switchers, Nixon in 1968 McGovern in 1972	42	26	32
All third-party voters and nonvoters in 1968	76	20	5
Third-party voters and nonvoters in 1968, McGovern in 1972	58	27	15

SOURCE: 1972 Ladd-Lipset survey.

On the other hand, faculty who had supported Humphrey in 1968 but shifted to Nixon seemed to have switched less directly as a result of the war policies or proposed programs of the 1972 contenders. Some did endorse Vietnamization, but the proportion of this group doing so was much smaller than the proportion among all Nixon voters. An unusually high percentage (26 percent) expressed reservations with both the withdrawal and the Vietnamization alternatives. McGovern's position on the war, so influential in bringing him faculty support, appears much less closely linked to the substantial erosion which he experienced among a category of Humphrey backers.

Nixon and McGovern adherents in the professoriate are very sharply differentiated in self-descriptions of their political philosophies (Table 74). Nearly 80 percent of those who voted for McGovern described their political views as "left" or "liberal," in striking contrast to just 13 percent of Nixon backers. A majority of all faculty who voted for Nixon in 1972 identified themselves as "conservatives," a label not especially in vogue in universities, one accepted by only a quarter of the professoriate. Professors switching from Nixon to McGovern (1968 and 1972 votes) as a group are considerably more liberal than those who stayed with Nixon, but considerably less liberal than the rank and file of McGovern's faculty supporters. Faculty who backed Humphrey in 1968 but switched to Nixon four years later paint a distinctive collective portrait of themselves as middle-of-the-roaders. As would be expected, professors who voted for third-party candidates in 1968 or sat the election out, and then went on to support McGovern in 1972, see themselves disproportionately as left of center; only 5 percent in this group are self-described conservatives.

We have described (Chapters 2 and 8) a strong link between general ideology, as reflected in views on national and international questions, and positions on a variety of campus controversies, such as the protests and demonstrations of the late 1960s, preferential hiring or admissions policies for underrepresented groups, more "student power" (that is, a broader voice by students in university decision making), and the like. The source of the high correlations between general liberalism-conservatism and positions on many campus issues is in one sense obvious enough. Commitment to egalitarian and popular causes in the larger society has its counterpart in a more egalitarian and popular posture on strictly intramural controversies. The extent of the correlation across an array of superficially disparate items again testifies to the highly constrained or ideological thinking of a large proportion of the faculty. Strong as the overall association is, however, significant numbers of academics who are national liberals strongly opposed protests and demonstrations and the new politicization of academic affairs on the grounds that such developments posed a threat to academic freedom and to a university committed to scholarly excellence.

We find (Table 75) an especially strong correlation between support for Nixon and opposition to the increase in campus activism in the late 1960s and early 1970s. Respondents to our 1972 survey were fairly evenly divided in their overall assessments of the student protests: 38 percent indicated general approval, 48 percent disapproved, and 14 percent displayed conflicting assessments. A full 80 percent of those in the approval category voted for McGovern, while 70 percent who described their position as one of disapproval backed Nixon. Just one-quarter of McGovern's voters among the faculty indicated opposition to student activism, compared with nearly three-fourths of Nixon voters.

The hypothesis was offered at the outset of this chapter that campus protests, but more generally the whole politicization of universities in recent years, had led to the emergence of new divisions among professors which would manifest themselves in the 1972 presidential voting. It was postulated that Senator McGovern, in part because activist students and young faculty furnished the core of his most visible supporters in many university communities, would find the faculty response to his candidacy significantly affected by these new internecine divisions, and, in particular, that he would experience some attrition of support among normally Democratic professors who had reacted negatively to the activism of recent years and its attendant manifestations.

TABLE 75 *Positions of faculty on campus political issues, by presidential vote choice (row percentages)*

	Percentage opposed to student activism*	Percentage opposed to preferential hiring for underrepresented groups†	Percentage opposed to faculty unionism‡	Percentage opposed to faculties taking collective stands on major controversies§
All McGovern voters	26	43	34	58
All Nixon voters	73	61	59	67
Switchers, Humphrey in 1968, Nixon in 1972	60	60	58	67
Switchers, Nixon in 1968, McGovern in 1972	25	50	40	52
All third-party voters and nonvoters in 1968	35	46	36	60
Third-party voters and nonvoters in 1968, McGovern in 1972	17	46	37	58

*"What has been your general position on the emergence of radical student activism in recent years, approval or disapproval?"

†"Do you agree or disagree . . . that groups which are underrepresented on the faculty—such as blacks, Chicanos and women—should be assigned a large share of future faculty vacancies until they are proportionately represented?"

‡"Do you agree or disagree . . . that the recent growth of unionization of college and university faculty is beneficial and should be extended?"

§"Do you agree or disagree . . . that it is desirable for college and university faculty to put themselves on record by vote on major political controversies?"

SOURCE: 1972 Ladd-Lipset survey.

Table 75 provides some tentatively confirming data on this. Whereas just 26 percent of those voting for McGovern expressed general opposition to student activism, 60 percent of the professors who had been for Humphrey in 1968 but switched to Nixon in the 1972 balloting expressed such opposition. The Humphrey-to-Nixon switchers, similarly, contained a notably high proportion who were against assigning "a large share of future faculty vacancies" to groups such as blacks and women that have been underrepresented, who rejected the proposition that "the recent growth of unionization of college and university faculty is beneficial and should be extended," and who disagreed with the position that "it is desirable for . . . faculty to put themselves on record by vote on major political controversies." McGovern's relative weakness among senior faculty of high scholarly attainment seems a product of this group's disproportionate opposition to aspects of the "new academic politics" and their association of the Democratic nominee with it.

Although it is hard to be precise on the matter, we also find in our data some indication that events of the last half decade or so may have contributed to the creation of a conservative attitude of a special sort among a segment of the professoriate. It is a special variety because it is not manifested in conventional policy areas such as support for civil rights and civil liberties, backing for social welfare measures, and adherence, in general, to programs commonly thought of as liberal. It involves something more nearly akin to the Burkean than to the post-New Deal concept of conservatism. The social turbulence of recent years appears to have impressed upon a portion of the faculty a greater sense of the fragility of societal institutions, more appreciation of unintended negative consequences of change, and a feeling for the importance of civil order. This surely does not indicate a swing to the right in the American professoriate, but rather indicates a change in conceptual orientation that touches strains historically associated with conservatism.

The ideological sources of Nixon's and McGovern's support, and of vote switching between the 1968 and 1972 presidential elections, are evident enough. McGovern drew his backing from left-to-liberal faculty, traditionally Democratic, and he significantly increased Humphrey's 1968 base by bringing left and antiwar professors back to the party fold. At the same time, he lost ground, as about a fifth of the academics who backed Humphrey over Nixon in 1968 switched to Nixon's camp in 1972. Table 76, along with data already presented, brings out the most salient ideological characteristics of the switchers. Academics who described their politics as left or liberal gave Nixon almost exactly the same proportion of their vote (just over 10 percent) in each election.

TABLE 76   *1972 and 1968 vote of professors, by political self-description and position on student activism (row percentages)*

	1972, for:			1968, for:		
	McGovern	Nixon	Other	Humphrey	Nixon	Other
Political self-description						
Left or liberal	88	12	1	82	11	7
Middle-of-the-road	37	62	1	54	45	1
Conservative	12	88	—	13	86	1
Position on student activism						
Approval	79	20	1	71	20	9
Uncertain, conflicting assessments	74	26	—	69	31	—
Disapproval	31	69	—	43	56	1

SOURCE: 1972 Ladd-Lipset survey.

Similarly, conservatives were overwhelmingly Republican in both 1968 and 1972. A major shift occurred, however, among self-described "centrists." A decisive majority voted for Humphrey over Nixon in 1968, but by a margin of more than six to four this group backed Nixon over McGovern four years later. McGovern also lost significant support among Humphrey voters of four years earlier who resented campus protests and politicization. Table 76 shows, for example, that *professors indicating opposition to student activism divided fairly evenly between Nixon and Humphrey in 1968, but voted overwhelmingly Republican in 1972.* In general, McGovern lost support exactly where it was expected, in view of his policies and the base upon which his candidacy was built: among middle-of-the-road Democrats and independents, including especially, it seems, those hostile to the "new academic politics" of the preceding half decade.

THE CHOICE IN 1972 AS PROFESSORS SAW IT

Thus far, the bases of Nixon's and McGovern's support in universities have been described in terms of personal and professional characteristics and ideological orientations. We now take our analysis one step further and examine the specific reasons our respondents themselves offered to explain their vote choices. All faculty interviewed in the 1972 study were asked, "In assessing your vote, what consideration(s) do you find of paramount importance? What, more than anything else, led you to make the choice you did?" Answers were unusually elaborate and precise, and together with responses to related questions, provide a comprehensive picture of the considerations most salient to our faculty sample.

There was a high level of voter apathy and general negativism in the 1972 presidential election (Ladd & Lipset, 1973*a*, pp. 33–65). The dynamic of such a landslide was such that a significant segment of the electorate felt dissatisfied with the choice it was being asked to make, and wound up either not voting or choosing reluctantly. This negativism pervaded faculty assessments of the 1972 presidential contest and indeed was the predominant response. Reading through the nearly 500 interviews, one is more than struck by the "anti" character of the 1972 vote—one is almost overwhelmed by it.

Distrust of Nixon and dissatisfaction with his Vietnam and domestic policies were McGovern's greatest assets among academics. Repeatedly, McGovern's backers cited inadequacies of the Republican incumbent as their prime reason for voting Democratic. A professor of civil engineering at a Southern university described his vote for McGovern as simply due to "a lack of a suitable alternative." Long standing "Nixonphobia" was frequently cited. Said a political scientist at a small Eastern college, "I have always found voting against Nixon one of my easiest tasks." As a professor of English at a Southwestern university put it, "I continue to regard Nixon as a threat to national sanity." Again: "I have voted against Nixon for years and did so again with enthusiasm. I dislike and distrust him intensely. Mine was a vote of 'no confidence' in the incumbent."

Other McGovern voters were more specific in their criticisms of Nixon. Even in November the issue of corruption was often raised. "The issues of integrity in government and credibility—rather than the lack of it," said a professor of classics. "Mr. Nixon has never deigned to comment on the charges of sabotage and espionage. No public official should feel he is above accountability." Interestingly enough, however, in view of developments to come, not a single respondent in our faculty survey referred specifically to Watergate. The relatively low saliency of the affair in late 1972, evident for the population at large, held as well for the professoriate. Many McGovern electors took issue with the record of the Nixon administration in the area of civil liberties. A professor of physics at a West Coast university asserted, "Constitutional rights are incompatible with Nixon." A psychologist at a Southern university cited "Nixon's erosion of freedom of speech, and his selection of Supreme Court Justices." Yet another McGovern voter, a molecular biologist, explained his choice this way: "Domestic issues; Nixon is no friend of the conservationists or the consumerists. His record on curbing inflation is awful." The comments of a professor of law at an East Coast institution captured the flavor of the comments of many faculty who voted for McGovern as they tried to explain their decision: "Nixon represented a greater evil and was surrounded by more dangerous men; McGovern's inabilities might have led to equally awful results, but at least his heart was more or less right. I wish there was a 'no vote' that would prompt new elections."

On the other hand, a large segment of Nixon's voters stressed dissatisfaction with McGovern as the prime reason for their choice. "Radicalism" and a general feeling that the South Dakota Democrat was not "up to the job" were the criticisms most commonly offered. For example:

McGovern is not up to the job; also, he is too radical.

I don't think McGovern could effectively take care of the problems of the Presidency. Also, he is too indecisive. He is okay as a Senator from South Dakota, but not as President.

My vote was one against McGovern's indecision, his style and his lack of integrity.

McGovern did not impress me as being responsible or capable.

Both candidates, of course, had ardent admirers. Faculty members who voted for McGovern and who offered positive reasons for doing so most often cited what they felt was the courage and correctness of his position on Vietnam. Nixon admirers, on the other hand, most frequently used the word "competent." A biological scientist at a Midwestern university spoke of his confidence in the President's "ability to lead the country effectively." A West Coast chemist said he voted for Nixon because of "the feeling that Nixon would be vastly more competent and decisive in dealing with the array of national and international problems." On more specific, substantive matters, the President received high marks from a number of his supporters for accomplishments in the area of foreign relations.

The explanations which our faculty respondents gave for their presidential choices in 1972 have been categorized in a number of different ways. Table 77 represents an effort to organize many disparate responses into four basic groups which together account for about 80 percent of all the individual evaluations. The first contains explanations of "the decisive factor" which focus upon positive attributes—personal and programmatic—of the favored candidate. The second comprises assessments stressing failures or inadequacies of the only viable alternative. The third group bears some resemblance to the second, but differs in its emphasis upon basic dissatisfaction with both major-

TABLE 77 *Explanations by faculty of the principal determinants of their 1972 presidential vote (row percentages)*

	Favorable references to the preferred candidate	Unfavorable references to the major alternative	Gross dissatisfaction with both candidates, but a choice must be made	Positions on the war in Vietnam
All McGovern voters	13	14	17	34
All Nixon voters	30	27	8	15
Switchers, Humphrey in 1968, Nixon in 1972	18	27	23	18
Switchers, Nixon in 1968, McGovern in 1972	19	10	14	43
Third-party voters and nonvoters in 1968, McGovern in 1972	19	8	11	49

NOTE: Row percentages do not equal 100 because of miscellaneous responses not included.
SOURCE: 1972 Ladd-Lipset survey.

party candidates: "A plague on both your houses." Faculty in this category wound up voting, but with a distinct lack of enthusiasm. Finally, there is a group of responses focusing upon the war in Vietnam. Some of these could have been grouped into categories one or two, since they involve both criticism and praise of Nixon and McGovern positions. But the war was such a prime determinant of the vote of so large a segment of the professoriate that it seemed desirable to include together all vote explanations which raised the war as the decisive consideration.

A full third of McGovern's faculty adherents cited the war in Vietnam as the main determinant of their voting decision. An even higher proportion (43 percent) of faculty who voted for Nixon in 1968 but switched to McGovern in the past election gave war-related matters this primacy. And a full half (49 percent) of professors who backed third-party candidates or were nonvoters in 1968 and moved to McGovern's camp in 1972 said that matters related to the war were decisive in their choice.

Nixon voters were influenced much more, Table 77 shows, by general reactions, favorable and unfavorable, to the two candidates. Of Nixon's backers, 30 percent cited accomplishments or positive attributes of the Republican incumbent as determining their choice, whereas only 13 percent of McGovern's supporters offered favorable assessments of the South Dakota Democrat as the primary reason for their decision. An almost equally high proportion (27 percent) of Nixon's adherents said that negative attributes of the Democratic nominee were decisive. The fact that a much higher share of Nixon than of McGovern backers gave positive or, conversely, negative candidate references of a general nature as the primary reasons for their vote has three main sources: (1) Nixon, as the incumbent President, had a concrete record, notably his attainments in foreign policy, for his proponents to applaud; (2) McGovern suffered a special loss of confidence in his abilities to handle the Presidency; and (3) most importantly, McGovern's position as an antiwar candidate loomed so large in his overall profile. Much of the support for the Democrat's position on Vietnam was coupled, of course, with negative assessments of administration policies.

Overall, Table 77 confirms the highly negative character of faculty voting in 1972. The dynamic leading to this "unnatural landslide" produced much the same effect, then, among professors as among the general public. The election was marked by absence of enthusiasm in a substantial sector of the professoriate. Especially striking is the underlying weakness of McGovern's appeal, in view of his position as a liberal, antiwar candidate who relied so heavily upon an activist stratum in the university.

Brief reference should be made to that 5 percent of our sample who indicated in early September an intention to vote Republican but wound up shifting to the Democratic nominee. These campaign switchers display a remarkably uniform profile. They are moderate liberals or centrists who voted for Humphrey in 1968 and who had serious reservations about both of the 1972 major-party candidates. Their shift to McGovern as the campaign progressed seems rooted in the negativism we have been describing. They were finally drawn to the Democratic camp, less as voters influenced by the positive appeals of McGovern's candidacy than as voters "returning to the fold" because of serious dissatisfactions concerning the choice before them. These intracampaign switchers were strongly cross-pressured. Their normal inclination was to vote Democratic, but they had reservations about the 1972 Democratic nominee. A decisive factor in their decision to return to the fold seems to have been the environment in which they moved. Of this small group, 90 percent were at elite schools whose faculties, as we have noted, were heavily for McGovern. The fact that the short-lived defections from Democratic ranks were concentrated at such schools also points up anew the way in which the campus controversies of the late sixties impinged on the more prestigious faculty and unsettled their long-standing liberal political commitments.

There may appear to be, on the surface, a contradiction between our earlier emphasis on the impact of new campus divisions upon

McGovern's candidacy and the failure of any significant segment of the professoriate to cite this factor in explaining their vote. While we have no data which deal conclusively with this, we doubt that there is in fact any inconsistency. It is more likely that a segment of the professoriate whose opposition to the "new campus politics" led them to an aversion to McGovern—whom they associated with this politics—chose not to engage in so involved an explanation of their presidential assessments, even if they were conscious of it, and instead expressed concern about McGovern's "competency" for the job of President.

CONCLUSIONS

On university campuses, the 1972 election was both "business as usual" and something quite new, reflecting currents in the larger society. As to the first, Nixon and McGovern drew heavily upon traditional Republican and Democratic bases of support in the professoriate, and the disproportionate liberalism of the faculty, compared with the public at large, resulted in an academic vote for the Democratic nominee far in excess of what he achieved in the entire electorate. On the other hand, McGovern's candidacy did not, ultimately, strike a strongly responsive chord in the universities, even though he had, of course, his strong partisans, as did Nixon.

University faculty had not swung to the right in any general ideological sense, but there had been a notable reaction to the "new campus politicization" of the late 1960s and early 1970s which redounded to McGovern's disadvantage. Probably no other matter had ever so divided the American university, severing social and intellectual relations, as the controversies over how to deal with student protest. Professors also divided over proposals to modify the traditional academic commitment to meritocratic standards. Many opposed efforts to establish quotas for groups—such as blacks, Chicanos, and women—underrepresented on faculties and in student bodies.

Data from our two national surveys, and from a number of more localized studies as well, indicate that the divisions among faculty were linked to general ideological orientations. The more leftist faculty tended to back student activism and favor official political action by professorial groups, while their more conservative colleagues opposed these positions. More interesting, however, is the fact that significant numbers of academics of liberal persuasion took the "conservative" or "moderate" position in the intramural debates. To a notable degree, the latter were older, often quite prestigious, individuals, heavily involved in research activities. For them, as we have seen, keeping the university a meritocratic "house of study" was a crucial matter.

Since many prominent figures associated with the antiwar "New Politics," such as Senators McGovern and Fulbright, backed the line of argument presented by the left faculty caucuses, we anticipated, as noted earlier, that the internecine cleavage would affect national political attitudes and behavior of more moderate professors, including their voting decisions. In fact, however, the effects which can be detected in the 1972 elections are limited.

In a sense, therefore, 1972 was a story of opportunities missed by the Republican party. The reasons for the failure are manifold. But to a considerable extent, we believe, the GOP was unable to take advantage of the divisions within the university because many of its leaders failed to differentiate among professors. Higher education was, simply, enemy territory. Some politicians in both parties exploited popular concern about campus protests, but Republicans were typically in the forefront. Ronald Reagan, for example, was elected governor of California in 1966 campaigning on the issue of campus disruption at Berkeley. In speeches before and after taking office, he blamed the faculty as a group both for not spending enough time with students and for not taking sanctions against student demonstrators. Various speeches by President Nixon and Vice President Agnew were interpreted as blanket attacks on faculty and administrators.

Republicans can argue, and rightly, that their party was in fact divided, and that some of its leaders have championed university interests. In view of the antipathy of faculty for the Republicans, however, a concerted effort by the minority party to win academic support was required. Instead, the *prevailing* Republican tone was one of suspicion, if not outright hostility.

It is not surprising, then, that in spite of the identification of George McGovern with student activism and support of the counterculture, a climate of distrust of Republicans continued, particularly in the predominantly liberal, upper-tier universities. Coupled with the long-standing Democratic ascendancy among academics, this produced a situation in which there were minimal Republican gains among faculty (and, probably, intellectuals generally) even when the party's presidential nominee was carrying the country so heavily.

The most striking feature of the 1972 presidential election among academics remains the lack of enthusiasm for both candidates, paralleling the reaction in much of the national electorate and attributable in large measure to the same dynamic. Despite the lopsided nature of the final results, American voters did not bestow an overwhelming mandate. Nor, for many of the same reasons, did the professoriate.

10. Issues of the 1970s: Unionism and the Professoriate

If student activism and reactions to efforts to politicize academic life explicitly proved to be the major developments affecting American campuses in the latter half of the 1960s, faculty trade union organization and formal collective bargaining appear to constitute the most important new intramural issues of the 1970s. Unionism has emerged as a potent force in higher education. At the end of 1974, faculty at approximately 350 campuses were represented by bargaining agents, and at over 150 of these campuses faculty were working under a bargaining contract ("Where College Faculties . . .," 1974, p. 24; *Collective Bargaining . . .*, 1974, pp. 2–3). Even more impressive than the sheer numbers of colleges now unionized is the placing of collective bargaining prominently on the political agenda of academe. A decade ago, professorial unionism was hardly even considered. Faculty behavior seemingly still confirmed Thorstein Veblen's (1918, p. 162) observation, made at the end of World War I, that professors would not join unions because of "a feeling among them that their salaries are not of the nature of wages, and that there would be a species of moral obliquity implied in overtly dealing with the matter." But today, in all but a small sector of higher education, the possibilities of unionization are actively considered.

The growth of interest in unionism among academics, its precipitants and its likely consequences, deserve attention. For one thing, this development testifies to important changes occurring in the larger context of academic life. Union norms and practices have been extended to an occupational stratum where they have had no place whatever historically because that stratum has seen its position transformed. Yet another reason for our special interest in the issue lies in the capacity of academic collective bargaining to reflect and reveal a number of salient

NOTE: We have discussed the subject at greater length in a monograph: Ladd and Lipset (1973b). This chapter summarizes much of the material presented in the monograph.

attitudinal structural divisions in the contemporary American professoriate.

FACTORS IN THE GROWTH OF FACULTY UNIONISM

The rapid growth of professorial unionism in the 1970s suggests a sharp reversal of the historic position of academics that their interests and status as professionals are basically incompatible with the spirit of trade unionism, identified in the past largely with manual workers. A prime characteristic of those occupations that are considered highly professional—in addition to their possession of bodies of generalized and systematic knowledge and the presence of a reward structure that involves "a set of symbols of work achievement [which are] ends in themselves, not means to some end of individual self interest"—is a high degree of independence, internal self-control, and evaluation (Barber, 1965, p. 18; Parsons, 1968). In the case of a pursuit based upon a high degree of knowledge, the understanding needed for effective evaluation and control is available only to persons trained in that body of knowledge.

It follows that some kind of self-control, by means of internalized codes of ethics and voluntary in-groups, is necessary. In the realms of professional behavior, such codes and such associations for the setting and maintaining of standards proliferate. Further controls on professional behavior exist, of course, in the informal agencies of public opinion and in government-legal agencies. But these other forms of social control are less important than in nonprofessional areas (Barber, 1965, p. 19).

Everett Hughes (1965, pp. 2–3) has discussed another aspect of this independence of the professions. The professional, not his clients, becomes the true judge of the value of the services rendered. Instead of *caveat emptor*, the motto of all professions is appropriately *credat emptor*—the buyer should trust the judgment of those privy to the requisite esoteric knowledge.

Perhaps the principal reason, then, for the long-standing aversion of college professors and other professionals to trade unions lies in the fact that the latter have been nourished by a condition of dependence—the need to organize and act collectively to achieve some measure of standing and voice vis-à-vis the dominant "outside" party, usually management of the large-scale business enterprise—whereas the former have operated in a situation of substantial independence or autonomy. The factor of social status is closely associated here. Members of an occupation characterized by a high degree of self-regulation draw from that position a sense of individual standing and importance that they guard jealously. The collectivism and accompanying egalitarian norms of trade unionism, in contrast, are acceptable, if not always appealing, to those whose personal status and freedom of action in any case must be low. If there is this link between the independence and high status of the professions and hostility to the spirit of unionism within their own ranks, then the current growth of faculty unionism would seem to indicate that the professoriate is becoming less "professional," and this growth should have achieved its greatest impetus in the least professional components of higher education—that is, in sectors such as the community colleges, which are closest in structure and function to the kindergarten to twelfth grade (K–12) part of education.

The K–12 system is solely concerned with teaching and has no long-standing tradition of professional control over work. At the other extreme is the world of advanced scholarship and research, whose institutions, the leading universities and research institutes of the world, operate as self-governing producers' cooperatives. Their members control most aspects of their working conditions and choose colleagues for their presumed competence as distinguished contributors to the world of scholarship or art. For such institutions, teaching is a function carried on to facilitate the continued growth of knowledge. In between, of course, are the myriad of institutions that attempt different combinations of emphases on teaching and scholarly creativity. We shall be returning to these distinctions repeatedly in the discussion that follows.

The egalitarian norms of unionism would appear to clash much more sharply with the standards and expectations that have prevailed in the professions than with those of the "semiprofessions," such as public school teaching and nursing. A primary distinction between the professions and the semiprofessions involves the so-called "replaceability factor." Doctors, lawyers, or scholars are not viewed as readily interchangeable. In contrast, a good nurse or public school teacher can more easily be replaced by another person with the same basic training and performance record (Etzioni, 1969).

FACULTY ASSOCIATIONS AND THE SWING TO UNIONISM

Unions are a new thing to them, but academics have long been organized into professional associations, many of which have undertaken economic and status representation functions. The largest of these is the American Association of University Professors, founded in 1915, which now has about 90,000 members. The AAUP took as its initial major task the protection of academic freedom in higher education. It was involved from the start with efforts to secure formally protected "job rights," perceived in academe as tenure.[1] Over the years, it demanded and in large measure secured the institutionalization of academic "due process," safeguards governing the conditions under which professors might lose their jobs—a concern not dissimilar to that which has occupied trade unions.[2] For much of its history, too, the AAUP has attempted to advance faculty salaries by fostering minimum standards and then publicizing the extent to which schools actually meet them. Its affiliated chapters also have pressed for incorporation of faculty into university governance, including involvement in the budgetary process and decisions on how the available funds are divided with respect to salaries and various fringe benefits.[3] Committee Z, the AAUP's committee on the Economic Status of the Profession, has not only attempted to analyze and publicize the salary situation, but also has lobbied with national government units which influence salary structures and has encouraged local AAUP chapters to press state legislatures for more funds. In 1971, for example, the committee sent "two urgent communications to the Cost of Living Council established to administer the [wage] freeze," seeking modification of the rules to permit the academic community to gain larger wage increases ("Coping with Adversity . . .," 1972).

Yet from its inception until 1972, the AAUP resisted the notion that it resembled a trade union, that it should engage in strikes or collective bargaining.[4] In 1972, the outgoing president of the organization, Sanford Kadish, gave a strong statement of the traditional "antiunion" precepts:

I will simply point out that the strike proceeds by deliberately harming the educational mission . . . in order to promote the personal employee interest, in contradiction to the service ideal of subordinating personal interest to the advancement of the purposes of the university. . . . More generally, the economic strike

[1]See Joughlin (1967) Metzger, (1965), and "Report of the Self-Survey Committee . . ." (1965). For a discussion of the AAUP as "an occupational association or quasi-union," see Strauss (1965–1966).

[2]An excellent discussion by one of labor's key intellectuals of the sources of faculty unionism and its relation to the concept of professionalism is Tyler (1971–1972). For a discussion of the similarities in function and degree of organization between professional organizations and trade unions, see Lipset (1967*b*).

[3]For a recent statement, see "The Role of the Faculty. . ." (1972).

[4]See "Council Position on Collective Bargaining" (1971), and Trombley (1972). A description of the way in which an AAUP chapter was transformed into a union and went on strike may be found in Pitts (1972).

constitutes a significant compromise with the mode of persuasion implicit in arguing entitlements through appeal to shared premises. . . . In dividing the university into worker-professors and manager-administrators and governing boards. . . [collective bargaining] imperils the premise of shared authority, encourages the polarization in interests and exaggerates the adversary concerns over interests held in common. . . . Moreover, the process itself as it functions tends to remit issues which faculty should themselves determine to outside agencies, such as state and federal boards, arbitrators, and union bureaucracies. In addition, since unions rest on continued support of their constituency, the process becomes susceptible to essentially political rather than essentially academic decision-making.[5]

Kadish made his remarks, however, just as most of the active members of the AAUP were abandoning the old posture in order to compete with their trade union rivals. At the May 1972 annual meeting in New Orleans, the Association decided by an overwhelming margin "to pursue collective bargaining as a major additional way of realizing [our] goals in higher education."

The largest professional organization of teachers in America is the National Education Association (NEA). From its formation in 1857, the NEA has been concerned with improving the position of teaching as a profession by enhancing training, requiring more and better education, formalizing the requirements for teachers' credentials, and the like. Although primarily an organization for those who taught or administered in elementary and secondary schools, the NEA established a higher education department in 1870 that lasted until the 1920s, when it was dissolved on the grounds that other groups were dealing more effectively with the college scene. (The department was re-created in 1943.) In large measure, the NEA's early efforts in higher education, like those at lower levels, were dedicated to improving the quality of education rather than the salaries or internal influence of teachers (Wesley, 1957). Its lack of interest in these problems in large part reflected the fact that much of its leadership came from school superintendents and college and university presidents.

Beginning early in this century, however, the NEA increasingly took up the cudgels to improve the salaries and working conditions of classroom teachers in public schools. It engaged in repeated publicized surveys of the salary situation and sought to establish appropriate salary schedules. In many ways, it gradually assumed a role at the primary

[5]See Kadish (1972, p. 122; 1969, pp. 34–68); Kadish, Webb, & Van Alstyne (1972, pp. 57–61); and "1968 Statement on Faculty Participation in Strikes" (1971, pp. 42–46).

and secondary level comparable with that of the AAUP in higher education, including emphasis on the work of its Defense Commission and its Committee on Tenure and Academic Freedom.

Perceived as the major organization of schoolteachers, the NEA did not pretend to compete with the AAUP for professorial membership. Its various higher education divisions were most successful in sectors linked to lower education—the teachers colleges and their successors among four-year state schools and junior or community colleges, often administered by the same boards that governed high schools.[6]

During the 1960s, in part responding to the growth of trade unionism through the American Federation of Teachers, the NEA began to give up some of its cherished emphasis on appropriate professional behavior for teachers who are concerned with the welfare of their students. It started authorizing strikes, first described as "refusals to work" without contracts guaranteeing minimum rights, salaries, and work standards. From these work stoppages the NEA moved to actual collective bargaining, competing in Labor Board elections, signing contracts, and explicitly using the strike weapon. By the end of the 1960s, the NEA was a full-fledged teachers' union, in fact if not in name. Recognition of this had led it to cooperate closely with the AFT in a number of situations and to the merger of NEA and AFT locals in some major cities. In January 1973, the NEA joined with the most rapidly growing union in the country, the 525,000-member American Federation of State, County and Municipal Employees, in a new group, CAPE (Coalition of American Public Employees), for joint organizing, collective bargaining, and political action.

This shift to the status of trade union also affected NEA involvement in higher education. Its professorial affiliates (now organized in a body called the Higher Education Association) began to function as a faculty union. Although, with 30,000 members, it was considerably smaller than the AAUP, the NEA became the largest faculty union of the early 1970s, representing many more professors in formal collective bargaining negotiations than its two principal rivals.[7] Moreover, its 1972 convention voted to give "priority" to organizing higher education ("NEA gives Top Priority . . .," 1972, p. 2).

[6]For a description of the operation of various wings of the NEA in the middle 1960s, before it accepted a role as a collective bargaining agent in higher education, see *Report of the Task Force on Higher Education* (1968).

[7]For detailed descriptions of these three groups, their attitudes toward collective bargaining, and membership estimates, see Marmion (1969, pp. 1–14) and Scully and Sievert (1971, pp. 1, 6).

The changes in the self-conception and activities of the AAUP and the NEA clearly have been precipitated by recent successes of the American Federation of Teachers (AFT), the oldest teachers' union. Founded in 1916 as an affiliate of the American Federation of Labor, the AFT made little progress until the 1960s. Its uncompromising insistence on equating the situation of teachers with that of manual workers held it back as long as few teachers were ready to accept that link.

The AFT has always included some professors among its membership, but since it was defined primarily as an organization of schoolteachers, it had minimal support in higher education until very recently. According to its own official history, faculty adherents in the 1920s were mostly persons interested "in broad social issues" rather than collective bargaining (*A Loose Leaf History . . .*, 1972, p. 1). Not surprisingly, in view of the strength of the Communist party and other left-wing groups among the intelligentsia of the 1930s, the AFT came to include some members primarily concerned with advancing radical causes. The college teachers' locals, which numbered 2,000 members, were particularly affected by the politicization of that era and were caught up in bitter factional strife between pro-Communist and liberal-Socialist factions. In the late thirties, "several locals, including a number of college locals, had their charters revoked" by the parent body for serving the interests of an external political organization. Commenting on the situation in the 1930s, the authors of the union's history write: "From the perspective of the seventies it is difficult to appreciate how radical the AFT appeared . . ." (ibid., pp. 3–4).

Not until the 1960s did teacher unionism really gain momentum, starting with the victory of the New York City AFT affiliate, the United Federation of Teachers, in a 1961 collective bargaining election. The union then began to win representation rights and contracts with school boards in many major cities and assorted communities across the country. It was able to carry through a number of major strikes, helped in large measure by the fact that other unions respected its picket line. Efforts to organize college teachers followed directly on the successes in the public schools. The United Federation of College Teachers, Local 1460, was formed in New York City in 1963. The national organization created a Colleges and Universities Department in 1967. In 1968, New York provided the initial major triumph in higher education when a collective bargaining election held for the City University of New York resulted in a division of representation rights between two groups, the AFT affiliate for lecturers and other part-time teachers and the Legislative Conference for those on the regular professorial ladder. The two groups merged in 1972, and the new unit affiliated with both the AFT and the NEA. (The New York State organizations of these groups merged as well.) The union also was successful in Chicago, where it won a collective bargaining election to represent faculty in the junior college system and subsequently (Fall 1966) was victorious in a prolonged strike. It claims over 20,000 faculty members nationally.

OPINIONS ON FACULTY UNIONISM

Although collective bargaining in higher education seems here to stay, its extension has hardly met with universal acclaim. Traditional grounds for opposition remain, and a large segment of the professoriate continues to be opposed. Not all elections are supporting unionization. All told, 29 out of 367 campuses which have been involved in such contests have voted for "no agent" ("Where College Faculties . . .," 1974, p. 24). The group includes some important schools. In October 1972, for example, the Michigan State University faculty overwhelmingly rejected collective bargaining—1,213 for no agent, 438 for the NEA, and 280 for the AAUP ("Results Mixed . . .," 1972, p. 1). In the fall of 1973, the faculties of the University of Massachusetts at Amherst, Syracuse, Villanova, Antioch, Albion, Randolph-Macon, the University of Detroit, and New York University all rejected union representation (Semas, 1973c, p. 1). It is by no means certain, then, or even likely, that unionization will move across academe with the same inevitability as an incoming tide. Rather, what we find is a deeply divided professoriate.

Nearly three-fifths (59 percent) of all academics in the 1969 Carnegie survey gave general endorsement to the principle of collective bargaining by rejecting the proposition that "collective bargaining by faculty members has no place in a college or university." On a more demanding question, where pro-unionism required agreement with the statement that "there are circumstances in which a strike would be a legitimate means of collective action for faculty members," almost half (47 percent) were in favor. Four years later, an American Council on Education survey posed the "collective bargaining has no place . . ." proposition in exactly the same form as the earlier Carnegie survey, and found a slight increase in probargaining sentiment—66 percent indicating general approval of the practice, with 34 percent definitely opposed.[8] This shift of 7 points toward acceptance of the legitimacy of bargaining for faculty (on the basis of data from the two surveys) is hardly enough to speak of a decided trend, but it suggests that the slowdown in victories for bargaining agents does not reflect increased opposition to collective

[8]For a further description of the 1973 ACE study, see Bayer (1973, p. 30).

bargaining. Our 1972 survey found professors evenly divided in their assessments of the extraordinary growth of unionism since the late 1960s—43 percent agreed "that the recent growth of unionization of college and university faculty is beneficial and should be extended," while 44 percent disagreed and 13 percent entertained conflicting assessments.

In examining the characteristics of those who are supportive of unionism and collective bargaining (see Tables 78 and 79), two factors stand out, the first related to aspects of professional standing and the second to political opinions generally. Faculty employed in the lower tier of academe—in terms of scholarly prestige, financial resources, and economic benefits—and those who are in the lower ranks, who lack tenure, and who are younger, are much more likely to favor organized collective action. Not surprisingly, considering the traditional association in society of support for trade unionism with liberal views, and the historic experience of the AFT, our data show liberal-to-left professors much more pro-union than their conservative colleagues. Those who perceive themselves as being on the political left, have backed liberal candidates, hold liberal attitudes on a variety of community political issues, support compensatory programs for blacks, are favorable to campus activism, support giving students greater power within higher education, and want to change the governance system of higher education to increase faculty power are more likely to endorse collective bargaining and faculty strikes and to view increased unionization as a good thing.

Class interests   The data presented in Table 78 testify to the strong linkage between "class interests" of academics and their receptivity to union practices in higher education. The association between "faculty power" and the scholarly standing of colleges and universities is well known. That is, professors at major schools are much less "employees," much more the controlling force in their institutions, than are their colleagues at lesser places. In the upper reaches of academe, faculty generally have acquired almost all the power to choose new employees (colleagues), to judge whether they should be retained (given tenure), and, to a lesser but still substantial degree, to determine individual salary increases. Naturally enough, they do not view the university administration and trustees as their *employer* in the way those working in industry or government look upon their top administrative hierarchies. All this is another way of stating that major college faculty have possessed in significant measure the independence and self-control characteristic of a *highly professional* occupational cohort.

TABLE 78 *Faculty attitudes toward collective bargaining and unionism, by professional characteristics and rewards (percentages of n)*

The 1969 survey	Disagree, "no place on campus for faculty collective bargaining"	Agree, "faculty strikes can be legitimate action"
ALL FACULTY (60,028 RESPONDENTS)	59	47
Quality of school at which professor teaches		
A (elite) (n = 19,089)	53	49
B (n = 25,224)	55	44
C (n = 13,110)	60	44
D (lowest tier) (n = 2,580)	67	52
Type of institution		
University (n = 44,871)	54	46
Four-year college (n = 13,020)	61	46
Two-year college (n = 2,133)	67	49
Tenure		
Tenured faculty (n = 29,853)	54	41
Untenured faculty (n = 26,766)	64	53
Received research grants, last 12 months		
Yes [received grant(s)] (n = 27,966)	54	49
No (n = 29,778)	61	47
Salary		
Over $20,000 (n = 6,420)	45	38
$14,000–$20,000 (n = 15,567)	52	42
$10,000–$14,000 (n = 21,417)	59	47
Under $10,000 (n = 15,312)	66	51
Age		
60 years and older (n = 4,398)	45	30
50–59 (n = 9,408)	53	35
40–49 (n = 16,113)	57	44
30–39 (n = 20,580)	62	52
Under 30 (n = 8,607)	68	60

TABLE 78 *(continued)*

| The 1972 survey | "Do you agree or disagree that the recent growth of unionization of college and university faculty is beneficial and should be extended?" | | |
	Agree	Uncertain; conflicting assessments	Disagree
ALL FACULTY (n = 471)	43	13	44
Quality of school at which professor teaches			
Major colleges and universities (n = 193)	39	19	43
Lower-tier colleges and universities (n = 278)	45	10	45
Received research grants, last 12 months			
Yes [received grant(s)] (n = 241)	36	15	48
No (n = 216)	50	11	39
Age			
50 years and older (n = 139)	32	11	58
35–49 (n = 227)	46	14	40
Under 35 years (n = 104)	51	14	35

SOURCES: 1969 Carnegie Commission Survey of Student and Faculty Opinion; 1972 Ladd-Lipset survey.

"We are the university" is a valid description of the standing of professors at the top of the academic hierarchy, but it decidedly does not hold for teachers at many lesser institutions. This is an important reason why the Carnegie survey data show faculty receptivity to unionization lowest at such elite centers of higher education as the major universities, and strongest at two-year colleges and other schools of low scholarly standing. Since the enormous expansion of higher education over the past decade has occurred disproportionately at the lower levels, in institutions where faculty independence, and hence professional standing, is tenuous at best, we have identified one component of the increased receptivity to unionism in the academic community.

Data on attitudes toward unionism by individual attainment are consistent with the "class interest" hypothesis. Thus, professors of low scholarly achievement give greater backing to the principles of collective bargaining than do their more productive colleagues, untenured

TABLE 79 *Faculty attitudes toward unionism, by general political orientations (row percentages)*

The 1969 survey	Disagree, "no place on campus for faculty collective bargaining"	Agree, "faculty strikes can be legitimate action"
Liberalism-Conservatism Scale		
1 *(very liberal)*	80	80
2	64	56
3	58	44
4	53	33
5 *(very conservative)*	42	24
	Gamma = .32	Gamma = .46
Campus Activism Scale		
1 *(strongly supportive)*	82	80
2	68	59
3	56	41
4	49	33
5 *(strongly opposed)*	40	23
	Gamma = .37	Gamma = .48
1968 presidential vote for:		
Left third-party candidate (n = 1,308)	87	84
Humphrey (n = 30,492)	64	56
Wallace (n = 456)	49	35
Nixon (n = 17,820)	47	29

professors give more backing than those with tenure, and academics with low salaries are more supportive than their better-rewarded associates.[9]

These differences in views of collective bargaining and faculty unionism, by achieved academic position, might be seen as largely due to the age variable—a result of the lower status and more liberal

[9]A. H. Halsey and Martin Trow describe a comparable pattern in Great Britain regarding support for the Association of University Teachers (AUT), an organization comprising about 60 percent of British university teachers, which is halfway between a full-fledged trade union and a traditional professional association. The AUT had its origins before World War I "among the non-professorial staff of the new civic universities led by Manchester men like J.S.B. Stopford and J.E. Myers." It has continued to be weakest among "the higher ranks" and in the ancient elite centers, Oxford and Cambridge (Halsey & Trow, 1971, pp. 184–185, 139–140). The major work on the AUT is Perkin (1969).

TABLE 79 *(continued)*

| | "Do you agree or disagree that the recent growth of unionization of college and university faculty is beneficial and should be extended?" | | |
The 1972 survey	Agree	Uncertain; conflicting assessments	Disagree
Political self-characterization			
Left-liberal (n = 221)	54	17	29
Middle-of-the-road (n = 118)	37	8	55
Conservative (n = 113)	29	11	60
Position on Vietnam			
Withdrawal (n = 255)	51	15	34
Vietnamization (n = 154)	32	11	57
Position on radical student activism			
Approve (n = 172)	55	13	32
Disapprove (n = 217)	36	9	55
1972 presidential vote for:			
McGovern (n = 237)	53	14	33
Nixon (n = 184)	29	10	60

SOURCES: 1969 Carnegie Commission Survey of Student and Faculty Opinion; 1972 Ladd-Lipset survey.

views of young professors. However, specifying the relationship between indicators of academic position and union support within the different age categories shows that both academic "class" position and age have independent effects. Young faculty are consistently more supportive of unionism in each quality stratum of institutions, and within each age cohort teachers at the lesser schools give more support than those at major scholarly centers. Age and tenure also exert consistent independent effects on attitudes toward faculty unionization.

Ideology General political orientations themselves are important determinants of views on faculty unionism (Table 79). Among professors scoring in the most liberal (or left) quintile on the Liberalism-Conservatism Scale (for national issues), 80 percent concurred that faculty strikes are a legitimate means of collective action, as against 24 percent of those in the most conservative quintile. Just 42 percent of the latter group rejected the proposition that collective bargaining is inappropriate to the university context, in contrast to 80 percent of the most liberal academics.

The variation in union support by position on campus protests and demonstrations is also large. Of faculty who gave the strongest backing to student activism 80 percent endorsed the legitimacy of strikes by professors, compared with only 23 percent of that fifth of academics most opposed to the protests and demonstrations of the late sixties.

Interestingly enough, the correlations are somewhat weaker between opinion on campus issues not directly connected to national affairs—as were the campus protests and demonstrations—and views on faculty unionism. The association between responses to questions subsumed by our University Governance Index—such matters as whether junior faculty are perceived as having too little say in decision making and whether the role of faculty in university governance should be augmented—and positions on unionism is notably weaker than the relationship of the latter with liberalism-conservatism generally. While the differences described are far from massive, they run contrary to what we suspected. There was reason to expect that professors who most strongly backed a bigger voice for faculty "backbenchers" in decision making would be notably supportive of unionism. In fact, the correlation between liberalism-conservatism and support for academic unionism is even stronger.

Both the AFT and the NEA argue that many college and university administrative structures are authoritarian, and that unionization is the way to achieve the necessary democratization. Although the association between support for governance reform and for unionism among faculty at large is not as high as was expected, it is still substantial. Academics who maintain that junior faculty have insufficient voice in department decisions, that senior professors have excessive control over university affairs, and that matters would be improved if colleges operated more as democracies governed by full faculty and student participation are notably more receptive to the idea of collective bargaining and strikes. And the strength of these associations is not significantly lessened when we control for age.

What is most striking, however, is that support for governance reform is greater at upper-tier schools—where objectively the situation is better in the sense that decisions are more collegial and less hierarchical—than at colleges of the lower range (Table 80). Of elite-school faculty, 38 percent agree that junior members have too little say, as compared with 26 percent and 29 percent, respectively, at institutions of the two lowest tiers. Support for unionism is greater at the lesser places

TABLE 80   **Dissatisfaction with governance practices, by quality of school at which faculty are located (row percentages)**

Quality of school	Agree, *"junior faculty have too little say in department decisions"*	Agree, *"a small group of senior faculty holds disproportionate influence"*	Agree, *"undergraduate education would be improved if faculty and students had full control"*
A (elite)	38	47	42
B	31	42	40
C	26	37	38
D (lowest tier)	29	38	38

SOURCE: 1969 Carnegie Commission Survey of Student and Faculty Opinion.

(Table 78), but there is not as strong a sense of need for governance reform at these schools as at major universities.

On first inspection, we might conclude that the data in Table 80 simply reflect the fact that elite-college professors are more liberal or left-of-center than their brethren at schools of lower standing and favor a "liberalization" in governance in much the same way they endorse liberal and egalitarian programs in the larger society. But essentially the same pattern applies when we hold ideology constant. Overall, conservatives at major universities are slightly more receptive to criticisms of existing governance practices than their ideological counterparts at lesser schools.

Clearly, the relatively strong support for faculty unionism at lower-tier institutions is not the product of a greater acceptance of the governance critique advanced by the NEA and AFT leadership. Elite-school faculty, while operating in environments that generally are more democratic—that is, with greater scope for individual initiative—are at the same time more demanding. They hold much higher expectations. College teaching at places of low academic standing less resembles a profession, and faculty in such positions therefore see less of a clash between their status and the norms of unionism. But they are not, at the same time, the most critical of existing governance practices.

PATTERNS IN SOURCES OF SUPPORT FOR UNIONISM

Analysis of the 1969 and 1972 surveys of academic opinion sustains the interpretation that support for faculty unionism and collective bargaining has two independent sources—apart from the general economic and political climate in which higher education finds itself. Large, apparently growing segments of the professoriate occupy positions that give them a kind of "class interest" in the development of unionism. They are at institutions where faculty have less professional independence, are relatively poorly compensated economically, or receive low recognition. The least professional—that is, "profession-like"—sectors of academe are the most supportive of faculty unions. At the same time, views on unionism are a function of general ideological orientations. Academics have long been distinguished by a disproportionate commitment to liberal-left politics, and this has deepened during the recent period of antiwar protest and student activism.

Liberal professors are more pro-union than their conservative brethren at all types of institutions and in all age and achievement groupings. At the same time, holding ideology constant, we find that faculty at major centers of research and scholarship are significantly less supportive of unionism than their colleagues at academically weaker institutions (Table 81). Again holding ideological orientations constant, professors of high status are less favorable to unions than those of more modest attainment, older academics are less supportive than younger, and relatively well-paid scholars show less sympathy than colleagues not so amply remunerated.

General ideology and career position join to affect the views and behavior of younger faculty, who are much more liberal politically and whose career expectations in the form of salary, tenure and promotion prospects, and various perquisites of academic life have been sharply reduced in a period of budget stringencies and little or no expansion. Young nontenured professors increasingly consider themselves a deprived group who might benefit from unionization. Someone else—senior faculty, the central administration, or the trustees—controls their future. The change in the labor market, with relatively few permanent openings, especially in more attractive schools, appears to have made many of them sympathetic to proposals to lessen the competitive character of faculty life. The sense of being relatively independent, high-status professionals probably has diminished significantly among young academics in recent years.

Table 82 shows an interesting interactive pattern among three variables that most strongly influence orientations to faculty unionism: age (with its interest or status components), type of institutional setting, and general ideology. Each of these factors independently affects propensity to back unionization. Ideology produces the sharpest dif-

TABLE 81 *Support for faculty unionism, by general ideology and academic career variables (percentages in each cell are, first, the proportion rejecting the proposition that collective bargaining has no place on a college campus, and second [in parentheses] the percentage agreeing that strikes are a legitimate means of collective action for faculty)*

Position on Liberalism-Conservatism Scale	School quality		
	C (lower tier)	B	A (elite)
Very liberal, liberal	79 (72)	73 (70)	67 (69)
Middle-of-the-road	67 (50)	53 (41)	45 (37)
Conservative	51 (31)	43 (25)	37 (24)

Position on Liberalism-Conservatism Scale	Scholarly publications last two years		
	None	1–4	5 or more
Very liberal, liberal	77 (72)	70 (69)	69 (69)
Middle-of-the-road	63 (46)	55 (42)	48 (40)
Conservative	50 (29)	44 (26)	39 (28)

Position on Liberalism-Conservatism Scale	Age		
	Under 35	35–49	50 and older
Very liberal, liberal	75 (76)	70 (68)	64 (56)
Middle-of-the-road	56 (46)	52 (41)	47 (34)
Conservative	48 (33)	43 (25)	37 (18)

Position on Liberalism-Conservatism Scale	Salary		
	Under $12,000	$12,000–$17,000	$17,000 and over
Very liberal, liberal	77 (75)	69 (67)	60 (58)
Middle-of-the-road	60 (47)	49 (39)	41 (33)
Conservative	48 (28)	41 (24)	33 (20)

SOURCE: 1969 Carnegie Commission Survey of Student and Faculty Opinion.

ferentiation, with between 20 and 25 percentage points separating liberal-left from centrist-conservative academics in each category defined by the interaction of type of school and age. In comparison, professors at upper-tier schools are consistently about 10 percentage points less supportive of collective bargaining than their colleagues at lower-tier institutions, controlling for both age and general ideological perspectives. Holding constant ideology and institutional setting, we find that young (under 35) faculty are more pro-union than the older

TABLE 82 *Percentage of faculty supporting collective bargaining,* by age, school quality, and general liberalism-conservatism (Liberalism-Conservatism Scale)*

[Percentages are centrist-conservative/ very liberal, liberal faculty]	Age	
Quality of school at which professor teaches	Over 35	Under 35
Upper tier	41/64	48/72
Lower tier	53/74	61/81

[Percentages are upper tier/lower tier faculty]	Age	
Position on Liberalism-Conservatism Scale	Over 35	Under 35
Centrist-conservative	41/53	48/61
Very liberal, liberal	64/74	72/81

[Percentages are over 35/under 35 faculty]	Position on Liberalism-Conservatism Scale	
Quality of school at which professor teaches	Centrist-conservative	Very liberal-liberal
Upper tier	41/48	64/72
Lower tier	53/61	74/81

*"Collective bargaining by faculty members has no place in a college or university." Percentages are those *disagreeing* with this proposition.

SOURCE: 1969 Carnegie Commission Survey of Student and Faculty Opinion.

(over 35) cohort by a margin of 6 to 8 percentage points in each category.[10]

Professional status and ideology: a basic tension An interesting and important tension exists in the relationship between ideology and support for unionism on the one hand and that between academic status and union sympathies on the other. Faculty of high scholarly standing, we

[10]Although we are dealing with scales and measures of varying structure, it is still informative to note that computation of partial correlation coefficients shows the same relative weights for the independent or "predictor" variables:

	Support for unionism
Age	.07
Index of Academic Standing	.15
Liberalism-Conservatism Scale	.32

have noted, show up in all measures as more supportive of a liberal-left "progressive" and egalitarian politics than their less highly achieving colleagues. On the whole, a "class theory of politics" is essentially inapplicable to academe. The source of the relative liberalism of American academics, compared with most other groups in the society, is not their objective deprivation but their intellectuality. Highly achieving faculty, then, are the most liberal, and there is a very strong relationship between liberalism and support for faculty unionism. But at the same time, scholars of high attainment are less supportive of unionism than their colleagues of lower professional standing. The liberalism of elite-school faculty pushes them one way with regard to unionism, but factors relating to their professional status at once shove them in the opposite direction.

The relative lack of support for faculty unionism at major colleges and universities is not solely a function of a more privileged economic and power position. The more research-oriented culture of academe is inherently meritocratic. Faculty are rewarded with tenure, promotions, and salaries from within, and with research grants and honorific rewards from without, according to judgments made about their scholarly activities. There is an important clash, then, between the interests and values of achieving academics and the normative system of trade unionism. The latter is largely egalitarian. Unions seek to limit salary and other differences among those doing similar work, using seniority as the prime base for differentiation. Initial appointments to a position are usually defined by unions as probationary, and once the appointee has demonstrated competence by some recognized minimum standard, he may not be fired or denied job security (tenure) simply because someone else better qualified becomes available. Unions press for increases in benefits for entire categories of employees. They seek to reduce the employer's power to differentially reward employees (discriminate among them) as a means of reducing arbitrary power.

The general outlook of unions—notably of the AFT and the NEA, which have their greatest strength in primary and secondary schools—is clearly relevant to the position and needs of faculty at lower-tier four-year colleges and two-year community colleges. As noted, faculty have much less autonomy at these institutions. Administrators and trustees exert a large measure of control over hiring and firing and over the various economic decisions. Because there is little or no research activity, faculty may be judged differentially only in terms of teaching competence and school service, much as in a high school. There are few external sources of recognition, such as competitive job offers dictated by national judgments about ability in a discipline. In this context, unions are a way of pressing for higher income and other benefits that will come for the collectivity or not at all.

The most consistent proponent of the collectivist ideology of the lower tier of academe, the American Federation of Teachers, has repeatedly sought to appeal to the resentment against the prestigious faculty of those with little personal bargaining power by complaining about academic "elitism," the "academic entrepreneur," "the 'star' scholar" who is able to "feather his own nest by job-skipping." Israel Kugler, a professor of social science in a New York community college and a leading AFT spokesman in higher education, has argued the case of the locally oriented teacher who is not involved in research, stating that "elitism . . . led to the 'flight from teaching,'" and resulted in little "loyalty to the institution" (Kugler, n.d., pp. 2–5). He praises faculty who "remain at an institution and engage in its reform rather than become academic entrepreneurs who hop to other institutions that are ready to pirate them away with the lure of individual betterment" (Kugler, 1968, p. 417). On another occasion, Kugler (1969, p. 184) wrote that the AFT "is appalled at the widespread practice of secret individual deals for a favored few."

The NEA has also sought to make an explicit appeal to the lower-status elements in academe against the higher. Thus, during the 1972 collective bargaining elections at the University of Hawaii, its campaign organ issued this appeal for votes from faculty in less prestigious fields and at community colleges:

Academia has traditionally looked down at the workers in the applied sciences and technologies with varying degrees of sufferance and snobbishness. Informally, the workers in theoretical disciplines have looked upon the likes of engineers with condescension, but placed them in a higher niche than the educationists. Now where do you suppose the people who teach business management, pre-med, pre-dental, physical education, military science, sugar technology, dental technology, and similar subjects end up in such a hierarchy.

It is now apparent that the College of Tropical Agriculture occupies a stratum of low esteem. . . .

[The University of Hawaii] created a Community College system, with among other arrangements, a separate classification for employees with a separate salary schedule [than that at the main Manoa campus]. . . .

It is interesting that the [status of the] college-transfer English instructor is different than the English instructor at Manoa. However, the student passed by the Community College instructor is totally acceptable to the Manoa instructor with full credit (Kiyosaki, 1972, p. 1).

These issues were also voiced in economic terms during the collective bargaining election campaign at Michigan State University in the fall of

1972. The strongest union group, the MSU Faculty Associates, an NEA affiliate, stated that it "unequivocally rejects the concept of rewarding scholars on the basis of 'market place' values." It repeatedly distributed data purporting to demonstrate the inequities in salary among the various segments of the university. Its platform proclaimed that it "is committed to . . . correct[ing] the many salary inequities that now exist at the University. The manner in which inequities may be resolved includes the provision of higher salary increases to lower paid faculty members while assuring that individuals who currently received high salaries would receive increases *at least* equal to the increasing cost of living." Its strongest opponent, the Committee of Concerned Faculty, which successfully urged a vote against collective bargaining, argued for the continuation of "a system of merit increases for extra rewards for outstanding faculty—young or old" ("Consensus 2 . . .," 1972; "Today and . . .," 1972).

Given the enormous differences in professional status and autonomy characteristic of the several levels of academe, the presence of "structural" variations in faculty response to unionism is readily understood. What complicates the development of unionization in higher education, and prevents the matter from being a simple "greater-lesser" relationship, is that academics at the less prestigious institutions, involved in teaching rather than scholarship, are decidedly more conservative in their political views generally—and hence ideologically less receptive to the norms of unionism—than their major-university, research-oriented colleagues.

Professors at upper-tier schools, and highly achieving academics in general, are significantly cross-pressured with regard to faculty unionism: Their liberalism would incline them to support it, but their objective interests and the general structure of their academic values bring them into opposition. And, as we have seen, *the latter considerations typically prove decisive.* The relative lack of support for unionization among professors of high attainment exists not because of, but in spite of, their broad ideological commitments and is testimony to the strength of competing interests and values.

Objective "deprivation" and union support   The presence of substantially greater backing for faculty unionism at the bottom than at the top of academe has been discussed in terms of contrasting status and interests: the fact that teachers at lower-tier institutions typically have less of the independence and self-regulation associated with being members of a profession, that they have less personal standing and bargaining power, and that they are not nearly so well appointed in salary and

TABLE 83   *Economic rewards, job demands, and scholarly standing of faculty, by the quality of the school at which they teach (row percentages)*

Quality of school	Salary: under $12,000	Research support received, last 12 months: none	Number of hours taught per week: 11 and up	Number of scholarly publications, last two years: none
A (elite)	37	37	10	24
B	44	52	23	40
C	66	82	50	67
D_1 (lowest tier, 4-year schools)	73	85	59	70
D_2 (lowest tier, 2-year schools)	73	95	78	88

SOURCE: 1969 Carnegie Commission Survey of Student and Faculty Opinion.

various perquisites of academic life. The latter point deserves further comment because objective differences in the position of faculty by type of school are so striking.

In Table 83, we compare academics in terms of formal rewards and achievements, by the quality of the institution at which they are located. Only 37 percent of elite-school professors, compared with 73 percent at the lowest-tier schools, received salaries of under $12,000 in 1969. Also, 95 percent of junior college faculty and 85 percent of those in four-year colleges of the lowest range had received no research support of any kind in the 12 months preceding the survey, contrasted with just over one-third (37 percent) of major-college academics. Only 10 percent in the top tier, but 78 percent in two-year institutions, taught 11 or more hours of classes per week. Scholarly output naturally varied greatly, with 88 percent of those in the junior colleges, as against just 24 percent of faculty in elite institutions, reporting no publications in the most recent two-year period.

The rewards at the top dwarf those at the bottom. These vast differences in objective standing are a powerful underlying factor behind the disproportionate growth of unions in the less-privileged sectors of the academy. It is important to recognize that the underpinnings of lower-tier unionization are located in these differences and not in more politicized job-related complaints or even in job satisfaction generally. We noted earlier in this chapter that elite-school professors are generally more critical of existing practices in university governance and more inclined to perceive and object to hierarchical or insufficiently democratic modes of decision making than their colleagues at lesser places.

Further, along this line, we find that a larger proportion of academics in major colleges and universities than in two-year colleges, according to the 1969 survey, see themselves as totally powerless "to influence the policies of [their] institution"—42 percent as against 24 percent. In addition, 35 percent of the former, compared with 24 percent of the latter, believe their departments are administered "autocratically." It is more striking, perhaps, that faculty at the less scholarly eminent places do not manifest greater overall dissatisfaction with their occupational situation. Among junior college teachers, 56 percent, in comparison with 54 percent of professors at elite institutions, maintain that the school at which they teach "is a very good place for me." And those at the bottom are as satisfied with their choice of career as colleagues at the upper reaches.

This reminds us strongly of the importance of contrasting reference groups and evaluation structures. Reference group analysis attends to "determinants and consequences of those processes of evaluation and self appraisal in which the individual takes *the values or standards of other individuals and groups as a comparative frame of reference.*"[11] The "other individuals and groups" serving as objects of reference for junior college faculty have included secondary school teachers. As Gus Tyler, a union leader and frequent commentator on higher education, noted recently, "the community college for both administration and faculty is a continuation of lower-grade experience, an extension of K–12 to K–14" (Tyler, 1971–1972, p. 24). Junior colleges, in one sense, are not the *bottom rung* of higher education but the *top rung* of the K–14 ladder. "Am I doing well?" "Is my college administration sufficiently democratic?" "Is my institution generally a good place to be?" Such questions are answered by teachers at two-year schools from a frame of reference that is very different from the one operative for major-university faculty.

Because of significant variations in reference points, the lower tier of academe does not appear more critical or dissatisfied than the top, although it is less well-appointed. Unionism has proceeded fastest at the bottom simply because the objective situation there, as a totality, makes it much more "natural." If, as Tyler has observed, the professoriate contains components of both priesthood and proletariat, the latter is much more prominent in the condition of teachers at the lesser schools.

---

[11]See Merton and Kitt (1950, p. 51). For a discussion of reference group theory applied specifically to unions, see Lipset and Trow (1957, pp. 391–411).

COLLECTIVE BARGAINING ELECTIONS IN ACADEME

As of spring 1975, faculty unionization has remained heavily skewed toward lower-tier schools, especially the junior colleges. Around 70 percent of all colleges and universities that formally bargain with their faculty are two-year institutions, even though this sector comprises only a third of all campuses in the country. Because these schools are relatively small, the disproportion in organized strength is less when judged by numbers of individual faculty covered. Still, approximately one-quarter of all academics included in bargaining units are in two-year institutions—which employ less than a sixth of faculty nationally. The NEA and the AFT dominate junior college bargaining, with the AAUP largely left out. Most large universities still are not under collective bargaining, the major exceptions being the two New York giants, the 20-campus City University and the 29-unit State University. Outside of these institutions, which owe their organization to a pro-union climate and very favorable legislation on bargaining by public employees, most of the four-year schools that negotiate collectively are state institutions, many of which were former teachers colleges, including 14 in Pennsylvania, 8 in Massachusetts, 8 in New Jersey, 4 in Nebraska, and 4 in Michigan. Again, the AFT and the NEA are dominant. The American Association of University Professors, the late-comer, represents the faculty of 29 schools, mostly private (16), but including a few middle-level public universities, such as Wayne State, Rhode Island, Rutgers, Hawaii, Cincinnati, Delaware, and Temple ("Where College Faculties . . .," 1974, p. 24).

In spite of the fact that unionism has touched only a relatively small segment of academe thus far, a rather substantial body of experience with collective bargaining elections has already developed. By examining several of these elections, we can locate patterns which are themselves instructive and which, even more importantly, provide a guide to what is likely to occur as unionization spreads to a much broader segment of higher education in the coming years.

The importance of constituency definition   As in most electoral situations, determination of the unit(s) in which the contest will be conducted is proving to be a prime factor in academic bargaining agent elections, and subsequently in the development of faculty unionism. There are two basic sets of constituency-definition issues. First, who will be included in the bargaining unit besides regular, full-time members of the instructional staff? Especially in larger universities, "nonteaching professionals" (NTPs)—librarians, full-time research personnel, student counselors—are a substantial group. Will the faculty and the NTPs form separate units or be included together? In the case of publicly supported institutions, this is a matter for state regulation, and there is substantial variation around the country.[12] A second issue also arises in state systems: whether the various campuses will be individual bargaining units or will be grouped together in one or more inter-campus units. The range of possible constituencies runs, then, from faculty at a single institution to all professional staff at the various campuses of an integrated statewide system.

The subject of constituency definition for bargaining representatives in higher education has a number of facets that lie beyond the scope of our study. It links, however, to one theme that has been our concern: the pronounced differences in general interests, and in support for unionization, among various groups in the academic community.

The move toward unionization is generating particular tensions within the growing number of heterogeneous statewide university systems. Although faculty at the more prestigious, research-oriented, and better-paying campuses of these systems generally seek to be separated from the lesser units in collective bargaining elections, they have been denied this in some states. Conflict among parts of such systems is endemic because those campuses not as involved in graduate education seek parity in salary, teaching loads, and other work conditions with the most prestigious units.

The CUNY elections   The first election in an integrated, heterogeneous, multicampus system, the City University of New York (CUNY) in 1968, furnishes an extremely good example of the contrasting interests of faculty at different units. At CUNY, two faculty groups—the Legislative Conference, a 30-year-old organization that had existed to represent the faculty in lobbying efforts, and the AFT affiliate, the United Federation of College Teachers—filed to take part in the first contest to be held under the then newly enacted Taylor Law, which requires public bodies to negotiate with representatives of their employees chosen in collective bargaining elections. Both groups agreed that there should be a single bargaining unit for all 20 campuses, but disagreed as to whether all teaching personnel, including the large number of part-time lecturers and other assistants, should be included within one constituency. The state agency decided to separate part-time faculty from those who held

[12]State practice in defining academic bargaining units is discussed by McHugh (1971, pp. 55–90). This entire issue of the *Wisconsin Law Review* is devoted to collective bargaining in higher education and is an unusually comprehensive source.

regular appointments, and placed nontenured full-time instructors in the latter category. The two constituencies were then faced with a choice between a union group that had previously succeeded in organizing the schoolteachers of the city and the old faculty organization, which had not previously operated as a union but which developed close ties with the NEA during the campaign as a means of securing professional assistance and funds. They also could vote for no representation.

The ensuing elections established a pattern that subsequently has been followed elsewhere: The lower the tier of academe, in terms of security, income, prestige, and involvement in the graduate scholarly-research culture, the stronger the vote for unionization, as represented by a regular union body; the higher the level, the greater the likelihood of votes for "no representation" or for the least "union-like" faculty organization on the ballot. An examination of the results broken down by the several tiers in CUNY demonstrates this clearly. Thus, among regular full-time faculty, only 38 percent voted for the AFT in the first election, whereas over three-fifths of the lecturers and other part-time staff chose the AFT as their representative. Since no alternative had a majority among the regular faculty, a runoff was necessary; it was won by the Legislative Conference. More interesting than these overall results, however, are variations among the regular line faculty linked to the status and nature of the campuses on which they taught. As Table 84 shows, those at the Graduate Center of the university, who were expected to devote themselves to scholarly research and who had the lightest teaching load and the highest salaries, showed a strong distaste for unionization. Almost half of them (46 percent) voted for "no representation" on the first ballot; only 17 percent opted for the AFT. A substantial majority of the faculty at the eight senior colleges also strongly rejected the AFT, while close to three-fifths at the two-year community or junior colleges voted for the union. Less than 10 percent of the latter chose the option of "no representation," as compared with over 15 percent of the senior college staff. Professors at the older and more prestigious senior colleges of the CUNY system were less favorable to the AFT than their colleagues at the new four-year institutions. In commenting on the results, AFT leaders noted that they would have won the contest had there been a single constituency, and that they had secured almost half the vote among the full-time faculty in the runoff. Conversely, the AFT would have been beaten severely in a constituency limited to senior college and Graduate Center faculty. The heartland of

TABLE 84 *Collective bargaining election returns at City University of New York (percentages of n)*

	First Election: December 5, 1968		
	Legislative Conference	UFCT (AFT)	Neither
Unit I (regular line appointees) (n = 4,431)	47	38	15
Unit II (lecturers and teaching assistants) (n = 2,715)	27	60	13
	Runoff: December 18, 1968		
Unit I (n = 3,841)	54	46	

	Unit I vote by category of college				
	First Election			Runoff	
	Legislative Conference	AFT	Neither	Legislative Conference	AFT
Graduate Center (n = 123; 99)	37	17	46	75	25
Four older senior colleges* (n = 2,353; 2,051)	57	28	16	65	35
Four younger senior colleges† (n = 516; 472)	47	38	15	54	46
Community colleges (n = 1,323; 1,219)	32	58	10	33	67

*Older senior colleges: Brooklyn, CCNY, Hunter, Queens.

†Younger senior colleges: Baruch, John Jay, Lehman, Richmond.

SOURCE: Raw data reported in "Election Analysis," (1969, pp. 1–2).

AFT backing was among the lower-tier faculty, lecturers and junior college teachers.

Without going into details, which we have reported elsewhere, it should be noted that four years later, in 1972, an almost identical scenario was played out 5,000 miles away at the multicampus University of Hawaii in a comparable two-election sequence. There, the AFT beat out a number of rivals, of which the AAUP was most important, securing the bulk of the vote from those in community colleges and other lesser-status applied schools and thus overwhelmed the support for "no representative" or for the AAUP, which was concentrated in the more research- and graduate student-centered parts of the university (Ladd & Lipset, 1973b, pp. 50–53). In October 1974, the AAUP, this time in alliance with the NEA, succeeded in reversing the 1972 results, winning 60 percent of the vote. But the sources of strength for the two major protagonists remained the same.

Rhode Island and Michigan elections An indication that the CUNY and Hawaiian returns did not simply represent fortuitous happenings in highly unionized communities may be drawn from results of elections in the public institutions of two states that do not have unified systems of higher education, Rhode Island and Michigan. In the smaller state, with each campus voting separately during 1971–1972, the AAUP won representation rights at the University of Rhode Island, the AFT came out on top at the four-year Rhode Island College, and the NEA was victorious over its two national rivals at Rhode Island Junior College.

Michigan has a variety of publicly supported institutions, and these differ considerably in faculty quality, working conditions, and function. They also vary in their response to unionization. The most prestigious campus, a long-time center of research and graduate studies, the University of Michigan, has been least affected. The union group has not felt strong enough even to call for a collective bargaining election. At the second-ranking state school, Michigan State, which succeeded after World War II in upgrading itself from an agricultural campus to major university status, 64 percent of the faculty voted for "no representation" in an election held in the fall of 1972. Moving one notch down the academic hierarchy, Wayne State University provides an example of a school that opted for collective bargaining but chose the AAUP over the AFT. At the "university college" unit of the state system, Oakland University, a campus with a strong sense that it provides an "elite" education resembling that at distinguished private undergraduate colleges, the AAUP again came out on top. The remaining lower-ranking four-year schools, as well as the various two-year community colleges, on the other hand, largely voted to be represented either by the NEA or the AFT. Had the public institutions of the state of Michigan or Rhode Island been linked within a statewide multicampus system, all their faculty would probably now be under collective bargaining.

The SUNY elections The experience of the second major multicampus New York public university, the 29-unit State University of New York (SUNY), points up the difficulties facing those who seek to maintain the independence of the more privileged or prestigious sectors in such heterogeneous systems. At SUNY, leaders of the statewide Faculty Senate first tried to head off unionization by offering the senate itself as a bargaining agent. At the same time, the nonteaching professionals (NTPs), who were totally unrepresented in university governance and who served at the pleasure of their appointment officer, formed the State University Professional Association (SUPA). In reaction to an AFT campaign to organize faculty and professional staff, the Faculty Senate quickly changed its rules and admitted the NTPs, an action which won over the SUPA. Faced with court action by the AFT against its use of university funds, the Senate (January 1970) created a separate organization, the Senate Professional Association (SPA), to include both faculty and NTPs. Formally unaffiliated at the start, the SPA found itself confronting well-financed competition from the AFT and was forced to look for some external support. An AAUP affiliation proved impossible because the AAUP then provided that only faculty and librarians could hold voting membership. So the SPA turned to the NEA, which agreed to provide financial backing. A group started by the senate leaders to avoid unionization and external affiliation found itself, then, dependent on a national union body.

As at other universities, the first decisive contest occurred over designation of the boundaries of the collective bargaining unit. Here, however, roles took on a reverse twist from those that developed in other statewide systems. The AFT had its main strength in a few of the four-year colleges, and requested separate bargaining elections. The SPA leadership, confident that it could win a statewide-system election with its threefold base among faculty at the four major university centers (Albany, Binghamton, Buffalo, and Stony Brook) and two medical centers, the NTPs, and NEA adherents in a number of the four-year colleges, insisted upon and secured a statewide constituency.[13] Although faculty at the university and medical centers were relatively uninterested in any form of unionization, their leaders did not believe separate representation would help them. They anticipated that a struggle over equalization would occur in any case. Their prior experience with the state legislature indicated that the politicians preferred to treat the system as one unit, to enact across-the-board general increases, and to be responsive to pressures from unions and civil service groups. Consequently, they felt they would be in a better position if they carried on their battles with the other campuses within the university, rather than competing with units represented by the AFT before the legislature.

In the first balloting in December 1970, the AFT led with 35 percent, followed by 31 percent for the SPA, 20 percent for the AAUP, 7 percent

[13]For a description of the SUNY situation, see Oberer (1969, pp. 138–140).

for the Civil Service Employees Association, and 6 percent for no representative. In the runoff in January, the SPA won by a narrow margin, securing 53 percent compared with 47 percent for its trade union rival. Over one-third of the 15,746 eligible to vote did not cast ballots in each election ("Faculty Association...," 1971, p. 4; "NEA Supported...," 1971, p. 4). The ballots at SUNY were not separated by campus or between faculty and nonteaching professionals. Some indication of the probable variation in orientation of the latter two strata may be seen, however, in the results at a smaller institution, Eastern Michigan University. There, 39 percent of the faculty voted for "no representative," as contrasted with 8 percent of the nonteaching professionals. The AFT and the NEA took 71 percent of the vote among NTPs but only 41 percent within the teaching staff ("... AAUP Loses Election," 1972, p. 3).

The SUNY election was defined by both major groups as a contest between a "professional" association, controlled by local faculty and stressing maintenance of the collegial atmosphere of the university, and a "trade union" insisting upon institutionalized collective bargaining conducted on an adversary basis and assisted by professional union representatives. But the differences declined greatly during the long representation campaign and afterwards. The SPA originally contended that it was a continuation of the senate, "the same organization that has bargained for you in the past." It argued that "allying with unions would dilute ... the faculty's role in university government." Many of its supporters, particularly those at the university centers, expressed fear that unionization would lead to efforts at "equalization" (Sievert, 1970, pp. 1, 5). Within a month after the election, the SPA formally affiliated with the NEA, thus following in the footsteps of the Legislative Conference at CUNY. And as at CUNY, the more senior and prestigious faculty, most involved in the Faculty Senate and basically uninterested in any forms of unionism, proved reluctant even to pay dues to the SPA. Faculty at the four-year colleges provided a higher proportion of the membership than did the university center professoriate. And nonteaching professionals were more disposed to join the union than were professors. As a result, the SUNY system was represented for some years by an organization headed by a nonteaching professional (a registrar) who was himself still a doctoral candidate.

The regular faculty at both major New York public universities first voted for an unaffiliated faculty association. As noted, however, the two independent associations soon affiliated with the NEA, finding that they required outside expert assistance to handle the complicated problems posed by collective bargaining. This affiliation, in turn, was followed in 1972 by the merger of the New York statewide organizations of the NEA and the AFT. The new organization is now affiliated with both national groupings. At CUNY, the Legislative Conference, representing the full-time regular line faculty, also merged in April 1972 with the AFT local, which was composed of lecturers and other part-time and nonregular faculty staff.

The SUNY SPA, though successful in defeating its rivals in the election, subsequently was unable to recruit a substantial membership. Faced with the considerable expense of collective bargaining, and under continued criticism from its AFT rival, the SPA governing body (the Representative Council) voted in March 1973 to conduct a membership referendum on merging with the State University Federation of Teachers (AFT). The representatives of the university centers initially resisted the proposal, fearing, among other things, that their influence would be swamped in the merged group, since the AFT membership was heaviest on the four-year campuses. The national NEA also strongly opposed the merger (Kiereck, 1972; "SPA Rep Council OK's Merger Referendum," 1973, p. 2). In the referendum held on April 4, merger was overwhelmingly approved by a vote of 1,157 to 379.

Although this referendum was obviously of major importance for the future direction of the university, it is striking to note that only 50 percent of the 3,061 eligible members of the SPA actually cast ballots. Not surprisingly, opposition to the merger within the faculty was greatest among those at the four university centers and the affiliated college at Syracuse University. Over one-third (36.5 percent) were against uniting with the AFT affiliate, whereas almost 90 percent of SPA faculty members at the six two-year agricultural and technical campuses voted for unification, as did 83 percent of those at the four-year colleges. Within the voting membership of the SPA, then, as among faculties nationally, support for more militant forms of unionism is greatest in the less prestigious, least research-involved sector and lowest in those units most involved with graduate training and basic research. These intrauniversity variations, plus the fact that literally over 90 percent of the 16,000 people covered by the collective bargaining unit were not involved in the referendum, do not, however, change the ultimate result. The initial effort of the leaders of the Faculty Senate at SUNY to find an approach to collective bargaining independent of outside groups and the larger labor movement has been a failure.

Future rounds of collective bargaining contests With the record of the recent past in mind, we anticipate that collective bargaining may spread to other elite sectors of public higher education—schools such as those at Berkeley and Madison. At the moment, their faculties are resisting efforts to include them in the same constituency as other segments of the state university system for the purpose of collective bargaining elections. At Berkeley and Madison, some have organized local faculty groups to avoid the issue of representation by a national organization that has standard union policies. Whether they will succeed is very much uncertain. There can be little doubt that at such schools the majority of academics do not see the need for formal collective bargaining representation, given the power of their faculty self-government institutions. But some of them face the prospect that their desires may be frustrated by inclusion in a collective bargaining unit with faculty at less prestigious parts of the state system or with the numerous NTPs. "Non-ladder" lecturers, librarians, research and extension "specialists," and the like, typically give more support to unionism than does the faculty: They have lower incomes and status and are largely unrepresented in professorial self-government organs.

Defining the representation unit has become a decisive issue in California and Wisconsin.[14] Faculty on the Berkeley campus, the oldest and most prestigious unit of the University of California, have been advantaged with respect to salaries, teaching loads, and research support, although the University's structure ostensibly provides for equality among the campuses. The larger California system of five-year state colleges and universities, in which faculty have lower salaries and higher teaching loads than those at the University of California, is a completely separate institution, as is the even more numerous body of two-year colleges. Although no organization has been designated as a collective bargaining agent in any of these, unionization has made considerable headway among the professors of the state college system.

In 1967, before the wave of unionization had really begun, the faculty of the state colleges, in a referendum sponsored by the Academic Senate, voted down collective bargaining by a narrow margin, 3,016 to 2,741. At that time, however, three organizations that had a considerable membership—the AAUP, the NEA-affiliated California College and University Faculty Association (CCUFA), and the California State Employees' Association (CSEA)—strongly opposed collective bargaining while it was backed by two other groups, the AFT and the Association of California State College Professors (ACSCP) (Haak, 1968, pp.

---

[14]Considerable information concerning the arguments and decisions determining constituency boundaries in many universities may be found in various articles and discussions in Tice (1972).

1, 19; Haehn, 1971). The latter two groups united in 1970 to form the United Professors of California (UPC), which has over 3,000 members among the 14,000 faculty in the system (Trombley, 1970). The California sections of the AAUP and the NEA have shifted their position, of course, in favor of collective bargaining.

In October 1972, following extensive discussion on the various campuses and an evaluation of the results of a questionnaire distributed to faculty concerning their views on unionism, the statewide Academic Senate of the system voted unanimously to call for legislation permitting faculty collective bargaining. An "exclusive negotiating agent," it was urged, should be chosen in an election in which all faculty of the 19-campus system would be in a single unit ("Document on Collective Negotiation," 1972). Since a large majority of the faculty belong to organizations that favor collective bargaining, there can be little doubt that the system will be unionized once appropriate legislation is enacted by the state of California. Meanwhile, the various faculty associations have been able to take part in negotiations with the Board of Trustees and state agencies and to represent faculty in grievance procedures involving issues of promotion and tenure.

The growth in support for collective bargaining in the statewide system has been gauged by James Haehn, who analyzed a series of votes and sample surveys of faculty opinions taken from 1966 to 1970. In the first one, taken in 1966, 37 percent opted for collective bargaining. In the most recent poll, the support figures reached 61 percent. The factors differentiating supporters from opponents corresponded generally to those indicated by our national surveys. Thus, collective bargaining was backed by the more politically liberal faculty, professors in the social sciences and humanities, and those below the rank of full professor. Reversing the national pattern, however, faculty who were more dedicated to research proved to be disproportionately pro-union, a phenomenon which may reflect their sense of grievance at the high teaching load and the lack of support for research in a teaching-oriented system. Organizations that are now part of the AFT United Professors of California were preferred as the bargaining representative by 33 percent of those queried in the 1970 poll. Some "new organization" was favored by 23 percent, 16 percent chose the statewide Academic Senate, 12 percent were for the AAUP, and 7 percent backed the NEA affiliate (Haehn, 1970).

Support for collective bargaining has also emerged within the elite sector of the state's higher education system, the University of California. Among the 7,289 faculty and librarians, the AAUP, as of 1973, had recruited 1,400, as contrasted with the AFT's 653 members (some of whom are nonfaculty academic employees other than librarians). The NEA has not tried to organize within the university. The AAUP, AFT, and NEA are much weaker in the University of California than at the five-year California State University and Colleges system. Within the latter, the AFT-affiliated United Professors of California had about 3,200 members, the NEA-linked California Higher Education Association had 2,300, while the AAUP included 1,400 out of the 11,250 faculty.[15] As in other state systems of public higher education, that segment that has less prestige, and whose faculty receive lower pay for many more hours of teaching per week, is more disposed to collective bargaining generally, and to the more "union-like" associations—the AFT and the NEA—rather than the AAUP.

Both the AFT and its opponents recognize that the issue of constituency boundaries, now under consideration by state authorities, may determine the results of future bargaining elections within the University. Aware that it probably will be unable to win a majority among the faculty, the AFT advocates that all "academic employees" should form one representation unit. Such a constituency, however, probably would not include the 3,000 teaching assistants. Professors, full- and part-time, still form a minority among the remaining 19,000 professional employees. The latter encompass lecturers, librarians, full-time research personnel, and other professional nonteaching staff ("The Necessity . . .," 1972, p. 4). Such a drawing of representation boundaries would give the AFT an opportunity to overwhelm faculty with the votes of nonteaching professionals who have a greater stake in unionization.

In self-defense, Berkeley's Academic Senate adopted a resolution endorsing collective bargaining and authorizing the creation of a local campus group, the Faculty Association, designed to organize the regular faculty to resist inclusion with the other less prestigious campuses of the University of California and, perhaps even more importantly, with the NTPs.[16] The association has been endorsed by the Berkeley AAUP. Testifying before the State Assembly Committee on Public Employee Relations, Lloyd Ulman of the Berkeley faculty, "speaking as an interim officer of the newly formed Faculty Association, UCB, urged that legislation permit separate bargaining units for faculty and non-Senate academic employees as well as campus rather than Universitywide units.

---

[15]These data were obtained from the records of the California State University and College system, the University Council of the AFT, and the Western regional office of the AAUP.

[16]Irving (1971); Moore (1972). For an analysis of the situation which led many Berkeley faculty to propose a Faculty Association, see the "Report on Possible Collective Action by the Faculty" (1972).

For example, Berkeley faculty might elect to bargain through its own unit, UCLA faculty through another and Davis through still a third unit" ("Major Push . . .," 1972, p. 3). Thus the Berkeley Senate leadership, while accepting the premise that some form of collective bargaining is inevitable, has chosen to follow a strategy totally opposite from that of their compeers at SUNY.

The Berkeley chancellor, Albert Bowker, who presided over CUNY when it was divided into two separate components in 1968, has favored only one constituency at Berkeley, in part to avoid having two recognized groups competing to demonstrate their weight with the university. This position is consistent with one that Bowker took four years earlier in New York when he foresaw that "the possibility of different agents representing the two units invites whipsaw tactics by the two organizations to enhance their power" (Hechinger, 1968).

Although it is difficult to make precise quantitative distinctions among the different units of the University of California because of the vagueness of potential membership bases (faculty, full-time and part-time, librarians, academic employees, etc.), the available data given us by the AFT and the AAUP do permit a reliable specification of the direction of the differences. Table 85 shows that the AFT is stronger within the six smaller, so-called emerging campuses while it is quite weak at the two major graduate and research centers, Los Angeles (including a large medical school) and Berkeley, and at the San Francisco Medical campus. The smaller campuses, though formally con-

TABLE 85   *AFT and AAUP membership in the University of California (February 1973) (percentages of n*)*

	AAUP	AFT
Los Angeles (including its medical school) (n = 2,299)	14	3
Berkeley and the San Francisco Medical campus (n = 2,084)	16	8
Four older small campuses (Davis, Riverside, Santa Barbara, and San Diego) (n = 2,235)	15	18
Two newest campuses (Irvine and Santa Cruz) (n = 671)	12	24
ALL CAMPUSES (n = 7,289)	15	9

*The number used as the base is the sum of the individuals, part- and full-time, who are members of the Academic Senate, plus librarians.

SOURCES: The membership data for the AAUP and the AFT were supplied by officers of each organization. The base figures are from the Personnel Office of the University of California.

gruent to the two large ones in salary schedules, in fact have a higher teaching load, slower promotion, fewer faculty receiving "star" salaries, and much less state support for research facilities. The AFT's University Council, on a number of issues, has opposed the statewide university administration's policy designed to protect the status of Berkeley and Los Angeles in a period of budget stringencies. The strengths on these two campuses have been maintained at the cost of cutting back on commitments to the smaller, growing units.

Data available only for Berkeley and Irvine indicate that a significant minority of the AFT members are not faculty. Over 20 percent of the union members at these two schools are librarians, twice their ratio to faculty among university personnel. As in CUNY and other multicampus institutions, the newest units with the youngest faculty—in this case, Irvine and Santa Cruz—are the foremost union strongholds.

Support for the most professionally oriented group, the AAUP, does not vary much among the campuses. Because all the campuses of the University of California are concerned with research and graduate education at a high level, their faculty as a whole belong to the category nationally that we have been referring to as upper tier. Presumably, the AAUP draws on the older men among them. Because senior scholars are much more heavily represented at the two major centers, AAUP strength in the six "emerging campuses" may actually constitute a larger fraction of the potential membership than at UCLA and Berkeley, in line with a national pattern indicated by the earlier analysis of AAUP membership.

The greater support for faculty organizations at Berkeley, compared with UCLA, is reflected in efforts at the former to counter systemwide collective bargaining. The Berkeley Faculty Association has recruited over 400 members, about 25 percent of the local Academic Senate. This greater propensity of the Berkeley academics to support diverse forms of faculty activism has been of long duration. A variety of protests within the university have received disproportionate backing on this campus for many decades (Lipset and Altbach, 1967, pp. 208–209; Lipset, 1972b, pp. 97–99).

Additional evidence sustaining our general analysis of the relationship between types of institutions and support for collective bargaining is available from a large-scale survey of California faculty in all levels of higher education—private institutions, the University of California, the California State University and Colleges system, and the community colleges—gathered in the spring of 1972. It was conducted for the Joint Committee on the Master Plan for Higher Education of the State Legislature. The poll included only one item relevant to unionism:

"State policy should be to enable and encourage collective bargaining on the part of faculty in California colleges (through a faculty union or other faculty association)." Respondents were asked to check whether they thought the matter (and many others) was "of no importance," "of low importance," "of medium importance," "of high importance," or "of extremely high importance" (Peterson, 1973). The distribution by type of school is given in Table 86.

In general, the results presented in Table 86 correspond to the national pattern in collective bargaining elections. The majority of the faculty in the five-year and two-year systems clearly favor collective bargaining, and presumably will vote that way should California pass the enabling legislation to permit representation elections. Those in the upper echelon of higher education, the University of California, are more ambiguous in their reaction. Faculty at the private institutions—excluding the two most eminent, Stanford and the California Institute of Technology, which were not in the sample—are least sympathetic to collective bargaining. This latter finding coincides both with the fact that unions have been least successful in such schools across the country and with the results of other recent as yet unpublished national surveys.

The situation in Wisconsin is even more complex. The state legislature has merged the two major public systems—the University of Wisconsin (UW), which resembled the University of California, and the Wisconsin State University (WSU), which comprised the more nu-

TABLE 86 *Responses by California faculty to question on importance of collective bargaining, Spring 1972 (percentages of n*)*

	Level of importance			
Type of school	*No or low*	*Medium*	*High or extremely high*	*Did not respond*
Private institutions (n = 740)	33	32	35	(21)
University of California (n = 532)	32	24	44	(18)
California State University and Colleges (n = 1,342)	22	16	62	(14)
Community colleges (n = 3,557)	21	21	58	(19)

*The percentages for the different levels of importance are based on the total who answered the question. These are not given in the published reports. We are indebted to Richard Peterson, the study director, for access to the computer printout. See Peterson (1973) for a detailed report on this survey, which dealt only peripherally with collective bargaining.

merous four-year state colleges—into one body under a single state-wide administration and board. About half of the 2,000 faculty in the WSU system belonged to an association that, though not affiliated with any national organization, is similar ideologically to the NEA. Since the merger, this group has been constituted as the Association of University of Wisconsin Faculty and is probably the largest single professorial body in the university. It has been quite influential with the legislature and governor. At Madison, the system's elite campus, two groups are actively preparing for the eventual representation struggle: the AAUP, and the United Faculty, which affiliated with the AFT in 1974. Before affiliation, the AAUP had 500 members and the United Faculty about 230. Both Madison organizations have sought to have each UW campus designated a separate representation unit. As at Berkeley, however, they differ on whether nonacademic professionals should be included in the unit. The AAUP derives the bulk of its support from older tenured faculty and wants to separate professors from the others. Close to half the United Faculty membership comes from the nontenured staff, including a substantial minority of the nonteaching professionals. In the long run, a combination of circumstances resembling those at CUNY, SUNY, and Hawaii may culminate in systemwide unionization of the highly disparate multicampus University of Wisconsin, although there is some possibility that the legislature will agree to separate the University into two constituencies, the graduate centers of Madison and Milwaukee, and the four-year schools.

The immediate future of collective bargaining in the less heterogeneous University of California system is in doubt. Since the California Master Plan designated all its campuses as centers of research and graduate work, it is likely to follow in the footsteps of comparable institutions that have remained uninvolved in the spread of unionization. Should the faculty feel pressed to opt for some form of collective bargaining, they are likely first to go the route of an independent faculty association or to vote for the AAUP, as at Rutgers, which separated itself in this way from the AFL-CIO and also from the local New Jersey union of the state college faculties. Rutgers sought to resist "statewide leveling tendencies . . . hope[d] to be able to lobby in the state capital to maintain their position vis-à-vis the rest of public higher education in the state" (Riesman, 1973, p. 424).

The efforts of academics at the most distinguished campuses of state universities to obtain a form of collective bargaining representation that is not part of a national union movement and does not include less prestigious parts of academe in their bargaining unit may still not resolve their concern with resisting the "leveling" tendencies that they see as inherent in unionization. They must face the likelihood that the faculty of the other state-supported institutions or the nonfaculty professionals at their campus will join a group that is part of, or allied to, the AFL-CIO in their state. An "unattached" elite main campus will be at a serious disadvantage in lobbying before the legislature when the several components of public higher education compete for a share of the state's budget. The two national union groups, the NEA and the AFT, have, in fact, made this case, arguing that effective negotiations over salaries must be conducted with the governor and state legislatures in public systems. They contend quite logically that power in the state capital will be decisive, and that the faculty, therefore, must choose a representative who is part of a larger power bloc—the labor movement as a whole, all the teachers of the state, or all civil service employees.

A final note on constituencies   As indicated in the above discussion, the boundaries for bargaining elections have often been crucial to the outcome. It is interesting to note, therefore, that affiliates of the three major national organizations and local independent faculty groups have not had a consistent policy with respect to defining boundaries. Not surprisingly, they have all been opportunistic, pressing for whatever definition would benefit them most in a given situation.

Thus, the AFT at SUNY proposed separate elections and bargaining representatives for each campus, while the Senate Professional Association and the AAUP favored a single statewide constituency. At CUNY, both the AFT and the Legislative Conference favored a systemwide election. In the New Jersey state colleges, the NEA, winner of the first elections on each campus in 1969, established systemwide bargaining. The AFT, seeking to break the NEA hold, filed petitions in 1972 demanding separate elections and bargaining in each of the eight schools. It stressed the virtues of local campus autonomy in enhancing faculty control over their own situation. At the University of Wisconsin, both the AFT and the AAUP favor separating the Madison campus from the rest of the system. On the other hand, at the University of California, the Berkeley-based Faculty Association favors making each campus a separate constituency, whereas the AFT wants to treat the entire university as one. In the California University and State Colleges System, however, the AFT first sought collective bargaining rights for schools in which it had strength. Only later did it shift to favoring one statewide unit.

Except for the AAUP, which has usually tried to limit a constituency to faculty, the AFT, the NEA, and local faculty groups have waffled over inclusion of nonteaching professionals in the unit.[17] NEA-linked groups in New York favored integrating them; the AFT preferred separating faculty from the NTPs in the SUNY unit and including them in CUNY. At Wayne State, the NEA backed the AAUP in its support of a "pure" faculty unit, while the AFT favored a broad constituency merging faculty and other academic personnel.

Belle Zeller, speaking in 1971 as president of the Legislative Conference, candidly stated why her organization had favored two constituencies: "We are not all in favor of the separation. Why did we ask the state agency for it? *It was just a case of arithmetic.* If we had combined all the part-time people with our full-time faculty in one unit, the part-time staff would have outnumbered the full-time personnel and the Legislative Conference would possibly have lost the election" (Zeller, 1972, p. 112).

PARTICIPATION

In considering the way in which the factors affecting the political behavior of academics have determined the patterns of support for a new form of faculty representation, trade unionism, it is important to note the impact on campus-related politics of variations in rates of participation. Faculty senates are generally dominated by small minorities of faculty oligarchs, who are often quasi-administrators primarily concerned with intramural politics—even though they are often the elected *pro forma* representatives of the whole faculty (most of whom do not bother to vote or attend meetings) in large schools (Clark, 1961, pp. 293–302; McConnell & Mortimer, 1971, pp. 24–39). Unionization generally involves a replacement of one clique of leaders, those of the senate, by another, the heads of the union. The latter, however, are chosen by a voting membership which is generally far from coterminous with the faculty as a whole. As noted earlier with reference to the SUNY situation, where only about one-fourth of those eligible for union membership actually belonged to the SPA, most professors typically do not join the union. And an even smaller percentage of the membership actually takes part in union meetings.

The selective nature of involvement in intramural faculty affairs may be illustrated with reference to rates of participation in the collective bargaining elections which took place at the multicampus University of

---

[17]At Rutgers, however, the AAUP represents faculty, all members of the research library, general extension and cooperative extension staffs, and, most surprisingly, teaching assistants, graduate assistants, and research interns.

Hawaii in 1972, and to characteristics of the membership of the CUNY union in 1973. The Hawaiian organization story resembles that at CUNY. The AFT, we noted, was originally able to defeat its AAUP rival, as well as the advocates of no representative, by securing extremely heavy majorities in the six two-year campuses and other less prestigious sectors.[18] This union victory, however, was made possible in part by the variation in faculty turnout. The proportion of those eligible who cast ballots decreased as the academic standing of the unit increased. Fully one-third of the faculty at Manoa, the pro-AAUP university center, did not even bother to express a choice, as contrasted with only 18 percent not voting in the community colleges. A report on a subsequent intraunion election to choose a bargaining committee in Hawaii indicated that "only 25 people voted in the College of Arts and Sciences" ("Memorandum to the Faculty," 1973, pp. 1–2).

Those who choose to become dues-paying and active members of the organization selected as the legal representative of all the faculty are often a strikingly unrepresentative subset. At CUNY, where the two rival union locals, the AFT and the NEA, voted to merge into the Professional Staff Congress (PSC) in April 1972, the pattern of membership as reported in the union paper is clear. The PSC is disproportionately composed of the less privileged groups within the university world—the younger, untenured faculty, those teaching at the two-year community colleges, minorities, and women (Grayson, 1973, p. 3). The more privileged have been less disposed to join up.

Differential participation may be a consequence of several factors. As we have seen, the less advantaged sectors of academe have more to gain from unionization and presumably are more interested in the outcome both of collective bargaining elections and of union meetings. Apart from this, as analyses of faculty behavior have demonstrated, academics not involved in research, who have little extramural visibility, tend to have a "local" orientation and to be much more committed to intramural politics. Conversely, the research-committed faculty are more cosmopolitan, more involved in the national and international research world, and are relatively unconcerned with day-to-day affairs of their local campus.[19] Since their reputations (and individual bargaining

[18]For a more detailed account of the Hawaiian situation with comprehensive statistics of elections there, see Ladd and Lipset (1973b, pp. 50–53).

[19]The concept of "locals" and "cosmopolitans" was first developed by Robert K. Merton (1968, pp. 441–474). It has been applied to the analysis of the varying behavior of academics in Gouldner (1957, pp. 281–306; 1958, pp. 444–480) and to scientists in Glaser (1964, pp. 15–30).

power) are largely determined by what scholars far removed from their university think of them, they devote as much time as possible to research and external academic activities. The lesser participation of these professors in union campaigns, even when they are strongly opposed to unionization, and their subsequent unwillingness to take part in the activities of collective bargaining units follow inevitably from their professional positions.

The shift from faculty representation through the committeemen of the academic senate to the officers of the union, from one "oligarchy" to another, does not end the phenomenon of a kind of self-coopting minority rule in faculty government, but it probably means a major change in the type of individual "representing" the professoriate. There is evidence that those who serve on faculty committees or who have been department chairmen are more conservative and more friendly to college administrations than the faculty as a whole. Lazarsfeld and Thielens (1958, pp. 151–152, 443) reported this pattern among a national sample of social scientists interviewed in 1955. And in our 1969 Carnegie survey of the professoriate, the relationships were somewhat similar. These findings reflect the fact that committeemen and chairmen, even when formally elected, are likely to be chosen from older faculty who are willing and even anxious to hold such "local" posts. In large measure, therefore, they come from the ranks of the less prestigious and less productive in scholarly terms, who, as noted earlier, tend to be more conservative politically. Heavily concerned with local status, they seek ways of getting along with the higher ranks of administration, a group that in itself is often recruited from the committeemen. Unionization, however, would appear to have opened a new avenue of prestige and power to another group of "locals," whose position will depend on their retaining the favor of union members drawn heavily from the less privileged and younger strata of the university. Presumably they will be more liberal politically, more inclined to take an adversary posture with administration, and more favorable to "a program of immediate across-the-board benefits for the existing majority" (Oberer, 1969, p. 143).

STUDENT-FACULTY TENSIONS

Any effort to anticipate the ultimate outcome of the unionization movement of the 1970s should be seen in the context of the way in which collective bargaining, though backed by the more left-disposed faculty, appears to lead inevitably to serious tension and even conflict with organized students. Many student groups, including the National

Student Association, have identified faculty unionism as a threat to the gains in "student power" secured in the 1960s, or to the "interests" of students with respect to such issues as tuition and teaching quality.

The assumption that unionization may stimulate student conflict with faculty is not simply a hypothetical prognostication (Semas, 1973*a*, p. 4). "Already, some student organizations are questioning the merits of faculty tenure, while others are looking askance at teaching efficiency, both in terms of classroom effectiveness and in terms of hours worked and classes taught" (Bonham, 1971–1972, pp. 13–14). Student leaders at the first major unionized university, CUNY, have openly expressed their opposition at times to the high pay package given to a "mediocre" faculty, arousing the natural ire of union leaders. In the spring of 1971, the student senate passed a resolution calling on the Board of Higher Education to rescind faculty pay increases and to use the money to offset proposed tuition increases ("On Faculty Unionism," 1971, p. 1). The University Student Press Service of CUNY released in January 1971 an article written by a student, George Mc-Cough, making a strong student-oriented case against faculty tenure.

A high ratio of tenured faculty will, in the long run, mean higher tuition and fees and a stagnant curriculum. Since neither of these can be regarded as being convergent with student interests, unconditional student support of faculty in tenure disputes is at least counter productive and clearly contradictory....

It must be concluded, that not only is student support or sympathy in faculty tenure disputes unwarranted, but students must actively seek to participate in those areas wherein tenure affects the character of the college and university community.... Students must become involved in collective bargaining as parties to the contract....

A predominant factor in the reappointment, promotion and tenure process must be its reliance upon student evaluations of faculty teaching ability.

In October 1972, Alan Shark, then chairman of the CUNY Student Senate, continued the attack, arguing that under current economic conditions, union demands for a reduced teaching load and higher salaries could only be met "through increases in fees and tuition costs." He criticized union insistence on separate faculty "elevators, private dining facilities, as well as private lavatories... [suggesting that] it is quite demeaning to see locked faculty bathrooms; it depicts an uncomfortable polarizing class distinction." He pointed out that the Board of Higher Education had stated that "students should have a participation role in the academic decision-making process...[while the union] has continually rejected new governance plans that provide for a greater sharing of academic responsibility with students" (Shark, 1972, pp. 552–558).

During the 1972–73 CUNY negotiations, the student senate sought permission to have observers present at bargaining sessions and to give testimony before the fact-finders. The Board of Higher Education supported the student request, the union opposed it. "The student leaders came away from the rebuff openly skeptical of the union's slogan, 'Professors Want What Students Need.' The union's president, Professor Belle Zeller of Hunter College, retorted: 'All the students have to do is holler, and the administration quivers. We are fighting to preserve the power of the faculty . . .'" (Raskin, 1973).

In an editorial in the union newspaper, the PSC argued vigorously against the CUNY administration's proposal to allow students "to participate in college governance," contending that the students had been responsible for a major blunder, Open Admissions: "Three years ago, CUNY students petitioned for Open Admissions and won. But we see now that Open Admissions was an empty promise, effected without plan or understanding. As a result, CUNY now has the highest dropout rate in its history, and there is no sign that the rate will be arrested" (F. B., 1973, p. 3).

At the State University of New York (SUNY), a comparable clash developed. Student representatives from the different SUNY campuses who met in Albany on February 6–7, 1972, to discuss the projected master plan for the university seemingly saw little good in the emergence of collective bargaining. A detailed report of that conference summarized their conclusions:

The formation of faculty and staff unions to further the self-interest of their members will inevitably clash with student interests. . . . The potential impact of these unions on university governance is particularly frightening. Negotiations between the University and the union on the terms and conditions of employment can and will cover every aspect of operation of the University. With students playing no role in these negotiations, the resulting contracts could nullify every gain which students have made in terms of increased participation in university governance . . .

Unfortunately, faculty and staff unions are a reality in American higher education. Now all possible steps must be taken to ensure that unionization does not lock students out of university governance. . . . It is unacceptable for students as consumers and participants in the learning process to be locked out of decision making ("Proceedings of the Student Conference . . .," 1972, pp. 5–6).

As at CUNY, the student representatives opposed bargaining solely at the systemwide level, demanding some form of local campus negotiations. They also challenged the tendency toward "leveling" inherent, as they saw it, in "an across-the-board increase." They argued for some rewards "on the basis of individual merit" as an incentive to improve "the quality of teaching and scholarship" (ibid., p. 6).

An explicit example of overt tension between a faculty union and students took place in the Chicago city college system. During an AFT strike in 1968, the union told students attending courses and planning to take exams that "grades and course credit which would be given without the certification of your teacher who is on strike would be invalid. A *college diploma issued to any of you on this basis will have no official standing*" (Finkin, 1971, p. 148). The subsequent contract between the union and the college system contained a specific clause limiting the scope of participation by students within individual departments to "curricular matters" only, and provided that departments could only deal with "democratically elected student governing bodies," that is, not with activist organizations. The departments were also forbidden to make any agreement with students that might "abrogate faculty rights" in the contract (ibid.).

More recently, in the fall of 1972, students at two community colleges in Pennsylvania sought injunctions against faculty strikes. Both sides in the disputes agreed that student pressure helped force the settlements (Semas, 1973a).

A report by a Central Michigan University faculty member on the background of the NEA victory there in September 1969 contends that the faculty were discontented with the new president's concern for students at the expense of faculty interests. The author argues that the faculty supported collective bargaining as a way of restricting the administration, holding back its pro-student initiatives (Hepler, 1971). The president, William Boyd, also emphasized as a cause of unionization "student demands for a share in decisions which were once the prerogative of faculties." And he noted the "danger... that contracts... may pay professors at the expense of students. ... How ironic it is that, just as students were achieving a share of power in campus governance the locus of decision-making should shift to a new location where they are unrepresented!" (Boyd, 1971, pp. 308, 315–316).

Clearly, some professors view the growth of faculty unionism favorably for the same reasons that student leaders fear it, seeing in it a way for the professoriate to regain power given up to students during the late 1960s. Writing from experiences at SUNY, William McHugh suggests that "unionism may well appeal to... traditional elements of a faculty as a reaffirmation of the faculty guild concept in face of student pressures. Faculty unionism may result in a collision course with the newly emerging tripartite governance patterns" (McHugh, 1973, pp. 135–136). A report by a Michigan State professor, Robert Repas, on the 1972 bargaining election there maintains that many MSU faculty "supported collective bargaining because they looked upon it as a device to keep students out of the decision making process" (Repas, 1973). During the campaign, an article in the campus newspaper made the same point from the student side, arguing that "unionization could jeopardize student gains in academic governance, [since] the faculty generally would not be swayed by any concern for student input . . ." (Fox, 1972).

The shift in power—or at least in representation—that excludes students may be seen in the Rutgers experience. There it was anticipated that collective bargaining "would develop as a new base for faculty power . . . because the university senate included representatives of faculty, students, and administration, and the AAUP could claim to be the sole universitywide faculty body" (McCormick, 1973, p. 280). A delegate assembly, with members elected by faculty from departments and campuses, was set up by the Rutgers AAUP. On January 29, 1973, the assembly "moved to strengthen its function as the only university-wide body that exclusively represents and expresses faculty opinion." It passed a resolution "to petition for a University Assembly called for the purpose of disbanding the University Senate and recognizing the Delegate Assembly as the Faculty Senate" (Howard, 1973, p. 6).

Conflict between students and unions already exists within the University of California. An official student lobby, an arm of the statewide university Council of Student Body Presidents, has offices in Sacramento. Interviews with AFT and student lobby officers indicate distrust between them. The student leaders argue the union is uninterested in student concerns and seeks to keep teaching loads low. The unionists report that the students complain to state officials about the "elitism" of the faculty, their emphasis on research rather than teaching, etc. A conflict also appears to be in the offing in the state of Washington, where student leaders contributed to the defeat of a collective bargaining bill in 1973 by demanding explicit student representation in the collective bargaining process (Semas, 1973a).

The AFT, from New York to California, has sharply opposed student involvement in judging the quality of their teachers. Thus Allan Netick, the editor of *The Advocate*, organ of the union for the California State University and Colleges system, objects to student evaluation of teaching as permitting a condition "whereby any chairman or dean, or PRT committee may judge a faculty member in comparison to other faculty members," thereby providing a supposedly objective basis for denying tenure or promotion. After reviewing the spread of such evaluations around the country, he concludes: "Student evaluation has become an important tool of management" (Netick, 1973, p. 10).

In Massachusetts, where state law until recently permitted collective bargaining on all issues except salaries, union groups agreed to student representatives participating in collective bargaining, in the expectation that students would back them on governance and other issues. The results of this experiment turned out to please representatives of administration and disappoint the unionists. Students have supported the administration on issues such as faculty workload and rejected the union argument that "students will get a better education if professors teach fewer and smaller classes. . ." (Semas, 1973*b*, p. 2).

The conflict between the interests of professors and students made evident with the growth of faculty unionism has served to modify the image presented during the 1960s by campus activists that students were the exploited "under-class" of the university, the equivalent of the workers in the factory. In fact, the students are the consumers, the buyers, the patrons of a product sold by the faculty through a middle-man, the university system. In economic class terms, the relationship of student to teacher is that of buyer to seller or of client to professional. In this context, the buyer or client seeks to get the most for his money at the lowest possible price. He prefers that an increased share of the payment to the institution should be channeled into more direct benefits for him—teaching, student activities, better housing, and so forth. The faculty seller of services, on the other hand, is obviously interested in maximizing his income and working conditions. Lower teaching loads and greater research facilities are to his benefit. Tenure not only reduces the power of administrators over faculty, it protects teachers from consumer (student) power as well.

The conception of students as consumers is not simply an analytic one. It has been explicitly argued in these terms by student leaders at CUNY and SUNY. Conversely, the CUNY union, in objecting to the students' demand to participate in negotiations, has said: "Management and labor do not invite consumers to the bargaining table, though consumers, of course, have rights and recourse elsewhere in the business sector" (F. B., 1973, p. 3).

Efforts, much more successful in Europe than in America, to give students a major role in university governance serve to weaken faculty power. Student power reduces the faculty's freedom to choose their colleagues, to determine the curriculum, to select research topics, and to control their work schedules. It does not, however, affect the power of those who control the purse strings to determine how much shall be spent on higher education and how it will be distributed among alternative sectors. Hence, even conservative politicians have been willing to support systems of student-faculty government in a number of European countries.

Student groups, of course, may ally with faculty factions for common extramural sociopolitical objectives. Given a similar political position—on racism or the Vietnam War, for example—they can work together against common opponents. Students may join with junior, nontenured faculty, close to students in age and style, in opposition to senior professors. Such alliances, too, often reflect similar ideological leanings in both strata. But where the issues are purely of the marketplace, where they revolve around the faculty's desire to maximize income and reduce the direct service (teaching) given to buyers (students), a conflict of interests exists that cannot be easily bridged. There may, in fact, often be a congruence of interests between the student buyers and the middlemen, public authorities and administrators. The latter may also be more interested in optimizing the services rendered to the students than in the conditions of the faculty. Students, their parents, and alumni form a much larger voting bloc than do professors. Thus, in spite of the "anti-Establishment" sympathies of most politically active students, tacit alliances between administrators and students against faculty have emerged.[20]

In the long run, it is likely that those who view faculty unionism as a way of enhancing faculty authority and reducing student power are right. Faculty unions, allied with the national labor movement and employing experienced permanent professional negotiators, public relations staff, and the like, are at a considerable advantage in contests with student groups dependent on a rotating leadership drawn from a highly transitory student population. The unions, once institutionalized, press on from year to year for "more." Student groups rise and fall, have little memory, and generally will be unable to best the faculty in any adversary relationship.

CONCLUSION

No discussion of the prospects for faculty unionism can ignore the fact that the academy differs from most other institutions in which unions and related employee groups operate. One major dissimilarity is that

[20]For a related discussion see Lipset (1972b).

faculties historically have contended, and not without reason, that they are the university. Other differences, however, are less clear and distinct today than in the past, in large part because of the enormous post-1945 expansion of American higher education and the extreme variety in types of institutions that now are comprised in it. As we noted earlier, faculty power and professional independence vary with school quality. The higher its academic standing, the more an institution resembles a professional guild; further down the hierarchy, colleges take on the characteristics of regular bureaucratic structures, with the "higher-ups" in charge.

Moreover, even in faculty-dominated schools, a broad range of decisions related to the amount of money available for salaries and how the "pie" is to be divided among the estates of the university (other employees, buildings, students, etc.) are usually made by the administration and trustees. With growth has come an inevitable bureaucratization of the multiversity. In public institutions, the legislature has considerable economic power, including the power to set salary scales.

There is also an existing political issue among professors within faculty-dominated schools, since power inherently is unequally distributed. For young, nontenured academics, there is a generational conflict of interest with senior members, who are often, de facto, their employers until they are voted regular membership (tenure). The efforts to "regularize" the granting of tenure, to permit those denied a permanency the right to file a grievance and to see the "record," are in many schools directed against the tenured faculty at least as much as against the administration (Bloustein, 1973). And as tenure vacancies become fewer, junior faculty grow more anxious to protect their access to them. The argument that faculty unions might meet some real interests of junior staff, but not of senior professors, was made in explicit terms by the president of the AAUP chapter at a private institution, Boston University.

[Unions cannot] offer tenured professors greater job security, since the instances of tenured faculty being fired are almost non-existent. . . . The only faculty group a union could really help are the junior, nontenured members, who tend to be exploited both on salary and working conditions, as well as having little job security. Unions might well lead to a higher percentage of these junior members being continued permanently in employment, but at a substantial price—the watering down of academic standards (McDowell, 1972).

The extension of trade union policies successfully applied in elementary and high schools to the research-oriented part of academe clearly would require some drastic modifications of practice. The more scholarly productive faculty, though much more liberal than other academics on societal questions and, hence, ideologically more receptive to the norms of unionism in general, tend to be opposed to intramural changes that will reduce the emphasis on research, meritocracy, and the ability of the academically successful to determine who will gain permanent status (tenure) in their institutions. Many of them see the competitive aspects of the system—the high regard given to presumed intellectual achievement as reflected in national and international peer judgments—as desirable ways of motivating the successful to continue to innovate and the able young to work hard to prove themselves. Further, as Riesman notes, "a college faculty needs to combine the individualism one associates with artists and free-floating intellectuals, with the cooperative-competitive collegiality, not of a submarine crew, but of a research group, a private medical clinic, or the partners in an elite law firm" (Riesman, 1973, p. 426).

Even these concerns may dwindle, however, in the face of the financial crunch that reaches all across academe. Confronted with declining monetary support, faculty may decide that unions are necessary. As Michigan State University economist Walter Adams, National President of AAUP, noted following the defeat of unionism in a MSU election in October 1972, economic hard times could quickly reverse the aversion of major university faculty: "Two bad years in the legislature and some disliked administrative action—no matter how trivial—will eventually put over unionization." What immediate success faculty unionism has at academically stronger colleges and universities will be determined significantly by the short-run economic positions in which these institutions find themselves.

In almost every state, the lesser parts of the public system argue vigorously for parity with the most prestigious public university in salaries, teaching loads, and research funds. With unionization, they should have greater power to affect variations in levels of support—and hence, in levels of quality—among state-funded schools. And this will probably serve more to downgrade the relative standing of the high achievers among public universities than to bring the lesser ones up to the level of their more affluent competitors.

Our discussion of the prospects and impact of unionization has centered on public rather than private institutions, since a variety of legal factors assure that the public sector will continue to be the principal battleground.[21] State legislative actions, notably reducing appropriations for higher education below the level faculty deem essential, provide a *raison d'être* for unions and a clarity of focus not present in the possibly more severe financial situation of private colleges and universities. Furthermore, the existence of multicampus state systems, with their extreme heterogeneity in academic standing and interests, and hence their great variations in orientations toward unionization, creates a potential for conflict not found in the private sector, where institutions are far more homogeneous internally. Finally, state legislatures across the country have been enacting statutes in recent years that provide for collective bargaining by public employees and establish the structure and the conditions that enable such bargaining to occur. This legislation is of great variety, comprising differences with important implications for the development of professorial unions.[22]

The greater pressures for unionization in the public sector have led one distinguished student of higher education to anticipate that "private colleges and universities might be able to far outstrip their distinguished public competitors, once unionization has embraced the latter" (Riesman, 1973, p. 427). David Riesman suggests that because unionization results in increased emphasis on adherence to diverse bureaucratic rules and regulations, whereas nonunionized major private universities are able to remain relatively undisciplined aggregates, the latter will become much more attractive places for creative scholars to work.

More important, perhaps, in fostering a variation in faculty quality between the upper rungs of the public and private sectors may be their strikingly different personnel policies. Although union contracts have almost invariably made it more difficult for schools to deny tenure, many of the leading private universities have placed an even greater emphasis on scholarly excellence, evaluated in a highly competitive context, as a requirement for tenure. From Stanford to Yale, administrators of such institutions have announced that the percentage of nontenured faculty who may expect to be promoted to a tenured position is

---

[21]Collective bargaining clearly has less appeal to faculty in private colleges, where presumably the total amount of money available for salaries is more fixed than in state institutions.

[22]For a description of state legislation providing for collective bargaining by public employees, see Le Francois (1970, pp. 14–16).

to be reduced sharply. In the absence of any faculty union, such proposals have met with little or no objection.

Efforts at comparable measures in unionized schools such as the City University of New York and the New Jersey State College system have, however, met with sharp opposition from the unions. The latter argue strenuously against proposals to set limits on the number of proportion of faculty who may receive tenure. The New Jersey Colleges AFT, for example, has insisted that higher education should not "operate in a cold and calculating manner towards its people," that "the traditional humane qualities which have characterized the academic community" call for "a *high* rate of award of tenure" (Memorandum to the New Jersey . . .," 1972, p. 2). At SUNY, the administration proposed limiting the number of tenured positions to 50 percent, and the Board of Higher Education adopted this policy in October 1973. But after a series of militant demonstrations by union members, who also lobbied vigorously with local political figures, the Chancellor, under bitter personal attack, capitulated and recommended to a newly appointed board (March 1974) that "all specific or implied numerical limits on the conferring of tenure" be rescinded, a proposal which was quickly enacted ("Kibbee to Recommend . . .," 1974, p. 1). This success of the New York union should sharply enhance the appeal of unionization to younger faculty around the country.

These issues will continue to affect the university world, even the highly prestigious research-oriented schools, in a period of economic stringency and no growth. Thus, efforts at the University of California to modify the policy that had existed during the decades of continual expansion, a policy under which any nontenured assistant professor could be promoted to a tenured associate professorship if he met the criteria of merit, have been strongly resisted by the AFT. With cessation of growth, and limitations on state funds, the University has proposed linking the number who could get tenure to such criteria as "the availability of funds," "fiscal considerations," "the University's need for an individual's services," "programmatic restrictions," and "budgetary restrictions." Following strong objections from the AFT and the Senate, the university administration sought to find a formula that might be more acceptable to faculty critics ("AFT-Senate . . .," 1973, pp. 1, 4). No acceptable compromise has been reached, and the union, therefore, has taken the university to court, arguing that the rights of nontenured faculty are abridged when decisions as to their promotion are subject to "programmatic and budgetary considerations" (AFT Section 52 Suit . . .," 1974, pp. 1, 8). On at least one previous occasion, an

AFT-financed lawsuit against a denial of tenure, brought on due process grounds, resulted in a concession by the university ("UC-AFT . . . , 1972, p. 5). The University of California is now faced with a situation in which it may have to repeatedly defend its procedures in tenure decisions in the courts, a fact which may affect the standards it seeks to uphold.

It should be noted that the president of Rutgers—one of the leading universities to be unionized, its faculty choosing the AAUP as the bargaining agent—stressed early in 1973 that collective bargaining has not affected the quality of the faculty. He indicated, however, that the Rutgers-AAUP contract had a special character. It did not affect "appointment and promotion of faculty and the development of most aspects of educational policy" (Bloustein, 1973). But soon after this article appeared, the Rutgers AAUP initiated a struggle to resist the university's efforts to tighten up tenure standards and, like other unions, opposed administration proposals for merit increases, preferring that much of the money allocated for salary increases be used for across-the-board gains. And in the California University and State Colleges system, the faculty unions successfully lobbied against a trustees' proposal for merit adjustments. The AFT representatives maintained in December 1972 that when there were not sufficient funds for a general step increase, "the choices should be made on some non-invidious basis, either seniority or by lot. Of the two possibilities, seniority seems preferable" ("On Implementation . . . , 1972, p. 1).

From the broadest perspective, the rapid growth of collective bargaining in higher education during the past half decade should be seen as the extension, to the level of university governance and faculty life, of the powerful trends toward equalization and away from elitism that have characterized many sectors of American society since the mid-sixties. As recently as 1968, Christopher Jencks and David Riesman stressed the extent to which the last several decades had witnessed throughout the entire system of higher education the triumph of meritocracy and of the values of the creative-research culture fostered by the leading faculty of the major institutions (Jencks & Riesman, 1968, pp. 15–20; Lee & Bowen, 1971, pp. 394–395).

They called attention to a "redistribution of power" within the universities that had given the faculty control over courses, curriculum, standards for admitting students and, most importantly, complete power with respect to selecting and rewarding colleagues. As they noted, at the better schools faculty were appointed "almost entirely on the basis of their 'output' and professional reputation. . . . The claims of localism, sectarianism, ethnic prejudice and preference, class back-ground, age, sex ... are largely ignored." These emphases and values, first largely centered in the major graduate institutions, permeated to the lesser ones. As a result, there was "a rapid decline in teaching loads for productive scholars, an increase in the ratio of graduate to under-graduate students at the institutions where scholars are concentrated, the gradual elimination of unscholarly undergraduates from these insti-tutions, and the partial elimination of unscholarly faculty." Administra-tors came to "see their institution primarily as an assemblage of schol-ars and scientists, each doing his work in his own way. Most university presidents see their primary responsibility as 'making the world safe for academicians'" (Jencks & Riesman, 1968, p. 17).

By the mid-seventies, it is obvious that the scene has changed consid-erably. The egalitarian pressures of the late 1960s have broken the hold of meritocratic values. Universities have altered their admissions policies to give special preference to students from "culturally de-prived" backgrounds, defined in ethnic, racial, sex, and class terms. Under pressure from the federal government, and reinforced by the belief of many faculty in liberal-left egalitarian values, affirmative ac-tion programs, often including informal but real quotas for people belonging to deprived groups, have been accepted by many leading in-stitutions in their faculty appointment policies. Moreover, the rapid spread of unionization has pressed to reduce meritocracy even further as a basis for differentiation within the professoriate itself. Organiza-tions of academics successfully oppose merit increases and seek to reduce the ability of the universities to emphasize competitive judg-ments about scholarly excellence as a basis for granting or refusing tenure. Such policies, of course, represent the interests of the less privileged and less prestigious components of the professoriate, who, as we have seen, not only form the base of the electorate which votes for collective bargaining, but also are much more disposed to become dues-paying and active members of organizations which have become the legal bargaining agents for the entire faculty and professional staff.

It may be argued that faculty unionization represents an effort by the mass of academe to overthrow the domination of a relatively small group of distinguished scholars. Writing in 1968, Jencks and Riesman (1968, p. 17) noted that "in the course of trying to strengthen their facul-ty, administrators of upwardly mobile institutions also usually offend many of the 'weak' faculty currently on the payroll." They did not antic-ipate, however, that the offended faculty so soon would be in a position to strike back. A combination of factors—the change in the larger sociopolitical atmosphere from the stress in the 1950s on achievement and meritocracy to that in the 1960s on egalitarianism and particularism, together with the drastic shift in the economic circumstances governing budgets, both for salaries and for research—has given the less privileged and younger academics the opportunity to challenge the main direction of much of higher education.[23]

Yet the reversal of emphasis was inherent in the earlier commitment of the society to widen access to higher education for the majority of youth, to make the academy a mass institution. Since World War II, the great growth has been (1) in the public rather than the private sector, and (2) in the lower-tier teaching institutions rather than in those concerned with basic research and the training of scholars. In the prototypical state of California, there are now 96 community colleges with 700,000 students and 13,000 faculty, 19 campuses of the State University and Colleges system with close to 300,000 students and over 11,000 faculty, and nine units of the University of California, which have over 100,000 students and 6,000 faculty. The community colleges and the State University and Colleges are explicitly defined as "teaching" institutions, with the latter system offering no work beyond the master's degree. Standards for both student and faculty selection appropriate to graduate and research-oriented universities clearly do not apply to the larger teaching systems. But as noted earlier, many of the policies implicit in unionization *do apply* to the latter. They need to institutionalize their relations with public authorities, to bargain collectively, for unlike the "scholars," they have little individual bargaining power.

The issues posed by unionization have been confused by the presence of quite disparate schools within such multicampus state systems as SUNY, CUNY, Hawaii, and the expanded, integrated University of Wisconsin. As two students of the "multicampus university" note, it is highly dubious "whether the differences . . . among campuses ranging from two-year technical schools to graduate-dominated university centers can be contained within a single system of collective bargaining" (Lee & Bowen, 1971, p. 293). There is some question, however, whether public authorities are willing explicitly to define and support major public centers of scholarship. At the moment, political pressures seem largely opposed to this. In California, proposals to revise the Master Plan for Higher Education call for increasing the "open enrollment"

---

[23]For a discussion of the shifting, semicyclical character of the interacting tension between the emphases on equality and achievement in American life, see Lipset (1967a, pp. 140–147).

component of the student body at the University of California. It may be extremely difficult for a publicly supported university, subject to legislative budgetary control, to remain a highly selective institution. Hence, Riesman's more recent anticipation of a growing gap in scholarly quality between the distinguished public and private universities has a good chance of being confirmed, not only because of changes inherent in unionization, but also because of the increased public support for equality of result.

The issues surrounding faculty unionism are far from resolved. Most of higher education is not yet organized. The more "profession-like" research-oriented sector, even in public universities, thus far has resisted incorporation into a unionized system. What is clear is that trade unionism, so long considered by professors to be totally inappropriate to their interests and status, will be the focus of major activity and conflict throughout academe during the current decade.

11. Concluding Observations

The political climate in American higher education during the fall of 1974, as we end this volume, differs sharply from what it was in 1967, when a large sample survey of faculty opinion was authorized by the Carnegie Commission, and in the spring of 1969, when data for the 60,000 sample were collected. The late sixties witnessed the height of the campus unrest engendered by opposition to the Vietnam War. Large numbers of students, supported by many faculty, were involved in massive demonstrations. Acts of civil disobedience, particularly seizures of university buildings, severely divided the estates of the university. And sharp conflict among academics characterized campus life. Faculty meetings were crowded as professors debated how to deal with student unrest, and whether and how they should react to a war which the large majority found unpalatable or immoral. The issues divided departments and led old friends and colleagues into bitter personal squabbles. Classrooms became political arenas. The delicate though often impersonal confidence between teachers and students, professors and professors, students and students, was severely breached. The community of scholarship appeared to be endangered.

But half a decade later, the campus scene was almost strikingly different. The headlines in newspaper stories dealing with universities now read, "Era of Turmoil Seems Dead on Campuses, Check of College Finds Grades, Jobs Are Now Students' Top Concerns" (Los Angeles *Times*, October 14, 1973); "'New Vocationalism' Now Campus Vogue" (*New York Times*, December 25, 1973); "The Frat Is Back" (*Newsweek*, November 12, 1973); "Rah Rah Revival: School Related Products Make a Comeback" (*Wall Street Journal*, October 4, 1973); "Black Studies Courses Now Obsolete" (Los Angeles *Sentinel*, November 22, 1973); "ROTC Apparently Making a Cautious Comeback at Many Colleges" (*New York Times*, October 25, 1973); "School of Theology Turning from Social Concerns" (Boston *Globe*, November 10, 1973); "Greeks [Fraternities] Making Comeback" (Boston *Globe,* January 6, 1974); "Becoming Popular Again: The Relevance of History Returns" (San Francisco *Examiner,* December 18, 1973); "Medical Education: Harvard Returns to Tradition" (*Science,* September 14, 1973); "The Mellow '70's Hit the Campus" (San Francisco *Chronicle,* October 11, 1973); "At Brown, Trend Is Back to Grades and Tradition" (*New York Times,* February 24, 1974); "Study of Greek and Latin Revived on Campus" (*New York Times,* February 10, 1974); "Youth, Once Disaffected, Looks Warily at Business" (*New York Times,* January 6, 1974); "Activism on U.S. Campuses Just a Memory in 1974. Students Buckle Down to Studies as Good Studies, Nostalgia Hold Sway" (*Christian Science Monitor,* February 11, 1974); "Trend Toward Individualism, Privacy Important to Students: 'Community Spirit' Lacking" (Lawrence University *Report,* February 1974); "Business Is Good at Business Schools" (Philadelphia *Inquirer,* January 28, 1974).

The change in mood among students came as a surprise to most friends and foes of militant campus activism. James Kunen, author of *The Strawberry Statement,* an activist's account of the Columbia uprising in 1968, reported in 1973 on the despair which the veterans of campus wars of the 1960s felt as they observed the "quiet seventies." Among this group, he noted "contempt for our successors in college." One of these "veterans," now teaching in a university, observed "that his undergraduates say they're right to be preoccupied with grades and success, that *we* were the aberration" (Kunen, 1973, p. 70).

As the headlines cited above indicate, students no longer form a mass base for activist protest. Those now on campuses know of the wave of militancy as a historic event to which they do not relate.

This change should not come as much of a surprise to those with any sense of history. As has been noted in various chronicles of university life, American higher education has witnessed a series of waves of student political and campus protest, some of which involved large proportions of students (Earnest, 1953; Lipset, 1972*b*; Altbach, 1974; Lipset, 1975). The protest of the early nineteenth century was perhaps more violent than that of the late 1960s (Lipset, 1972*b*, pp. 128–133). In the twentieth century, the pre-World War I decade and the era of the Great Depression witnessed relatively high levels of radical student activism. The 1920s and the 1950s, on the other hand, produced a moderate to low level of campus protests (Altbach, 1974, pp. 7–10). Writing in 1953 during the "quiet" of the McCarthy era, Ernest Earnest concluded that "unless history fails to repeat itself, there will be another revolt of youth" (Earnest, 1953, p. 337). During the 1960s, student radicals bitterly resented and attacked efforts at scholarly analysis which pointed up the cyclical character of campus activism, a conclusion which implied that their wave would also ebb, that they were not living in an age of revolution. On the other hand, Bettina Aptheker, a leader of the Berkeley Revolt in 1964–65 and a self-declared member of the Communist party, took heart in 1973 from the fact that "all social movements go in waves. You cannot sustain a level of intensity for an indeterminate length of time. . . . If that analysis is right the movement will recur" (Stephen, 1973).

To attempt to analyze the sources of political cycles would be to move beyond the scope of this book. It may be noted, however, that the historical evidence bearing on both campus and societal politics suggests that waves of protest constitute responses to politically relevant events —wars, depressions, inflations, and the like—more than to basic structural trends. As events change, and particularly as the issue or situation giving rise to a particular wave or movement is satisfied, the movement ebbs, the cycle shifts.[1] Beyond this, as Bettina Aptheker noted following considerable Communist writing on the subject, revolutionary periods rarely last more than a short while. Conflict situations are painful, and people move away from them if at all possible.

Political cycles take on a peculiar pattern in universities because the student population turns over almost completely within half a decade. The freshman class of 1969–70, which witnessed the final major events of the ebbing antiwar activity, the Cambodian protest, and the killings at Kent State and Jackson State, graduated in June 1973. The seniors returning to campus in the mid-decade year 1975 for the most part entered college in 1972—after the militancy was totally over. For them Vietnam and the "movement" are part of history. They are responding to a different political era, and even more importantly, to a period of economic uncertainty in a depressed labor market. This latter consideration has seemingly pressed students entering in the 1970s to study hard and compete strenuously with one another for the good grades which may affect their personal futures.

Faculty, on the other hand, as the more or less permanent estate of the university, should be less likely to reflect drastic fluctuations in views and behavior. Although they too respond to changes in the overall mood and to varying salient events and issues, the large majority of them carry the experiences and commitments which form their un-

---

[1]For a discussion of the sources of such changes in the context of a historical analysis of American right-wing movements, see Lipset and Raab (1970, pp. 484–487, 498–501).

derlying values with them into new eras. And, as mentioned earlier, since academe has entered a "no growth" period in the 1970s with a relatively young senior faculty, the turnover rate for the next two decades will be very low. Earlier moods, waves, and experiences should continue to inform academic orientations for a long time to come.

The steadier character of faculty political predispositions was demonstrated during previous cycles. Thus, during the quiet and more conservative fifties, surveys of academic opinion indicated that faculty remained consistently to the left of the electorate generally and of most subgroups in the population. In 1948 and 1952, left third parties were considerably stronger among professors than among other groups. The same cannot be said for the undergraduates of the period, who were much more likely than their teachers to have preferred Thomas Dewey and Dwight Eisenhower.

Faculty also were more disposed to take part in campus protests against violations of academic freedom than were students. Thus, the celebrated fight against the imposition of an anti-Communist loyalty oath at the University of California in 1949–50 was almost entirely a faculty affair. Student groups did little to support the faculty in its opposition. The study of social scientist's reactions to McCarthyism conducted by Lazarsfeld and Thielens concluded that supporters of McCarthy stood more risk of being sanctioned (ostracized) by their colleagues than did Communists (Lazarsfeld & Thielens, 1958, pp. 95, 104). Liberal faculty were critical of the mood of students. Thus in May 1953, Arthur Schlesinger, Jr., then a history professor at Harvard, wrote to the Harvard *Crimson* complaining about student groups canceling an appearance by author Howard Fast and a movie starring Paul Robeson. Schlesinger stated: "I gather that in these cases the students acted on their own, without orders or even hints from the Faculty. It is a stirring commentary on the courage of this new generation that the faculties and governing boards of the university should be more in favor of free speech than the students" (Halberstam, 1953, p. 62). In 1972, when the country swung to the right, faculty gave a slightly larger majority to McGovern than did college students. The shift of the students from undergraduate preferences four years earlier put them more in conformance with the mood of the electorate than were the professors.

The sense of alienation from the dominant establishment culture, identified with business and materialistic values, strongly felt in academe, may be reinforced during the late seventies and possibly the eighties by two factors discussed earlier—the financial squeeze and the disproportionate weight which those faculty who entered in the 1960s will continue to have in a period of no expansion. The decline in financial support during a period of rapid inflation, which implies reductions in real income, the laying off of some tenured faculty, and increasing difficulty in securing tenure, has led many academics to support collective bargaining and to vote for faculty unions. The primary academic professional organization, the AAUP, has moved significantly from its historic anti-collective bargaining posture. Meanwhile, faculty unions, currently the AFT and the NEA, have jumped directly into the political arena in ways which faculty bodies avoided before the Vietnam War. The NEA campaigned strongly for McGovern, as did many of the AFT college teacher locals. Linked directly to trade union political action groups, both organizations should constitute a continuing force for liberal political action among faculty. And the apparent tendency of unions to draw their leadership selectively from the ranks of more militant and left-disposed academics indicates that faculty unions will act as a left force both within academe and outside in the larger labor movement.

"Class" or vocational interests in the late seventies may, therefore, enhance the traditional "adversary culture" associated with higher education. One may even identify in this process a counter-cyclical trend in the academic community whereby the more conservatively inclined "teacher" segment at less research-involved schools takes on socially critical views in harmony with their support for militant unionism. The initially more liberal views of the younger faculty, reflecting the dominant orientations of the period when they entered the profession, the 1960s, may be reinforced rather than moderated as these faculty suffer frustrations imposed by a declining labor market and scarce financial resources.

The growth in vocational consciousness and consequent union organization among faculty appears, however, to have quite different political effects among students. The recognition by student groups that their interests as consumers run counter to those of the organized faculty may lead them into alliances with conservative forces—administrations, alumni, and politicians. Thus, the cooperation of two liberal strata, faculty and students, against the extramural powers which characterized the Vietnam War period may have ended for some time to come.

This does not mean an end to student organization. The example of an organized faculty pressing directly for its interests in ways which are perceived by many undergraduates as antithetical to their interests is precipitating organization for "self-defense." As an example of this process, the students at one of the New Jersey colleges, Stockton State, finding themselves faced with the prospect of an AFT-called faculty strike, formed the Stockton Student Union, which insisted not only "that professors protect student course credit during the strike" but also that the Stockton AFT negotiate any concessions won by their job action with the student union. The student union won contract guarantees which stipulated "1) that students must be given credit for all work done during the strike; 2) that faculty must supply students with syllabi and work booklets before the strike; and 3) that the union must make a major effort to negotiate overtime provisions with the state in order to help students catch up" (Klotz, 1974, p. 5).

In stressing the changes which have occurred between the late 1960s and the mid-1970s, it is important to note that some of the issues and sentiments which came to the fore in the earlier period are continuing in force (Yankelovich, 1974). The decline in student militancy and radicalism has had relatively little effect on the cultural liberalization which occurred as a by-product of the politicized era. This may be seen not only with respect to the new and freer sexual morality, but also in continued student insistence on procedural rights—their willingness to fight both faculty and administrators when their interests are affected.

More important than these developments, however, for the future political life of the university is the continued emphasis on some of the egalitarian tendencies which arose during the militancy of the sixties, particularly rights for ethnic and racial minorities and for women. The demand of these groups that they be accorded rights as a *group* has had extraordinary consequences for general conceptions of equal rights in America and for the traditional values of academe. Historically, minority groups that have suffered discrimination, institutionalized prejudice, or handicap with respect to education or jobs have demanded the elimination of barriers denying *individuals* access to opportunity. Jews, Orientals, and Italians objected in previous decades to the *numerus clausus* (quota) established by institutions of higher learning against qualified members of their ethnic groups (Steinberg, 1974).

Liberal and socialist opinion had always assumed that the egalitarian creed meant advocacy of a universal meritocracy, enabling all to secure positions for which they qualified in open, fair competition. Felix Frankfurter, who came to Harvard Law School from CCNY as an immigrant Jewish youth before World War I, never lost his awe of the meritocratic system. "What mattered was excellence in your profession to which your father or your face was equally irrelevant. And so rich man, poor man, were just irrelevant titles to the equation of human relations. The thing that mattered was what you did professionally" (Frankfurter, 1960, pp. 26–27). Randolph Bourne, a Columbia graduate and the most creative and celebrated of the young socialist intellectuals of the pre-World War I period, also argued in similar terms: "Scholarship is fundamentally democratic. Before the bar of marks and grades, penniless adventurer and rich man's son stand equal" (Bourne, 1913, p. 318).

Scholarship emphasizes the need to apply pure meritocratic and universalistic criteria (treatment of all according to impersonal standards) in evaluating those who would take part in its world. For scholarship, intellectual abilities and achievements—not family, race, wealth, or other aspects of social background—must be the primary quality associated with any award within its scope. Committed to advancing the frontiers of knowledge, the scholar ideally seeks only the best available (Merton, 1968, pp. 273–278).

This standard for university life has been rejected in recent years by those who argue that it is necessary to speed up the process of gaining equality for underprivileged minorities and women by applying the standard of "equality of results," requiring institutions to establish quotas for admission and for hiring which would bring the proportion of such groups in the university up to their percentage in the population. Compliance with these demands, which have increasingly become government policy, means denial of access to some with greater qualifications for study or creative scholarship. It involves the acceptance of a version of the principle of *ascription*, or hereditary placement, as a method of advancing opportunity (Lipset, 1974, pp. 16–27).

Not surprisingly, specific issues stemming from the emphasis on ascription as distinct from achievement have sharply divided academe. Giving preference to some means denying position to others. And in a declining labor market, filling black or female quotas reduces the chances of white males. Admitting less qualified students at given levels of higher education affects the level and nature of teaching. Introducing standards other than the meritocratic as criteria for choosing faculty may reduce the general emphasis on scholarship.

The more intellectually oriented, research-involved scholars, though generally more liberal than others, are highly committed to the competitive emphasis on originality and creativity. They seek for themselves and their students the rewards for being the best scholars, in much the same framework an athletic contest is conducted. To deny access to the best qualified, to the brightest, is for them comparable to dropping a player from a championship sports competition because of some social characteristic. Hence, though often quite liberal on other social issues, they seek to retain the principle of meritocracy in their university, department, or research team.

Few in academe openly resist the policy of judging the commitment of universities to equality for minorities and women in terms of willingness to use quotas. In fact, however, many white males and some members of minority groups are troubled. Their resistance often appears in discussions of specific candidates for admission, hiring, or promotion. And as a form of covert but real politics, the issues stemming from efforts at affirmative action for minorities will continue for many years to come.

Our examination of the politics of academics was not intended solely to discover sources of division within the stratum. Rather, as we noted earlier, academia has had a considerable impact on the larger body politic. This impact has clearly grown over the years, as polity and society have come increasingly to rely upon the universities as centers of expertise as well as of new knowledge. Since the Depression, many of the great debates on such issues as the economy, welfare, science policy, or weaponry have had academics among the principal protagonists. Though it is obviously possible to find a professorial authority for almost any position, very often the predominant weight of relevant academic opinion comes down on one side of an issue, establishing it as the "scientifically correct" response.

Beyond the immediate influence derived from playing the expert role, leading scholars, together with nonacademic intellectuals, have been able to affect the general climate of political opinion, both through their access to the media and through their impact on other elites who look to academe for guidance.

To appreciate the intellectuals' potential for social change, it is necessary to consider their functions and their relationships to other social elites and to the body politic generally. A key function of intellectuals is to provide symbolic formulations for the cultural construction of reality. Hence, they may play a role in "restructuring" people's conceptions of themselves and their society. Beyond that, they may be able to apply sanctions to motivate others to act toward their favored ends. The sanctions which they possess have three principal bases: power derived from the threat of withholding needed services, influence derived from possession of high prestige, and value commitments generated through the elaboration of ideology.

With respect to the first, it is clear that academic intellectuals supply services vitally needed by various social collectivities and their elites.

At the same time, they are dependent on others for resources, especially financial support in the form of remuneration or grants. The extent to which they come to exercise power depends on the degree to which their services are needed, whether they constitute a relatively unified monopolistic supplier (that is, control the market), and the extent of their dependency upon services or resources which others supply. Although in all advanced industrial countries the state is particularly reliant upon intellectuals for skills and expertise in many areas, including military research and weapons development, the intellectual community for the most part comprises many separate suppliers rather than being a single monopolistic force. For that reason, their power vis-à-vis the state has been obscured by the more manifest power of the political authorities over them. The relationship, however, is not a constant and may not always be so asymmetrical.

Contributing to the increased political importance of intellectuals has been the growing significance of science and other branches of knowledge, evidenced by the rapid expansion of those occupational groups which are engaged in knowledge production. This development, noted at the outset of our study, has led some to posit the beginning of a new social era. Daniel Bell (1973) speaks of a "postindustrial" society in which theoretical knowledge becomes the principal source of social and economic change, the "matrix of innovation," thereby permitting the scientific-technological intelligentsia to gain great prominence, prestige, and power. In a similar vein, Zbigniew Brzezinski (1970) writes of the onset of a "technetronic" age, in which technology and especially electronic communication increasingly becomes the principal determinant of change, altering social structure, values, mores, and the global outlook of society.

The impact of the "scientific-technological revolution" has been gaining greater attention recently among scholars in Communist countries. The most comprehensive and significant study, perhaps, is that conducted by Radovan Richta and his associates in the mid-sixties under the auspices of the Czechoslovakian Academy of Sciences. According to the authors, the work, entitled *Civilization at the Crossroads: Social and Human Implications of the Scientific and Technological Revolution*, was "conceived in an atmosphere of critical, radical searching and intensive discussion on the way forward for a society that has reached industrial maturity while passing through a phase of far-reaching socialist transformation" (Richta, 1968, p. 21). The central thesis of the study is that "science is emerging as the leading variable in the national economy and [is] the *vital dimension* in the growth of civilization. There are signs of a *new* [postindustrial] *type of growth*, with a new dynamic stemming from continual structural changes in the productive forces, with the amount of means of production and manpower becoming less important than their changing quality and degree of utilization. Herein lie the intensive elements of growth, the acceleration intimately linked with the onset of the scientific and technological revolution" (Richta, 1968, p. 39).

Coinciding with the scientific-technological revolution are major changes in occupational structure. Demonstrating the "disparity between the scientific and technological revolution and industrialization," the authors point out, is "the turn to a relative *decline* in the amount of labour absorbed by *industry* and associated activities" and the prospect that the tertiary sector will encompass 40 to 60 percent of the national labor force in industrial countries in the coming decades —already the case in the United States. Particularly noteworthy is the rapid expansion of that portion of the labor force engaged in science, research, and development: Until recently a fraction of 1 percent, these experts now constitute about 2 percent in the technologically advanced countries; by the end of the century they may account for 10 percent, and in the first half of the next century 20 percent or more (Richta, 1968, pp. 120–124).

"The fantastic forecast of a drastic, tenfold expansion in scientific activity made by Professor Bernal in 1939—received with incredulity at the time—was soon outdone by reality," comment Richta and his associates. "In most industrial countries the work force in science, research and development is doubled within eight to twelve years..." (Richta, 1968, p. 217). In the United States, the number of engineers rose from 217,000 in 1930 to more than a million in the mid-1970s, while during the same period, the number of scientists increased from 46,000 to over a half million. Otherwise stated, whereas the general work force increased by about 85 percent between 1930 and 1974, the number of engineers increased by 500 percent and the number of scientists by 1,100 percent (Bell, 1973, pp. 212–235; U.S. Bureau of the Census, 1973, pp. 231, 527).

Not only have the knowledge-producing occupations been increasing in number at a phenomenal rate, but such intellectuals have become more conscious of their social role and more widely valued by the general population. A signal event in the United States was the Soviet Union's successful launching of Sputnik in 1957. As Richard Hofstadter (1963, pp. 4–5) observed: "The Sputnik was more than a shock to American national vanity: It brought an immense amount of attention to bear on the consequences of anti-intellectualism in the school system and in American life at large. . . . In 1952 [during the height of McCarthyism] only intellectuals seemed much disturbed by the specter of anti-intellectualism; by 1958 the idea that this might be an important and even a dangerous failing was persuasive to most thinking people."

In appraising the social significance of the expanding intellectual stratum, it is important to realize that though the scientist's or scholar's specialized knowledge may be comprehensible only to relatively few, his personal prestige is widely appreciated. That prestige may provide the basis for the exercise of influence, in the sense specified by Talcott Parsons, or social leadership more generally. According to Parsons (1967, pp. 355–382), when information suggesting a course of action but not offering a clear inducement is transmitted by an actor, the receiver differentially appraises the information in terms of the actor's prestige. Prestige, as a code, changes not the content of information but the evaluation of it. If such information is transmitted by someone of higher status, action in accordance with it is more compelling than if it is transmitted by someone of lower status; that is, the message is more "persuasive." Thus, people tend to "look up" to those whom they respect and to defer to their judgments on important matters. In this way, the prestige of knowledge producers contributes to the political and social importance of intellectuals and the critical intelligentsia in both capitalist and Communist countries.

The greater impact of intellectuals and the university community on the body politic of many nations is not a function simply of increased numbers, of the vital services provided, or even of increased general social prestige. Both serving, as we have noted, to certify other elites as technically competent through their control of formal education, and helping to produce the ideational and cultural resources that various collectivities need, the leading universities and intellectuals have been gaining in their ability to exercise great influence over the other elites, whether in government, the churches, business establishments, or the mass media. They are more readily able to disseminate their values and ideas and to assure their acceptance by others in elite positions. The most visible and distinguished scholars and scientists constitute important reference individuals for those who respect intellectual accomplishment.

In the West, the influence of the universities and the intellectual community generally with respect to the churches appears as another chapter in the historic process of secularization. Both the Protestant and Catholic churches are currently under severe internal tensions as they seek to adjust their identity, theology, and ritual to contemporary conditions. Although the complex changes occurring in the churches have a variety of causes, one of the major sources of change stems from the fact that increasingly the leaders of the churches—those concerned, above all, with questions of theology and dogma—conceive of themselves as "intellectuals" and include the secular intellectuals in their reference group. While the university is a secular and critical institution which is modern in the sense of constantly being in the forefront of the elaboration of new ideas, churches by their nature emphasize continuity, tradition, and the legitimacy of revelation. Numerous dilemmas confront those churches seeking to maintain belief in revelation and tradition while also aligning themselves with the critical, innovative approach of the universities. The modernization of many religious denominations reflects the extent to which theology has become a branch of general intellectual life. Surely the changes in the church have important consequences for the value system of the larger society. Organized religion, rather than being simply a conservative structure, increasingly emerges as an institution pressing for social reform, often of a radical nature.

As suggested at the beginning of this volume, a second sphere of activity where the elite show strong signs of being affected by ties to the intellectual and university world is in the mass media. To an increasing degree in the United States and in other Western countries, the men and women who write for the major papers and journals and who are in charge of broadcasting have the same values and political orientations as the critical intellectuals. A survey by the Harris poll of mass media editors reports that 40 percent describe themselves as "liberals" and only 13 percent as "conservatives," a pattern which puts them far to the left of the public but to the right of leading intellectuals. Harris reports, however, that 63 percent of those in charge of major organs located in the principal cities are liberal (Harris Survey, 1970). It appears that those who have achieved prominence in the national communications media consider themselves intellectuals. They identify prestige as being at the summit of an intellectual institution, not as being successful in business. The "working press," then, is increasingly composed of individuals sympathetic to social change. Consequently, though the most influential American communications media—the Columbia Broadcasting System, National Broadcasting Company, Washington *Post, New York Times*, and the like—are big business establishments, they present views sympathetic to those who seek to change society from the left.

A third elite group on which the intellectual community exerts a growing influence is the government bureaucracy. Commenting on the way in which the antibusiness values of the intellectuals were undermining the legitimacy of capitalism, Joseph Schumpeter (1962, p. 155) stressed the "direct relationship between the intellectual group and the bureaucracy.... Except for inhibitions due to professional training and experience, they are therefore open to conversion by the modern intellectual with whom, through a similar education, they have much in common.... Moreover, in time of rapid expansion of the sphere of public administration, much of the additional personnel required has to be taken directly from the university." The government bureaucracy has become increasingly dependent on the expertise cultivated by higher education, so that it is now staffed, particularly at its upper levels, by persons with close ties to academia. Since many of them seek the approbation of that community, they too appear responsive to the changing orientations and generally leftist dispositions of prominent figures in the academic world.

In the United States, one leadership group resistant to this liberalizing influence of the university is business management. One would expect business executives to provide support for conservative values, since they manage the dominant economic institutions of the society. Yet even business is beginning to face problems deriving from the functions and prestige of the university. Particularly in capitalist society, as Schumpeter (1962) noted, and as was later reiterated by the radical sociologist J. P. Nettl (1969), the business establishment finds it necessary to protect the right of intellectuals to undermine the system. These scholars argued:

In a capitalist society... any attack on the intellectuals must run up against the private fortresses of bourgeois business which, or some of which, will shelter the quarry. Moreover such an attack must proceed according to bourgeois principles of legislative and administrative practice which no doubt may be stretched and bent but will checkmate prosecution beyond a certain point. Lawless violence the bourgeois stratum may accept or even applaud when thoroughly roused or frightened, but only temporarily... because the freedom it disapproves cannot be crushed without also crushing the freedom it approves....

From this follows both the unwillingness and the inability of the capitalist order to control its intellectual sector effectively ... the intellectual group cannot help nibbling ... and criticism of persons and of current events will, in a situation in which nothing is sacrosanct, fatally issue in criticism of classes and institutions....

In defending the intellectuals as a group—not of course every individual—the bourgeoisie defends itself and its scheme of life. Only a government of a non-bourgeois nature and non-bourgeois creed—under modern circumstances only a socialist or fascist one—is strong enough to discipline them (Schumpeter, 1962, pp. 150–151; Nettl, 1969, p. 57).

One cannot preclude the possibility of a right-wing reaction to severe challenges from the intelligentsia, but in the United States at least, as David Riesman (1960, pp. 506–507) has suggested, it appears that the top business executives show increasing respect and concern for "intellectual values" as articulated by those in universities. Being respectful of intellectuals and sharing at least some of their values, the business elite is significantly affected by criticism emanating from the academy and the intellectual world. Preliminary results from the Columbia University study of the American elite, directed by Charles Kadushin and Alan Barton, strongly reinforce these assumptions.

Academics and their apprentices, university students, have never been as numerous as they are today. Given the increased requirements of postindustrial society for university-trained people and continuing high levels of innovative research, the university is needed more than ever before. While the society is becoming more dependent on intellectuals, it is also more influenced by them.

It may be argued that the growth of a critical intelligentsia disposed to support the "adversary culture" and reject the worth of dominant political and economic institutions is undermining the capacity of governing systems in modern societies to maintain social equilibrium. Leadership itself, the primary function of authority, is under question by intellectuals everywhere. Castro, Mao, Tito, Franco, the Japanese governing elite, the leaders of Western Europe, no less than those who head the governments of the United States and the Soviet Union, have found themselves at odds with their intellectuals.

The critical intellectual questions the possibility of participating in government without betraying the ideals of the society. Although faced with attacks on their legitimacy from intellectuals, many in the governing elites still find it difficult to ignore or suppress groups to whose values of scientific and intellectual progress they are committed. The basic tensions, the contradictions within the system, then, come increasingly from within the elite itself—from its own intellectual leaders, often supported by large segments of its student children. If in Hegelian terms the contradiction of capitalism was its dependence on an ever-growing, potentially hostile, working class brought together in large factories, the contradiction of postindustrial society, whether Communist or non-Communist, may be its dependence on trained intelligence, on research and innovation, which requires that it bring together large numbers of intellectuals and students on great campuses and in a few intellectual communities located at the centers of communication and influence.

Such assertions made during the "calm" of the mid-seventies may appear as an exaggerated projection from the turmoil of the sixties. Clearly, the extent to which leading academics and other intellectuals give voice to the "adversary culture" varies over time in an irregular fashion. As noted earlier, periods of intense politicization and criticism are self-exhaustive. Academics, like other people, tend to withdraw into a protective shell, the ivory tower, after experiencing the punitive effects of involvement in highly controversial disputations. As particular issues, such as the Vietnam War, work themselves out, many persons who were once active drop out of politics to return to their basic work, scholarship and teaching. Trends in the larger society which foster conservative or nonpolitical orientations discourage academics and other critics from voicing their discontent with the powers. But new issues, new crises, new types of popular discontent inevitably occur; and the now massive intellectual stratum, centered around the university, remains available to reenter the political arena voicing dissatisfaction with the "established," as Whitelaw Reid suggested over 100 years ago.

Joseph Schumpeter has argued that authority could not win over the allegiance of the intellectuals, no matter how successful the economic and social order it managed (Schumpeter, 1962, pp. 154–155). Unlike other groups who have challenged the system at various times, the antagonism of the intellectual does not appear to be reduced by success and the rewards it brings; if anything, as we have seen, success associated with intellectual achievement is actually linked to a propensity for social criticism. Almost certainly, the intellectual stratum will provide in a continuing fashion the principal nexus from which pressures for social change will emanate in postindustrial America.

Appendix A: The Carnegie Commission Faculty Study Questionnaire

THE CARNEGIE COMMISSION ON HIGHER EDUCATION

THE AMERICAN COUNCIL ON EDUCATION

Dear Colleague:

American higher education is currently undergoing its greatest changes in a hundred years. The extent and rapidity of these changes are causing severe strains and grave problems in our colleges and universities. But while we can see the broad outlines of these problems in over-crowded classrooms, rising costs, student rebellions, and threats to academic feeedom from sev-eral quarters, there is very little detailed information on the form they take in different kinds of institutions, or in different disciplines and professions. Nor do we have firm knowledge of how the people most directly affected, the students and faculty, feel about these problems and issues.

To meet this need for more and better knowledge, the Carnegie Commission on Higher Educa-tion, in cooperation with the American Council on Education, is conducting a national survey of students and faculty in a broad sample of colleges and universities. The information we are gath-ering will be of help to the Carnegie Commission and to other bodies concerned with public policy in this area, as well as to scholars who are studying current problems and developments in Ameri-can higher education. Our findings will be published in books and reports; the data we collect will be made available in an anonymous form to other scholars and students of higher education.

We have no illusion that even a broad survey of this kind will answer all our questions. We know the limits of questionnaires, and are conducting other studies, in other ways, to supplement this survey. Nevertheless, a broad survey such as this provides information that can be obtained in no other way. We know how busy faculty members and administrators are. And we know also that other surveys may have made similar demands on your time. But the present survey is unique in its scope and purposes: it is the first to ask similar questions of students and faculty in the same in-stitutions, and it is the first to explore a variety of these issues on a national scale. The accur-acy of the survey and the worth of its findings are dependent on your willingness to answer our questions. We believe the importance of the study will justify the time you give it.

One other matter. It is impossible to frame questions all of which are equally relevant to faculty members in many different fields and kinds of institutions; you may find some that seem inappro-priate to your situation. We urge you to answer all the questions as well as you can; in our analy-sis we will be able to take into account special circumstances that affect replies to some questions.

Finally, we assure you that your answers will be held in strictest confidence. We are inter-ested only in statistical relationships and will under no circumstances report responses on an in-dividual or departmental basis. Any special markings on your form are used solely for internal data processing.

We hope you will find the questionnaire interesting to answer, and that you will complete and return it to us while you have it at hand.

With our thanks for your cooperation.

Sincerely,

Logan Wilson   *Clark Kerr*

Logan Wilson
President
American Council
  on Education

Clark Kerr
Chairman
Carnegie Commission
  on Higher Education

MARKING INSTRUCTIONS:

This questionnaire will be read by an auto-
matic scanning device. Certain marking requirements are essential to this process.
Your careful observance of these few simple
rules will be most appreciated.

Use soft black lead pencil only. (No. 2½
or softer)

Make heavy black marks that completely
fill the circle.

Erase completely any answers you wish to
change.

Avoid making any stray marks in this
booklet.

1. What is your present rank?

Instructor ....O
Assistant Professor ....O
Associate Professor.....................O
Professor ....O
Lecturer ....O
No ranks designated ....O
Other ....O

2. What kind of appointment do you have here?

Regular with tenure.....................O
Regular without tenure ....O
Acting ....O
Visiting..............................O

3. During the spring term *, how many hours per
week are you spending in formal instruction in
class? (Give actual, not credit hours)

None.. O   7-8 ......O   13-16........O
1-4 ...O   9-10 .....O   17-20 ....O
5-6 ...O   11-12 ....O   21 or more...O

4. Are your teaching responsibilities this
academic year

Entirely undergraduate ....O
Some undergraduate, some graduate ..O ⌐Skip to
Entirely graduate..................O ⌐ No. 7
Not teaching this year ....O→ Skip to
                                        No. 8

5. How much do you control the content of your
undergraduate courses?

Almost completely.. O   Somewhat ......O
Substantially ......O   Hardly at all...O

6. In about how many of the undergraduate courses
you teach do you use the following?

Most Some None

Term papers ................O...O..O
Frequent quizzes............O...O..O
Graduate teaching assistants ..O...O..O
Closed-circuit television ......O...O..O
Computer or machine-aided
instruction................O...O..O

* Quarter, semester, trimester, etc.

7. About how many students, at all levels,
are enrolled in your courses this term?

None....O   Under 25 ..O   100-249 .....O
            25-49 .....O   250-399 .....O
            50-99 .....O   400 or more ..O

8. Do you discourage undergraduates from seeing
you outside your regular office hours?

Yes, almost always ....O
Yes, but with many exceptions............O
No ....O

9. Please indicate your agreement or disagreement with each of the following statements.

1. Strongly Agree
2. Agree With Reservations
3. Disagree With Reservations
4. Strongly Disagree
①②③④

Most undergraduates are mature
enough to be given more responsibility for their own education.....①②③④

Graduate students in my subject do
best if their undergraduate major
was in the same general field.....①②③④

Most graduate students in my department*are basically satisfied
with the education they are getting...........................①②③④

Most Ph.D. holders in my field get
their degrees without showing
much real scholarly ability.......①②③④

My department*has taken steps to
increase graduate student participation in its decisions...........①②③④

The graduate program in my department*favors the bright, imaginative
student ....①②③④

Many of the best graduate students
can no longer find meaning in
science and scholarship ....①②③④

Graduate education in my subject
is doing a good job of training
students ....①②③④

Some of the best graduate students
drop out because they do not want
to "play the game" or "beat the
system".......................①②③④

The female graduate students in my
department*are not as dedicated as
the males.....................①②③④

The typical undergraduate curriculum has suffered from the specialization of faculty members ....①②③④

This institution should be as concerned about students' personal
values as it is with their intellectual development ....①②③④

*
If no graduate program in your department, leave blank.

9 Continued.

Most undergraduates here are basically satisfied with the education they are getting .... ①②③④

A man can be an effective teacher without personally involving himself with his students .... ①②③④

Most faculty here are strongly interested in the academic problems of undergraduates .... ①②③④

Most American colleges reward conformity and crush student creativity .... ①②③④

This institution should be actively engaged in solving social problems .... ①②③④

More minority group undergraduates should be admitted here even if it means relaxing normal academic standards of admission .... ①②③④

Any institution with a substantial number of black students should offer a program of Black Studies if they wish it .... ①②③④

Any special academic program for black students should be administered and controlled by black people .... ①②③④

Undergraduate education in America would be improved if:

a) All courses were elective ..... ①②③④

b) Grades were abolished .... ①②③④

c) Course work were more relevant to contemporary life and problems .... ①②③④

d) More attention were paid to the emotional growth of students .. ①②③④

e) Students were required to spend a year in community service at home or abroad .... ①②③④

f) Colleges and universities were governed completely by their faculty and students .... ①②③④

g) There were less emphasis on specialized training and more on broad liberal education .... ①②③④

10. For each of these areas, should present academic standards in your institution (a,b) and your graduate department (c,d) be--
(Mark one in each row)

1. Much higher
2. Somewhat higher
3. Left as they are
4. Somewhat lower
5. Much lower
①②③④⑤⑥— 6. No graduate department

a) Undergraduate admissions .. ①②③④⑤

b) Bachelor's degrees .... ①②③④⑤

c) Graduate admissions....... ①②③④⑤⑥

d) Advanced degrees .... ①②③④⑤⑥

11. Do you feel that the administration of your department*is:

Very autocratic .... ○

Somewhat autocratic..................... ○

Somewhat democratic .... ○

Very democratic .... ○

*Here and hereafter, if you have a joint appointment, answer for your main department. If your institution has no departments, answer for the equivalent administrative unit (e.g., division for junior colleges).

12. Is the chairman of your department appointed for a fixed short term (3 years or less) or for a long or indefinite period?

Long/Indefinite... ○   Short term...... ○

13. Roughly how many regular members (at the rank of instructor or above) does your department have this year?

3 or fewer........ ○	16 - 20 .... ○
4 - 5 .... ○	21 - 25 .... ○
6 - 7 .... ○	26 - 30 .... ○
8 - 10 .... ○	31 - 40 .... ○
11 - 15 .... ○	41 or more ..... ○

14. How much has your department changed in size in the last 3 years? Is it:

Much larger .... ○

Somewhat larger .... ○

About the same .... ○

Smaller............................. ○

15a Do you think your department is now

Too big............................. ○

About right.......................... ○

Too small........................... ○

b Do you think your institution is now

Too big............................. ○

About right.......................... ○

Too small........................... ○

16. How active are you (a) in your own department's affairs? (b) in the faculty government of your institution (committee memberships, etc,)?
(Mark one in each column)

	Department	Institution
Much more than average......	○	○
Somewhat more than average..	○	○
About average	○	○
Somewhat less than average .	○	○
Much less than average	○	○

17. How much opportunity do you feel you have to influence the policies (a) of your department? (b) of your institution?

(Mark one in each column)

Department Institution

	Department	Institution
A great deal	O	O
Quite a bit	O	O
Some	O	O
None	O	O

18. How many of the people you see socially are:
(a) members of the faculty here?

Almost all ......O   Some........O
Most ....O   Almost none ..O
About half ......O

(b) members of your department?

Almost all ......O   Some ....O
Most ....O   Almost none ..O
About half ......O

19. What do you think of the emergence of radical student activism in recent years?

Unreservedly approve..................O
Approve with reservations.............O
Disapprove with reservations ....O
Unreservedly disapprove ....O

20. With respect to the student revolt at Columbia last year, were you in sympathy with

the students' aims and their methods ....O
their aims but not their methods.........O
neither their aims nor their methods .....O
I don't know enough about it to judge ....O

21. Have any of your children been active in civil rights, anti-Vietnam, or other demonstrations?

Yes...................................O
None active ....O
None of that age ....O

22. Has your campus experienced any student protests or demonstrations during the current academic year?

Yes...O   No....O (if no, skip to No. 25)

23. How would you characterize your attitude toward the most recent demonstration?

Approved of the demonstrators' aims and methods ....O
Approved of their aims but not their methods ....O
Disapproved of their aims ....O
Uncertain or mixed feelings ....O
Indifferent ....O

24. What was your role in this demonstration? (Mark all that apply)

Helped to plan, organize, or lead the protest ....O
Joined in active protest with the demonstrators ....O
Openly supported the goals of the protestors.............................O
Openly opposed the goals of the protestors..O
Tried to mediate in the protest ....O
Was not involved actively in any way ......O

25. What effect have student demonstrations (on your campus or elsewhere) had on each of the following? (Mark one in each row)

1. Very favorable
2. Fairly favorable
3. Fairly harmful
4. Very harmful
①②③④⑤— 5. No effect

Your research.................①②③④⑤
Your teaching.................①②③④⑤
Your relations with departmental colleagues ....①②③④⑤
Your relations with other colleagues ....①②③④⑤
Your relations with students .....①②③④⑤
Your view of your campus administration ....①②③④⑤
Your institution's relations with the local community ....①②③④⑤

26a. What role do you believe undergraduates should play in decisions on the following?

1. Control
2. Voting power on committees
3. Formal consultation
4. Informal consultation
①②③④⑤—5. Little or no role

Faculty appointment and promotion ....①②③④⑤
Undergraduate admissions policy.①②③④⑤
Provision and content of courses .①②③④⑤
Student discipline.............①②③④⑤
Bachelor's degree requirements ..①②③④⑤

b. What role do you believe graduate students should play in decisions on the following?

Faculty appointment and promotion......................①②③④⑤
Departmental graduate admissions policy ....①②③④⑤
Provision and content of graduate courses ....①②③④⑤
Student discipline.............①②③④⑤
Advanced degree requirements ..①②③④⑤

27. **Please indicate your agreement or disagreement with each of the following statements.**

1. Strongly agree
2. Agree with reservations
3. Disagree with reservations
① ② ③ ④ — 4. Strongly disagree

The normal academic requirements should be relaxed in appointing members of minority groups to the faculty here . . . . ① ② ③ ④

Opportunities for higher education should be available to all high school graduates who want it . . . . . ① ② ③ ④

Most American colleges and universities are racist whether they mean to be or not . . . . ① ② ③ ④

Public colleges and universities must be more responsive to public demands than are private institutions . . . . ① ② ③ ④

Junior faculty members have too little say in the running of my department . . . . ① ② ③ ④

A small group of senior professors has disproportionate power in decision-making in this institution ① ② ③ ④

This institution would be better off with fewer administrators . . . . ① ② ③ ④

There should be faculty representation on the governing board of this institution . . . . ① ② ③ ④

Trustees' only responsibilities should be to raise money and gain community support . . . . ① ② ③ ④

The administration here has taken a clear stand in support of academic freedom . . . . ① ② ③ ④

Faculty unions have a divisive effect on academic life . . . . ① ② ③ ④

Teaching assistants' unions have a divisive effect on academic life . . ① ② ③ ④

Faculty members should be more militant in defending their interests . . . . ① ② ③ ④

Collective bargaining by faculty members has no place in a college or university . . . . ① ② ③ ④

Most rules governing student behavior here are sensible . . . . ① ② ③ ④

Campus rules here are generally administered in a reasonable way . . ① ② ③ ④

Undergraduates known to use marijuana regularly should be suspended or dismissed . . . . ① ② ③ ④

Political activities by students have no place on a college campus ① ② ③ ④

27 Continued.

Student demonstrations have no place on a college campus . . . . ① ② ③ ④

Students who disrupt the functioning of a college should be expelled or suspended . . . . ① ② ③ ④

Most campus demonstrations are created by far left groups trying to cause trouble . . . . ① ② ③ ④

College officials have the right to regulate student behavior off campus . . . . ① ② ③ ④

Respect for the academic profession has declined over the past 20 years . ① ② ③ ④

A student's grades should not be revealed to anyone off campus without his consent . . . . ① ② ③ ④

Faculty members should be free on campus to advocate violent resistance to public authority . . . . ① ② ③ ④

Faculty members should be free to present in class any idea that they consider relevant . . . . ① ② ③ ④

Campus disruptions by militant students are a threat to academic freedom . . . . ① ② ③ ④

28. **Have you known of a case here within the past two years in which a man's politics affected his chances for retention or promotion?**

I know definitely of a case . . . . ○
I've heard of a case . . . . ○
I don't know of a case . . . . ○
I'm sure it hasn't happened . . . . ○

29. **In recent years, have you ever felt intimidated in your classes by students with strong political or racial views?**

Yes . . . . ○   No . . . . . . ○

30. **In what year did you obtain your highest degree?**

1928 or before . . ○   1949-1953 . . . . . . ○
1929-1933 . . . . . . ○   1954-1958 . . . . . . ○
1934-1938 . . . . . . ○   1959-1963 . . . . . . ○
1939-1943 . . . . . . ○   1964-1966 . . . . . . ○
1944-1948 . . . . . . ○   1967 or later . . . . ○

31. **How many years elapsed between your obtaining your bachelor's degree and your highest degree?**

No degree higher than bachelor's . . . . ○
I am still working for a higher degree . . . . . . ○
1 - 2 years . . . . ○
3 - 4 years . . . . ○
5 - 7 years . . . . ○
8 - 10 years . . . . ○
11 - 15 years . . . . ○
Over 15 years . . . . ○

32. On the following list, please mark
    1. (If any) the degree(s) for which you are currently working
    2. **All** degrees that you have earned
    3. **All** degrees you have earned at **this** institution

Working Toward / *Now hold* / *Earned here*

Less than Bachelor's (A.A., etc.) ....①②③
Undergraduate Bachelor's ....①②③
First professional law degree ....①②③
First professional medical degree (e.g. M.D., D.D.S.)......................①②③
Other first professional beyond under- graduate bachelor's ....①②③
Master's (except first professional)...①②③
Doctor of Arts or equivalent for doc- torate degree without dissertation ..①②③
Ph.D........................①②③
Ed.D............................①②③
Other doctorate (except first profes- sional)............................①②③
None ....①②③

33. From the following list, mark **one** subject in each column; mark the most appropriate **fine** categories, if applicable; where your precise field does not appear, mark the most similar category.

    1. Undergraduate major
    2. Highest postgraduate degree
    3. Present principal teaching field
    4. Present primary field of research, scholarship, creativity
    5. Department*of teaching appointment

①②③④⑤
NONE ....①②③④⑤
Agriculture and/or Forestry.....①②③④⑤
Architecture and/or Design .....①②③④⑤
Biological Sciences (General Biology) ....①②③④⑤
Bacteriology, Molecular biology, Virology, Micro- biology....................①②③④⑤
Biochemistry ....①②③④⑤
General Botany ....①②③④⑤
Physiology, Anatomy ....①②③④⑤
General Zoology ....①②③④⑤
Other Biological Sciences ①②③④⑤
Business, Commerce and Management ....①②③④⑤
Education ....①②③④⑤
Elementary and/or Secondary ..①②③④⑤
Foundations ....①②③④⑤
Educational Psychology and Counseling ....①②③④⑤
Educational Administration ....①②③④⑤
Other Education fields ....①②③④⑤

Engineering ....①②③④⑤
Chemical...................①②③④⑤
Civil ....①②③④⑤
Electrical ....①②③④⑤
Mechanical.................①②③④⑤
Other Engineering fields ......①②③④⑤
Fine Arts ....①②③④⑤
Art........................①②③④⑤
Dramatics and Speech ....①②③④⑤
Music.....................①②③④⑤
Other Fine Arts ....①②③④⑤
Geography..................①②③④⑤
Health Fields...............①②③④⑤
Medicine ....①②③④⑤
Nursing ....①②③④⑤
Other Health fields ....①②③④⑤
Home Economics ....①②③④⑤
Humanities ....①②③④⑤
English language & literature..①②③④⑤
Foreign languages & literature .①②③④⑤
French....................①②③④⑤
German ....①②③④⑤
Spanish...................①②③④⑤
Other foreign languages (in- cluding linguistics).........①②③④⑤
History ....①②③④⑤
Philosophy ....①②③④⑤
Religion & Theology ....①②③④⑤
Other Humanities fields ......①②③④⑤
Industrial Arts ....①②③④⑤
Journalism ....①②③④⑤
Law......................①②③④⑤
Library Science ....①②③④⑤
Mathematics and Statistics .....①②③④⑤
Physical & Health Education ....①②③④⑤
Physical Sciences...........①②③④⑤
Chemistry...................①②③④⑤
Earth Sciences (incl. Geology).①②③④⑤
Physics.....................①②③④⑤
Other Physical Sciences ......①②③④⑤
Psychology...................①②③④⑤
Clinical...................①②③④⑤
Experimental ....①②③④⑤
Social ....①②③④⑤
Counseling and Guidance......①②③④⑤
Other Psychology fields ......①②③④⑤
Social Sciences ....①②③④⑤
Anthropology & Archaeology ....①②③④⑤
Economics ....①②③④⑤
Political Science, Government ..①②③④⑤
Sociology ....①②③④⑤
Other Social Sciences.........①②③④⑤
Social Work, Social Welfare......①②③④⑤
ALL OTHER FIELDS..........①②③④⑤

* Mark main department, if you have a joint appointment.

34. On the following list of large American universities, mark one in each column; if the names
of your institutions do not appear, mark appropriate "other" categories.

　　　　　1. Bachelor's degree
　　　　2. Highest degree
①②③ — 3. First regular teaching job

NONE or not appropriate...........①②③
Boston University ....①②③
Brown University, R.I. ....①②③
California Institute of Technology ..①②③
California, University of, at Berkeley①②③
California, University of, at Los
　Angeles........................①②③
Carnegie Institute of Technology, Pa.①②③
Catholic University of America, D.C..①②③
Chicago, University of ....①②③
Colorado, University of.............①②③
Columbia University Teachers'
　College, N.Y....................①②③
Columbia University, N.Y. ....①②③
Cornell University, N.Y. ....①②③
Duke University, N.C...............①②③
Florida, University of..............①②③
Fordham University, N.Y............①②③
Harvard University, Mass ....①②③
Illinois, University of..............①②③
Indiana University at Bloomington ...①②③
Iowa State University ....①②③
Iowa, University of ....①②③
Johns Hopkins University...........①②③
Kansas, University of..............①②③
Louisiana State University..........①②③
Maryland, University of.............①②③
Massachusetts Institute of Technology①②③
Michigan State University...........①②③
Michigan, University of.............①②③
Minnesota, University of............①②③
Missouri, University of, at Columbia .①②③
Nebraska, University of ....①②③
New York University ....①②③
North Carolina, University of........①②③
Northwestern University, Ill........①②③
Notre Dame University, Ind ....①②③
Ohio State University ....①②③
Oklahoma, University of............①②③
Oregon State University ....①②③
Oregon, University of ....①②③
Pennsylvania State University.......①②③
Pennsylvania, University of.........①②③
Pittsburgh, University of ....①②③
Princeton University, N.J...........①②③
Purdue University ....①②③
Rochester, University of............①②③
Rutgers University, N.J.............①②③
Southern California, University of....①②③
Stanford University, Calif..........①②③

34 Continued

Syracuse University, N.Y............①②③
Texas, University of ....①②③
Utah, University of.................①②③
Virginia, University of..............①②③
Washington University, Mo..........①②③
Washington, University of, Wash .....①②③
Western Reserve University, Ohio.....①②③
Wisconsin, University of ....①②③
Yale University, Conn ....①②③
Other private Ph.D.-granting univer-
　sity.............................①②③
Other state Ph.D.-granting university ..①②③
Other private college (no Ph.D.
　program)........................①②③
Other public college (no Ph.D.
　program).........................①②③
A foreign institution................①②③
A junior or community college ....①②③

35. How long have you been employed (beyond
the level of teaching or research assistant):
a. in colleges or universities?

1 year or less..... O	10-14 years ...... O
2-3 years .... O	15-19 years ...... O
4-6 years......... O	20-29 years ...... O
7-9 years .... O	30 years or more.. O

b. at this institution?

1 year or less..... O	10-14 years ...... O
2-3 years......... O	15-19 years ..... O
4-6 years......... O	20-29 years ...... O
7-9 years .... O	30 years or more.. O

36. At how many different colleges or universities
have you been employed full-time (beyond the
level of teaching or research assistant)?

None .... O	Four ....O
One .... O	Five ....O
Two.............. O	Six.............O
Three .... O	Seven or more ... O

37. Comparing yourself with other academic men of
your age and qualifications, how successful do
you consider yourself in your career?
Very successful ... O
Fairly successful .. O
Fairly unsuccessful. O
Very unsuccessful .. O

38. In general, how do you feel about this
institution?
It is a very good place for me............. O
It is fairly good for me.................. O
It is not the place for me................ O

39. Do you think you could be equally or more satisfied with life in any other college or university?

Definitely yes .... O
Probably yes .... O
Probably no .... O
Definitely no .... O

40. If you were to begin your career again, would you still want to be a college professor?

Definitely yes .... O
Probably yes .... O
Probably no .... O
Definitely no .... O

41. (a) Mark all types of work that you have engaged in for a year or more since earning your bachelor's degree (not counting part-time work while in graduate school). (b) What were you doing immediately prior to taking a job at this institution? (Mark one)

	Have Done	Did Last
Teaching in a university	O	
Teaching in a 4-year college	O	O
Teaching in a junior or community college	O	O
Full-time non-teaching research position in a college or university	O	O
Post-doctoral fellowship or traineeship in a university	O	O
Full-time college or university administration	O	O
Teaching or administration in an elementary or secondary school	O	O
Research and development outside educational institutions	O	O
Executive or administrative post outside educational institutions	O	O
Other professional position	O	O
Student	O	O
Other	O	O

42. Please indicate your agreement or disagreement with each of the following statements.

1. Strongly agree
2. Agree with reservations
3. Disagree with reservations
① ② ③ ④ — 4. Strongly disagree

My field is too research oriented . . ① ② ③ ④
I prefer teaching courses which focus on limited specialties to those which cover wide varieties of material . . . . ① ② ③ ④

42 Continued

I consider myself an intellectual . . . . . ① ② ③ ④
I hardly ever get the time to give a piece of work the attention it deserves . . . . ① ② ③ ④
I tend to subordinate all aspects of my life to my work . . . . ① ② ③ ④
A man's teaching and research inevitably reflect his political values . . . . . ① ② ③ ④
My commitments to different aspects of my job are the source of considerable personal strain . . . . ① ② ③ ④
I am in frequent communication with people in my own academic specialty in other institutions . . . . ① ② ③ ④
Many of the highest-paid university professors get where they are by being "operators", rather than by their scholarly or scientific contributions . . . . ① ② ③ ④
By and large, full-time professional researchers in universities are people who couldn't quite make it on the faculty . . . . ① ② ③ ④
Genuine scholarship is threatened in universities by the proliferation of big research centers . . . . ① ② ③ ④
The concentration of federal and foundation research grants in the big institutions (Mark each line)
1) is unfair to other institutions . . . . . ① ② ③ ④
2) is corrupting to the institutions and men that get them . . . . ① ② ③ ④
3) contributes substantially to the advancement of knowledge . . . . ① ② ③ ④
Many professors in graduate departments exploit their students to advance their own research . . . . ① ② ③ ④
In my department it is very difficult for a man to achieve tenure if he does not publish . . . . ① ② ③ ④
Teaching effectiveness, not publications, should be the primary criterion for promotion of faculty . . . . ① ② ③ ④
Faculty promotions should be based in part on formal student evaluations of their teachers . . . . ① ② ③ ④
A professor at a junior college or state college ought to get the same pay as a university professor of equal seniority . . . . ① ② ③ ④
Classified weapons research is a legitimate activity on college and university campuses . . . . ① ② ③ ④
Big contract research has become more a source of money and prestige for researchers than an effective way of advancing knowledge . . . . ① ② ③ ④

43. Given the following four possible activities of academic men, please mark the first three in order:
    1. According to their importance to you personally
    2. According to your understanding of what your institution expects of you
       (Mark one in each column)

	Importance to Me			Institution's Expectation		
	First	Second	Third	First	Second	Third
Provide undergraduates with a broad liberal education	O	O	O	O	O	O
Prepare undergraduates for their chosen occupation	O	O	O	O	O	O
Train graduate or professional students	O	O	O	O	O	O
Engage in research	O	O	O	O	O	O

44. **Within the past two years have you received an offer of another job or a serious inquiry about your availability for another position?**
    An offer..O
    Not an offer, but a serious inquiry.........O
    Neither ....O

45. **In a normal week, what proportion of your work time is devoted to the following activities:**
    a. Administration (departmental or institutional, including committee work)

    None .....O 1-10% ...O   41-60% ......O
              11-20%...O   61-80% ......O
              21-40%...O   81-100% .....O

    b. Consulting (with or without pay)
    None .....O 1-10%....O   41-60% ......O
              11-20%...O   61-80% ......O
              21-40%...O   81-100%.....O

    c. Outside professional practice
    None .....O 1-10%....O   41-60% ......O
              11-20%...O   61-80% ......O
              21-40%...O   81-100% .....O

46. **To how many academic or professional journals do you subscribe?**
    None .....O 3-4 ......O   11-20........O
    1-2.......O 5-10 .....O   More than 20 .O

47. **How many articles have you published in academic or professional journals?**
    None .....O 3-4 ......O   11-20........O
    1-2.......O 5-10 .....O   More than 20 .O

48. **How many books or monographs have you published or edited, alone or in collaboration?**
    None ....O   3-4 ....O
    1-2............O   5 or more ....O

49. **How many of your professional writings have been published or accepted for publication in the last two years?**
    None ..O   3-4 ....O   More than 10 .O
    1-2.....O 5-10 ......O

50. **Do your interests lie primarily in teaching or in research?**
    Very heavily in research.................O
    In both, but leaning toward research.......O
    In both, but leaning toward teaching.......O
    Very heavily in teaching................O

51. **Are you currently engaged in any scholarly or research work which you expect to lead to publication?**
    Yes.....O   No.....O (If no, skip to No. 55)

52. **Which of these statements applies to your current major piece of research or scholarship?**
    I am essentially working alone ....O
    I am working with one or two colleagues ....O
    I am a member of a larger group...........O

53. **Are any of the following working with you on any research project? (Mark all that apply)**
    Graduate research assistants.............O
    Post-doctoral fellows or trainees ....O
    Full-time professional level research personnel...........................O

54. **In the past 12 months, did you receive research support from: (Mark all sources that apply)**
    Institutional or departmental funds ....O
    Federal agencies ....O
    State or local government agencies........O
    Private foundations ....O
    Private industry ....O
    Other ....O
    None..................................O

55. **During the past two years, have you served as a paid consultant to: (Mark all that apply)**
    Local business, government or schools .....O
    A national corporation..................O
    A non-profit foundation ....O
    Federal or foreign government ....O
    A research project ....O
    Other ....O
    No paid consulting.....................O

56. Are you a member of any of the following organisations? (Mark all that apply)

American Association of University
Professors............................○

American Federation of Teachers.......○

A National Education Association
affiliate...........................○

A local or state association or union of
college teachers.....................○

A state, county or city employees' association or other association not confined to
college teachers.....................○

An association limited to teachers at your
institution (other than the Academic
Senate)............................○

57. Do you feel that there are circumstances in which a strike would be a legitimate means of collective action:

a. for faculty members

Definitely yes.........................○
Probably yes..........................○
Probably not ....○
Definitely not ....○

b. for teaching assistants

Definitely yes.........................○
Probably yes ....○
Probably not ....○
Definitely not ....○

58. Please indicate your agreement or disagreement with each of the following statements.

1. Strongly agree
2. Agree with reservations
3. Disagree with reservations
①②③④ — 4. Strongly disagree

Where de facto segregation exists,
black people should be assured
control over their own schools ..①②③④
Racial integration of the public
elementary schools should be
achieved even if it requires
busing.......................①②③④
Meaningful social change cannot be
achieved through traditional
American politics.............①②③④
With a few exceptions, the Chicago
police acted reasonably in curbing
the demonstrations at the Democratic National Convention .....①②③④
Hippies represent an important
criticism of American culture ...①②③④
Marijuana should be legalized ...①②③④

58 Continued

Some form of Communist regime is
probably necessary for progress
in underdeveloped countries......①②③④
In the USA today there can be no
justification for using violence to
achieve political goals...........①②③④
The main cause of Negro riots in
the cities is white racism........①②③④

59. Which of these positions on Vietnam is closest to your own?

The U.S. should withdraw from Vietnam
immediately........................○
The U.S. should reduce its involvement,
and encourage the emergence of a coalition government in South Vietnam......○
The U.S. should try to reduce its involvement, while being sure to prevent a
Communist takeover in the South.......○
The U.S. should commit whatever forces
are necessary to defeat the Communists ○

60. How active were you in last year's political campaigns:

a. before the conventions?

Very active.........................○
Fairly active ....○
Not very active.....................○
Not active at all...................○

b. after the conventions?

Very active.........................○
Fairly active.......................○
Not very active.....................○
Not active at all...................○

61.

1. Left
2. Liberal
3. Middle-of-the-road
4. Moderately conservative
①②③④⑤ — 5. Strongly conservative

a. How would you characterize
yourself politically at the
present time?................①②③④⑤

b. What were your politics as a
college senior? ....①②③④⑤

c. What were your father's politics
while you were growing up?.....①②③④⑤

d. How would you describe the prevailing political sentiments of
undergraduates here?..........①②③④⑤

62. Whom would you have favored:
    a. At the Republican convention:
       Nixon.........O   Rockefeller......O

    b. At the Democratic convention:
       Humphrey......O   McCarthy........O

63. Whom did you vote for in November?
    Humphrey...O   Another candidate.....O
    Nixon......O   Did not vote.........O
    Wallace ....O   No answer ....O

64. Whom did you vote for in 1964?
    Johnson....O   Another candidate.....O
    Goldwater ..O   Did not vote.........O
                    No answer ....O

		Yes	No
65.	a. Are you a United States citizen?...O		O
	b. IF YES: Have you ever been a	Yes	No
	citizen of another country?........O		O

66. Have you ever been a member of a   Yes   No
    student political club or group?........O   O

67. Have you ever attended a junior or   Yes   No
    community college as a student? ......O   O

68. During your career as a graduate student:
    Were you ever a teaching assis-   Yes   No
    tant?..........................O   O
    Were you ever a research   Yes   No
    assistant?......................O   O
    Were you ever awarded a fellow-
    ship or scholarship worth $1,000   Yes   No
    per year or more?................O   O
    Was there a faculty member who acted
    as your "sponsor" when you were   Yes   No
    looking for your first job?.........O   O

69. Do you have a working association
    with any research institute or center   Yes   No
    within your institution?.............O   O

70. In your department, are decisions other
    than personnel matters normally made
    by the vote of the whole department,   Yes   No
    including junior members?...........O   O

71. a. Are you now chairman or head of   Yes   No
       your department?...............O   O
    b. IF NO: Have you ever been chair-
       man or head of a university or   Yes   No
       college department?............O   O

72. a. Do you hold a full-time adminis-
       trative position outside your own   Yes   No
       department?...................O   O
    b. IF NO: Do you hold a part-time
       administrative position outside   Yes   No
       your own department?...........O   O

73. a. Are you now negotiating for, or
       have you already found or ac-
       cepted, another position for   Yes   No
       the fall of 1969 ?...............O   O
    b. IF NO: Are you looking for   Yes   No
       another position?...............O   O
    c. IF NO: Would you seriously
       consider a reasonable offer of   Yes   No
       another position?...............O   O

74. Would you describe yourself as con-   Yes   No
    servative in your religious beliefs?....O   O

75. How would you rate each of the following?
    1. Excellent
    2. Good
    3. Fair
    ①②③④ — 4. Poor

    Your own salary ....①②③④
    Your own graduate education ......①②③④
    The academic reputation of your de-
    partment outside your institution ..①②③④
    At your institution--
    The intellectual environment ......①②③④
    Faculty salary levels.............①②③④
    Teaching load ....①②③④
    Ratio of teaching faculty to students①②③④
    The administration...............①②③④
    The effectiveness of your campus
    senate or faculty council ....①②③④
    General research resources (e.g.,
    library, labs, computers, space,
    etc.) ....①②③④
    Availability of research funds from
    all sources.....................①②③④
    Cultural resources ....①②③④
    In your department--
    The intellectual environment ......①②③④
    Personal relations among faculty...①②③④
    Faculty/student relations ....①②③④

76. How often, on average, do you

    1. Once a week or more
    2. Two or three times a month
    3. About once a month
    4. A few times a year
    ①②③④⑤ — 5. Once a year or less
    See undergraduates informally
    (for meals, parties, informal
    gatherings) ?..................①②③④⑤
    Spend 4 hours uninterruptedly on
    professional reading, writing or
    research?.....................①②③④⑤
    Attend:
    1. A religious service ....①②③④⑤
    2. A concert ....①②③④⑤
    3. An "art" film ....①②③④⑤
    4. A play ....①②③④⑤
    5. An art exhibition ....①②③④⑤
    6. An athletic event...........①②③④⑤

77. Do you consider yourself
    - Deeply religious .... ○
    - Moderately religious .... ○
    - Largely indifferent to religion .... ○
    - Basically opposed to religion .... ○

78. a. In what religion were you raised?
    - Protestant....... ○   Other............. ○
    - Catholic .... ○   None .... ○
    - Jewish.......... ○   No answer ...... ○

    b. What is your present religion?
    - Protestant....... ○   Other............. ○
    - Catholic .... ○   None .... ○
    - Jewish.......... ○   No answer .... ○

79. What is the highest level of formal education reached by your spouse? Your father? Your mother? (Mark one in each column)

    Spouse / Father / Mother

    - No spouse........................ ○
    - 8th grade or less .... ○○○
    - Some high school.................. ○○○
    - Completed high school............. ○○○
    - Some college .... ○○○
    - Graduated from college............. ○○○
    - Attended graduate or professional school .... ○○○
    - Attained advanced degree .... ○○○

80. What is (was) your father's principal occupation? (Mark one)
    - College or university teaching, research or administration .... ○
    - Elementary or secondary school teaching or administration .... ○
    - Other professional...................... ○
    - Managerial, administrative, semiprofessional .... ○
    - Owner, large business .... ○
    - Owner, small business .... ○
    - Other white collar: clerical, retail sales... ○
    - Skilled wage worker .... ○
    - Semi- and unskilled wage worker, farm laborer............................... ○
    - Armed forces .... ○
    - Farm owner or manager................. ○

81. What is your basic institutional salary, before tax and deductions, for the current academic year?
    - Below $7,000..... ○ $17,000-$19,999.. ○
    - $7,000-$9,999.... ○ $20,000-$24,999.. ○
    - $10,000-$11,999... ○ $25,000-$29,999.. ○
    - $12,000-$13,999... ○ $30,000 and over . ○
    - $14,000-$16,999... ○

82. Is this based on
    - 9/10 months....... ○   11/12 months ...... ○

83. In recent years, roughly how much have you earned over and above your basic salary? (Please estimate as a percentage of your basic salary.)
    - 0%..... ○   Under 10%. ○   30%-39% ..... ○
    -                10%-19% .. ○   40%-49% ..... ○
    -                20%-29% .. ○   50% and over . ○

84. What are the two largest sources of your supplementary earnings? (Mark one in each column)

	Largest	Second Largest
Summer teaching	○	○
Teaching elsewhere (extension, etc.) other than summer teaching	○	○
Consulting	○	○
Private practice	○	○
Royalties (from publications, patents)	○	○
Fees for speeches and lectures	○	○
Research salaries and payments	○	○
Other	○	○
None	○	○

85. What is your marital status?
    - Married (once only)..................... ○
    - Married (remarried) .... ○
    - Separated .... ○
    - Single (never married) .... ○
    - Single (divorced)...................... ○
    - Single (widowed)...................... ○

86. How many dependent children do you have?
    - None .... ○   Two .... ○
    - One .... ○   Three or more ..... ○

87. What is your date of birth?
    - 1903 or before ..... ○   1924-1928 .... ○
    - 1904-1908......... ○   1929-1933 .... ○
    - 1909-1913......... ○   1934-1938 .... ○
    - 1914-1918......... ○   1939-1943 .... ○
    - 1919-1923......... ○   1944 or later ...... ○

88. Your sex: Male .... ○   Female ...... ○

89. Your race:
    - White/Caucasian....................... ○
    - Black/Negro/Afro-American .... ○
    - Oriental .... ○
    - Other............................... ○

If you have comments on any of the issues covered in this questionnaire please send them under separate cover to:

Survey of Higher Education
The Carnegie Commission on Higher Education
National Computer Systems Processing Center
1015 South Sixth Street
Minneapolis, Minnesota 55415

THANK YOU FOR YOUR COOPERATION

Appendix B: The 1972 Faculty Study Questionnaire

August-September Telephone Survey "Wave"

1. Do you plan to vote in this November's Presidential Election?

    1. Yes

    2. No

    3. Uncertain

    0. Not answered

2. [IF YES, ASK:] For whom do you plan to vote?

    1. Nixon

    2. McGovern

    3. Other

    4. Undecided

    5. Not applicable

    0. Not answered

3. [IF UNDECIDED, ASK:] Which candidate are you leaning toward at this time?

    1. Nixon

    2. McGovern

    3. Other

    4. Completely undecided

    5. Not applicable

    0. Not answered

4. [IF NO, ASK:] Is your reason for nonvoting ineligibility, lack of interest, or dissatisfaction with the candidates entered in the race?

    1. Not eligible

    2. Not interested

    3. Dissatisfied

    4. Not applicable

    0. Not answered

5. Thinking back prior to the Democratic National Convention, who was your first choice for the Democratic Presidential nominee this year?

    1. McGovern

    2. Humphrey

3. Kennedy

4. Jackson

5. Muskie

6. Wallace

7. Lindsay

8. Chisholm

9. Mills

10. Yorty

11. Hartke

12. Other

13. No first choice; not interested; etc.

0. Not answered

6. For whom did you vote in the 1968 Presidential Election?

1. Humphrey

2. Nixon

3. Wallace

4. Another candidate

5. Did not vote

0. Not answered

7. [ASK OF 1968–1972 SWITCHERS ONLY]

Could you tell me the main reason you plan to vote _____ [REP/DEM] in 1972 whereas you voted _____ [DEM/REP] four years ago?

_____

_____

8. In politics today do you think of yourself as a Democrat, a Republican, as a member of some other political party, or as an independent?

1. Democrat

2. Republican

3. Another party

[IF ANOTHER PARTY, ASK:] Which party is that?

4. Independent

0. Not answered

Now, I would like to turn to other matters of national politics.

9. Which of these positions on Vietnam is closer to your own: That the United States should unilaterally withdraw from Vietnam at once; or that the United States should continue with the present "Vietnamization" program?

   1. Withdrawal
   2. Vietnamization
   3. Some other program distinctly different
   4. Uncertain
   0. Not answered

10. How would you characterize yourself politically at the present time: As left or radical, as liberal, as middle-of-the-road, as moderately conservative or as strongly conservative?

    1. Left or radical
    2. Liberal
    3. Middle-of-the-road
    4. Moderately conservative
    5. Strongly conservative
    6. None of these
    0. Not answered

The next questions concern campus politics.

11. What has been your general position on the emergence of radical student activism in recent years, approval or disapproval?

    1. Strongly approve
    2. Approve with reservations
    3. Approve, no indication whether 1 or 2
    4. Uncertain; conflicting assessments
    5. Disapprove, no indication whether 6 or 7
    6. Disapprove with reservations

7. Strongly disapprove

0. Not answered

12. Do you agree or disagree that groups which are underrepresented on the faculty—such as blacks, Chicanos and women—should be assigned a large share of future faculty vacancies until they are proportionately represented?

    1. Strongly agree
    2. Agree with reservations
    3. Agree, no indication whether 1 or 2
    4. Uncertain; conflicting assessments
    5. Disagree, no indication whether 6 or 7
    6. Disagree with reservations
    7. Strongly disagree
    0. Not answered

13. Do you agree or disagree that the recent growth of unionization of college and university faculty is beneficial and should be extended.

    1. Strongly agree
    2. Agree with reservations
    3. Agree, no indication whether 1 or 2
    4. Uncertain; conflicting assessments
    5. Disagree, no indication whether 6 or 7
    6. Disagree with reservations
    7. Strongly disagree
    0. Not answered

14. Do you agree or disagree that it is desirable for college and university faculty to put themselves on record by vote on major political controversies?

    1. Strongly agree
    2. Agree with reservations
    3. Agree, no indication whether 1 or 2
    4. Uncertain; conflicting assessments
    5. Disagree, no indication whether 6 or 7
    6. Disagree with reservations
    7. Strongly disagree

0. Not answered

Finally, I have a few questions on your academic career and interests.

15. How would you describe your principal area of specialization within
    _____? [RESPONDENT'S FIELD]

    _____
    _____

16. What is your present rank?

    1. Instructor
    2. Assistant Professor
    3. Associate Professor
    4. Professor
    5. Lecturer
    6. Other
    0. Not answered

17. Do your interests lie primarily in teaching or in research?

    1. In research
    2. In teaching
    3. In both, but leaning toward research
    4. In both, but leaning toward teaching
    0. Not answered

18. Approximately how many of your professional writings have been
    published or accepted for publication in the last two years?

    1. None
    2. 1-2
    3. 3-4
    4. 5-10
    5. More than 10
    0. Not answered

19. In the past 12 months, did you receive research support from any agency of
    the federal government?

    1. Yes

2. No

0. Not answered

20. In the past 12 months, did you receive research support from any other agency or foundation?

1. Yes

2. No

0. Not answered

21. What is your date of birth?

1. 1903 or before

2. 1904–1908

3. 1909–1913

4. 1914–1918

5. 1919–1923

6. 1924–1928

7. 1929–1933

8. 1934–1938

9. 1939–1943

10. 1944 or later

0. Not answered

22. Lastly, in what religion were you raised?

1. Protestant

2. Catholic

3. Jewish

4. Other

5. None

0. Not answered

23. [Sex of Respondent:]

1. Male

2. Female

November–December Mailed Questionnaire "Wave"

1. Did you vote in the Presidential election November 7?

    1. Yes

    2. No

2. [IF YES:] For whom did you vote?

    1. McGovern

    2. Nixon

    3. Other

        [Please Specify] _____

3. [IF YES:] In assessing your vote, what consideration(s) do you find of paramount importance? What, more than anything else, led you to make the choice you did?

    _____
    _____
    _____
    _____

4. [IF NO:] What were your reasons for not voting?

    _____
    _____
    _____

5. How would you guess faculty in your department voted:

    1. Heavily for McGovern

    2. A modest majority for McGovern

    3. A modest majority for Nixon

    4. Heavily for Nixon

6. In the Congressional election in your district, which Party's candidate did you vote for?

    1. Republican

    2. Democratic

    3. Other

        [Please Specify] _____

4. Did not vote

Turning now to several other questions of national and campus politics:

At the height of your concern, how deeply did (do) you feel about each of the following issues?

[Please locate your position on the seven point scale]

7. American involvement in Vietnam

						Largely
Very deeply						*uncon-*
concerned						*cerned*
1	2	3	4	5	6	7

8. Busing of children to achieve greater racial balance in public schools

						Largely
Very deeply						*uncon-*
concerned						*cerned*
1	2	3	4	5	6	7

9. Campus protests and demonstrations

						Largely
Very deeply						*uncon-*
concerned						*cerned*
1	2	3	4	5	6	7

10. How would you evaluate the effects of the wave of campus political activism of the late 1960s on higher education?

_____
_____
_____
_____

11. What would you describe as the most pressing problem confronting American colleges and universities today?

_____
_____
_____
_____

Finally, a few questions on professional and personal orientations:

12. In most academic fields, scholars vary between a more "rigorous," "hard," or scientific approach on the one hand, and a more "qualitative," "soft," or humanistic approach on the other. Where would you locate your approach on this "hard-soft" continuum?

"Hard," "rigorous," or scientific					"Soft," "qualitative," or humanistic	
1	2	3	4	5	6	7

13. In many disciplines, faculty differ as to whether their work is primarily in the area of *theory,* or involves a largely *substantive* or *experimental* approach. Is your work:

    1. Largely theoretical

    2. Largely substantive or experimental

    3. The distinction is not applicable to my discipline

14. Comparing yourself with other academic men of your age and qualifications, how successful do you consider yourself in your career?

    1. Very successful

    2. Fairly successful

    3. Fairly unsuccessful

    4. Very unsuccessful

Appendix C: Background and Attitudinal Characteristics of Faculty by Selected Disciplines

	Age		
	Over 50	*35–49*	*Under 35*
Anthropology	20	51	30
Economics	20	42	38
Political science	16	38	46
Psychology	18	46	36
Clinical	8	53	39
Experimental	11	38	50
Social	11	43	47
Sociology	25	41	34
Law	22	39	40
English	25	37	38
History	24	42	34
Philosophy	23	37	40
Fine arts	24	43	33
Education	31	49	20
Mathematics	18	35	48
Chemistry	20	38	42
Physics	15	49	36
Bacteriology	25	45	30
Biochemistry	23	46	32
Botany and zoology	25	50	25
Physiology	22	52	26
Medicine	23	59	18
Civil engineering	23	48	29
Electrical engineering	14	46	40
Mechanical engineering	24	43	34
Business	22	47	32
Agriculture	26	48	27
ALL FIELDS	24	44	33

Percentage who are women	Percentage having college-educated fathers
15	61
4	45
11	40
18	37
20	45
6	37
11	38
16	28
3	48
30	43
11	44
13	43
24	41
27	33
12	39
11	36
3	41
25	46
6	41
10	39
17	40
6	59
—	44
0.3	44
0.5	41
16	32
0.2	22
19	39

	Religion raised				
	Protestant	*Catholic*	*Jewish*	*Other*	*None*
Anthropology	68	8	14	1	10
Economics	60	16	18	2	5
Political science	70	11	11	4	4
Psychology	58	18	17	3	4
Clinical	41	9	45	3	2
Experimental	54	17	14	5	10
Social	64	10	17	—	9
Sociology	53	23	12	6	6
Law	51	18	24	4	3
English	67	18	9	3	4
History	64	22	8	2	3
Philosophy	48	38	7	1	6
Fine arts	72	15	7	3	3
Education	71	17	6	4	2
Mathematics	66	18	8	4	4
Chemistry	68	18	6	5	3
Physics	60	13	13	6	8
Bacteriology	63	14	15	6	3
Biochemistry	58	11	21	4	8
Botany and zoology	76	13	3	5	3
Physiology	65	16	12	3	3
Medicine	59	14	21	2	3
Civil engineering	64	18	4	9	4
Electrical engineering	52	20	15	5	8
Mechanical engineering	70	15	7	6	3
Business	67	19	9	4	0.9
Agriculture	87	9	0.3	2	1
ALL FIELDS	66	18	9	4	3

	Frequency of attending a religious service				
Weekly	2–3 times a month	Once a month	Few times a year	Once a year or less	
8	6	8	15	63	
23	13	6	17	42	
22	7	6	17	47	
20	8	5	16	52	
7	4	6	25	58	
10	7	2	13	68	
18	4	—	8	70	
32	14	5	13	36	
21	13	5	14	47	
30	9	5	16	41	
33	11	3	10	43	
45	7	3	9	36	
37	11	6	15	32	
43	15	6	14	22	
39	9	6	12	34	
34	14	6	15	31	
29	12	7	10	42	
28	13	6	8	45	
31	10	8	14	37	
26	7	6	25	38	
32	13	4	13	38	
22	11	8	23	37	
41	17	8	15	19	
31	11	11	13	34	
37	15	9	16	23	
38	15	9	16	24	
51	15	8	13	12	
36	12	7	14	32	

	Frequency of attending a concert			
	2–3 times a month or more	Once a month	Few times a year	Once a year or less
Anthropology	4	21	47	28
Economics	5	20	51	24
Political science	9	23	46	22
Psychology	8	20	49	23
Clinical	6	26	48	20
Experimental	11	16	42	31
Social	10	11	40	39
Sociology	7	25	42	26
Law	9	26	40	25
English	13	22	50	15
History	13	24	46	18
Philosophy	14	22	47	17
Fine arts	39	22	31	8
Education	9	24	47	21
Mathematics	9	16	47	28
Chemistry	8	22	47	23
Physics	9	25	41	24
Bacteriology	10	25	43	21
Biochemistry	8	26	48	18
Botany and zoology	9	15	50	26
Physiology	12	20	46	22
Medicine	11	22	47	21
Civil engineering	4	11	46	40
Electrical engineering	6	17	50	28
Mechanical engineering	7	12	51	31
Business	4	14	49	33
Agriculture	1	16	51	32
ALL FIELDS	12	21	46	22

Frequency of attending an athletic event			
2–3 times a month or more	*Once a month*	*Few times a year*	*Once a year or less*
6	11	37	47
12	17	39	32
14	18	34	35
12	17	31	41
15	12	31	42
8	16	34	43
11	7	30	52
4	19	33	44
17	18	34	32
7	11	32	51
14	14	31	41
15	9	34	42
10	12	32	46
19	19	36	26
21	16	29	34
12	21	35	32
5	19	32	44
13	16	27	44
13	14	33	40
10	12	35	43
23	10	30	38
12	18	41	29
20	17	38	25
13	18	30	38
19	21	38	22
22	19	39	20
23	28	38	11
17	16	33	34

	Hours spent per week in class			
	4 or less	5–8	9–12	13 or more
Anthropology	31	43	20	7
Economics	24	34	33	10
Political science	17	34	38	11
Psychology	29	33	26	13
Clinical	36	36	26	2
Experimental	27	41	23	9
Social	34	30	31	6
Sociology	22	28	37	13
Law	28	57	13	3
English	9	21	54	16
History	11	29	41	19
Philosophy	11	25	49	15
Fine arts	7	19	25	49
Education	31	27	28	14
Mathematics	16	28	34	22
Chemistry	23	23	23	32
Physics	35	27	18	20
Bacteriology	41	20	18	22
Biochemistry	55	19	16	10
Botany and zoology	20	28	27	26
Physiology	35	19	20	27
Medicine	59	21	10	10
Civil engineering	18	41	25	16
Electrical engineering	26	32	19	23
Mechanical engineering	18	27	26	29
Business	14	25	30	31
Agriculture	41	19	13	28
ALL FIELDS	22	25	29	24

Percentage primarily committed to research (versus teaching)	Percentage receiving research grants (last 12 months)
60	65
34	49
27	37
38	67
31	56
64	76
52	64
34	42
20	35
12	17
24	32
26	21
18	33
12	46
23	27
33	57
47	60
55	73
70	85
36	78
44	66
38	72
28	61
36	55
27	51
11	21
40	60
24	58

	Percentage receiving federal research grants (last 12 months)
Anthropology	33
Economics	23
Political science	11
Psychology	36
Clinical	22
Experimental	46
Social	34
Sociology	18
Law	7
English	2
History	4
Philosophy	3
Fine arts	7
Education	24
Mathematics	19
Chemistry	31
Physics	46
Bacteriology	51
Biochemistry	71
Botany and zoology	41
Physiology	41
Medicine	54
Civil engineering	39
Electrical engineering	38
Mechanical engineering	25
Business	4
Agriculture	38
ALL FIELDS	29

Percentage serving as paid consultants (last 2 years)	Percentage consulting for federal government (last 2 years)
49	17
49	19
35	12
56	17
78	20
40	13
46	23
47	10
49	16
17	2
19	3
17	2
35	3
60	11
23	5
28	7
37	12
23	8
36	17
33	8
26	13
56	28
70	18
52	11
61	10
50	8
39	6
37	8

	Number of books published/edited			
	None	*1–2*	*3–4*	*5 or more*
Anthropology	41	30	16	13
Economics	51	27	10	13
Political science	54	28	10	7
Psychology	67	23	6	4
Clinical	66	29	3	2
Experimental	72	20	4	5
Social	59	23	11	7
Sociology	56	28	7	9
Law	58	27	11	4
English	68	22	5	5
History	62	24	8	6
Philosophy	64	27	5	4
Fine arts	77	15	4	4
Education	58	28	8	6
Mathematics	79	15	3	3
Chemistry	77	18	3	2
Physics	79	15	5	2
Bacteriology	69	24	4	3
Biochemistry	69	23	7	2
Botany and zoology	68	28	3	1
Physiology	68	25	4	3
Medicine	64	25	7	5
Civil engineering	74	20	4	2
Electrical engineering	67	26	7	0.4
Mechanical engineering	70	24	5	1
Business	68	21	5	6
Agriculture	69	22	5	4
ALL FIELDS	69	22	6	4

Number of publications (last two years)				Percentage strongly satisfied with career choice
None	*1–2*	*3–4*	*5 or more*	
15	27	31	28	70
39	33	20	8	58
51	29	13	7	49
39	28	18	15	58
41	28	21	10	64
17	30	23	30	63
30	23	30	18	58
45	28	15	13	67
41	32	16	10	46
61	24	9	7	61
55	30	10	6	66
59	24	9	8	58
67	21	7	6	51
52	28	12	8	56
64	20	10	7	56
46	20	14	19	60
36	25	22	17	59
28	24	22	26	54
17	26	25	32	59
29	30	24	18	57
29	34	18	19	53
17	25	24	34	45
38	34	16	12	44
40	32	16	11	37
48	29	13	10	46
67	19	8	6	55
36	22	20	22	41
53	24	12	11	54

	Percentage who believe the administration of their department is autocratic
Anthropology	29
Economics	25
Political science	24
Psychology	30
Clinical	40
Experimental	26
Social	32
Sociology	27
Law	23
English	37
History	26
Philosophy	15
Fine arts	31
Education	29
Mathematics	29
Chemistry	29
Physics	28
Bacteriology	38
Biochemistry	43
Botany and zoology	25
Physiology	35
Medicine	50
Civil engineering	35
Electrical engineering	41
Mechanical engineering	38
Business	26
Agriculture	31
ALL FIELDS	30

Percentage considering themselves intellectuals	Agree, most colleges reward conformity, crush student creativity
83	60
83	56
86	59
76	62
80	70
82	45
72	64
81	66
82	48
78	57
86	56
88	55
63	61
68	59
67	48
75	46
82	47
80	46
72	45
77	49
77	51
74	43
56	35
64	51
59	44
55	46
54	37
70	52

	Disagree, most undergrads are basically satisfied with education they are getting
Anthropology	34
Economics	32
Political science	40
Psychology	37
Clinical	46
Experimental	34
Social	52
Sociology	37
Law	33
English	33
History	30
Philosophy	41
Fine arts	29
Education	36
Mathematics	27
Chemistry	22
Physics	27
Bacteriology	30
Biochemistry	32
Botany and zoology	26
Physiology	27
Medicine	22
Civil engineering	13
Electrical engineering	21
Mechanical engineering	14
Business	18
Agriculture	12
ALL FIELDS	27

Agree, undergrad education be improved if less specialized training	Agree, undergrad education be improved if grades abolished
79	40
69	29
82	34
63	42
72	56
56	31
77	45
76	43
67	29
81	38
77	32
83	41
61	43
57	50
49	26
43	17
45	20
54	34
45	19
63	16
45	24
54	25
29	15
32	19
30	11
35	28
28	22
57	33

	Agree, undergrad curriculum has suffered from specialization of faculty members
Anthropology	55
Economics	55
Political science	61
Psychology	51
Clinical	58
Experimental	43
Social	69
Sociology	53
Law	47
English	58
History	55
Philosophy	65
Fine arts	44
Education	56
Mathematics	50
Chemistry	49
Physics	44
Bacteriology	59
Biochemistry	46
Botany and zoology	54
Physiology	55
Medicine	56
Civil engineering	41
Electrical engineering	47
Mechanical engineering	46
Business	44
Agriculture	50
ALL FIELDS	51

Agree, field is too research oriented	*Agree, highest paid professors get there by being "operators" rather than by scholarly, scientific contributions*
20	52
33	39
44	50
24	43
25	41
11	48
17	60
31	48
14	37
43	44
37	47
29	46
17	50
15	50
44	41
37	51
29	46
16	50
15	55
21	56
26	50
17	50
18	49
30	50
17	58
12	47
18	48
25	48

	Agree, research grants corrupting to institutions and men that get them
Anthropology	43
Economics	36
Political science	45
Psychology	36
Clinical	36
Experimental	28
Social	45
Sociology	43
Law	35
English	48
History	46
Philosophy	54
Fine arts	37
Education	34
Mathematics	36
Chemistry	37
Physics	30
Bacteriology	29
Biochemistry	28
Botany and zoology	37
Physiology	29
Medicine	32
Civil engineering	36
Electrical engineering	46
Mechanical engineering	37
Business	33
Agriculture	33
ALL FIELDS	37

Disagree, weapons research is legitimate activity on college campuses	Agree, undergrads should play formal role in faculty appointments and promotions
76	31
56	28
66	32
67	35
72	47
60	30
81	38
63	36
54	25
72	27
66	28
70	41
66	20
55	27
59	20
61	17
64	20
66	16
62	14
52	21
51	20
43	17
36	7
56	16
40	8
39	15
35	9
57	21

	Agree, undergrads should play formal role in deciding provision and content of courses
Anthropology	60
Economics	54
Political science	53
Psychology	64
Clinical	71
Experimental	61
Social	77
Sociology	62
Law	50
English	56
History	52
Philosophy	58
Fine arts	47
Education	60
Mathematics	45
Chemistry	43
Physics	51
Bacteriology	49
Biochemistry	55
Botany and zoology	43
Physiology	52
Medicine	55
Civil engineering	32
Electrical engineering	39
Mechanical engineering	26
Business	40
Agriculture	43
ALL FIELDS	49

Agree, relax normal academic requirements in appointing minorities to faculty	*Agree, admit more minority students even if relaxing normal academic standards required*
32	58
28	51
46	61
31	50
39	56
21	45
53	71
38	63
27	58
27	49
28	45
34	55
22	39
28	48
19	38
11	30
19	46
19	41
19	43
13	34
15	40
24	35
14	24
17	32
9	23
14	28
8	25
21	39

	Agree, most American colleges and universities are racist, whether they mean to be or not
Anthropology	54
Economics	42
Political science	44
Psychology	49
Clinical	57
Experimental	42
Social	70
Sociology	57
Law	31
English	45
History	48
Philosophy	49
Fine arts	43
Education	40
Mathematics	38
Chemistry	27
Physics	29
Bacteriology	41
Biochemistry	34
Botany and zoology	29
Physiology	37
Medicine	37
Civil engineering	21
Electrical engineering	34
Mechanical engineering	26
Business	29
Agriculture	31
ALL FIELDS	38

Disagree, faculty collective bargaining has no place on a college campus	Approve the emergence of radical student activism
79	60
66	55
69	67
68	56
79	66
62	57
75	79
78	72
40	42
67	58
66	53
61	63
61	47
63	46
65	39
49	35
57	46
49	38
44	48
55	36
52	40
52	36
25	26
44	35
41	27
56	28
48	18
59	43

	Disagree, disruptive students on campus should be expelled
Anthropology	33
Economics	25
Political science	31
Psychology	33
Clinical	45
Experimental	34
Social	50
Sociology	44
Law	16
English	31
History	26
Philosophy	34
Fine arts	21
Education	25
Mathematics	19
Chemistry	12
Physics	20
Bacteriology	24
Biochemistry	16
Botany and zoology	13
Physiology	12
Medicine	12
Civil engineering	12
Electrical engineering	16
Mechanical engineering	14
Business	12
Agriculture	9
ALL FIELDS	20

Agree, marijuana should be legalized	*Disagree, use of violence to achieve political goals never justified in U.S.*
64	47
48	38
53	48
57	32
71	33
68	37
74	42
64	42
48	30
49	34
43	39
51	44
38	26
26	28
33	28
29	24
37	25
36	26
34	19
28	25
25	22
32	18
17	17
31	24
18	22
23	22
12	17
33	27

	1964 Presidential vote for Johnson	1968 Presidential vote for Humphrey
Anthropology	91	85
Economics	86	68
Political science	91	76
Psychology	87	76
Clinical	93	86
Experimental	89	77
Social	89	74
Sociology	90	74
Law	87	65
English	86	70
History	90	79
Philosophy	89	73
Fine arts	79	62
Education	83	60
Mathematics	74	55
Chemistry	73	52
Physics	88	71
Bacteriology	73	52
Biochemistry	88	61
Botany and zoology	75	52
Physiology	78	58
Medicine	74	54
Civil engineering	58	28
Electrical engineering	72	51
Mechanical engineering	52	33
Business	64	40
Agriculture	60	36
ALL FIELDS	78	58

SOURCE: 1969 Carnegie Commission Survey of Student and Faculty Opinion.

		Political self-characterization		
Left	Liberal	Middle-of-the-road	Moderately conservative	Strongly conservative
15	56	16	13	—
8	56	21	13	2
13	59	17	10	0.1
7	59	22	12	0.4
8	74	15	3	2
10	56	28	7	—
13	69	9	8	2
17	60	18	5	0.1
7	48	29	14	3
10	51	21	16	3
12	54	21	13	1
15	53	21	8	4
4	46	22	26	3
3	41	29	26	0.3
5	36	30	27	2
2	37	33	23	5
4	49	24	22	2
3	43	26	25	3
2	43	34	18	3
2	37	29	31	1
3	41	29	26	1
2	40	29	27	2
—	22	40	33	5
3	37	31	25	6
2	23	25	44	6
1	30	29	34	6
0.1	17	30	48	5
5	41	27	25	3

References

Aaron, Daniel: *Writers on the Left, Episodes in American Literary Communism,* Harcourt, Brace & World, New York, 1961.

". . . AAUP Loses Election," *Higher Education and National Affairs,* Apr. 7, 1972.

Adams, Charles Francis (ed.): *The Works of John Adams,* vol. VIII, Little, Brown and Company, Boston, 1853.

Ad Hoc Committee of Sociologists for Peace in Vietnam: "To the President of the United States, the Vice President and the Members of Congress . . . ," Nov. 1, 1967. (Pamphlet.)

"AFT Section 52 Suit to Uphold Merit Promotions," *University Guardian,* vol. 3, pp. 1, 8, March 1974.

"AFT-Senate Protests Block 'Floating Bottom,'" *University Guardian,* vol. 2, pp. 1, 4, January 1973.

Altbach, Philip: *Student Politics in America, A Historical Analysis,* McGraw-Hill Book Company, New York, 1974.

"The American Jew Today: Poll of Jewish Attitudes," *Newsweek,* vol. 77, pp. 46–48ff., Mar. 1, 1971.

American Sociological Association: "Constitutional Procedure," *American Sociologist,* vol. 2, p. 223, November 1967.

Anderson, Charles H.: "Kitch and the Academic," *Sociology and Social Research,* vol. 51, pp. 445–452, July 1967.

Aristotle: "The Rhetorica," in Richard McKeon (ed.), *The Basic Works of Aristotle,* Random House, Inc., New York, 1941.

Armor, David J., Joseph B. Giacquinta, R. Gordon McIntosh, and Diana E. H. Russell: "Professors' Attitudes Toward the Vietnam War," *Public Opinion Quarterly,* vol. 31, pp. 159–175, Summer 1967.

Aron, Raymond: *The Opium of the Intellectuals,* W. W. Norton & Company, Inc., New York, 1962.

Aubery, Pierre: *Milieux juifs de la France contemporaine,* Plon, Paris, 1962.

Avineri, Shlomo: "Feuer on Marx and the Intellectuals," *Survey*, no. 62, pp. 152–155, January 1967.

Barber, Bernard: "The Sociology of the Professions," in Kenneth S. Lynn (ed.), *The Professions in America*, Houghton Mifflin Company, Boston, 1965.

Bayer, Alan: *College and University Faculty: A Statistical Description*, American Council on Education, vol. 5, no. 5, Washington, 1971.

Bayer, Alan: *Teaching Faculty in Academe: 1972–73*, American Council on Education, vol. 8, no. 2, Washington, 1973.

Becker, Carl: *Progress and Power*, Stanford University Press, Stanford, Calif., 1936.

The Behavioral Sciences and the Federal Government, National Academy of Sciences, Washington, 1968.

The Behavioral and Social Sciences: Outlook and Needs, National Academy of Sciences, Washington, 1969.

Behrendt, R.: "Die öffentliche Meinung und das Generationsproblem," *Kölner Vierteljahrshefte für soziologie*, vol. 11, pp. 290–309, 1932.

Bell, Daniel: "The Background and Development of Marxian Socialism in the United States," in Donald D. Egbert and Stow Persons (eds.), *Socialism and American Life*, vol. I, Princeton University Press, Princeton, N.J., 1952.

Bell, Daniel: *The Coming of Post-Industrial Society*, Basic Books, Inc., Publishers, New York, 1973.

Bendix, Reinhard: "Sociology and the Distrust of Reason," *American Sociological Review*, vol. 35, pp. 831–843, October 1970.

Berger, Bennett M.: "How Long Is a Generation?" from his *Looking for America*, Prentice-Hall, Inc., Englewood Cliffs, N.J., 1971.

Berman, Ronald: *America in the Sixties: An Intellectual History*, The Free Press, New York, 1968.

Bettelheim, Bruno: "The Problem of Generations," in Erik Erikson (ed.), *Youth: Change and Challenge*, Basic Books, Inc., Publishers, New York, 1963.

Bidwell, Charles E.: "Faculty Responses to Student Activism: Some Preliminary Findings from a Survey of American Professors," mimeographed paper presented at the 7th World Congress of Sociology at Varna, Yugoslavia, in 1970.

Bloland, Harland G., and Sue M. Bloland: *American Learned Societies in Transition*, McGraw-Hill Book Company, New York, 1974.

Bloustein, Edward J.: "Unionization in Academe," *The New York Times*, Feb. 2, 1973.

Bohlke, Robert H.: "The Activity Value–Committed Sociologist: An Emerging Role," paper presented at the Annual Meeting of the Eastern Sociological Society, Boston, April 1968.

Bonham, George W.: "The New Class," *Change*, vol. 3, pp. 13–14, Winter 1971–1972.

Bourne, Randolph: *Youth and Life*, Houghton Mifflin Company, Boston, 1913.

Boyd, William: "Collective Bargaining in Academe: Causes and Consequences," *Liberal Education*, vol. 57, pp. 306–318, October 1971.

B. P.: "College Professors and the Public," *Atlantic Monthly*, vol. 89, pp. 282–288, February 1902.

Brooks, Van Wyck: "Harvard and American Life," *Living Age*, vol. 259, pp. 643–649, Dec. 12, 1908.

Broun, Heywood, and George Britt: *Christians Only*, Vanguard Press, Inc., New York, 1931.

Brown, Carol: "A History and Analysis of Radical Activism in Sociology, 1967–1969, with Special Reference to the Sociology Liberation Movement, the Black Caucus, the Executive Council, the War in Vietnam and a Few Other Things," *Sociological Inquiry*, vol. 40, pp. 27–33, Winter 1970.

Brzezinski, Zbigniew: *Between Two Ages: America's Role in the Technetronic Era*, The Viking Press, Inc., New York, 1970.

Buckley, William F.: *God and Man at Yale: The Superstitions of Academic Freedom*, Henry Regnery Company, Chicago, 1951.

Burns, James MacGregor: "Candidate on the Eve: Liberalism without Tears," *New Republic*, vol. 143, pp. 14–16, Oct. 31, 1960.

"Campus '65," *Newsweek*, vol. 65, pp. 43–48ff., Mar. 22, 1965.

Cantarow, Ellen, with help from Jim Goldberg, Louis Kampf, Kathryn Kremen, and the Radical Caucus: *The Great Training Robbery*, New University Conference, Chicago, n.d.

Cartter, Allan M.: "Faculty Needs and Resources in American Higher Education," *Annals of the American Academy of Political and Social Sciences*, vol. 404, pp. 71–87, November 1972.

Chomsky, Noam: *American Power and the New Mandarins*, Pantheon Books, Inc., New York, 1967.

Clark, Burton: "Faculty Authority," *AAUP Bulletin*, vol. 47, pp. 293–302, Winter 1961.

Clark, Peter B.: "The Opinion Machine: Intellectuals, The Mass Media and American Government," in Harry M. Clor (ed.), *The Mass Media and Modern Democracy*, Rand McNally & Company, Chicago, 1974.

Cohn, Werner: "The Politics of American Jews," in M. Sklare (ed.), *The Jews*, The Free Press, Glencoe, Ill., 1958.

Coleman, James S., et al.: *Equality of Educational Opportunity*, U.S. Government Printing Office, Washington, 1966.

Collective Bargaining in Postsecondary Educational Institutions, Education Commission of the States, no. 45, Denver, Colo., 1974.

"Consensus 2. The Platform of the MSU/Faculty Associates," *State News*, Michigan State University, East Lansing, Oct. 23, 1972.

Converse, Philip E.: "The Nature of Belief Systems in Mass Publics," in D. Apter (ed.), *Ideology and Discontent*, The Free Press, New York, 1964.

"Coping with Adversity: Report on the Economic Status of the Profession, 1971–72," *AAUP Bulletin*, vol. 58, pp. 182–186, Summer 1972.

"Cornell University Survey Conducted for Special Trustee Committee," Douglas Williams Associates, New York, 1969.

"Council Position on Collective Bargaining," *AAUP Bulletin*, vol. 57, pp. 511–512, Winter 1971.

Crittenden, John: "Aging and Party Affiliation," *Public Opinion Quarterly*, vol. 26, pp. 648–657, Winter 1962.

Diamond, Stanley: "A Revolutionary Discipline," *Current Anthropology*, vol. 5, pp. 432–437, December 1964.

"Document on Collective Negotiation," Academic Senate of California State University and Colleges, Oct. 12, 1972.

Drew, David E.: *A Profile of the Jewish Freshman*, American Council on Education, Washington, 1970.

Earnest, Ernest: *Academic Procession: An Informal History of the American College, 1636–1953*, The Bobbs-Merrill Company, Inc., Indianapolis, 1953.

The Editors of Fortune Magazine: "The Scientists," vol. 48, pp. 106–112, 166–176, October 1948.

Eisenstadt, S. N.: *From Generation to Generation*, The Free Press, Glencoe, Ill., 1956.

Eitzen, D. S., and G. M. Maranell: "The Political Party Affiliations of College Professors," *Social Forces*, vol. 47, pp. 145–153, December 1968.

"Election Analysis," *Action* (UCFT), vol. 6, pp. 1–2, February 1969.

Emmerson, Donald K.: "Conclusions," in Donald K. Emmerson (ed.), *Students and Politics in Developing Nations*, Frederick A. Praeger, Inc., New York, 1968.

Engels, Friedrich: *The German Revolutions*, The University of Chicago Press, Phoenix Edition, Chicago, 1967.

Ernst, Morris L., and David Loth: *Report on the American Communist*, Henry Holt and Company, Inc., New York, 1952.

Erskine, Hazel: "The Polls: Recent Opinion on Racial Problems," *Public Opinion Quarterly*, vol. 32, pp. 696–703, Winter 1968–1969.

Erskine, Hazel: "The Polls: Is War a Mistake?," *Public Opinion Quarterly*, vol. 34, pp. 134–150, Spring 1970.

Etzioni, Amitai (ed.): *The Semi-Professions and Their Organizations: Teachers, Nurses, Social Workers*, The Free Press, New York, 1969.

"Faculty Association and Union Face Run-off in SUNY Bargaining Election: AAUP Out," *The Chronicle of Higher Education*, vol. 5, p. 4, Jan. 11, 1971.

F. B.: "Students: Why We Care," *Clarion*, vol. 2, p. 3, Feb. 5, 1973.

Felix, David: *Protest: Sacco-Vanzetti and the Intellectuals*, Indiana University Press, Bloomington, 1965.

Feuer, Lewis: *The Conflict of Generations*, Basic Books, Inc., Publishers, New York, 1969a.

Feuer, Lewis: *Marx and the Intellectuals*, Anchor Books, Doubleday & Company, Inc., Garden City, N.Y., 1969b.

Field, John O., and Ronald E. Anderson: "Ideology in the Public's Conceptualization of the 1964 Election," *Public Opinion Quarterly*, vol. 33, pp. 380–398, Fall 1969.

Finkin, Matthew W.: "Collective Bargaining and University Government," *Wisconsin Law Review*, vol. 1971, no. 1, pp. 125–149, 1971.

Fox, Michael: "Wharton Taints Union Vote," *State News*, Michigan State University, East Lansing, Oct. 27, 1972.

Frankfurter, Felix: *Felix Frankfurter Reminisces*, ed. by Harlin B. Phillips, Reynal and Company, Inc., New York, 1960.

Freidel, Frank: "Dissent in the Spanish-American War and the Philippine Insurrection," in Samuel Eliot Morison et al., *Dissent in Three American Wars*, Harvard University Press, Cambridge, Mass., 1970.

Fuchs, L. H.: *The Political Behavior of American Jews*, The Free Press, Glencoe, Ill., 1956.

Fulbright, J. William: "The War and Its Effects—II," *Congressional Record*, vol. 113, p. S36182, Dec. 13, 1967.

Galbraith, John Kenneth: "An Adult's Guide to New York, Washington and Other Exotic Places," *New York*, vol. 4, p. 52, Nov. 15, 1971.

Gallup Opinion Index, Report no. 49, Gallup International, Inc., N.J., p. 26, July 1969.

Gallup Opinion Index, Report no. 58, Gallup International, Inc., N.J., p. 9, April 1970.

Gallup Opinion Index, Report no. 65, Gallup International, Inc., N.J., p. 17, November 1970.

The Gallup Poll: Public Opinion 1935–1971, vol. 3, Random House, Inc., New York, 1972.

"Gallup Poll Release," June 29, 1968. (Newspaper release.)

Geiger, Theodore: *Aufgaben und Stellung der Intelligenz in der Gesellschaft,* Ferdinand Enke Verlag, Stuttgart, 1949.

"Gilbert Youth Survey Release," August 1972. (Newspaper release.)

Glaser, Barney G.: *Organizational Scientists: Their Professional Careers,* The Bobbs-Merrill Company, Inc., Indianapolis, 1964.

Glazer, Nathan: "The Jewish Role in Student Activism," *Fortune,* vol. 79, pp. 112–113ff., January 1969.

Glazer, Nathan, and Daniel P. Moynihan: *Beyond the Melting Pot,* The M.I.T. Press, Cambridge, Mass., 1970.

Gouldner, Alvin W.: "Cosmopolitans and Locals—I," *Administrative Science Quarterly,* vol. 2, pp. 281–306, December 1957.

Gouldner, Alvin W.: "Cosmopolitans and Locals: Toward an Analysis of Latent Social Roles—II," *Administrative Science Quarterly,* vol. 2, pp. 444–480, March 1958.

Gouldner, Alvin W.: *The Coming Crisis of Western Sociology,* Basic Books, Inc., Publishers, New York, 1970.

Gouldner, Alvin W., and J. Timothy Sprehe: "Sociologists Look at Themselves," *Trans-action,* vol. 2, pp. 42–44, May–June 1965.

Grayson, Gerald, "Review: Ladd and Lipset," *Clarion,* vol. 3, p. 3, Dec. 12, 1973.

Haak, Harold H.: *Collective Bargaining and Academic Governance: The Case of the California State Colleges,* San Diego State College Public Affairs Institute, April 1968.

Haehn, James O.: *A Survey of Faculty and Administrator Attitudes on Collective Bargaining,* A Report to the Academic Senate, California State Colleges, May 1970.

Haehn, James O.: "Faculty Organizations," in Donald R. Gerth and James O. Haehn (eds.), *An Invisible Giant: The California State Colleges,* Jossey-Bass Inc., Publishers, San Francisco, 1971.

Halberstam, Michael J.: "The Undergraduate," *Harvard Alumni Bulletin,* vol. 55, p. 623, May 9, 1953.

Halsey, A. H., and Martin Trow: *The British Academics,* Harvard University Press, Cambridge, Mass., 1971.

Harris, Louis: *The Harris Survey,* Chicago Tribune–New York News Syndicate Incorporated, Nov. 27, 1972.

Harris, Seymour E.: *A Statistical Portrait of Higher Education,* McGraw-Hill Book Company, New York, 1972.

Harris Survey: "Report on Study of Culture Critics and Editors," released by United Church of Christ, Mar. 16, 1970.

The Harris Survey Yearbook, 1970, Louis Harris Associates, New York, 1971.

Heberle, Rudolf: *Social Movements,* Appleton-Century-Crofts, Inc., New York, 1951.

Hechinger, Fred M.: "Unions Due to Get Key at City U," *The New York Times,* Nov. 24, 1968.

Helson, Ravenna, and Richard Crutchfield: "Mathematicians: The Creative Researcher and the Average Ph.D.," *Journal of Consulting and Clinical Psychology,* vol. 34, pp. 250–257, April 1970.

Hepler, John C.: "Timetable for a Take-over," *Journal of Higher Education,* vol. 42, pp. 103–115, February 1971.

Hicks, Granville: *Where We Came Out,* The Viking Press, Inc., New York, 1954.

Himmelfarb, Milton: "The Jewish Vote (Again)," *Commentary,* vol. 55, pp. 81–85, June 1973.

Hodge, Robert W., Paul M. Siegel, and Peter M. Rossi: "Occupational Prestige in the United States," in Reinhard Bendix and Seymour Martin Lipset (eds.), *Class, Status and Power,* The Free Press, New York, 1966.

Hofstadter, Richard: *Anti-intellectualism in American Life,* Alfred A. Knopf, Inc., New York, 1963.

Hofstadter, Richard: "Discussion," in A. Alvarez (ed.), *Under Pressure,* Penguin Books, Inc., Baltimore, 1965.

Hook, Sidney: "Nixon Is the Lesser Evil—'An Open Letter to George McGovern,'" *New America,* vol. 10, pp. 4–5, 7, Sept. 30, 1972.

Horowitz, Irving Louis (ed.): *The Use and Abuse of Social Science,* Transaction Books, E.P. Dutton & Co., Inc., New Brunswick, N.J., 1971.

Howard, Daniel F.: "Delegate Assembly Meets, Explores Possible Role as Faculty Senate," *Rutgers AAUP Newsletter,* vol. 4, March 1973.

Howard, Lawrence C.: "The Academic and the Ballot," *School and Society,* vol. 86, pp. 415–419, Nov. 22, 1958.

Howe, Irving, and Lewis Coser: "The Intellectuals Turn Left," in their *The American Communist Party: A Critical History, 1919-1957,* Beacon Press, Boston, 1957.

Hughes, Everett C.: "Professions," in Kenneth S. Lynn (ed.), *The Professions in America,* Houghton Mifflin Company, Boston, 1965.

Irving, Carl: "California Professors Turn to Unions," *San Francisco Examiner,* Dec. 26, 1971.

Jencks, Christopher, and David Riesman: *The Academic Revolution,* Anchor Books, Doubleday & Company, Inc., Garden City, N.Y., 1968.

Joughlin, Louis (ed.): *Academic Freedom and Tenure: A Handbook of the American Association of University Professors,* University of Wisconsin Press, Madison, 1967.

Kadish, Sanford H.: "The Strike and the Professoriate," in Walter Metzger et al. (eds.), *Dimensions of Academic Freedom,* University of Illinois Press, Urbana, 1969.

Kadish, Sanford H.: "The Theory of the Profession and Its Predicament," *AAUP Bulletin,* vol. 58, pp. 120–125, Summer 1972.

Kadish, Sanford H., Robert Webb, and William Van Alstyne: "The Manifest Unwisdom of the AAUP as a Collective Bargaining Agency," *AAUP Bulletin,* vol. 58, pp. 57–61, Spring 1972.

Kaufman, Laura: "Labour Leads by 11 Percent on Campus," *The Times Higher Education Supplement,* no. 155, p. 1, Oct. 4, 1974.

Kerr, Clark: *The Uses of the University,* Torchbooks, Harper & Row, Publishers, Incorporated, New York, 1966.

"Kibbee to Recommend End to Tenure Quotas," *Clarion,* vol. 3, p. 1, Feb. 28, 1974.

Kiereck, Mary: "Two College Groups to Merge," *The Democrat and Chronicle,* Rochester, N.Y., Dec. 3, 1972.

Kiyosaki, Ralph H.: "Faculty Faces Locus of Tenure Menace," *CUPA Voice of the Faculty,* p. 1, September 1972.

Klotz, Neil: "Unions S.S.U. Is First," *Stockton Alumni Journal,* vol. 1, p. 5, Spring 1974.

Knowledge into Action: Increasing the Nation's Use of the Social Sciences, National Science Board—National Science Foundation, Washington, 1969.

Kornhauser, Arthur: "Attitudes of Economic Groups," *Public Opinion Quarterly,* vol. 2, pp. 260–268, April 1938.

Kraft, Joseph: "Washington Insight: Kennedy and the Intellectuals," *Harper's Magazine,* vol. 227, pp. 112–117, November 1963.

Kugler, Israel: *Higher Education and Professional Unionism,* American Federation of Teachers, Washington, n.d.

Kugler, Israel: "The Union Speaks for Itself," *Educational Record,* vol. 49, pp. 414–418, Fall 1968.

Kugler, Israel: "Unionism: A New Instrument for Faculty Governance," *ISR Journal,* vol. 1, p. 184, Summer 1969.

Kugler, Israel: "Collective Bargaining for the Faculty," *Liberal Education,* vol. 56, pp. 75–85, March 1970.

Kunen, James S.: "The Rebels of '70," *The New York Times Magazine,* vol. 123, pp. 22–23, 67–72, 78, Oct. 28, 1973.

Ladd, Everett C.: "Professors and Political Petitions," *Science*, vol. 163, pp. 1425–1430, Mar. 31, 1969.

Ladd, Everett C.: "American University Teachers and Opposition to the Vietnam War," *Minerva*, vol. 8, pp. 542–556, October 1970a.

Ladd, Everett C.: *American Political Parties: Social Change and Political Response*, W. W. Norton & Company, Inc., New York, 1970b.

Ladd, Everett C.: *Ideology in America: Change and Response in a City, a Suburb and a Small Town*, W. W. Norton & Company, Inc., New York, 1972.

Ladd, Everett C., and Seymour Martin Lipset: "The Politics of American Political Scientists," *PS*, vol. 4, pp. 135–144, Spring 1971a.

Ladd, Everett C., and Seymour Martin Lipset: "American Social Scientists and the Growth of Campus Political Activism in the 1960's," *Social Science Information*, vol. 10, pp. 105–120, April 1971b.

Ladd, Everett C., and Seymour Martin Lipset: "Politics of Academic Natural Scientists and Engineers," *Science*, vol. 176, pp. 1091–1100, June 9, 1972.

Ladd, Everett C., and Seymour Martin Lipset: *Academics, Politics and the 1972 Election*, American Enterprise Institute for Public Policy Research, Washington, 1973a.

Ladd, Everett C., and Seymour Martin Lipset: *Professors, Unions, and American Higher Education*, Carnegie Commission on Higher Education, Berkeley, Calif., 1973b.

Ladd, Everett C., and Seymour Martin Lipset: "Unionizing the Professoriate," *Change*, vol. 5, pp. 38–44, Summer 1973c.

Ladd, Everett C., and Seymour Martin Lipset: "Portrait of a Discipline: The American Political Science Community," Part I, *Teaching Political Science*, vol. 2, pp. 3–39, October 1974.

Ladd, Everett C., and Seymour Martin Lipset: "Portrait of a Discipline: The American Political Science Community," Part II, *Teaching Political Science*, vol. 2, pp. 123–144, January 1975.

Lappé, Marc: "Biological Warfare," in Martin Brown (ed.), *The Social Responsibility of the Scientist*, The Free Press, New York, 1971.

Lazarsfeld, Paul F., and Wagner Thielens, Jr.: *The Academic Mind*, The Free Press, Glencoe, Ill., 1958.

Lee, Eugene C., and Frank M. Bowen: *The Multicampus University*, McGraw-Hill Book Company, New York, 1971.

Le Francois, Richard H.: "Bargaining in Higher Education: A Maze of State Legislation," *NSP Forum*, vol. 4, November–December 1970.

Lenski, Gerhard: *The Religious Factor*, Anchor Books, Doubleday & Company, Inc., Garden City, N.Y., 1963.

Leuba, James H.: *The Belief in God and Immortality*, The Open Court Publishing Company, La Salle, Ill., 1921.

Leuba, James H.: "Religious Beliefs of American Scientists," *Harper's Magazine* vol. 169, pp. 291–300, August 1934.

Leuba, James H.: *The Reformation of the Churches*, Beacon Press, Boston, 1950.

Lichtman, Richard: "Ideological Functions of the University," *Upstart*, no. 1, pp. 27, 29–31, January 1971.

Liebman, Charles S.: "Toward a Theory of Jewish Liberalism," in Donald R. Cutler (ed.), *The Religious Situation: 1969*, Beacon Press, Boston, 1969.

Linton, Ralph: *The Study of Man*, D. Appleton-Century Company, Inc., New York, 1936.

Lipset, Seymour Martin: *Political Man: The Social Bases of Politics*, Anchor Books, Doubleday & Company, Inc., Garden City, N.Y., 1963.

Lipset, Seymour Martin: *The First New Nation: The United States in Historical and Comparative Perspective*, Anchor Books, Doubleday & Company, Inc., Garden City, N.Y., 1967a.

Lipset, Seymour Martin: "White Collar Workers and Professionals—Their Attitudes and Behavior Towards Unions," in William A. Faunce (ed.), *Readings in Industrial Sociology*, Appleton-Century-Crofts, Inc., New York, 1967b.

Lipset, Seymour Martin: *Revolution and Counterrevolution*, Anchor Books, Doubleday & Company, Inc., Garden City, N.Y., 1970a.

Lipset, Seymour Martin: "The Politics of Academia," in David C. Nichols (ed.), *Perspectives on Campus Tensions*, American Council on Education, Washington, 1970b.

Lipset, Seymour Martin: "Academia and Politics in America," in T. J. Nossiter et al. (eds.), *Imagination and Precision in the Social Sciences*, Faber and Faber, Ltd., London, 1972a.

Lipset, Seymour Martin: *Rebellion in the University*, Little, Brown and Company, Boston, 1972b.

Lipset, Seymour Martin: *Opportunity and Welfare in the First New Nation*, American Enterprise Institute for Public Policy Research, Washington, 1974.

Lipset, Seymour Martin: "Political Controversies at Harvard, 1636–1974," in Seymour Martin Lipset and David Riesman, *Education and Politics at Harvard*, McGraw-Hill Book Company, New York, 1975.

Lipset, Seymour Martin, and Philip Altbach: "Student Politics and Higher Education in the United States," in Seymour Martin Lipset (ed.), *Student Politics*, Basic Books, Inc., Publishers, New York, 1967.

Lipset, Seymour Martin, and Philip Altbach (eds.): *Students in Revolt*, Houghton Mifflin Company, Boston, 1969.

Lipset, Seymour Martin, and Richard B. Dobson: "The Intellectual as Critic and Rebel," *Daedalus*, vol. 101, pp. 137–198, Summer 1972.

Lipset, Seymour Martin, and Everett C. Ladd: "Politics and Polarities: And What Professors Think," *Psychology Today*, vol. 4, pp. 49–51ff., November 1970.

Lipset, Seymour Martin, and Everett C. Ladd: "Jewish Academics in the United States: Their Achievements, Culture and Politics," *American Jewish Year Book*, vol. 72, pp. 89–128, 1971*a*.

Lipset, Seymour Martin, and Everett C. Ladd: "The Divided Professoriate," *Change*, vol. 3, pp. 54–60, May–June 1971*b*.

Lipset, Seymour Martin, and Everett C. Ladd: "The Politics of American Sociologists," *American Journal of Sociology*, vol. 78, pp. 67–104, July 1972*a*. This article also appeared in *Varieties of Political Expression in Sociology*, University of Chicago Press, Chicago, 1972.

Lipset, Seymour Martin, and Everett C. Ladd: "The Political Future of Activist Generations," in Philip G. Altbach and Robert S. Laufer (eds.), *The New Pilgrims*, David McKay Company, Inc., New York, 1972*b*.

Lipset, Seymour Martin, and Everett C. Ladd: "The Myth of the Conservative Professor," *Sociology of Education*, vol. 47, pp. 203–213, Spring 1974.

Lipset, Seymour Martin, and Earl Raab: *The Politics of Unreason*, Harper and Row, Publishers, Inc., New York, 1970.

Lipset, Seymour Martin, and Martin Trow: "Reference Group Theory and Trade Union Wage Policy," in Mirra Komrarovsky (ed.), *Common Frontiers of the Social Sciences*, The Free Press, Glencoe, Ill., 1957.

A Loose Leaf History of the American Federation of Teachers, American Federation of Teachers, Washington, 1972.

Lubell, Samuel: "The People Speak," syndicated columns published in the spring of 1966.

Lyons, Eugene: *The Red Decade: The Stalinist Penetration of America*, The Bobbs-Merrill Company, Inc., Indianapolis, 1941.

Lyons, Gene M.: "The Social Science Study Groups," in Irving Louis Horowitz (ed.), *The Use and Abuse of Social Science*, Transaction Books, E.P. Dutton & Co., Inc., New Brunswick, N.J., 1971.

"Major Push for Public Employee Collective Bargaining Law in 1973," *University Guardian*, vol. 2, p. 3, October 1972.

Man, Henri de: *The Psychology of Socialism*, Henry Holt and Company, Inc., New York, 1927.

Mandel, Ernest: "The New Vanguard," in Tariq Ali (ed.), *The New Revolutionaries*, William Morrow & Company, Inc., New York, 1969.

Mannheim, Karl: *Ideology and Utopia,* Harcourt, Brace and Company, Inc., New York, 1936.

Mannheim, Karl: "The Sociological Problem of Generations," in his *Essays on the Sociology of Knowledge,* Oxford University Press, New York, 1952.

Marmion, Harry A.: "Faculty Organizations in Higher Education," in Stanley Elam and Michael H. Moscow (eds.), *Employment Relations in Higher Education,* Phi Delta Kappa, Bloomington, Ind., 1969.

Matza, David: "Subterranean Traditions of Youth," *Annals of the American Academy of Political and Social Sciences,* vol. 338, pp. 102–118, November 1961.

May, Henry: *The Discontent of the Intellectuals: A Problem of the Twenties,* Rand McNally & Company, Chicago, 1963.

McClintock, Charles G., Charles B. Spaulding, and Henry A. Turner: "Political Orientations of Academically Affiliated Psychologists," *American Psychologist,* vol. 20, pp. 211–221, March, 1965.

McConnell, T. R., and Kenneth P. Mortimer: *The Faculty in University Governance,* Center for Research and Development in Higher Education, University of California, Berkeley, 1971.

McCormick, Richard: "Rutgers," in David Riesman and Verne Stadtman (eds.), *Academic Transformation,* McGraw-Hill Book Company, New York, 1973.

McCracken, Paul W.: "The New Equality," *Michigan Business Review,* vol. 26, pp. 2–7, March 1974.

McDowell, Banks: "Should University Faculties Be Unionized?" *The Boston Globe,* June 18, 1972.

McHugh, William F.: "Collective Bargaining with Professionals in Higher Education: Problems in Unit Determinations," *Wisconsin Law Review,* vol. 1971, no. 1, pp. 55–90, 1971.

McHugh, William F.: "Faculty Unionism," in Bardwell C. Smith (ed.), *The Tenure Debate,* Jossey-Bass Inc., Publishers, San Francisco, 1973.

Meier, Richard L.: "The Origins of the Scientific Species," *Bulletin of the Atomic Scientists,* vol. 7, pp. 169–173, June 1951.

"Memorandum to the Faculty," *CUPA Voice of the Faculty,* pp. 1–2, Jan. 4, 1973.

Memorandum to New Jersey Board of Higher Education from the Council of New Jersey State College Locals MJSFT-AFT, Nov. 2, 1972.

Mentré, François: *Les Générations sociales,* Editions Bossard, Paris, 1920.

Merton, Robert K.: *Social Theory and Social Structure,* The Free Press, New York, 1968.

Merton, Robert K., and Alice Kitt: "Contributions to the Theory of Reference Group Behavior," in Robert Merton and Paul Lazarsfeld (eds.), *Continuities in Social Research,* The Free Press, Glencoe, Ill., 1950.

Metzger, Walter: *Academic Freedom in the Age of the University*, Columbia University Press, New York, 1961.

Metzger, Walter: "Origins of the Association," *AAUP Bulletin*, vol. 51, pp. 229 – 237, June 1965.

Meyers, Bert: "Is Research Counterrevolutionary?" *The Radical Teacher*, New University Conference, Chicago, pp. 10–11, n.d..

Milbraith, Lester: *Political Participation*, Rand McNally & Company, Chicago, 1965.

Minar, David: "Ideology and Political Behavior," *Midwest Journal of Political Science*, vol. 5, pp. 317–331, November 1961.

Moore, Barrington, Jr.: "Barrington Moore Asks for Student Restraint," *Harvard Crimson*, vol. 146, pp. 1, 4, Nov. 8, 1967.

Moore, William: "UC Faculty Organization Like a Union Is Proposed," *San Francisco Chronicle*, Mar. 21, 1972.

Moynihan, Daniel Patrick: *Maximum Feasible Misunderstanding*, The Free Press, New York, 1969.

Murphy, Gardner, and Rensis Likert: *Public Opinion and the Individual*, Harper & Brothers, New York, 1938.

Nagai, Michio: "The Development of Intellectuals in the Meiji and Taishō Periods," *Journal of Social and Political Ideas in Japan*, vol. 2, pp. 28–32, April 1964.

Namier, Lewis: *1848: The Revolution of the Intellectuals*, Anchor Books, Doubleday & Company, Inc., Garden City, N.Y., 1964.

"NEA Gives Top Priority to Higher Education Organizing," *NSP Forum*, vol. 6, p. 2, October–November 1972.

"NEA Supported Unit Wins Bargaining Vote at SUNY," *The Chronicle of Higher Education*, vol. 5, p. 4, Feb. 1, 1971.

The Necessity of Organization: American Federation of Teachers or Faculty Association, Berkeley Faculty Union, AFT Local 1474, 1972.

Netick, Allan: "The Student Grades the Prof," *The UPC Advocate*, vol. 3, pp. 7–11, April 1973.

Nettl, J. P.: "Ideas, Intellectuals, and Structures of Dissent," in Philip Rieff (ed.), *On Intellectuals*, Doubleday & Company, Inc., Garden City, N.Y., 1969.

Neumann, Sigmund: "The Conflict of Generations in Contemporary Europe," *Vital Speeches*, vol. 5, pp. 623–628, August 1939.

Neumann, Sigmund: *Permanent Revolution*, Harper & Brothers, New York, 1942.

"1968 Statement on Faculty Participation in Strikes," *AAUP Policy Documents and Reports*, American Association of University Professors, Washington, 1971.

Nisbet, Robert: *The Degradation of the Academic Dogma*, Basic Books, Inc., Publishers, New York, 1971.

Noll, C. Edward, and Peter H. Rossi: *General Social and Economic Attitudes of College and University Faculty Members*, National Opinion Research Center, University of Chicago, November 1966. (Private report.)

Nomad, Max: *Apostles of Revolution*, Collier Books, The Macmillan Company, New York, 1961.

Oberer, Walter E.: "Faculty Participation in Academic Decision Making: As to What Issue, by What Forms, Using What Means of Persuasion?" in Stanley Elam and Michael H. Moscow (eds.), *Employment Relations in Higher Education*, Phi Delta Kappa, Bloomington, Ind., 1969.

"On Faculty Unionism," *Measure*, no. 15, p. 2, November 1971.

"On Implementation of New Academic Salary Structure," testimony presented by United Professors of California before the Faculty and Staff Affairs Committee of the CSUC Trustees on December 8, 1972.

Oppenheimer, J. Robert: "Science and the Human Community," in Charles Frankel (ed.), *Issues in University Education*, Harper & Brothers, New York, 1959.

Ortega y Gasset, José: *Man and Crisis*, W. W. Norton & Company, Inc., New York, 1958.

Page, Charles A.: "Sociology as a Teaching Enterprise," in Robert K. Merton et al. (eds.), *Sociology Today*, Basic Books, Inc., Publishers, New York, 1959.

Parry, Albert: *The New Class Divided: Science and Technology versus Communism*, The Macmillan Company, New York, 1966.

Parsons, Talcott: *Sociological Theory and Modern Society*, The Free Press, New York, 1967.

Parsons, Talcott: "Professions," in David L. Sills (ed.), *International Encyclopedia of the Social Sciences*, vol. 12, The Macmillan Company, New York, 1968.

Perkin, H. J.: *Key Profession: The History of the Association of University Teachers*, Routledge and Kegan Paul, Ltd., London, 1969.

Peterson, Richard E.: *Goals for California Higher Education: A Survey of 116 College Communities*, The Joint Committee on the Master Plan for Higher Education, California Legislature, Sacramento, 1973.

Pitts, Jesse R.: "Strike at Oakland University," *Change*, vol. 4, pp. 16–19, February 1972.

Pool, Ithiel de Sola: "The Necessity for Social Scientists Doing Research for Government," in Irving Louis Horowitz (ed.), *The Rise and Fall of Project Camelot*, The M.I.T. Press, Cambridge, Mass., 1967.

"Preliminary Tabulations, CBS News Election Day Survey," CBS News, New York, 1972. (Mimeographed.)

"Proceedings of the Student Conference on the 1972 Master Plan," on file in the Planning Office of the State University of New York, 1972.

Rahv, Philip: "American Intellectuals in the Postwar Situation," reprinted in his *Literature and the Sixth Sense,* Houghton Mifflin Company, Boston, 1969.

Raskin, A. H.: "Unionism and the Content of Education: What Are the Bounds?" *The New York Times,* Jan. 8, 1973.

Reed, John: "The Harvard Renaissance," *The Harvard Progressive,* March 1939.

Reichley, A. James: "Our Critical Shortage of Leadership," *Fortune,* vol. 84, pp. 88–93ff., September 1971.

Reid, Whitelaw: "The Scholar in Politics," *Scribner's Monthly,* vol. 6, pp. 605–616, September 1873.

Reid, Whitelaw: *American and English Studies,* vol. 1, Charles Scribner's Sons, New York, 1913.

Repas, Robert: personal correspondence, 1973.

"Report on Possible Collective Action by the Faculty," submitted by a subcommittee on faculty organization to a meeting of the Berkeley Senate Representative Assembly, Mar. 20, 1972.

"Report of the Self-Survey Committee of the AAUP," *AAUP Bulletin,* vol. 51, pp. 99 – 209, May 1965.

Report of the Task Force on Higher Education, National Education Association, Washington, June 1968.

Reston, James: "Washington: On Kennedy's Discontented Intellectuals," *The New York Times,* Oct. 8, 1961.

"Results Mixed in Union Votes by Six Faculties," *The Chronicle of Higher Education,* vol. 7, p. 1, Oct. 30, 1972.

Richta, Radovan, et al.: *Civilization at the Crossroads: Social and Human Implications of the Scientific and Technological Revolution,* International Arts and Sciences Press, White Plains, N.Y., 1968.

Riesman, David: "The Spread of 'Collegiate' Values," in George B. de Huszar (ed.), *The Intellectuals,* The Free Press, Glencoe, Ill., 1960.

Riesman, David: "Commentary and Epilogue," in David Riesman and Verne Stadtman (eds.), *Academic Transformation,* McGraw-Hill Book Company, New York, 1973.

Robinson, John: "Public Reaction to Political Protest: Chicago 1968," *Public Opinion Quarterly,* vol. 34, pp. 1–9, Spring 1970.

"The Role of the Faculty in Budgetary and Salary Matters," *AAUP Bulletin,* vol. 58, pp. 170–172, Summer 1972.

Rosenberg, Morris: *Occupations and Values,* The Free Press, Glencoe, Ill., 1957.

Ruchames, Louis: "Jewish Radicalism in the United States," in Peter Rose (ed.),

The Ghetto and Beyond: Essays on Jewish Life in America, Random House, Inc., New York, 1969.

Schirmer, Daniel B.: *Republic or Empire?*, Schenkman Publishing Co., Inc., Cambridge, Mass., 1972.

Schumpeter, Joseph: *Capitalism, Socialism and Democracy*, Torchbooks, Harper & Row, Publishers, Incorporated, New York, 1962.

Schwartz, Charles: "The Movement vs. the Establishment," *The Nation*, vol. 210, pp. 747–751, June 22, 1970.

Schwartz, Charles: "Professional Organization," in M. Brown (ed.), *The Social Responsibility of the Scientist*, The Free Press, New York, 1971.

Scully, Malcolm G., and William A. Sievert: "Collective Bargaining Gains Converts among Teachers: Three National Organizations Vie to Represent Faculties," *The Chronicle of Higher Education*, vol. 5, pp. 1, 6, May 10, 1971.

Selvin, Hanan C., and Warren O. Hagstrom: "Determinants of Support for Civil Liberties," in Seymour Martin Lipset and Sheldon Wolin (eds.), *The Berkeley Student Revolt*, Anchor Books, Doubleday & Company, Inc., Garden City, N.Y., 1965.

Semas, Philip W.: "Students Consider Own Bargaining Role as Faculty Units Dominate Key Issues," *The Chronicle of Higher Education*, vol. 7, p. 4, Apr. 30, 1973a.

Semas, Philip W.: "3 Mass. Colleges Allow Students to Sit In on Faculty Bargaining," *The Chronicle of Higher Education*, vol. 8, pp. 1–2, Oct. 29, 1973b.

Semas, Philip W.: "Four More Faculties Reject Unionization," *The Chronicle of Higher Education*, vol. 8, p. 1, Nov. 26, 1973c.

Shark, Alan: "A Student's Collective Thought on Bargaining," *Journal of Higher Education*, vol. 43, pp. 552–558, October 1972.

Shenker, Israel: "Anthropologists Clash over Their Colleagues' Ethics in Thailand," *The New York Times*, Nov. 21, 1971.

Shepard, Herbert A.: "The Engineer and His Culture," *Explorations in Entrepreneurial History*, ser. 1, vol. 4, pp. 211–218, May 1952.

Sievert, William A.: "Four Groups Competing to Represent Faculty at State University of New York," *The Chronicle of Higher Education*, vol. 5, pp. 1, 5, Dec. 14, 1970.

Sklar, Martin J.: "On the Proletarian Revolution and the End of Political-Economic Society," *Radical America*, vol. 3, pp. 23–36, May–June 1969.

Snow, C. P.: *The New Men*, Macmillan Co., Ltd., London, 1954.

"SPA Rep Council OK's Merger Referendum," *New York Teacher*, State Edition, vol. 14, Mar. 4, 1973.

Spaeth, Joe L., and Andrew M. Greeley: *Recent Alumni and Higher Education,* McGraw-Hill Book Company, New York, 1970.

Spiegel, John: *Transactions: The Interplay between Individual, Family, and Society,* Science House, Inc., New York, 1971.

Sprehe, J. T.: *The Climate of Opinion in Sociology: A Study of the Professional Value and Belief Systems of Sociologists,* Ph.D. dissertation, Department of Sociology, Washington University, St. Louis, Mo., 1967; obtainable through University Microfilms, Ann Arbor, Michigan.

Steinberg, Stephen: *The Academic Melting Pot: Catholics and Jews in American Higher Education,* McGraw-Hill Book Company, New York, 1974.

Stephen, Beverly: "Veterans of the Student Revolution," *San Francisco Chronicle,* Oct. 31, 1973.

Strauss, George: "The AAUP as a Professional Occupational Association," *Industrial Relations,* vol. 5, pp. 128–140, 1965–1966.

"Technical Report: Carnegie Commission National Surveys of Higher Education," Survey Research Center, University of California, Berkeley, April 1971. (Mimeographed.)

Teitelboim, V.: "Problems Facing Latin American Intellectuals," *World Marxist Review,* vol. 11, pp. 68–75, December 1968.

Thelen, David P.: "The Academic Freedom Crisis of the 1890s and the Process of Change," paper delivered to the Organization of American Historians, Washington, April 1972.

Tice, Terrence (ed.): *Faculty Power: Collective Bargaining on Campus,* The Institute of Continuing Legal Education, Ann Arbor, Mich., 1972.

Time College Graduate Study, 1947, data made available through the Roper Public Opinion Research Center, Williamstown, Mass.

Tocqueville, Alexis de: *The Old Regime and the French Revolution,* Anchor Books, Doubleday & Company, Inc., Garden City, N.Y., 1955.

Tocqueville, Alexis de: *Democracy in America,* Phillips Bradley (ed.), Vintage Books, Inc., Alfred A. Knopf, Inc., New York, 1958.

"Today and Tomorrow the Decision Is Still Ours," *State News,* Michigan State University, East Lansing, Oct. 23, 1972.

Toffler, Alvin: *The Culture Consumers,* St. Martin's Press, Inc., New York, 1964.

Trilling, Lionel: *Beyond Culture,* The Viking Press, Inc., New York, 1965.

Trombley, William: "Professors from 23 Colleges in California Form New Group," *Los Angeles Times,* May 11, 1970.

Trombley, William: "Professors' Group Reverses Stand on Collective Bargaining," *Los Angeles Times,* May 21, 1972.

Trow, Martin: "Conceptions of the University: The Case of Berkeley," *The American Behavioral Scientist,* vol. 11, pp. 14–21, May–June 1968.

Turner, Henry A., Charles B. Spaulding, and Charles G. McClintock: "Political Orientations of Academically Affiliated Sociologists," *Sociology and Social Research,* vol. 47, pp. 273–289, April 1963a.

Turner, Henry A., Charles G. McClintock, and Charles B. Spaulding: "The Political Party Affiliation of American Political Scientists," *Western Political Quarterly,* vol. 16, pp. 650–665, September 1963b.

Tyler, Gus: "The Faculty Joins the Proletariat," *Change,* vol. 3, pp. 40–45, Winter 1971–1972.

"UC-AFT Brief on Faculty Tenure and Due Process at U.C.," *University Guardian,* vol. 2, p. 5, October 1972.

Ulam, Adam: *The Fall of the American University,* The Library Press, Freeport, N.Y., 1972.

"Upsurge of the Youth Movement in the Capitalist Countries," *World Marxist Review,* vol. 11, pp. 3–32, July 1968.

U.S. Bureau of the Census: *Historical Statistics of the United States, Colonial Times to 1957,* 1960.

U.S. Bureau of the Census: *Statistical Abstract of the United States: 1966,* 1966.

U.S. Bureau of the Census: *Statistical Abstract of the United States: 1973,* 1973.

U.S. Department of Health, Education and Welfare, Office of Education: *Teaching Faculty in Universities and Four-Year Colleges, Spring, 1963,* 1966.

Veblen, Thorstein: *The Higher Learning in America: A Memorandum on the Conduct of Universities by Business Men,* B. W. Huebsch, New York, 1918.

Veblen, Thorstein: *Essays on Our Changing Order,* The Viking Press, Inc., New York, 1934.

Veysey, Laurence: "The Emergence of the University," Ph.D. thesis, Department of History, University of California, Berkeley, 1962.

Veysey, Laurence: "The American Professor: A Study in Long Term Social Deviance," paper prepared for the American Historical Association, Dec. 29, 1969.

Walum, Laurel R.: "Sociologists as Signers: Some Characteristics of Protesters of the Vietnam War Policy," *American Sociologist,* vol. 5, pp. 161–164, May 1970.

Weber, Max: *From Max Weber: Essays in Sociology,* ed. and trans. by H. H. Gerth and C. Wright Mills, Oxford University Press, New York, 1946.

Welles, Sam: "The Jewish Elan," *Fortune,* vol. 61, pp. 134–139ff., February 1960.

Wesley, Edgar B.: *NEA: The First Hundred Years,* Harper & Row, Publishers, Incorporated, New York, 1957.

Wessler, Ira Eli: *The Political Resolutions of American Learned Societies,* doctoral dissertation submitted to the Graduate Faculty of Arts and Sciences, New York University, 1973.

Weyl, Nathaniel: *The Creative Elite in America,* Public Affairs Press, Washington, 1966.

Weyl, Nathaniel: *The Jew in American Politics,* Arlington House, New Rochelle, N.Y., 1968.

"Where College Faculties Have Chosen or Rejected Collective Bargaining Agents," *The Chronicle of Higher Education,* vol. 8, p. 24, June 10, 1974.

Williams, Gereth, Tessa Blackstone, and David Metcalf: *The Academic Labour Market: Economic and Social Aspects of a Profession,* Elsevier Scientific Publishing Co., New York, 1974.

Wilson, James Q.: *The Amateur Democrat,* The University of Chicago Press, 1962.

Wolfe, Alan: "Unthinking about the Thinkable: Reflections on the Failure of the Caucus for a New Political Science," *Politics and Society,* vol. 1, pp. 393–406, May 1971.

Wolff, Robert P.: *The Ideal of the University,* Beacon Press, Boston, 1969.

Wright, Charles: "Scientists and the Establishment of Science Affairs," in R. Gilpin and C. Wright (eds.), *Scientists and National Policy-Making,* Columbia University Press, New York, 1964.

Yankelovich, Daniel: *The New Morality: A Profile of American Youth in the 70's,* McGraw-Hill Book Company, New York, 1974.

Zeller, Belle: "Panel Discussion," in Terrence Tice (ed.), *Faculty Power: Collective Bargaining on Campus,* The Institute of Continuing Legal Education, Ann Arbor, Mich., 1972.

Index

About the Authors

EVERETT CARLL LADD, JR., is professor of Political Science and director of the Social Science Data Center at the University of Connecticut. He is the author or coauthor of numerous books and journal articles on American politics and the political process listed in the front of this book. Professor Ladd has been a visiting professor at Yale University and has held fellowships from the Social Science Research Council, the Ford Foundation, and the Guggenheim Foundation. In addition, he is a research fellow of the Center for International Affairs, Harvard University. He is currently a member of the Executive Council of the Inter-University Consortium for Political Research (ICPR).

SEYMOUR MARTIN LIPSET is the George D. Markham Professor of Government and Sociology and a member of the Executive Committee of the Center for International Affairs, Harvard University. He has held fellowships from the Social Science Research Council, the Ford Foundation, the Guggenheim Foundation, and the Center for Advanced Study in the Behavioral Sciences. He has been elected to the American Academy of Arts and Sciences, the National Academy of Education, and the National Academy of Sciences. He is currently vice-president of the American Academy of Arts and Sciences and chairman of the Section on the Social and Economic Sciences of the American Association for the Advancement of Science. He has been on the councils of the American Political Science and the American Sociological Associations. Two of his works have received awards: *Political Man* (the MacIver Award) and *The Politics of Unreason* (the Myrdal Prize). *The First New Nation* was a National Book Award finalist. His books have appeared in eighteen languages.

Carnegie Commission on Higher Education

Sponsored Research Studies

THE UNIVERSITY AND THE CITY:
EIGHT CASES OF INVOLVEMENT
George Nash, Dan Waldorf, and Robert E.
Price

THE BEGINNING OF THE FUTURE:
A HISTORICAL APPROACH TO GRADUATE
EDUCATION IN THE ARTS AND SCIENCES
Richard J. Storr

ACADEMIC TRANSFORMATION:
SEVENTEEN INSTITUTIONS UNDER PRESSURE
David Riesman and Verne A. Stadtman (eds.)

WHERE COLLEGES ARE AND WHO ATTENDS:
EFFECTS OF ACCESSIBILITY ON COLLEGE
ATTENDANCE
C. Arnold Anderson, Mary Jean Bowman, and
Vincent Tinto

NEW DIRECTIONS IN LEGAL EDUCATION
Herbert L. Packer and Thomas Ehrlich
abridged and unabridged editions

THE UNIVERSITY AS AN ORGANIZATION
James A. Perkins (ed.)

THE EMERGING TECHNOLOGY:
INSTRUCTIONAL USES OF THE COMPUTER
IN HIGHER EDUCATION
Roger E. Levien

A STATISTICAL PORTRAIT OF HIGHER
EDUCATION
Seymour E. Harris

THE HOME OF SCIENCE:
THE ROLE OF THE UNIVERSITY
Dael Wolfle

EDUCATION AND EVANGELISM:
A PROFILE OF PROTESTANT COLLEGES
C. Robert Pace

PROFESSIONAL EDUCATION:
SOME NEW DIRECTIONS
Edgar H. Schein

THE NONPROFIT RESEARCH INSTITUTE:
ITS ORIGIN, OPERATION, PROBLEMS, AND
PROSPECTS
Harold Orlans

THE INVISIBLE COLLEGES:
A PROFILE OF SMALL, PRIVATE COLLEGES
WITH LIMITED RESOURCES
Alexander W. Astin and Calvin B. T. Lee

AMERICAN HIGHER EDUCATION:
DIRECTIONS OLD AND NEW
Joseph Ben-David

A DEGREE AND WHAT ELSE?
CORRELATES AND CONSEQUENCES OF A
COLLEGE EDUCATION
Stephen B. Withey, Jo Anne Coble, Gerald
Gurin, John P. Robinson, Burkhard Strumpel,
Elizabeth Keogh Taylor, and Arthur C. Wolfe

THE MULTICAMPUS UNIVERSITY:
A STUDY OF ACADEMIC GOVERNANCE
Eugene C. Lee and Frank M. Bowen

INSTITUTIONS IN TRANSITION:
A PROFILE OF CHANGE IN HIGHER
EDUCATION
(INCORPORATING THE 1970 STATISTICAL
REPORT)
Harold L. Hodgkinson

EFFICIENCY IN LIBERAL EDUCATION:
A STUDY OF COMPARATIVE INSTRUCTIONAL
COSTS FOR DIFFERENT WAYS OF ORGANIZ-
ING TEACHING-LEARNING IN A LIBERAL
ARTS COLLEGE
Howard R. Bowen and Gordon K. Douglass

CREDIT FOR COLLEGE:
PUBLIC POLICY FOR STUDENT LOANS
Robert W. Hartman

MODELS AND MAVERICKS:
A PROFILE OF PRIVATE LIBERAL ARTS
COLLEGES
Morris T. Keeton

BETWEEN TWO WORLDS:
A PROFILE OF NEGRO HIGHER EDUCATION
Frank Bowles and Frank A. DeCosta

BREAKING THE ACCESS BARRIERS:
A PROFILE OF TWO-YEAR COLLEGES
Leland L. Medsker and Dale Tillery

ANY PERSON, ANY STUDY:
AN ESSAY ON HIGHER EDUCATION IN THE
UNITED STATES
Eric Ashby

THE NEW DEPRESSION IN HIGHER
EDUCATION:
A STUDY OF FINANCIAL CONDITIONS AT 41
COLLEGES AND UNIVERSITIES
Earl F. Cheit

FINANCING MEDICAL EDUCATION:
AN ANALYSIS OF ALTERNATIVE POLICIES
AND MECHANISMS
Rashi Fein and Gerald I. Weber

HIGHER EDUCATION IN NINE COUNTRIES:
A COMPARATIVE STUDY OF COLLEGES AND
UNIVERSITIES ABROAD
Barbara B. Burn, Philip G. Altbach, Clark Kerr,
and James A. Perkins

BRIDGES TO UNDERSTANDING:
INTERNATIONAL PROGRAMS OF AMERICAN
COLLEGES AND UNIVERSITIES
Irwin T. Sanders and Jennifer C. Ward

GRADUATE AND PROFESSIONAL EDUCATION,
1980:
A SURVEY OF INSTITUTIONAL PLANS
Lewis B. Mayhew
(Out of print, but available from University Microfilms.)

THE AMERICAN COLLEGE AND AMERICAN
CULTURE:
SOCIALIZATION AS A FUNCTION OF HIGHER
EDUCATION
Oscar Handlin and Mary F. Handlin

RECENT ALUMNI AND HIGHER EDUCATION:
A SURVEY OF COLLEGE GRADUATES
Joe L. Spaeth and Andrew M. Greeley
(Out of print, but available from University Microfilms.)

CHANGE IN EDUCATIONAL POLICY:
SELF-STUDIES IN SELECTED COLLEGES AND
UNIVERSITIES
Dwight R. Ladd

STATE OFFICIALS AND HIGHER EDUCATION:
A SURVEY OF THE OPINIONS AND
EXPECTATIONS OF POLICY MAKERS IN NINE
STATES
Heinz Eulau and Harold Quinley
(Out of print, but available from University Microfilms.)

ACADEMIC DEGREE STRUCTURES,
INNOVATIVE APPROACHES:
PRINCIPLES OF REFORM IN DEGREE
STRUCTURES IN THE UNITED STATES
Stephen H. Spurr

COLLEGES OF THE FORGOTTEN AMERICANS:
A PROFILE OF STATE COLLEGES AND
REGIONAL UNIVERSITIES
E. Alden Dunham

FROM BACKWATER TO MAINSTREAM:
A PROFILE OF CATHOLIC HIGHER
EDUCATION
Andrew M. Greeley

THE ECONOMICS OF THE MAJOR PRIVATE
UNIVERSITIES
William G. Bowen
(Out of print, but available from University Microfilms.)

THE FINANCE OF HIGHER EDUCATION
Howard R. Bowen
(Out of print, but available from University Microfilms.)

ALTERNATIVE METHODS OF FEDERAL
FUNDING FOR HIGHER EDUCATION
Ron Wolk
(Out of print, but available from University Microfilms.)

INVENTORY OF CURRENT RESEARCH ON
HIGHER EDUCATION 1968
Dale M. Heckman and Warren Bryan Martin
(Out of print, but available from University Microfilms.)

The following technical reports are available from the Carnegie Commission on Higher Education, 2150 Shattuck Ave., Berkeley, California 94704.

RESOURCE USE IN HIGHER EDUCATION:
TRENDS IN OUTPUT AND INPUTS, 1930–1967
June O'Neill

TRENDS AND PROJECTIONS OF PHYSICIANS
IN THE UNITED STATES 1967–2002
Mark S. Blumberg

MAY 1970:
THE CAMPUS AFTERMATH OF CAMBODIA
AND KENT STATE
Richard E. Peterson and John A. Bilorusky

MENTAL ABILITY AND HIGHER EDUCATIONAL
ATTAINMENT IN THE 20TH CENTURY
Paul Taubman and Terence Wales

AMERICAN COLLEGE AND UNIVERSITY
ENROLLMENT TRENDS IN 1971
Richard E. Peterson

PAPERS ON EFFICIENCY IN THE
MANAGEMENT OF HIGHER EDUCATION
Alexander M. Mood, Colin Bell, Lawrence
Bogard, Helen Brownlee, and Joseph McCloskey

AN INVENTORY OF ACADEMIC INNOVATION
AND REFORM
Ann Heiss

ESTIMATING THE RETURNS TO EDUCATION:
A DISAGGREGATED APPROACH
Richard S. Eckaus

SOURCES OF FUNDS TO COLLEGES AND
UNIVERSITIES
June O'Neill

THE NEW DEPRESSION IN HIGHER
EDUCATION—TWO YEARS LATER
Earl F. Cheit

PROFESSORS, UNIONS, AND AMERICAN
HIGHER EDUCATION
Everett Carll Ladd, Jr. and
Seymour Martin Lipset

A CLASSIFICATION OF INSTITUTIONS
OF HIGHER EDUCATION

POLITICAL IDEOLOGIES OF
GRADUATE STUDENTS:
CRYSTALLIZATION, CONSISTENCY, AND
CONTEXTUAL EFFECT
Margaret Fay and Jeff Weintraub

FLYING A LEARNING CENTER:
DESIGN AND COSTS OF AN OFF-CAMPUS
SPACE FOR LEARNING
Thomas J. Karwin

THE DEMISE OF DIVERSITY?:
A COMPARATIVE PROFILE OF EIGHT
TYPES OF INSTITUTIONS
C. Robert Pace

TUITION: A SUPPLEMENTAL
STATEMENT TO THE REPORT
OF THE CARNEGIE COMMISSION
ON HIGHER EDUCATION ON
"WHO PAYS? WHO BENEFITS?
WHO SHOULD PAY?"

THE GREAT AMERICAN
DEGREE MACHINE
Douglas L. Adkins

The following reprints are available from the Carnegie Commission on Higher Education, 2150 Shattuck Ave., Berkeley, California 94704.

ACCELERATED PROGRAMS OF MEDICAL EDUCATION, by Mark S. Blumberg, reprinted from
JOURNAL OF MEDICAL EDUCATION, vol. 46, no. 8, August 1971.*

*The Commission's stock of this reprint has been exhausted.

SCIENTIFIC MANPOWER FOR 1970–1985, by Allan M. Cartter, reprinted from SCIENCE, vol. 172, no. 3979, pp. 132–140, April 9, 1971.*

A NEW METHOD OF MEASURING STATES' HIGHER EDUCATION BURDEN, by Neil Timm, reprinted from THE JOURNAL OF HIGHER EDUCATION, vol. 42, no. 1, pp. 27–33, January 1971.*

REGENT WATCHING, by Earl F. Cheit, reprinted from AGB REPORTS, vol. 13, no. 6, pp. 4–13, March 1971.*

COLLEGE GENERATIONS—FROM THE 1930S TO THE 1960S, by Seymour M. Lipset and Everett C. Ladd, Jr., reprinted from THE PUBLIC INTEREST, no. 25, Summer 1971.*

WHAT'S BUGGING THE STUDENTS?, by Kenneth Keniston, reprinted from EDUCATIONAL RECORD, American Council on Education, Washington, D.C., Spring 1970.*

THE POLITICS OF ACADEMIA, by Seymour Martin Lipset, reprinted from David C. Nichols (ed.), PERSPECTIVES ON CAMPUS TENSIONS: PAPERS PREPARED FOR THE SPECIAL COMMITTEE ON CAMPUS TENSIONS, American Council on Education, Washington, D.C., September 1970.*

INTERNATIONAL PROGRAMS OF U.S. COLLEGES AND UNIVERSITIES: PRIORITIES FOR THE SEVENTIES, by James A. Perkins, reprinted by permission of the International Council for Educational Development, Occasional Paper no. 1, July 1971.*

FACULTY UNIONISM: FROM THEORY TO PRACTICE, by Joseph W. Garbarino, reprinted from INDUSTRIAL RELATIONS, vol. 11, no. 1, pp. 1–17, February 1972.*

MORE FOR LESS: HIGHER EDUCATION'S NEW PRIORITY, by Virginia B. Smith, reprinted from UNIVERSAL HIGHER EDUCATION: COSTS AND BENEFITS, American Council on Education, Washington, D.C., 1971.*

ACADEMIA AND POLITICS IN AMERICA, by Seymour M. Lipset, reprinted from Thomas J. Nossiter (ed.), IMAGINATION AND PRECISION IN THE SOCIAL SCIENCES, pp. 211–289, Faber and Faber, London, 1972.*

POLITICS OF ACADEMIC NATURAL SCIENTISTS AND ENGINEERS, by Everett C. Ladd, Jr., and Seymour M. Lipset, reprinted from SCIENCE, vol. 176, no. 4039, pp. 1091–1100, June 9, 1972.

THE INTELLECTUAL AS CRITIC AND REBEL, WITH SPECIAL REFERENCE TO THE UNITED STATES AND THE SOVIET UNION, by Seymour M. Lipset and Richard B. Dobson, reprinted from DAEDALUS, vol. 101, no. 3, pp. 137–198, Summer 1972.

*The Commission's stock of this reprint has been exhausted.

THE POLITICS OF AMERICAN SOCIOLOGISTS, *by Seymour M. Lipset and Everett C. Ladd, Jr.,* *reprinted from* THE AMERICAN JOURNAL OF SOCIOLOGY, *vol. 78, no. 1, July 1972.*

THE DISTRIBUTION OF ACADEMIC TENURE IN AMERICAN HIGHER EDUCATION, *by Martin* *Trow, reprinted from* THE TENURE DEBATE, *Bardwell Smith (ed.), Jossey-Bass, San Francisco, 1972.*

THE NATURE AND ORIGINS OF THE CARNEGIE COMMISSION ON HIGHER EDUCATION, *by* *Alan Pifer, based on a speech delivered to the Pennsylvania Association of Colleges and* *Universities, Oct. 16, 1972, reprinted by permission of the Carnegie Foundation for the Advancement of Teaching.*

AMERICAN SOCIAL SCIENTISTS AND THE GROWTH OF CAMPUS POLITICAL ACTIVISM IN THE 1960s, *by Everett C. Ladd, Jr., and Seymour M. Lipset, reprinted from* SOCIAL SCIENCES INFORMATION, *vol. 10, no. 2, April 1971.**

THE POLITICS OF AMERICAN POLITICAL SCIENTISTS, *by Everett C. Ladd, Jr., and Seymour* *M. Lipset, reprinted from* PS, *vol. 4, no. 2, Spring 1971.**

THE DIVIDED PROFESSORIATE, *by Seymour M. Lipset and Everett C. Ladd, Jr., reprinted* *from* CHANGE, *vol. 3, no. 3, pp. 54–60, May 1971.**

JEWISH ACADEMICS IN THE UNITED STATES: THEIR ACHIEVEMENTS, CULTURE AND POLITICS, *by Seymour M. Lipset and Everett C. Ladd, Jr., reprinted from* AMERICAN JEWISH YEAR BOOK, *1971.**

THE UNHOLY ALLIANCE AGAINST THE CAMPUS, *by Kenneth Keniston and Michael Lerner,* *reprinted from* NEW YORK TIMES MAGAZINE, *November 8, 1970.**

PRECARIOUS PROFESSORS: NEW PATTERNS OF REPRESENTATION, *by Joseph W. Garbarino,* *reprinted from* INDUSTRIAL RELATIONS, *vol. 10, no. 1, February 1971.**

. . . AND WHAT PROFESSORS THINK: ABOUT STUDENT PROTEST AND MANNERS, MORALS, POLITICS, AND CHAOS ON THE CAMPUS, *by Seymour Martin Lipset and Everett C. Ladd, Jr.,* *reprinted from* PSYCHOLOGY TODAY, *November 1970.**

DEMAND AND SUPPLY IN U.S. HIGHER EDUCATION: A PROGRESS REPORT, *by Roy Radner and* *Leonard S. Miller, reprinted from* AMERICAN ECONOMIC REVIEW, *May 1970.**

RESOURCES FOR HIGHER EDUCATION: AN ECONOMIST'S VIEW, *by Theodore W. Schultz,* *reprinted from* JOURNAL OF POLITICAL ECONOMY, *vol. 76, no. 3, University of Chicago,* *May/June 1968.**

*The Commission's stock of this reprint has been exhausted.

INDUSTRIAL RELATIONS AND UNIVERSITY RELATIONS, *by Clark Kerr, reprinted from* PROCEEDINGS OF THE 21ST ANNUAL WINTER MEETING OF THE INDUSTRIAL RELATIONS RESEARCH ASSOCIATION, *pp. 15–25.**

NEW CHALLENGES TO THE COLLEGE AND UNIVERSITY, *by Clark Kerr, reprinted from Kermit Gordon (ed.),* AGENDA FOR THE NATION, *The Brookings Institution, Washington, D.C., 1968.**

PRESIDENTIAL DISCONTENT, *by Clark Kerr, reprinted from David C. Nichols (ed.),* PERSPECTIVES ON CAMPUS TENSIONS: PAPERS PREPARED FOR THE SPECIAL COMMITTEE ON CAMPUS TENSIONS, *American Council on Education, Washington, D.C., September 1970.**

STUDENT PROTEST—AN INSTITUTIONAL AND NATIONAL PROFILE, *by Harold Hodgkinson, reprinted from* THE RECORD, *vol. 71, no. 4, May 1970.**

COMING OF MIDDLE AGE IN HIGHER EDUCATION, *by Earl F. Cheit, address delivered to American Association of State Colleges and Universities and National Association of State Universities and Land-Grant Colleges, Nov. 13, 1972.*

MEASURING FACULTY UNIONISM: QUANTITY AND QUALITY, *by Bill Aussieker and J. W. Garbarino, reprinted from* INDUSTRIAL RELATIONS, *vol. 12, no. 2, May 1973.*

PROBLEMS IN THE TRANSITION FROM ELITE TO MASS HIGHER EDUCATION, *by Martin Trow, paper prepared for a conference on mass higher education sponsored by the Organization for Economic Co-operation and Development, June 1973.**